Dante's Testaments

Figurae

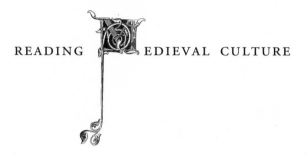

READING MEDIEVAL CULTURE

Dante's Testaments

ESSAYS IN SCRIPTURAL IMAGINATION

Peter S. Hawkins

Stanford University Press, Stanford, California, 1999

Stanford University Press
Stanford, California
© 1999 by the Board of Trustees of the Leland Stanford Junior University

Printed in the United States of America
CIP data appear at the end of the book

To Luis Roberto Varela (1954–1990),
who had nothing in particular to do with Dante
but everything in the world to do with me.

"colà dove gioir s'insempra"

(*Paradiso* 10.148)

Acknowledgments

A project this long in the making inevitably accrues many debts of gratitude. As I say in the prologue, my list of thanks must begin with John Freccero, the teacher who first set me on the way to Dante studies. Following close behind my initial mentor are the colleagues I had at the Dante Institutes held for three years at Dartmouth and Stanford: Kevin Brownlee, Rachel Jacoff, Jeffrey Schnapp, William Stephany, and Nancy Vickers. In the mid-1980s we worked through the *Commedia* in blocks of six weeks, covering each canto in twenty minutes, three or four a day. Such a "folle volo" could never be taken alone, but to find such fellow travelers as these meant that I had a great deal more than company: I discovered the richest intellectual joy I have ever known in the academy. Footnotes have enabled me to acknowledge my reliance on their published scholarship, but I can only suggest here the extent to which my knowledge of the poem, and indeed my love for it, were nourished by the five of them, my own "bella scola."

I would like to express my particular appreciation of Rachel Jacoff. Since our times together at Yale, Dartmouth, and Stanford she has been, whether in person or in early morning telephone calls between New Haven and Boston, my most regular interlocutor, an unfailing source of intellectual energy, encouragement, and laughter. Given her great contribution to my life and work, it seems only fitting that among her many helpful suggestions should be the title of his book.

Along with Rachel Jacoff, a number of stalwart friends read earlier versions of my manuscript and made it better by doing so: Nora Anthony, Stephen Henderson, Leslie Moore, Ann Monroe, Barbara Mowat, and Lee Palmer Wandell. Nora Anthony and Stephen Henderson were especially painstaking in their readings, pointing out the weakness of an argument here and rewriting an artless phrase there. They reminded me of a truth I have known over the course of almost 25 years at Yale Divinity School: a teacher can learn a great deal from his students, not only about his prose but about himself.

I need to name other friends as well, who may not have read my work in progress but who dealt lovingly with me in the course of it: Lucia Ballantine and Ron Walden, Richard Belitsky, Barbara Butera Ferriter, K. D. Codish, John and Phyllis Cook, Robert Dance, Ellen Davis, Martha Dewey, Margot Fassler, Stephen and Jane Garmey, Michael Hendrickson, James Hood, Valerie Komor, Gretchen Law, Helene MacLean, Michael Malone and Maureen Quilligan, J. D. McClatchy and Chip Kidd, Peggy McEvoy, Andrea Nightingale, Carol Pepper, LeAnne Schreiber, Cynthia and Gardner Shattuck, Nicolas Shumway, Leland and Laura Torrence, Richard Ward, Scott Westrem, and Diana Wylie.

Throughout this time I have also been the recipient of other kinds of support. The Henry Luce Foundation and the Association of Theological Schools gave me the means to take a year off for uninterrupted concentration on this project, while the Stonington Village Improvement Association provided the perfect place to enjoy it—James Merrill's extraordinary house at 107 Water Street. Marjorie Perloff has shared her Stanford home with me over a decade of summers, during which Dante's earthly paradise "e suo stato felice" have come to make sense in a way they simply never could in New Haven. The faculty of Princeton Theological Seminary invited me in 1995 to give the annual Stone Lectures, which later developed into chapters in this book. In earlier years, the Conant Fund and the Lilly Endowment awarded me research money and encouraged my studies. During the latter days of preparing this manuscript I have been assisted by Ann Napoli, Laurie Holst, and Sheryl Serviss. Jim Forsyth patiently took me through the looking glass of Windows 98 and always came back to pick up the pieces. Nancy A. Young went through the finished manuscript with a demand for clarity, an eye for detail, and an ear for the way a sentence should sound. Every author should be so blessed in a copy editor. Finally, thanks go to Helen Tartar of Stanford University Press, who for years over dinner has asked to see my Dante manuscript and, once I agreed to hand it over, published it with the care for which she is renowned.

I gratefully acknowledge permission to reprint earlier versions of portions of this book that have appeared in scholarly journals or critical anthologies. The original titles and places of publication are as follows. Prologue, "Dante: Poet-Theologian," *Princeton Seminary Bulletin*, n.s., 16, no. 3 (1995): 327–37. Chapter 1, "Dante and the Scriptural Self," in *The Papers of the Henry Luce III Fellows in Theology*, vol. 2, ATS Series in Theological Scholarship and Research, edited by Jonathan Strom, pp. 63–86 (Atlanta: Scholars Press, 1997). Chapter 2, "Dante and the Bible," in *The Cambridge Companion to Dante*, edited by Rachel Jacoff, pp. 120–35 (Cambridge, Eng.: Cambridge University Press, 1988), copyright Cambridge University Press; reprinted with the permission of Cambridge University Press. Chapter 3, "Scripts for the Pageant," *Stanford Literature Review*, 5 (Spring-Fall 1988): 75–92. Chapter 4, "Self-Authenticating Artifact: Poetry and Theology in *Paradiso* 25," *Christianity and Literature*, 41, no. 4 (Summer 1992): 387–94. Chapter 6, "Dido, Beatrice, and the Signs of Ancient Love," and Chapter 8, "Watching Matelda," in *The Poetry of Allusion: Virgil and Ovid in Dante's "Commedia,"* edited by Rachel Jacoff and Jeffrey T. Schnapp, pp. 113–30 and 181–201 (Stanford, Calif.: Stanford University Press, 1991), with the permission of the publishers; copyright The Board of the Trustees of the Leland Stanford Junior University. Chapter 7, "The Metamorphosis of Ovid," in *Dante and Ovid: Essays in Intertextuality*, edited by Madison Sowell, pp. 17–34, MRTS, vol. 82 (Binghamton, N.Y.: Medieval and Renaissance Texts & Studies, 1991), copyright Arizona Board of Regents for Arizona State University. Chapter 9, "Transfiguring the Text: Ovid, Scripture and the Dynamics of Allusion," *Stanford Italian Review*, 5 (Fall 1985): 115–40. Chapter 10, "Divide and Conquer: Augustine in the 'Divine Comedy,'" *PMLA*, 106, no. 3 (May 1991): 471–82. Chapter 11, "Dante's *Paradiso* and the Dialectic of Ineffability," in *Ineffability: Naming the Unnamable from Dante to Beckett*, edited by Peter S. Hawkins and Anne Howland Schotter, pp. 5–22 (New York: AMS Press, 1984). Chapter 12, " 'By Gradual Scale Sublim'd': Dante's Benedict and Contemplative Ascent," in *Monasti-*

cism and the Arts, edited by Timothy Verdon, pp. 255–69 (Syracuse, N.Y.: Syracuse University Press, 1984). Chapter 13, "Crossing Over: Dante's Purgatorial Threshold," in *Rule of Faith, Rule of Order*, edited by Nathan Miller and John Baldovin, pp. 140–60 (Collegeville, Minn.: The Liturgical Press, 1996). Chapter 14, " 'Out upon Circumference': Discovery in Dante," in *Discovering New Worlds: Essays on Medieval Exploration and Imagination*, edited by Scott D. Westrem, pp. 193–220 (New York: Garland, 1991).

P.S.H.

Contents

Abbreviations

Aen.	Virgil, *Aeneid*
CHB	*Cambridge History of the Bible*, vol. 2, *The West from the Fathers to the Reformation*, ed. G. W. H. Lampe (Cambridge, Eng.: Cambridge University Press, 1969)
DB	*Dante e la Bibbia*, ed. Giovanni Barblan (Florence: Olschki, 1988)
Dict. B.	*Dictionnaire de la Bible*, ed. F. Vigouroux, 5 vols. in 10 (Paris: Letouzey, 1922–28)
DSARDS	*Dante Studies with the Annual Report of the Dante Society*
DTC	*Dictionnaire de théologie catholique*, ed. A. Vacant, E. Mangenot, and E. Amann; 15 vols. in 20 (Paris: Letouzey, 1908–50)
ED	*Enciclopedia Dantesca*, dir. Umberto Bosco, ed. Giorgio Petrocchi, 5 vols. and appendix (Rome: Enciclopedia Italiana, 1970–78)
Inf.	Dante, *Inferno*
Met.	Ovid, *Metamorphoses*
MLN	*Modern Language Notes*
NCE	*New Catholic Encyclopedia*, 17 vols. (New York: McGraw-Hill, 1967)
PA	*The Poetry of Allusion: Virgil and Ovid in Dante's "Commedia,"* ed. Rachel Jacoff and Jeffrey T. Schnapp (Stanford, Calif.: Stanford University Press, 1991)
Par.	Dante, *Paradiso*

PL   *Patrologiae Cursus Completus, Series Latina*, ed. J. P. Migne, 221
            vols. (Paris: Vrin, 1844–64, with later printings)

Purg.   Dante, *Purgatorio*

SL   *A Select Library of the Nicene and Post-Nicene Fathers of the
            Christian Church*, ed. Philip Schaff, 1st series, 14 vols.; 2nd
            series, 14 vols. (Grand Rapids, Mich.: William B. Eerdmans,
            1978)

ST   St. Thomas Aquinas, *Summa Theologiae*, Blackfriars Edition,
            with Latin text and English translation, 61 vols. (New York:
            McGraw-Hill, 1964–76)

A Note on Citations and Translations

All citations from the *Commedia* are from Singleton's version of the Petroc-chi text as published in *The Divine Comedy*, translation and commentary by Charles S. Singleton (Princeton, N.J.: Princeton University Press, 1970–75). Translations from the Latin Vulgate Bible are adapted with minor modifications from the Douay/Rheims edition. Texts and translations of Virgil and Ovid are from the Loeb Library editions. Translations of other works listed in original-language versions in the bibliography are my own unless otherwise noted.

Dante's Testaments

Prologue: Scripts for the Pageant

"Take it and read, take it and read . . ." When St. Augustine first heard these words in a garden in Milan, he assumed they must have come from the house next door. But what did they mean? It was impossible even to tell whether the voice was male or female. Perhaps the weird refrain was part of some child's play all the rage in Milan but foreign to his own North African youth. Or was it part of the lost world of childhood itself, and therefore a world away from the anguish he now felt as a tormented 32-year-old, locked in an agony of indecision over the direction of his life?

Or again, maybe "Take it and read" came not from a child playing behind the house next door but from God. In his moment of despair, Augustine dared a leap of interpretation. He recalled how St. Anthony of Egypt had walked by the open door of a church as the gospel was being read and then stood dumbfounded at what he chanced to hear: "Go home and sell all that belongs to you. Give it to the poor, and so the treasure you have shall be in heaven; then come back and follow me" (Matt. 19:21). Through those words Anthony had been converted: Scripture turned his life around, showed him what he was meant to do and who he was to become.

Similarly, might the childish singsong overheard by Augustine in fact be heaven's call to him to open the Bible at random and read the first passage that met his eye? Here the games of Augustine's childhood *did* come into play. For it had been common practice to treat the poetry of Virgil in exactly this way: to charge into the *Aeneid* and encounter, amid the fall of Troy or Aeneas's journey through the underworld, a line infused with some surprising personal relevance. Augustine recalled, "People sometimes opened a book of poetry at random, and although the poet had been thinking, as he wrote, of some quite different matter, it often happened that the reader placed his finger on a verse which had a remarkable bearing on his problem" (*Confessions* 4.3).

But that was at a time when the "fancies dreamed up by poets" (*Confessions* 1.13) enthralled both him and his schoolboy friends. Now, putting away childish things, Augustine turned not to poetry but to the Bible, to God's Book. Picking up the text he had put aside in his distraction—the Epistles of Paul—he read in silence the first passage that met his eyes: "Not in reveling and drunkenness, not in lust and wantonness, not in quarrels and rivalries. Rather, arm yourselves with the Lord Jesus Christ; spend no more thought on nature and nature's appetites" (Rom. 13:13–14). In this text Augustine found his oracle: "I had no wish to read more and no need to do so," he later wrote; "for in an instant, as I came to the end of the sentence, it was as though the light of confidence flooded into my heart and all the darkness of doubt was dispelled" (*Confessions* 8.12).

Augustine's moment in that Milanese garden, when he discovered a text that in turn found him, is the most memorable encounter with the Bible in all of Christian tradition.[1] But it is not only Scripture that has turned around the lives of those who randomly take up a book and read it: there is also Dante's *Commedia*. I am thinking of the extraordinary scene described by theatrical producer and director Norman Bel Geddes in his memoir, *Miracle in the Evening*. Bel Geddes recalls a time in 1921 when he, too, like Augustine in *Confessions* 8, languished in profound turmoil over the course of his life and work. One night, after a year of "concentrated idleness," he found himself feverish, almost in a state of delirium:

> The room seemed a block wide. I suddenly started to fall. I clutched for some sort of support but there was nothing to grab, and I fell headlong into a bookcase. Dazed and scared, I lay still for some moments, then pulled myself into a sitting position. I discovered that I was holding a book in my right hand. I opened it and, bemusedly, read the same passage over and over again before I realized what it was. . . . None other than Norton's translation of Dante's *The Divine Comedy*.[2]

The passage that caught his eye was *Inferno* 2.127–32: "As flowerlets, bent and closed by the chill of night, straighten themselves all open on the stem, so I became with my weak virtue. And such good daring hastened to my heart, that I began like one enfranchised."

Given that the *Commedia* provides 14,233 lines to choose from, Bel Geddes was fortunate to stumble upon this brief passage—a description of Dante's own move from fear to courage, of the moment when he resolved to take the journey that would transform his own mortal life. To be sure, Bel Geddes was alone in his study, with only words on a page. No Virgil emerged to rescue him from his dark wood, nor heaven's "three blessed ladies" (*Inf.* 2.124) to care for him. And yet, just as Augustine was set free by a verse from St. Paul, so Bel Geddes discovered in lines from the *Commedia* a way out of his predicament and into his future. After reading the same few verses over and over again, as if determined to find in them some kind of buried treasure, he turned back to the beginning of the poem: "Before the night was out, I had read the three volumes of my edition from beginning to end. And the next day . . . I was embarking upon a plan of [theatrical] production for the poem that would occupy at least half my waking hours for the next two years."[3]

Bel Geddes is not the only accidental reader of Dante who found himself "discovered" by the poem. In August 1944, mystery writer Dorothy L. Sayers heard the familiar howl of the air-raid siren and knew German bombs were once again falling on London. Rushing through her house on the way to shelter, she snatched up a dusty book that had once belonged to her grandmother—Dante's *Inferno*. Once safely below ground, she began to read a work she could not put down, even after the "all clear." "However foolish it may sound," she later recalled, "the plain fact is that I bolted my meals, neglected my sleep, work, and correspondence, drove my friends crazy, and paid only distracted attention to [Hitler's bombs], until I had panted my way through the Three Realms of the dead from top to bottom and from bottom to top."[4]

This obsession lasted for the rest of her life. From 1944 until her death, in 1957, Sayers translated almost the entire poem for the new Penguin paperback series, wrote notes and commentary, lectured over the radio as well as before audiences in London, Oxford, and Cambridge, and even worked on a novel about Dante and his daughter during the poet's latter years in Ravenna.[5] The *Commedia* gave Sayers the final chapter of her own life's work.

Not everyone who devotes a career to Dante, however, can claim such spectacular discoveries or such immediate enchantment. My own first encounter is now lost in the deep oblivion of my undergraduate education. A marked-up paperback *Inferno* with my name on the flyleaf proves that I studied at least part of the poem as a freshman in 1963, but I remember nothing more of it than of the other classics of "Western World Literature" routinely wasted on the young. Two years later I took a summer-school course and read the entire *Commedia* in translation. My professor, an Italian himself, had a native speaker's passion for Dante and the *bellezza* of his language. The poetry indeed "sounded" beautiful, but sadly, this go-round with the poem was also my introduction to the guild's preoccupation with scholarly commentary, with the barrage of authority that always threatens to preempt direct experience of the text itself. Although at the time I would admit it to no one, the poem left me untouched, even bored. Despite 600 years' worth of footnotes—all those names, dates, and diagrams!—I suspected there might be a great deal *less* here than met the eye. Maybe one had to be in the middle of the journey of life to get the point. In any event, to twist Augustine's words wildly out of context, it seemed to me that "I had no wish to read more and no need to do so."

Then something happened. In September 1972, while I was studying for my Ph.D. examinations in the Yale English department, my friend Nancy Vickers suggested that I go with her to the first session of John Freccero's yearlong Dante course. I explained my sad earlier history with the poem and argued that my examiners in the English department would certainly ask me nothing about an Italian poem. But she prevailed in the end. Or was it that somewhere I heard a still small voice saying, "Take it and read, take it and read"? In any case, I checked out a bilingual edition of the *Inferno* from Sterling Library and justified attendance at this first meeting as a "study break" from English literature. I would go, just this once.

Little did I know what the impact of that initial meeting would be: how I would audit not only the second class but every one after it; how I would go to Italy that very summer to begin my study of Dante's language; how my English department dissertation on *The Faerie Queene* would eventually be held hostage by Dante for two chapters; how I, too, once I became a professor at Yale Divinity School in 1976, would regularly teach a yearlong course on the *Commedia*. Moreover, the poem became not only the center of my teaching, lecturing, and publication, but an inspiration for my own life as a Christian second only to Scripture. Indeed, Dante seemed to bring the Bible to life for me precisely by appropriating it so boldly for himself. He saw the Exodus of Israel out of Egypt as none other than *his* story, chose Good Friday as the day that he, too, would descend into hell, and appointed Easter dawn as the time of his emergence on the shores of purgatory. I found myself reading the Bible because of what I found in the *Commedia*.

This is not to say that Dante made me a believer, any more than he turned me into a "medieval man." Nonetheless, coming to the poet in my late twenties had an enormous impact on the way I came to understand not only my Christian faith but my own self. Over the intervening 25 years, my relationship to both poet and poem has inevitably changed, becoming more complicated and at times even contentious. But the intensity of the connection has not faltered. On every count my debt remains constant.

I wonder now what made the huge difference back in the autumn of 1972. Certainly, I was fortunate enough to find a brilliant teacher, one whose eloquence moved my heart as well as my mind. John Freccero not only dazzled me with the poem's erudition but also involved me in its intellectual and spiritual drama. Perhaps because he presented the *Commedia* as an Augustinian story of conversion, I found myself willy-nilly being turned around by it. As a student of literature, for instance, I could see in Dante's genius all that a poet might do. But I also experienced the limits of art, saw that there was a point at which even the greatest human language falls short or runs headlong into silence. Likewise, as a young man who was for the first time in love, I understood the daring, even dangerous, truth of what Dante was attempting in the figure of Beatrice: how *eros* could be transfigured into *caritas* without spurning the erotic; how we might even come to know the divine face, however tentatively and imperfectly, by looking deeply into the faces of those we are given to love. Perhaps because the poem was a journey with an ineluctable sense of direction, I found myself pulled along, moved, and confronted. I recalled Moses' words in the book of Deuteronomy: "See, I have set before you this day life and good, death and evil" (30:15). Reading Dante made that choice urgent and vivid, made me want to choose life.

Twice a week, for two hours a class, Freccero gave the *Commedia* the most sustained and impassioned exegesis of a text I had ever encountered. As Dante students traditionally say of the teachers who guide them through the poem, he taught me to "see the stars." More than idle praise or mere hyperbole, this accolade reminds us that teaching others to read the *Commedia* inevitably means turning them into stargazers. For this reason, perhaps, Dante decided that each of the three canticles should conclude with the word *stelle*. At the end of the *Inferno*, for instance, as Dante and Virgil leave behind the nightmare of hell, the narrator says, "E quindi uscimmo a riveder le stelle" ("from thence we came forth to see again the stars," *Inf.* 34.139). After the ascent of Mount Purgatory, Dante (now without Virgil) is said to be "puro e disposto a salire a le stelle" ("pure and ready to mount up to the stars," *Purg.* 33.145). And then, as the entire poem culminates in a vision of God that the poet can neither remember nor describe adequately, Dante finds that he is revolving in accord with the heavens, as if *he* were one of the constellations. In the end, his will and desire are brought together by "l'amor che move il sole e l'altre stelle" ("the love that moves the sun and the other stars," *Par.* 33.145).

What may at first glance seem only a minor detail—the recurrent use of the word *stelle* as end marker of each of the canticles—in fact reveals major features of the *Commedia*. It suggests Dante's interest not only in symmetry but most especially in triads; his penchant for repetitions that also reveal difference; and, most important, his orientation of the reader heavenward, so that working one's way through the poem also becomes a movement *con sidera*, a "consideration."

Pondering the literal heavens requires from most of us a stretch of the imagination. To begin with, the stars themselves, at least for city dwellers, are seldom very visible. Victims of urban sprawl, they disappear behind light pollution and dirty air. Further, our cosmos, unlike Dante's, is a desolate and abstract void pocked with the likes of black holes, neutrino showers, and gravitational warpage—phenomena not only unviewable by the eye but nearly inconceivable to the lay mind. The Hubbell Space Telescope, too, provides us with data that regularly numbs the mind: 50 billion galaxies and still counting. Further complicating the view, especially for Americans, is our notion of the heavens as a territory to divide and conquer, whether with "Star Wars" defense strategies, commercial telecommunications satellites, or a space shuttle named "Challenger."

Dante's notion of the universe, on the other hand, is at once intimate and transcendent—a Chinese box of crystalline spheres, each governed by an angelic order, and all centered on earth. Thus to our sensibility, inured to strange and impersonal vastness, the universe of the *Commedia* is a little world made cunningly. Dante's model was ancient, an amalgam of theology and "science" that belongs to a bygone time when no evening, to recall Wallace Stevens, was "without angels."[6]

Why, then, was I so drawn into Dante's world? Was it because the vacancy of my own era did not, despite Stevens, "[glitter] round us everywhere"? In truth, part of me mistrusted the joy I felt in leaving my own century and worldview behind and worried that it flowed from mere nostalgia for the Christian Middle Ages. I wondered if the radiance I found in the *Commedia* was in reality only a posthumous glow, cast by what were, after all, *dead* stars. Nonetheless, I entered into the poem's three-storied universe as if it were brand new. Indeed, it became part of my own present tense, one of the worlds in which I continue to live my life—a place where I stargaze.

In the *Commedia*, it is Dante himself—the character whom critics have come to call the "pilgrim"—who learns to see the stars and to walk in their light. At the outset of the poem we discover him trying unsuccessfully to escape the dark wood in which he finds himself lost and terrified and to climb a radiant mountain that looms within view. On his own he can do nothing. But heaven sends him a rescuer and guide in the person of Virgil, "l'altissimo poeta" ("the loftiest poet," *Inf.* 4.80) of the Latin world. In Virgil's company he learns that the ascent must be prefaced by a descent, for to move toward the light he must confront everything that is murky and tangled not only within himself but within all of humanity.

The way down leads through hell. Step by step he follows his guide into the bowels of darkness as well as into its heart. This is the section of the *Commedia* that readers have always liked best, in part because of Dante's titillatingly gruesome dissection of each fresh horror, and in part, perhaps, because we feel most at home here. For what the *Inferno* describes is our world without grace, our cities without love, our will to power without mercy. In hell, the self is sovereign, cut off, frozen in obsession and monomania, always alone no matter how dense the crowd. The journey through *Inferno* also engages Dante's empathy by reminding him how often evil is a mystery of flawed goodness. But by the time he comes into the grotesque presence of Satan, hell has been exposed for what it is—a world where earth's atrocities rage unchecked for all eternity.

Purgatory represents an awakening from this nightmare. Reversals of the first canticle are everywhere. Having coursed down through the circles of *Inferno*, Dante now spirals up, ascending the radiant mountain that had proved so inaccessible at the opening of the poem. Readers typically find themselves disappointed in this movement: a penitent seems less "interesting" than the damned, spiritual therapy less riveting than torture. Likewise, the poem's new concern with big questions—what is the nature of the good? of love? of free will?—often proves less compelling than the verbal magic of hell's narcissistic spellbinders.

The *Purgatorio* does, however, afford some new pleasures. Because the obsessions of the individual ego are no longer the only focus, the reader's mind is stretched towards a larger understanding. We also begin to imagine human community as it might be if grace were given the upper hand. Gone are the operatic soloists of *Inferno*, each singing the words of his or her life song, and nobody listening to anyone else. In their place are individuals discovering what it means to be members of a choir, to make music together. Communion becomes a way of life.

And it is communion, carefully and sometimes uncomfortably learned, that becomes the sublime play of the *Paradiso*. Even after the transformation of heart and mind attained along the mountain terraces, Dante cannot take in this radiance all at once. Nor can Virgil lead him any farther along the mind's road to God. Thus, for the final part of his journey Dante gains a new guide, Beatrice, an earthly beloved who, now in death as she had in life, initiates him into the ways of glory. These lessons in beatitude are ones the pilgrim can learn only gradually. Therefore, as the blessed appear to him in the concentric spheres of the material heavens, they bring him slowly, patiently, into the life of the Trinity. The fact that the realities of earth continue to cast their shadow almost until the end of *Paradiso* surprises many readers. It is a sign, perhaps, that Dante would not allow the final canticle to be an escape from the world, a "time out" from reality. Still, the paradise he imagines, at least for the blessed, is a realm in which light plays upon light. Its only real shadow is that "deep but dazzling darkness" that belongs to God—the essential Mystery who can never be solved.

Not that Dante entirely resists the temptation. In the final canto of the poem, he wants to understand how the Incarnation "fits" within the Blessed Trinity; he is like a geometer determined to do the impossible by squaring the circle (*Par.* 33.133–35).[7] The attempt fails. But no matter: in the final moment of the poem, grace overwhelms Dante's intellect just as it rescued him from his dark wood at the outset. Face to face with God, as well as with the failure of his own "alta fantasia" ("high fantasy," 33.142), all he can do is acknowledge heaven's conquest. The rest is silence.

In assaying this brief summary of the poem, I have been speaking its language and entering into its world of discourse as if both were my own. I have become Dante's spokesman. So do most other critics, even those who, unlike me, do not share the essentials of Dante's religion. Does this process of assimilation take place because his voice is so strong that sooner or later one begins, quite unconsciously, to imitate it? I believe so. Perhaps because Dante's "I" is doubled in the dual roles of character and poet—and because he covertly plays all the other parts as well—it is almost impossible *not* to be overtaken by him.

Certainly, my own first readings were very much under his spell. I was overwhelmed, to begin with, by the structural symmetries and patterns that famously characterize the *Commedia*. They seemed a sign that God was undoubtedly in Dante's heaven, and therefore that all was ultimately right with his world. The poet also seemed to know everything. Problems first raised in the *Inferno* were worked out in the *Purgatorio* and then made sublime in the *Paradiso*. Nothing was out of place; every question had an answer.

I remember a moment during the Dartmouth Dante Institute of 1985 when this conviction of the poet's absolute control seemed almost too much to bear. A budding Dantista announced that the middle word of the central line of the entire poem was *amor*—"love" in both of Dante's languages, Latin and Italian. But that was not enough. When *amor* was spelled backward, as someone else quickly noticed, it revealed Dante's imperial remedy for the disaster of contemporary Italian politics: *amor* became *Roma*! Sighs of awe went up around the seminar room. All of us, whatever may have been either our religious conviction or our skepticism, recognized that here we were in the presence of a higher power. At a later time, the number crunching that produced this revelation was thrown into doubt; yet another candidate for the poem's central word was proposed—a word, alas, that made no sense when spelled backward. But by this time the question did not seriously matter. We knew that everything fit.[8]

Or did it? I cannot say that it was "Yale Deconstruction" that challenged my enthrallment with Dante's omniscience, my almost pious belief in the airtight way the poem held together. I think, rather, it was deeper experience with the text itself. On closer reading, the poem seemed more problematic than I had once imagined, and infinitely stranger.[9] Not everything made sense: there were difficulties that were not "worked out" or conveniently resolved into some larger pattern. I also discovered that Dante often took liberties with his venerable authorities. Therefore, to naively offer the *Glossa ordinaria* on a line would tell only half a truth: it would suggest what the authorities had to offer, but not necessarily what the poet was doing with this legacy. For rather than simply reiterating theological tradition, Dante felt himself free at times to devise it anew, according to the quirky and often self-serving needs of his own imagination. Moreover, the theological tradition he was working with turned out, on closer examination, to be a great deal less monolithic than I had first understood. There were options to choose among, room for the *sed contra* and individual *responsio*.

What also became increasingly interesting to me was the poetics of the poem, the way it created its world—the way, in particular, it had managed to turn *me* into so compliant a reader. I found myself beginning to talk back to Dante rather than simply to impersonate him. I was almost as interested in the "how" of his vision as in what he claimed to see. I fell in love with the *artifice* of his eternity.

I have described here two stages in my own work with the *Commedia* as if they represented a "before" and an "after." But sincere awe and cultivated suspicion are, in fact, poles between which I continue to move back and forth. It is impossible for me to disregard the religious core of the poem or discount what I take to be the poet's genuinely evangelical impulses. I believe the author of the epistle to Can Grande della Scala when he says "the end of the whole and of the part is to remove those living in this life from the state of misery and lead them to the state of joy."[10] I see Dante working within a complex religious tradition and toward an unabashedly theological end—the conversion of the reader to a deeper knowledge and love of God. Indeed, it is precisely this deepening that has been at the heart of my own experience with the text.

On the other hand, I cannot ignore the fact that the *Commedia* is openly a literary endeavor (however carefully it may work to conceal its status as fiction), and one that is designed to celebrate not only the glory of God but the poet's own *ingegno*. Boldness and risk infuse Dante's entire enterprise, a sense of almost reckless presumption that never ceases to astonish me. Despite the assiduous efforts of commentators to marshal precedents and analogues for his venture—in effect, to make the poem appear less daring than it is—both poet and poem keep striking me as something decidedly new.

In his essay "Of the Difference Between a Genius and an Apostle," Kierkegaard was adamant that these two identities shared no common ground.[11] The apostle passes on a tradition, the genius makes one up. The apostle cares only about the truth of the message, the genius about its beauty and originality. The apostle is uniquely concerned about the Word that is proclaimed, while the genius is seductive, courting our wonder and forcing our admiration. Kierkegaard's antithesis has its uses, and there is no denying the power of his austere either/or. Nonetheless, the Dante I have come to know over the last 25 years thoroughly collapses these two identities into one: he is Apostle-Genius, *Theologus-Poeta*. He fuses the antitheses in his own person as well as within the "sacred poem" to which, he claims, heaven and earth have each set a hand (*Par.* 25.1–2). Implicitly, he dares anyone to put asunder what God has joined together.

It may seem strange in these latter days of literary theory to consider an author and his intentions. Surely, few Shakespeareans any longer speak with assurance about the Bard of Avon or what he *meant* to do. Instead, all is confounded in that great sea of textuality (quartos, folios, myriad variant readings and editions) which, by way of shorthand, we continue to call "Shakespeare's plays"—unless, of course, the alleged author is actually Francis Bacon, the Earl of Oxford, or somebody else. But with Dante the case is different. The authorship of the *Commedia* is contested by no one, and surprisingly few variant readings compete within this lengthy and complicated text. Furthermore, a single intelligence continues to confront us early and late in Dante's career, as the poet-commentator of the *Vita nuova* goes on to develop and refine a recognizable set of concerns in one work after another. Throughout this corpus we meet an "I" that remains consistent and coherent, despite the changes in attitude or evaluation that distinguish the *Commedia* from his earlier writings. Moreover, a single life story develops in and between his lines: his meeting with a particular woman, a miraculous vision that seems to radiate from her, the various callings of philosophy, politics, and poetry, a sense of mission that looks beyond personal disaster to glimpse a divine end that can never be fully comprehended.

These elements of autobiography all coalesce in the *Commedia*. Dante sets his narrative during Holy Week of 1300, when he was, at the age of 35, still a young poet on his way to attaining public office in Florence and a place of prominence in its affairs.[12] Only two years later he was brought up on false charges of malfeasance and exiled from Florence, made a victim not only of power struggles within the commune but of the papal politics of Boniface VIII. He would not forgive this wrongdoing. For the rest of his life he moved between the cities of central and northern Italy; if legend is to be believed, he even journeyed as far north as Paris and Oxford. For roughly twenty years, from 1302 until his death, in Ravenna in 1321, he learned the difficulty of climbing another man's stairs and the salty taste of another man's bread, to recall the "prophecy" of his own exile in *Paradiso* 17.

During this time he was also engaged in a number of ambitious writing projects that suggest the range of his talents and concerns. One of the first, the *De vulgari eloquentia*, defends the vernacular tongue but is written in Latin to impress the scholars he was trying to win over to the linguistic possibilities of his own Italian. At roughly the same time he was also at work on the *Convivio*, in which he attempted in both poetry and prose to present serious philosophical reflections in the spoken language of the people, so that what he had to say could be read by "women no less than men, a vast number of both sexes, whose language is not that acquired through education, but the vernacular" (*Convivio* 1.9.5).[13]

Neither of these two projects was ever completed: the *Convivio* ends a third of the way through its projected length, and the *De vulgari* breaks off in midsentence. At a somewhat later time, and again in Latin, Dante wrote his *Monarchia*, a treatise on world government that argues not only for the revival of universal empire but for the divine authority of imperial rule: he was adamant that the emperor received his power directly from God, not through the pope. For this rejection of papal supremacy the *Monarchia* was publicly burned at Bologna in 1329, placed on the church's Index of Prohibited Books, and kept off limits to the pious until Benedict XV finally lifted the censure in 1921.[14]

Somewhere between 1307 and 1314 Dante began work on the poem that would be his sublime taskmaster for the rest of his life. We can only guess at the original inspiration for this work. Was it a grand idea, a "brainstorm," a dream, a vision?[15] Or was it the kind of rapture described by the prophet Ezekiel? "And the likeness of a hand was put forth and took me by a lock of my head: and the spirit lifted me up between the earth and heaven, and brought me in the vision of God into Jerusalem" (8:3). Clearly the author of the *Commedia* wanted his readers to take seriously this latter option, to believe that, like Ezekiel, he had been raised up by the hand of God, had "seen the light," and then received heaven's commission to tell what he had seen and heard.

Dante wrote at a time when divine visions were by no means unusual, and, indeed, when the claim to rapture or "spiritual illumination" was used by lay people to authorize otherwise suspect speech.[16] No doubt some contemporaries, like the credulous ladies of Verona mentioned by Boccaccio, took the poet at his literal word, and thought his dark complexion was the result of the time he had spent in the "heat and smoke down there": "Do you see the man who goes down into hell and returns when he pleases, and brings back tidings of them that are below?"[17] The earliest commentators, such as Dante's son Pietro Alighieri, were in fact eager to maintain that the poet was speaking metaphorically and therefore only feigning the journey. Others finessed the issue and concentrated on the ultimate source of Dante's vision—God. According to Guido da Pisa, Dante was like the Psalmist David in Psalms 44:22 ("my tongue flows readily as the pen of a swift writer"): "he himself was the pen of the Holy Spirit with which the Spirit speedily wrote for us the punishment of the damned and the glory of the blessed."[18]

Where *did* the *Commedia* come from? Imagine it this way: An exiled Dante paces the precincts of someone else's northern Italian garden, in a state of intense turmoil not only over his larger reversal of fortune but over his inability to bring to fruition two of the works he had begun. Suddenly, he hears the strange voice that may well come from a garden of the house next door, but that, more likely, wells up from deep within himself. He makes out the repeated refrain, "Take it and read, take it and read." Remembering Augustine's famous moment in Milan, he decides that these words are meant for him, that they issue a command he is meant to take literally. And so he rushes headlong to retrieve a book he had distractedly set aside sometime earlier—a book that would lead him beyond his present impasse and inspire the work he was meant to do.

Following breathlessly behind the poet, the eager Dante scholar strains to make out the identity of that crucial text. Given the prominence of Virgil in the poem, many have assumed the *Aeneid* to be the book in question. Ulrich Leo even proposed that it was a rereading of Aeneas's descent into the realms of the dead that specifically inspired Dante to leave behind his prose treatises and strike off along the narrative path of Virgil's epic: "to go himself, as a poet, to Hell and Heaven."[19]

Other works have also come to mind. Augustine's *Confessions*, for instance, has been suggested, in view of its story of spiritual conversion, its exploration of an author's double identity—the self who was and the present self who tells his tale of transformation. A good case might also be made for Dante's own *Vita nuova*, the "libello" of his youth, in which he described his meetings with Beatrice, the vision that followed upon her death, and his vow at a later time "to compose concerning her what has never been written in rhyme of any woman."[20] One might also point to the many accounts of voyage through the afterlife that enjoyed such popularity in the centuries before Dante—*St. Patrick's Purgatory*, for example, or the vision of Tundale.[21]

And what if the book that Dante took up and read—the text that more than any other generated the rest of his life's work—was none other than God's Book, the Bible? In spinning out this fantasy, I am not suggesting that there would have been a single passage that inspired his course in the *Commedia*, but rather that the poem took shape against the panorama of the entire canon—with Christ's descent into hell and resurrection on the third day making possible the story of his own redemption, Israel's Exodus from Egypt enabling him to transfigure his personal experience of exile and wandering, and Paul's rapture to the third heaven providing a precedent both for Dante's vision and for his "apostleship."

Because poetic influence works in strange ways—and because the poet in question is the polymath Dante—no single version of this Augustinian scenario can possibly give a definitive account of the *Commedia*'s origin. Nor need there be just a single precursor text. Indeed, the purpose of this collection of essays is to explore the range of Dante's reading, the extent to which he rewrote what he found in the pages he turned, whether in Scripture, in the poetry of Virgil and Ovid, in such luminaries of the Christian tradition as Augustine and Benedict, or in the "book of the world" itself—the globe traversed by pilgrims and navigators.

If there is a figure in my carpet, however—any overarching interest that brings this diverse body of work into focus—it is Dante's intense engagement with the Christian Scriptures. Here I mean not only scriptural text and commentary but also the Bible as experienced in sermon and prayer, hymn and song, fresco and illumination, or, less consciously, in everyday aphorism. Even my chapters devoted to Virgil and Ovid, in which I investigate patterns of allusion and strategies of citation, explore these classical poets with an eye to how Dante views them in the light of biblical revelation. Dante's grounding in Scripture, I believe, helps to explain how he is able to pick and choose among classical and Christian traditions, to manipulate arguments and time lines, and to forge imaginary ties between the ancient world and his own "moderno uso" (*Purg.* 16.42).

My title, *Dante's Testaments*, plays off the pilgrim's reply to St. Peter's question about the source of his faith. It is, Dante says, "La larga ploia/de lo Spirito Santo, ch'è diffusa/in su le vecchie e 'n su le nuove cuoia" ("The plenteous rain of the Holy Spirit which is poured over the old and over the new parchments," *Par.* 24.91–93). The "parchments" specifically referred to, of course, are the Old and New Testaments; but to their venerable and inspired pages Dante also dares to add his own "testamental" postscript, most richly in the *Commedia* but also in his other works. He may rewrite Virgil and Ovid in the sense that he corrects their vision, reorients their understanding of history or love. With the Bible, on the other hand, correction is unthinkable. Instead, the poet rewrites Scripture by reactivating it, by writing it again. He keeps the biblical imagination vital and fecund, open to the possibilities of a new vernacular—the language of his time. What most intrigues me is the complex adventure of Dante and his sources, whereby every old or received parchment becomes a script for his dazzling pageant, a new account of everything old.

PART I

Dante and the Bible

CHAPTER I

The Scriptural Self

It may be impossible for us to imagine how deeply the world of the Christian Scriptures permeated Dante's late-thirteenth-century culture. Today there are, of course, Orthodox Jews still very much defined by Torah and tradition, as well as various Protestant Christians who move comfortably inside their own "Bible-based" subcultures. Nonetheless, such groups also participate in a larger culture that by all accounts has lost the Bible as a living subtext. To be sure, the hotel nightstand may still hold the familiar Gideon volume, or a witness in court may swear to tell the whole truth by placing a right hand on that same distinctive cover. New translations also appear with astonishing regularity, as if more colloquial or politically acceptable language might slow the decline in biblical literacy. Yet putting the Christ child in "baby clothes" and laying him in "a bed of straw" does not seem to be reversing the trend. The stories and characters that until recently were common knowledge are, in truth, rapidly passing out of currency, even as the literary style of the Bible, its imagery and cadences, evaporate from our speech.

Here the contrast with Dante's world could not be greater. For his contemporaries the Bible was not an ancient text placed on a bookstore shelf crowded with other equally valuable esoterica. Nor was it subject to "Higher Criticism," the weekend deliberations of the Jesus Seminar, or magazine cover stories that find a news hook in the Christmas season by asking, "Is the Bible Fact or Fiction?" On the contrary, Scripture was, to quote Dante in his *Monarchia*, "infallible truth" (1.5) and "divine authority" (2.1). Although individual books were recorded over time by various human authors, there was no question about the Bible's ultimate authorship: "For although there are many who record the divine word, it is God alone who dictates, deigning to reveal his pleasure to us through the pens of many men" (3.4).

Given the Scripture's status, it is not surprising that the Bible was the most studied book in the Middle Ages, both the primer with which the young clerk learned to read and the "sacred page" that for centuries dominated every branch of higher learning.[1] But it would be a mistake to limit the Bible's centrality to the schools, to books, or to those relative few who understood Latin. As the sacred text of the church, Scripture was the primary source of all authoritative proclamations, from papal bulls to parish homilies. Furthermore, it constituted a complex symbolic network that extended far beyond the reach of words. Long before it appeared in vernacular translation, Scripture was available in a variety of forms that did not require Latin or, indeed, literacy of any kind. This "People's Bible" was known through ritual, pageant, and drama; in the iconographic programs of church facades and stained glass; in hymn and song. Therefore, no matter how important the actual biblical text may have been for clergy, monastics, and the educated layperson, the Bible was far more readily seen and heard than it was ever read. Its story was always *already* known, and known by people who, whatever the extent of their learning or the depth of their piety, were its "living concordances."[2]

Unlike the vast majority of laypeople who got their Bible by osmosis, Dante knew the Scripture intimately, and in ways that suggest years of reading and study. A good example of this knowledge is found in the brief introduction to the final section of the *Monarchia*. Throughout the first two books of this treatise, Dante makes his case for a single world government, primarily with the support of such esteemed pagan authorities as Aristotle, Virgil, and other great poets of antiquity. But when he turns to his last and most controversial thesis—that temporal world-rule comes authorized directly from God and *not* through the papacy—he changes his dominant frame of reference by opening with a quotation from the Bible: "He shut the lions' mouths, and they did not harm me, for in his sight righteousness was found in me" (Dan. 6:22).

In the book of Daniel these words are spoken from the depths of the lions' den, where the prophet was sent to his death for having dared to worship God rather than Darius the Mede. The verses that immediately precede the quoted text recount how the king went to the sealed pit on the day after Daniel's imprisonment and, fully expecting that his words would fall on dead ears, spoke the following taunt: "Daniel, servant of the living God, hath thy God, whom thou servest always, been able, thinkest thou, to deliver thee from the lions?" (6:20). Instead of a dead man's silence, however, Darius receives the reply, quoted above, of a prophet still very much alive. Astonished, the king commands his subjects to "dread and fear the God of Daniel" (6:26). The prophet then walks out of the lion's den unscathed, while his adversaries suffer the grisly fate heaven had spared him.

Dante does not hesitate to appropriate all of this text for himself, not only the specific verse he quotes but also the entire scenario.[3] He is Daniel, in whom can be found "no fault or suspicion," just as his detractors in the papal party, the canon lawyers and decretalists, play the parts of King Darius and his malicious royal counselors. As in the world of Scripture, so now in the vicissitudes of early-fourteenth-century politics. The machinations of the unjust are doomed to failure; the lions roar in vain.

This strategic use of Daniel's story might well be thought sufficient to make the point. But the young prophet of Israel is by no means Dante's only biblical role model. In addition to taking heart "from the words of Daniel cited above, in which a divine power is said to be a shield of the defenders of truth," he is bolstered by still other exemplars:

> "Putting on the breast-plate of faith" as Paul exhorts us, afire with that burning coal which one of the seraphim took from the heavenly altar to touch Isaiah's lips, I shall enter the present arena, and by his arm who freed us from the power of darkness with his blood, before the eyes of the world I shall cast out the wicked and the lying from the ring. What should I fear, when the Spirit who is coeternal with the Father and the Son says through the mouth of David: "the righteous shall be in everlasting remembrance and shall not be afraid of ill report."
>
> (*Monarchia* 3.1)

Dante wrote these fighting words from the no-man's-land of exile, cut off from earthly power. His sole vantage point was the high ground of his own convictions, his only authority that which he could borrow from Scripture. Nonetheless, he locates himself boldly in the arena of conflict and persecution. Surrounded by hostility, he shows himself neither naked nor defenseless. Rather, he takes from St. Paul the "breast-plate of faith," as well, presumably, as the remaining "whole armor of God" that Paul enjoins the soldier of Christ to wear against "the rulers of this world of darkness" (Eph. 6:12). With this protection Dante is ready to enter any arena, to take on all comers, ready even "before the eyes of the whole world . . . [to] cast out the wicked and the lying from the ring" (*Monarchia* 3.1).

Lest his readers take this battle cry against the papacy as irreverent— which is precisely how it *was* taken—Dante assumes a third biblical persona as a "cover." He proclaims himself another Isaiah, a man of unclean lips, dwelling "in the midst of a people that hath unclean lips" (Isa. 6:5), who is purified by heaven in order to take up the divine mission. By implication, therefore, he is also a prophet in the making, even if no seraph has yet touched his mortal lips with a burning coal.

In closing, the author of the *Monarchia* then asks, "What should I fear?" Placing himself in the company of Daniel, Paul, and Isaiah, he squares off against the hierarchy by asserting in no uncertain terms that the Triune God has summoned him to speak. And so he ends this brief introduction even as he began it, with a verse of Scripture designed to warrant what he is about to do in the rest of book three. He appeals to the Psalmist, whose words, he reminds the reader, were spoken by God "through the mouth of David" ("per os David"). It does not matter if the wicked gnash their teeth in rage; after all, "The just shall be in everlasting remembrance: he shall not fear the evil hearing" (Ps. 111 [112]:6–7). Consequently, readers of the *Monarchia* should not be distracted by those who malign the author unjustly, or who refuse to give his message a fair hearing. Rather, they must listen with assurance to the Word of the Lord, as it is heard in Scripture in the words of Isaiah and Daniel, Paul and David—and as it is spoken now "through the mouth of Dante."

This construction of a "scriptural self," to use John Alford's term, may seem highly presumptuous: who does the author think he is?[4] But, in fact, taking on a biblical identity—or even, as we see here, a plurality of such identities—was by no means uncommon in the Middle Ages. Hagiographers routinely told the lives of the saints against a template of Scripture, so that in effect the saint became "another" patriarch or apostle, or even, as in the biographies of St. Francis, another Christ. Nor did individuals hesitate to use the Bible for their own self-definition.[5] Thus Gregory the Great writes in his *Moralia in Iob*: "Scripture tells the deeds of the saints and excites the hearts of the weak to imitate them. . . . We ought to transform what we read into our very selves."[6] Scripture, after all, is a *speculum* in which to see the self, either as it is in actuality or only as it might be someday. And so Dante looks into the mirror of Scripture and finds himself reflected there in other selves. He is Daniel in the lion's den, Paul dressed up in the "whole armor of God," Isaiah at the moment of his call to prophecy, and David staring down his enemies without fear.

How did a Florentine layman around the year 1300 attain this degree of biblical knowledge, and such facility in the personal appropriation of Scripture? For what we find in Dante is a familiarity with the Bible far more profound than what could be picked up from the liturgy, from ordinary parish preaching, or from the general culture. His deep knowledge seems more like that of a monastic, who might well take on the Bible as second nature given the weekly recitation of the entire Psalter, the repeated readings of the various divine offices, and the annual cycle of the liturgy—not to mention the practice of *ruminatio* that kept the words of Scripture literally on one's lips, "like the buzzing of bees."[7] But how could a layman, living outside the monastery's round of worship and study, cultivate so deep a "biblical imagination"?[8]

We know almost nothing for certain about the poet's formal education, let alone the particular ways he was formed as a Christian.[9] However, study of popular religious life in the thirteenth century shows what André Vauchez has called a "rehabilitation of the lay status" taking place in the 50 years or so before Dante's birth.[10] In 1199, for instance, Pope Innocent III ordered the bishop of Metz to reverse a decision handed down against a group of laymen called the *Humiliati*. With an eye to the freedom and authority that heretical religious groups held out to Catholics dissatisfied with what the church offered them, Innocent approved the *Humiliati*'s desire to know the Scripture in the vernacular, "lest these simple people should be forced into heresy."[11] He also encouraged them to "exhort" one another with the gospel, while carefully restricting the office of preaching to the clergy. In other words, laypeople might "bear witness" to their faith and legitimately call one another to repentance; what they could not do, however, was publicly discuss matters of doctrine or the more controversial aspects of theology, which were considered too dangerous for them and were therefore kept as the privilege of the clergy alone.

Also in 1199, Pope Innocent canonized a man named Homobonus, renowned for his emulation of the apostolic life, his charitable works, and his opposition to heresy. What is startling here is not the reasons for the canonization but the fact that Homobonus, a mere artisan, was neither a monk nor a priest, nor had he been attached to a religious order or bound by a vow of celibacy. Rather, for the very first time, the church canonized a married layman. Shortly afterward, in 1215, the Fourth Lateran Council declared that a fully Christian life might be lived at home and in normal domestic relationships, that is, exactly as the majority of the faithful actually lived their lives: "For not only virgins and the continent but also married persons find favour with God by right faith and good actions and deserve to attain to eternal blessedness."[12]

The Lateran Council's calls for more frequent and more accessible preaching were part of a broad attempt to turn disaffected Catholics into people of "right favor and good actions." Undertaking precisely this mission were the newly formed Franciscan and Dominican orders, which set out to bring the gospel not only into the streets and public squares but also into the vernacular language of the people.[13] The impulse to popularize began with the founders of the two Mendicant orders. Contemporary accounts of St. Francis recall the power of his street preaching, the way he grabbed the attention of a crowd with gesture, act, or narrative. It was noted that "his discourse did not belong to the great genre of sacred eloquence" but more resembled the buttonhole techniques of *concionatores*, or "haranguers," public speakers who worked an audience to move it in one political direction or another.[14] Nor was St. Dominic less fervent, even if his style, like that of his Order of Preachers, pitched the gospel to a higher, more erudite level. In his canonization proceedings, for instance, he was remembered for having "devoted himself to preaching with such fervor that he exhorted and constrained his friars to announce the Word of God day and night, in churches and in homes, in the fields and on the road, everywhere, in short, and never to speak of anything but God."[15]

The result of this evangelizing zeal was the formation of a new kind of Christian, the *laicus religiosus*. It was now possible, as one cardinal wrote around 1255, "to use the term 'religious' for people who live in a holy and religious manner in their own homes, not because they are subject to a precise rule but because their life is simpler and more rigorous than that of other laypeople, who live in a purely worldly manner."[16] In Dante's Florence, where both literacy and religious interest were uncommonly high among the laity, such persons might choose to join one of the *laudesi*, or devotional groups, that publicly sang *laude*, or praises, to the Virgin Mary and the other saints. Others might seek out a charitable organization, called a *misericordia*, or join one of the many penitential confraternities affiliated with the Mendicants but structurally independent of them. An even closer connection with the Franciscans or the Dominicans might be found in their "tertiary," or third, orders, which attracted both men and women to the spiritual life of their communities. Although not bound by any vow, such laypeople lived according to a voluntary rule, whether privately in their own homes or communally with others.[17]

According to a fourteenth-century commentator on the *Commedia*, Francesco da Buti, Dante intended in his youth to become a Franciscan but never actually took vows.[18] Whatever the case, he was probably among the many who flocked to the great churches of the Mendicants, Dominican as well as Franciscan, where both women and men could find an intensity of Christian life not offered by the ordinary parish church. Preaching was at the center of this experience; lay people gathered en masse in the new piazzas built in front of the churches to accommodate their numbers, or met together in the more intimate setting of confraternities. In one sense, the monks' task was basic catechesis: the teaching of the faith, the conversion of the nominally Christian to a deeper (and more orthodox) life. But the Mendicants were also engaged in a wider translation of their own clerical training into forms that were available to a more or less sophisticated lay audience. Their effort was to turn the Latin erudition of the schools, as well as the devotional life of the cloister, into a dynamic spiritual vernacular that could speak to the concrete realities of secular life.[19]

Preachers' manuals in the thirteenth century on the *artes praedicandi* emphasized that the sermon was meant to target a particular audience and reach out to it at an appropriate level. Preaching was to be a kind of song ("quasi quidam cantus"), the preacher to be as agreeable as a jester and as sharp as a merchant ("accettato come un giullare, abile come un mercante").[20] Apparently, a number of the Mendicants actually met these high expectations, even if the transcriptions that have come down to us largely omit the amusing stories and asides that made this preaching so popular. A case in point is Giordano da Pisa, more than 700 of whose sermons still remain, all of them preached in the vernacular at the outset of the four-teenth century, and all taken down by anonymous laypeople who wanted to preserve at least the serious essence of the passing homiletic moment.[21]

There is no question of Dante himself having heard Giordano preach at Santa Maria Novella: the poet left the commune in late 1301, never to return, whereas the Dominican friar only arrived on the Florentine scene two years later. But while the influence of the one on the other is not at stake, nonetheless the similarity between the poet and the preacher is quite striking. Most notably, both men alternate freely between, on the one hand, the reality of everyday life in city and countryside and, on the other hand, an encyclopedic range of interest in the weightier matters of science, philosophy, and theology.

Among those whom Dante would certainly have encountered in Flor-ence was Giordano's superior at Santa Maria Novella, Remigio de' Giro-lami, who was master of theology at the Dominican convent school for nearly 40 years (from 1280 to 1320) and who also served as *protoretore* of the commune, preaching the funeral orations of important citizens and ex-tending formal welcome to visiting dignitaries.[22] Likewise, it would have been hard for Dante to miss Petrus dell' Olivi and Ubertino da Casale, Franciscans of great renown and influence, who were active at Santa Croce during the 1280s.[23] Whether or not Dante was actually in the Dominican church when Remigio preached on the Song of Songs, for instance, or whether he listened as Petrus dell' Olivi used the book of the Apocalypse to lambaste the corruption of the church, is simply not known. Yet evidence of their work in his suggests that at the very least he was well acquainted with their writings.

By Dante's account, moreover, we know that he had firsthand famil-iarity with both Mendicant centers where these men held forth. In the second book of the *Convivio* he writes that after the death of Beatrice (in 1290), he turned in his quest for solace to Lady Philosophy, first through his private reading of Boethius and Cicero, then by frequenting "the schools of the religious and the disputations of the philosophers" for a period of "perhaps some thirty months" (2.12.7). The "schools" ("scuole") referred to here are most certainly the *studia generale* of the Mendicant orders, in particular the Franciscans at the church of Santa Croce and the Domini-cans at Santa Maria Novella.[24] By the end of the thirteenth century, these two houses were among the most important places of learning in their respective communities, ranked second only to the *studia principalia* at Paris, Oxford, and Cambridge.

Established to train clerics, both schools drew teachers as well as students from all over Europe. But as we know from Dante's account, they were also open to lay people. To be sure, such access would have been limited. Contemporary statutes from the Roman Province of the Dominican order, for example, explicitly ban "seculars" (both clergy and lay) from attending lectures in philosophy and science. Likewise, at Pisa the chapter prohibited "the admission of any secular person to any lectures *except theological* ones without the special license of the provincial prior."[25] According to Charles Davis, however, these various prohibitions suggest that laypeople were in fact welcomed at lectures on Scripture and theology, even if they were officially excluded—perhaps because of their too enthusiastic attendance?—from the "disputations of the philosophers."[26]

Granted that Dante was among those who managed to make their way into the Mendicant schools, whether actually to attend lectures or only to benefit from the general ambiance, what might he have found there? From the Franciscans at Santa Croce he would have received not only the cult of Francis but the legacy of Plato and Augustine, especially as filtered through the works of St. Bonaventure. In addition, there was the teaching of Joachim of Fiore, especially as taken up by the later Franciscan "Spiritualists," with their radical emphasis on the virtue of poverty, their acute sense of historical crisis within the contemporary church, and their apocalyptic expectation of a new age at hand. The Franciscans also offered a style of *sermo humilis* preaching that reveled in narrative, in emotion, and in the commonplace. The Friars Minor focused on a very human Christ both in his incarnation and in the mystery of his passion.[27]

The Dominicans, on the other hand, had different emphases: they turned to Aristotle and Aquinas, upheld intellectual rigor and zeal in scholarship, had a much greater openness to classical learning and the legacy of pagan Rome, and stressed a belief in the constructive possibilities of human reason and secular life. Their preaching embraced the more abstract techniques of the *sermo modernus*, with its delight in intellectual argument, logic, and Scholastic methodology ("divisions and authorities").[28] Not surprisingly, the two orders appealed to different social and economic groups: the Franciscans to the humbler ranks of artisans, craftspeople, and shopkeepers, the Dominicans to an *haute bourgeoisie* of merchants and bankers.[29]

The two Mendicant orders offered, in other words, not only a study in contrasts but a richly diverse world of thought and sensibility from which Dante would go on to make his own highly eclectic synthesis in the *Commedia*. The poet does this quite explicitly in *Paradiso*'s heaven of the sun, where we find a celestial version of the schools blessedly free of the rivalry that on earth made these two very different orders competitive, if not openly antagonistic to one another.[30] Reflecting an actual "goodwill" practice observed on the feast days of Francis and Dominic, whereby a representative of one order praised the founder of the other, Dante brings the two Mendicant worlds together in a celebration of difference in harmony. The Dominican Aquinas eulogizes St. Francis, while the Franciscan Bonaventure accords the same honor to St. Dominic. Both theologians go on to denounce the present-day corruption of their own communities rather than find fault with each other's orders. The point is a glorification of mutuality, of "l'uno e l'altro," the one *and* the other—both heart and intellect, the ardor of the seraph and the cherub's splendor, the call to poverty and the mandate to teach the orthodox faith.

Indeed, as the souls appear one after another in these cantos, it becomes clear that Dante is orchestrating an extensive reconciliation of opposites.[31] Once-bitter theological adversaries—Aquinas and Siger of Brabant, Bonaventure and Joachim of Fiore—appear standing next to one another in the same beatific company. Representatives of the active life join those of the contemplative, even as the illiterate first followers of Francis are sprinkled among the church's greatest theological minds; for example, not only Aquinas and Bonaventure but Albertus Magnus, Anselm, Isidore of Seville, and the Venerable Bede. Even the poet's choice of descriptive metaphor strikes a note of reciprocity, for when this group of male celibates makes its initial appearance (*Par.* 10.76–81), they are collectively likened to young ladies in a dance who are delicately poised between one melody and another. At least in metaphor, the theologians are graceful, lyric, and unmistakably feminine.

We do not know if Dante had a foretaste of such harmony in his own experience of the "schools of the religious," or if the *studium* he presents in paradise was an ideal intended to reproach the Florentine reality. What is certain is that his debt to the Mendicant orders was profound. Nor should we forget the deep similarities between his project in the *Commedia* and theirs. Both were involved in the popular translation of "official" Latin culture;[32] both addressed not only those urban laypeople who had a formal education (such as judges, notaries, and clerks) but the far larger number who were "monolingual literates" in the vernacular: "merchants, artisans, shopkeepers, artists, accountants, shop or banking employees, as well as some workers and some women."[33]

I have been stressing Dante's debt to the Mendicant orders and the ways in which his project as poet and theologian coincided with theirs. Yet distinctions between them are no less important. Dante was not an ordained member of any religious order and had no authorized mission; he was only a layman who constructed his own authority—and at a time when the church's early-thirteenth-century openness to the laity had already begun to shut down. In this conservative retrenchment the Mendicant orders also, paradoxically, played a powerful part, for their evangelizing mission to the laity was used eventually to reassert the hegemony of the clergy, to encourage listening but not public speech. Lay silence would have to be golden, for as Giordano da Pisa proclaimed in Santa Maria Novella in 1304, "the office of preaching is not granted to just any man; and, more especially, it is everywhere and always forbidden for women to preach; next, forbidden to all laymen and fools who cannot read; so that no one can be a preacher who is not literate and learned; and to trespass in this regard is to face a serious excommunication and to commit a serious sin; because the Scripture is serious, and profound, and most subtle to understand, and not given to just any person."[34]

By no stretch of the imagination, of course, could Dante ever be described as one of these uneducated, benighted *idiotae,* "fools who cannot read." Nonetheless, as a layman he would have undoubtedly fallen outside Giordano's charmed clerical circle and been unable to take advantage of what was arguably the most important mode of mass communication in his day—the public sermon. But if denied the opportunity to preach in church, Dante the poet and prose-writer was quite free to construct for himself a literary pulpit that he could climb into at will. We have already seen an example of this freedom in the passage from the Latin *Monarchia,* where in a relatively few lines he assumes a number of biblical identities and speaks to his reader by means of an essentially scriptural discourse; that is, where he "speaks Bible." But there were limitations to writing in Latin, and so when it came to his "sacred poem," the *Commedia,* he aimed for a much wider audience by composing a text in his own Florentine vernacular—in a tongue that could be understood "by princes, barons, knights and many other of like nobility, women no less than men, a vast number of both sexes, whose language is not that acquired through education, but the vernacular" (*Convivio* 1.9.5).

The voice of the vernacular preacher is easy to catch throughout the *Commedia*.[35] Sometimes it is audible in the poet's own occasional interventions, when he interrupts the narrative to address the reader directly, either to raise a jeremiad ("Ahi serva Italia," *Purg.* 6.76–151) or to draw attention to what otherwise might be missed (*Par.* 10.22–27). But more often the preacher in question is a heavenly authority the likes of Saints Peter, John, Benedict, Peter Damian, Aquinas, and Bonaventure—characters Dante took from history and then turned into his own irrefutable spokesmen.

Perhaps none of these oratorical set pieces is more stunning than the diatribe in *Paradiso* 29 (vv. 85–126), where Dante gives to Beatrice—a gift from layman to laywoman—an opportunity to denounce the contemporary church hierarchy for having abandoned the gospel and the people it was meant to serve. The target here is not a master of theology, such as Giordano da Pisa or Remigio de' Girolami. Rather it is the pulpit show-offs, Franciscan and Dominican alike, who neglect the Word of God either by actively perverting its meaning or by drowning it in a barrage of rhetorical display. What these preachers shout from their pulpits are mere fables ("favole," v. 104), trash ("ciance," v. 110), jests and buffoonery ("con motti e con iscede," v. 115), outright folly ("stoltezza," v. 121). Instead of feeding their flocks with real biblical nourishment, they pasture the sheep in their charge on wind ("tornan del pasco pasciute di vento," v. 107). This "pastoring" is a travesty of the mission entrusted to the apostles and passed down within the church:

> Non disse Cristo al suo primo convento:
>   'Andate, e predicate al mondo ciance';
>   ma diede lor verace fondamento.
>   (*Par.* 29.109–11)

(Christ did not say to his first company, "Go, and preach idle stories to the world," but he gave them the true foundation.)

"Go, and preach idle stories to the world": the charge that Christ did *not* give to his disciples is, of course, a parody of the one he did proclaim at the end of his earthly ministry, according both to Matthew ("Going therefore, teach ye all nations," 28:19) and Mark ("Go into all the world and preach the gospel to all creatures," 16:15). In place of Scripture, however, the "new disciples" proclaim gossip and chatter, tell stories about St. Anthony's pig or entertain pointless theories about the eclipse that darkened the earth at Christ's death—what the New Testament refers to as "foolish and old wives' fables" ("ineptas . . . et aniles fabulas," 1 Tim. 4:7) and as "artificial fables" ("doctas fabulas," 2 Pet. 1:16). Given this kind of adulteration, the pulpit may well be an unlikely place from which to hear the Word of God.

In the *Commedia*, Dante himself presumes to fill this void: the responsibility that so many licensed preachers have thrown away, *he* will take up. He may be only a private individual, a single "lowly" voice crying in an early-fourteenth-century wilderness, as he presents himself in his epistle to the Italian Cardinals who were setting about to elect a new pontiff in Avignon. But the urgency of the day forces him to be bold—not only to speak out but to speak in the name of the Lord.

It takes almost the entire length of the poem for the character we call "Dante Pilgrim" to become authorized as the poet-prophet of the *Commedia*. Nonetheless, as early as *Inferno* 19 we see signs of the one who is to come. In a canto devoted to punishing the sin of simony, the buying and selling of church office, Dante takes on the papacy with a sense of religious and moral outrage shared by many others. Initially it is the poet who commands our attention: the canto's opening words are his denunciation of Simon Magus (Acts 8:9–13) and his "wretched followers" who prostitute for gold and silver the things of God. This same authorial voice goes on to praise the justice of God's peculiar punishment of the simonists—their burial upside down in holes that are shaped like baptismal fonts—as if to prepare us for the hard sayings that will come fast and furious as the text unfolds.

But if the canto opens with the words of the poet, it is soon the character Dante who claims our attention. The layman takes his place above the inverted form of a once-supreme pontiff, Nicholas III, with Dante likened to a friar summoned to hear the confession of a convicted

assassin just moments before the man is buried alive. The encounter be-
tween the two, however, is less that of a dying convict's confession to his
priest—after all, neither repentance nor absolution are available in hell—
than it is Dante's opportunity to pronounce a stirring anathema. At first it
is Nicholas alone who receives the brunt of the pilgrim's rage; but when, in
verse 106, his accusatory "you" shifts from the singular "tu" to the plural
"voi," it is clear that the hierarchy of the church is collectively being called
to account, exposed as a perverse apostolic succession of "lawless pastors."

Dante delivers a homily *ad hominem* that is largely a string of biblical
rebukes.[36] In the course of only 28 lines, he moves from the prophet Hosea,
to 2 Maccabees, to the Gospel of Matthew, to the Acts of the Apostles—all
the while weaving a web of scriptural allusion in which to catch the con-
science (or, at least, to establish the culpability) of the papacy:

> Io non so s'i' mi fui qui troppo folle,
>   ch'i' pur rispuosi lui a questo metro:
>   "Deh, or mi dì: quanto tesoro volle
> Nostro Segnore in prima da san Pietro
>   ch'ei ponesse le chiavi in sua balìa?
>   Certo non chiese se non 'Viemmi retro.'
> Né Pier né li altri tolsero a Matia
>   oro od argento, quando fu sortito
>   al loco che perdé l'anima ria.
> Però ti sta, ché tu se' ben punito."
>   (*Inf.* 19.88–97)

> (I do not know if here I was overbold in answering him in just this strain:
> "Pray now tell me how much treasure did our Lord require of Saint Peter
> before he put the keys into his keeping? Surely he asked nothing save:
> 'Follow me.' Nor did Peter or the others take gold or silver of Matthias
> when he was chosen for the office which the guilty soul had lost.
> Therefore stay right here, for you are justly punished.")

This is an extraordinarily confident denunciation, delivered with a
bravura that might well be considered premature for Dante Pilgrim at this
early stage of his journey through the afterlife. Perhaps for this very reason,
the tirade begins with an admission of doubt and humility. The soli-
tary layman wonders if perhaps he will be reckless, overbold, even mad—
"troppo folle" (v. 88)—as he turns the sharp blade of Scripture against the

keeper of the keys. At the end of this attack, he claims that he actually held back, out of reverence for the holy office that Nicholas once held "in the glad life." When he finishes speaking, he uses Virgil's approval to validate his own "hard words" ("parole . . . gravi," v. 103). The validation comes quickly: once the requisite "notes" (v. 118) of Dante's harsh but unmistakably biblical song have all been intoned, the ancient master clasps his disciple and lets his manifest pleasure serve as reassurance:

> I' credo ben ch'al mio duca piacesse,
>   con sì contenta labbia sempre attese
>   lo suon de le parole vere espresse.
> Però con ambo le braccia mi prese;
>   e poi che tutto su mi s'ebbe al petto,
>   rimontò per la via onde discese.
>
>   (*Inf.* 19.121–26)

(And indeed I think it pleased my guide, with so satisfied a look did he keep listening to the sound of the true words uttered. Thereupon he took me in his arms, and when he had me quite on his breast, remounted by the path where he had descended.)

One cannot miss the intended embrace of authority here. Yet Dante does not finally need the approval of an ancient, not to mention pagan, poet. His words are "true words," "parole vere," not because they come from some private "note" book of his own invention but because ultimately they come from God's Book, the Bible.

Where, then, does this leave the *Commedia*, which, though laced with Scripture, is not God's Book but only the work of a demonstrably human author? Dante's response, I believe, would be rather like Scripture's own: the poem is the Word of the Lord because it says it is. This self-affirmation is negotiated gradually, and in ways that are specific to each of the three canticles: it is only late in the *Paradiso*, moreover, that Dante actually claims for his own work the adjective "sacred" (*Par.* 23.62 and 25.1). But in this move toward "scripturality" the poet does not rely primarily on his own overt affirmations. In the end, he receives his authority to speak out against the abuses of the papacy from none other than St. Peter, the first pope.

In *Paradiso* 27, after the court of heaven has celebrated the Christian orthodoxy that Dante demonstrates over the course of three cantos of theological examination, the papacy makes its final appearance in the poem in the person of Christ's first chosen vicar. Peter offers Dante no sign of disapproval for his temerity in the *bolgia* of the simonists. On the contrary, Peter uses even harsher words here than either Dante Poet or Dante Pilgrim spoke in *Inferno* 19 when denouncing the church's hierarchy. But again, this bitter speech placed in the mouth of St. Peter is not without a biblical warrant. The first pope thunders against his fourteenth-century successors in language that echoes unmistakably the Temple sermon preached by Jeremiah against the priesthood of his own day (Jer. 7:1–15):[37]

> Quelli ch'usurpa in terra il luogo mio,
>   il luogo mio, il luogo mio che vaca
>   ne la presenza del Figliuol di Dio,
> fatt' ha del cimitero mio cloaca
>   del sangue e de la puzza; onde 'l perverso
>   che cadde di qua sù, là giù si placa.
>   (*Par.* 27.22–27)

(He who on earth usurps my place, my place, my place, which in the sight of the Son of God is vacant, has made my burial-ground a sewer of blood and of stench, so that the Perverse One who fell from here above takes comfort there below.)

Like so many of the other souls in paradise, Peter goes on to contrast the catastrophe of Dante's day with the church's brighter beginnings: he recalls popes like Linus and Cletus, who cared nothing for gold (vv. 40–42), or those popes (such as St. Peter himself) who were martyred for their faith. But then the sad reality of Dante's own historical moment becomes overwhelming, so that Peter blushes to think of the rapacious wolves now dressed in shepherds' clothing, who use the "seal of Peter" as a cover for essentially private business deals ("privilegi venduti e mendaci," v. 53). With such abysmal successors in the high office, where might the church look for guidance? Where might it seek the apostolic witness recorded in the Gospels and the Book of Acts? The reader does not have to look far for an answer. The disciple now called by Christ to feed his sheep, to be the church's rock, to hold the keys of a kingdom against which the powers of hell cannot prevail, is none other than Dante.

e tu, figliuol, che per lo mortal pondo
   ancor giù tornerai, apri la bocca,
   e non asconder quel ch'io non ascondo.
                     (*Par.* 27.64–66)

(And you, my son, who, because of your mortal weight will again return below, open your mouth and do not hide what I hide not.)

Earlier in the journey, Beatrice had told the pilgrim that when he returned to earth he must write down the apocalypse shown to him in the Garden of Eden, so that his afterlife vision might be shared with those on earth (*Purg.* 32.103–5). Then, in the heaven of Mars, his great-great-grandfather, Cacciaguida, charged him not to be a timid friend to truth but to make manifest everything he had witnessed over the entire course of his journey (*Par.* 17.127–29). Here in *Paradiso* 27, that call to prophesy attains its final imprimatur, as the first pope recognizes not only a spiritual successor but also a son. In a tour de force of self-authorization, Dante charges himself through the figure of St. Peter to produce his own Book of Revelation. No matter what the opposition, he is to be openmouthed and hide nothing. With a scriptural self grounded in the Bible's two Testaments, he has only to sing God's Word in the vernacular notes of his poem's *terza rima*.

CHAPTER 2

Old and New Parchments

When Dante's writings are considered as a whole, the Christian Scriptures turn out to be the source of more reference and allusion than any other work: by one count the poet's *opera* contains 575 citations of the Bible, as compared to 395 citations of Aristotle and 192 of Virgil.[1] Calculations of this sort, however, cannot begin to suggest the extraordinary degree to which Dante absorbed the world of Scripture. This is most notable in the *Commedia*, where the Old and New Testaments, both in Latin and in vernacular translation, so permeate his language as almost to become one with it. Sometimes the poet quotes the Bible openly or draws attention to its relevance; far more often, however, he allows its presence to go unannounced, relying on the reader to catch the biblical reference and make something of it.

A case in point is the very first line of the *Commedia*, coming immediately before Dante tells the reader of his terrifying experience in the dark wood and of his resolve to recall it, "because of the good that I found there." Without apparent resort to any other text or authority—indeed, in a line that comes to personalize him as readily as his own name—he begins, "Nel mezzo del cammin di nostra vita." Here the poet opens his work by telling time: he is "in the middle of the journey of our life." Annotating this line, commentators remind the reader that the journey through the afterlife is set during Holy Week of 1300, that the poet was born in 1265, and therefore that he is 35 years old at the time of the narrative. But none of this additional information is necessary for one who remembers that the span of "our life" is given in the Psalms: "the days of our years are seventy years" (Ps. 89 [90]:10).

Nor is this verse the only biblical text at play here. Dante's recollection of the events that took place for him "in the middle of the journey of our life" also echoes King Hezekiah's song of thanksgiving, as recorded by the prophet in Isaiah 38:10 to commemorate the king's rescue from mortal illness: "I said: in the middle of my days I shall go to the gates of hell." In this biblical passage we find a great deal more than a commonplace allusion to life's three score and ten; we have a scriptural subtext for Dante's larger effort in the *Commedia*. In opening his own story of salvation from the powers of death, Dante appropriates the parallel experience of Hezekiah, a man saved from the "pit of destruction" by God's intervention, who afterward looks back and writes about his deliverance. Moreover, St. Jerome noted in his influential commentary on Hezekiah's song that while a good man dies at the end of his days, the sinner comes to the gates of hell in the midst of his life. Dante's losing his way "nel mezzo del cammin," therefore, is a confession of his spiritual loss, a tacit admission at the very outset that he was (to quote Jerome's gloss on Isaiah 38:10) "in the shadow of errors that lead to hell."[2]

The opening line of the *Commedia* reveals in miniature the biblical matrix of Dante's imagination. He assumes the psalm's estimation of our lifespan, draws not only upon a single verse in the book of Isaiah but upon an entire narrative situation, and then adapts for his own use an ancient exegetical commonplace on what it means to face hell in the middle of one's days. Does it follow, then, that he consciously deployed all these texts, patristic as well as biblical, when he sat down to begin the poem? Centuries of scholarship would have us imagine so, as if the poet marshaled his meanings from the outset and wrote with footnotes in mind. It seems quite as likely, however, that Dante called upon his knowledge of scriptural metaphor, narrative, and traditional interpretation in a much less calculating, more spontaneous and fluid way. His knowledge would have been so deeply assimilated as to inform his thought reflexively, almost unconsciously, more a mother tongue of the imagination than a technical lexicon deliberately acquired. In this regard he was no doubt like most of his contemporaries, whose experience of Scripture came primarily from the whole sensorium of medieval culture rather than from study, who continuously "overheard" the Bible or saw its visual representation in passing, or had it somewhere in mind.

But unlike the vast majority of laymen in the Middle Ages, as we saw in the previous chapter, "The Scriptural Self," Dante also seems to have stud-

ied the Scriptures, and done so according to the major interpretative tra-
ditions of his time and place. In the "schools of the religious" (*Convivio*
2.22.7) at Santa Croce and Santa Maria Novella, moreover, he would have
encountered a common biblical culture shared by Franciscans and Domini-
cans. Scripture stood at the center of the curriculum and informed all three
aspects of the traditional clerical education: *lectio*, the reading of Scripture
with commentary; *disputatio*, the discussion of questions arising out of
problematic texts; and *praedicatio*, the preaching of Scripture. Such study
was also based on certain assumptions: the Bible's divine inspiration, the
typological relationship between Old Testament "figure" and New Testa-
ment "fulfillment," and a fourfold interpretation of Scripture, whereby the
literal text is regarded not only as true in itself but as concealing a set of
spiritual mysteries. Dante refers to this standard fourfold approach to bibli-
cal exegesis in his epistle to Can Grande, when he elaborates upon one of
the textbook examples of biblical "polysemy," Psalm 113 [114]:1, "In exitu
Israel de Aegypto." The literal sense of this text, "When Israel went out of
Egypt, the house of Jacob from a barbarous people," refers to the historical
event of the Exodus. Within this factual record of something that once
happened in time and space, however, other meanings are also to be found.
According to the allegorical sense, the Exodus signifies "our redemption
through Christ"; according to the moral sense, "the conversion of the soul
from the sorrow and misery of sin to a state of grace"; and according to the
anagogic or mystical sense, "the passing of the sanctified soul from the
bondage of the corruption of this world to the liberty of everlasting glory."[3]

These approaches to the Bible were ancient, with roots in the New
Testament's reading of the Old, as well as in the exegetical practice of
Augustine and the other church fathers. But in the thirteenth century one
had to reckon with new developments in biblical study as well. Particularly
in university circles, the biblical text largely lost its own formal integrity.
Instead, Scripture was abstracted in a *Summa*, or dissected into a multitude
of component parts (called the *divisiones per membra varia*), or employed
as an illustration or proof text taken wholly out of its original context. The
practice of massing together parallel passages and chains of citations—that
is, passages joined only by reason of a common word—served to reinforce
the notion of the Bible as a source that could be divided and reassembled
according to a theologian's need. So did the increasing number of research
tools developed to help the scholar and preacher use biblical text more effi-

ciently: glossaries, concordances, *florilegia*, *postillae*, collections of *exempla* and *distinctiones*.[4]

Nor should we underestimate the impact of the "glossed" text on the way the Scripture came to be treated. It had long been common practice to insert between the lines of the Bible a brief definition or explanation of its meaning. Gradually, scribes also added lengthier material taken from the *Glossa ordinaria*—the standard compendium of (largely patristic) commentary on the Bible—and placed it in the margins, or at the top and bottom of the page. By the end of the twelfth century, not only the *Glossa ordinaria* but two other works that were heavily based upon it—Peter Comestor's *Historia scholastica* and Peter Lombard's *Sententiarum*—came virtually to supplant the "sacred page" itself. At least in university circles, scholars tended to gloss not the Scripture itself but the several glosses upon it.[5] With citations both from the church fathers and from more contemporary exegetes filling the margins and running between the lines, the text was quite literally surrounded by interpretation. To read the Bible, therefore, was to encounter a cloud of other witnesses: there was meant to be no unmediated encounter.[6]

This discussion raises the inevitable question of what Bible Dante would have known. The answer is complicated, given the shadowy existence of vernacular translations in the mid–thirteenth century, not to mention our uncertainty about the many variant versions of St. Jerome's Latin (Vulgate) Bible.[7] If Dante had access to the renowned cathedral library in Verona, for instance, the Bibles found there would most likely have been multivolume editions, usually of monumental size, and lavishly decorated—books intended more for ceremony and display than for practical reading. By contrast, the so-called *exemplar Parisiensis*, or "Paris Bible," developed in Paris in the early thirteenth century, was intended to meet the needs both of the student in the university classroom and the Mendicant preacher on a mission.[8] Although full of textual errors that subsequently led to the formation of *correctoria*, the Paris Bible was an immediate and enduring success. Its compact, one-volume edition of the Scripture made crucial innovations in how the Bible would continue to be presented even to our own time.[9] Small in size, written on thin parchment, the Paris Bible and its thirteenth- and fourteenth-century offshoots normalized the order of the sacred books and (thanks to Stephen Langton, d. 1228) made chapter divisions virtually the same as today's. They often included the prefaces of St. Jerome, as well as an array of tools that made them eminently "searchable" and thus of great practical use: lists of biblical names, concordances, short passages intended to combat heretical teaching. For the first time in the Middle Ages, a book was designed both for reading and for reference.

Such material transformations suggest changes in the way Scripture was read and in its readership.[10] If stable religious communities continued to favor the large volumes in monastic libraries, these new and more portable texts became the traveling Bibles of the Mendicant Orders. Many were indeed small enough to be carried among the itinerant preacher's personal effects. The great proliferation of Paris Bibles also signals a growing number of individual (rather than communal) readers—an educated elite who gravitated to the universities and Mendicant schools, filled administrative positions in church and state alike, and actively used their Bibles in what André Vauchez has called the "diffusion of the evangelical word."[11]

Was Dante such a person? We do not know whether he himself possessed one of these portable Bibles, or whether he had access to some kind of vernacular translation, as his frequent citations of Scripture in Italian suggest.[12] Studies of his citations show that most often he used the Paris Bible, either when quoting the Latin directly or when rendering it into Italian.[13] Nonetheless, the citations provide evidence that he used other versions of the Scripture, such as the Old Latin (*Vetus Latina*) that was largely supplanted by Jerome's Vulgate but that remained current in trace form throughout the Middle Ages, largely because it was firmly fixed in the liturgy. Most such textual variations in Dante's practice of biblical citation are by no means momentous but only a matter of word order ("duo gladii" as opposed to "gladii duo") or of prepositions ("In exitu Israel *de* Aegypto" rather than "In exitu Israel *ex* Aegypto"). Most likely, Dante used whatever version of the Scripture was at hand, drawing upon the manuscripts he was able to consult personally or quoting from that internalized Bible treasured in memory and known by heart. In this latter regard, we should also recall the powerful, almost subliminal influence of the liturgy, with its biblical readings, hymnody, prayers, and sequences.[14] In fact, the Scriptures that Dante uses most often come precisely from those books that were privileged in the church's worship: the Gospels, the Psalms, and the Epistles of Paul.

The poet's use of Scripture varies in importance and technique from work to work, but the most striking contrast is that between the prose treatises and the *Commedia*. Both the *Convivio* and the *Monarchia*, for instance, are extremely rich in their use of biblical exegesis, showing real skill in the maneuvering of the "sacred page" to advance an argument or bolster a claim. While the poet of the *Commedia* is perfectly able to do the same, he characteristically makes use of Scripture less as a source of proof texts than as a divine "pretext" for the story. Instead of following the lead of medieval commentary in its move from particularity to abstraction—that is, from character and event to theological interpretation—Dante typically allows the Bible to generate his own narrative in the *Commedia*.

An example of this contrast is found in Dante's differing uses of the Gospel account of the Transfiguration. In *Convivio* 2.1.5, the event is said to illustrate the moral sense of the text: because Christ went up to the mountain with only three of his twelve disciples, "we should have few companions in matters that touch us most deeply." Dante refers to this episode again in *Monarchia* 3.9.11, but this time for quite a different purpose: Peter's "hasty and unthinking impulsiveness" on Mount Tabor becomes a way of arguing that in matters of temporal responsibility, the empire and not the church should hold sway. In *Purgatorio*, however, the entire biblical episode is evoked not to substantiate a particular polemical point but to construct Dante's identity and suggest the apostolic mystery into which he is being called:

> un splendor mi squarciò 'l velo
> del sonno, e un chiamar: "Surgi: che fai?"
> Quali a veder de' fioretti del melo
> che del suo pome li angeli fa ghiotti
> e perpetüe nozze fa nel cielo,
> Pietro e Giovanni e Iacopo condotti
> e vinti, ritornaro a la parola
> da la qual furon maggior sonni rotti,
> e videro scemata loro scuola
> così di Moïsè come d'Elia,
> e al maestro suo cangiata stola;
> tal torna' io.

> (*Purg.* 32.71–82)

(A splendor rent the veil of my sleep, and a call, "Arise, what are you doing?" As when brought to see some of the blossoms of the apple tree that makes the angels greedy of its fruit and holds perpetual marriage feasts in Heaven, Peter and James and John were overpowered, and came to themselves again at the word by which deeper slumbers were broken, and saw their company diminished alike by Moses and Elias, and their Master's raiment changed, so I came to myself.)

In the course of a densely scriptural simile that draws the Gospel episode into contact with the Song of Songs, the Apocalypse, and other New Testament texts, the Transfiguration associates Dante with the disciples Peter, James, and John; joins Beatrice typologically with Christ; and presents the events of Dante's poetic narrative in the light of a complex tradition of allegorical interpretation. Nor should it be forgotten that the three disciples recalled here in simile will later be encountered by Dante in person. Their appearance in *Paradiso* 24–26 suggests how in the *Commedia* Scripture can move from recollected text to dramatized encounter, from citation to scenario.

Not all uses of Scripture in the poem, of course, are so straightforward or so extensive. A substantial biblical text, with many implications for the poem, can be called up by a single word (as when the term "Miserere" in *Purgatorio* 5.24 conjures up Psalm 50 [51] "verse by verse") or by a bare phrase (as when "*et coram patre*" in *Paradsio* 11.62 recalls Matthew 10:32–33). It can also be made present in any number of ways: exact or near quotation, paraphrase, allusion, echo.[15] However, the sheer number of citations (or lack thereof) does not necessarily convey the extent of Dante's reliance on any particular book. For instance, although Exodus is cited only once in the *Commedia*—Exodus 33:19 in *Paradiso* 25.55–56—the paradigm of Israel's escape from bondage in Egypt provides one of the deep structures of the entire poem. Likewise with the Apocalypse: while the Revelation to John is cited only eight times, both the book and the exegetical traditions that grew up around it offer a massive subtext for the last cantos of the *Purgatorio*, as well as informing the general sense of apocalyptic crisis that impels the mood of the *Commedia* with increasing intensity.

But if simple enumeration of biblical references is not in itself definitive, noting patterns of citation within the three canticles can be instructive nonetheless. Given Dante's overt dependence on classical sources in the *Inferno*, as well as the rejection of God exemplified in those who have lost the "good of the intellect" (3.18), it should come as no surprise that hell is the least biblical realm of the afterlife. Nor is it difficult to see why in *Paradiso* biblical allusion is far more common than actual citation. The blessed have become so completely one with God's Word as to assimilate it into their own speech, to pass beyond the mediation of the Scriptures and into the reality they signify. Where the Bible plays its most overt and important role is in the middle space of the *Purgatorio*, with its 30 direct citations and roughly 40 allusions. In this realm of time and change, the souls have not yet reached their eternal destination; they remain *in via*, needing guidance and instruction. Small wonder, then, that in the second canticle Dante should pay sustained attention to God's Book, showing the power of its transforming word among the penitents and thereby suggesting its importance for the living.

In the *Purgatorio*, moreover, Dante stages a series of "meetings" with the Bible that stretches from antepurgatory at the base of the mountain to the Garden of Eden at its summit. In canto 2, the Pilgrim observes a boat heading for shore and piloted by an angel. In hell he saw Charon, the terrifying ferryman of the Virgilian underworld, carrying the damned over the river Styx and thence to their place of eternal torment. Here, instead of an angry monster, the Pilgrim sees a single "whiteness" on the horizon, then "un vasello snelletto e leggero" ("a vessel swift and light," v. 41) skimming the surface of the sea. When the boat comes closer he realizes that it has neither sail nor oar; rather, it races to shore by the fan of an angel's "etterne penne" ("eternal wings," v. 35). Just as the boat makes land, he hears the hundred souls on board all chanting the words of Scripture:

> Da poppa stava il celestial nocchiero,
>   tal che parea beato per iscripto;
>   e più di cento spirti entro sediero.
> "*In exitu Isräel de Aegypto*"
>   cantavan tutti insieme ad una voce
>   con quanto di quel salmo è poscia scripto.
>   (*Purg.* 2.43–48)

(At the stern stood the celestial steersman, such, that blessedness seemed to be inscribed upon him; and within sat more than a hundred spirits. "*In exitu Israel de Aegypto*" all of them were singing with one voice, with the rest of the psalm as it is written.)

One canto earlier, in the opening lines of the *Purgatorio*, Dante presented himself as a seafarer and his poem as a ship; both had survived the *Inferno*'s "cruel sea" to set forth over "miglior acque" ("better seas," 1.1).

Here we begin to understand what this change in watery element, this new setting forth, actually means. It is not only that an angel rather than a demon commands the first boat we come upon in the second canticle; it is also that everyone in the vessel is singing the Lord's song. Because Dante identifies this text by its *incipit*, "In exitu Israel de Aegypto"—and then says outright that the souls continued to sing "with the rest of that psalm as it is written"—our attention is drawn to the entirety of Psalm 113 as it appears in the Vulgate, a sweep of verses that in present-day Bibles is divided between Psalms 114 and 115:

> 1 When Israel went out of Egypt, the house of Jacob from a barbarous people: 2 Judea was made his sanctuary, Israel his dominion. 3 The sea saw and fled: Jordan was turned back. . . . 15 Blessed be you of the Lord, who made heaven and earth. 16 The heaven of heaven is the Lord's: but the earth he has given to the children of men. 17 The dead shall not praise thee, Lord: nor any of them that go down to hell. 18 But we that live bless the Lord: from this time now and forever.

These verses of Scripture provide a gloss on the new reality of the *Purgatorio*. Whereas the first canticle introduced us to a kingdom of death where none of the damned could say God's name let alone "bless the Lord," here we are put in the company of those who, however imperfectly at present, nonetheless "live" in God, as the psalm has it, "from this time now and forever." Dante also emphasizes that everyone in the angel's boat sings the Scripture "with one voice." In hell, whether the damned spoke in eloquent monologue or only uttered gibberish, all were in some radical sense soloists doomed to repeat their own private stories, to sing the songs of themselves. But as the angel speeds the redeemed to the shores of their spiritual transformation, the souls discover how private speech becomes the corporate Word of God. In hell there were echoes of Scripture, though often undermined by irony and always translated into the *Commedia*'s vernacular. In purgatory the Vulgate Bible sails into the text, "beato per iscripto," inscribing blessedness in its wake.

Dante could not have chosen a biblical text better able to suggest the plenitude of Scripture's meaning or the vital connection between the Bible and liturgy. To begin with, like the single word "Jerusalem," Psalm 113 was a stock example of the four senses of Scripture, as Dante himself demonstrates in his epistle to Can Grande. Here the souls who chant the psalm as they arrive on the shores of purgatory illustrate the multiple significance of the biblical text. Leaving the "Egypt" of this mortal world behind them, they set out as pilgrims for heaven's Promised Land. What enables them to take on the Scripture so that its multiple senses in effect become their own story is baptism—that "portal of faith" (to recall Virgil's words in *Inferno* 4.36) through which any pilgrim *in exitu* must pass. Exodus and the sacrament of Christian initiation are joined quite explicitly in the baptismal liturgy of Easter Eve, where Psalm 113 plays an important part in an extended fusion of the Old and New Testaments, so that the Hebrews' safe passage through the Red Sea becomes a figure of the baptismal crossing through sacramental waters. Nor is the Easter Vigil the psalm's only relevant liturgical setting: according to Jacques Le Goff, the text was "commonly sung in the Middle Ages when a body was moved from its home to the church and then to the cemetery."[16] "In exitu Israel de Aegypto" suggests the entryway of faith and the direction of eternity.

When Dante invokes this particular biblical text in *Purgatorio* 2, therefore, he is making no simple acknowledgment of the importance of God's Book. Rather, he is drawing upon Psalm 113's surplus of associations—exegetical, typological, and liturgical. He augments this abundance of meaning by setting his own journey through the afterlife at the time of the triduum, the Christian Holy Week's culmination. Having descended into hell on the afternoon of Good Friday, he emerges from its "deep and savage way" on Easter dawn; almost immediately thereafter he discovers more than a hundred souls chanting a psalm inextricably tied to the great Vigil of Easter and the sacrament of baptism. Thus, given the intersection of liturgical with narrative time, "In exitu Israel de Aegypto" becomes Dante's personal pilgrim song as well.

Spiritual exodus begins in earnest once the souls pass through the gates of purgatory in canto 10. Within the "second kingdom" proper they let God's Word dwell in them "abundantly," to recall St. Paul in Colossians 3:16, by "teaching and admonishing one another in psalms, hymns, and spiritual canticles." To this is added the power of what they now *see*—not only images carved into the sides of the mountain or depicted in pavement underfoot, but others quite immaterial, audible in voices that "pass flying" (13.28) or visible only in the mind's eye (17.13–45).

On the terrace of pride (*Purg.* 10–12), for instance, Dante finds numerous examples of biblical (as well as pagan) figures who either enjoin the virtue of humility or demonstrate the wages of arrogance. As if in illustration of how the Middle Ages "storiated" (10.73) the text of Scripture in the visual arts, Dante first presents a program of bas-reliefs that "tells" biblical narrative in the fashion of a carving, painting, or manuscript illumination. In the first of these, a portrait of the Virgin Mary and the archangel Gabriel at the Annunciation, the poet deliberately emphasizes the scripted nature of such visual representation by having the silent images seem to speak the words of the Vulgate Luke (1:28–38):

> Giurato si saria ch'el dicesse "*Ave!*";
>   perché iv' era imaginata quella
>   ch'ad aprir l'alto amor volse la chiave;
> e avea in atto impressa esta favella
>   "*Ecce ancilla Dei!*" propriamente
>   come figura in cera si suggella.
>   (*Purg.* 10.40–45)

(One would have sworn that he was saying "*Ave!*"; for there she was imaged who turned the key to open supreme love, and these words were imprinted in her attitude: "*Ecce ancilla Dei!*" expressly as a figure is stamped on wax.)

This "visible speech" (10.95) heightens our sense of the image's preternatural vitality, its refusal to be inarticulate marble. It reminds the reader of the many actual renderings of the Annunciation that show the words "Ave" and "Ecce ancilla Dei" coming out of the mouths of Gabriel and Mary—that give a "scripted" image of Scripture. Dante may also be drawing attention here to the achievement of his own craft: his skill at turning words into flesh, silence into sound, the ability of his poetry, that is, to "speak" to us. In any event, what the penitents on the terrace of pride contemplate in this visible translation of biblical narrative into graven image is the possibility of a new identity, a self more like Mary's than the one they left behind in the mortal world. Gradually, they read themselves into her script, step into her picture, and cross over that threshold she opened up when she "turned the key to open supreme love."

"Taking on" Scripture, moreover, is precisely what happens when the souls exit from the seven terraces of the mountain. When each successive stage of purgation is completed, the angel who guards that terminus uses a wing to brush away one of the seven P's (for *peccati*, sins) marking each soul's forehead. As the penitents move up Mount Purgatory, they come closer to a knowledge of God's kingdom as revealed by Christ in his Sermon on the Mount (Matt. 5:3–12, Luke 6:20–23): blessed are the poor in spirit, the meek, those who hunger and thirst after righteousness, and so on. Leaving each terrace, therefore, souls receive a particular Beatitude appropriate to their new level of understanding. The Scripture they receive signals both the virtue they have obtained and the capital sin that has been purged.

In all cases but one, the Beatitudes are indicated by a single Latin word or catchphrase that recalls the entire saying, so that the listener supplies the whole of a verse that is given only in part. The souls, therefore, complete what the angel says; they become the fulfilled promise of the Beatitude. After the purgation of pride, for instance, Dante notes that " ' *beati pauperes spiritu* ' was sung so sweetly as no words could tell" (*Purg.* 12.110–11). Only the initial phrase of the first Beatitude is given, but in keeping with the common liturgical practice of versicle and response, the proclamation "Blessed are the poor in spirit" is meant to elicit the remainder of the verse: "for theirs is the kingdom of heaven."

Dante repeats this simple citation of the Vulgate once again on the seventh and last terrace of the mountain ("he sang '*Beati mundo corde,* '" 27.8); otherwise he varies his linguistic practice. Sometimes Vulgate quotation dissolves into the vernacular, as on the terrace of sloth when "the angel moved his feathers and fanned us, declaring '*Qui lugent*' to be blessed, for they shall have their souls possessed of consolation" (19.49–51). Elsewhere the Latin is dropped entirely, as on the terrace of gluttony, where the angel does not so much translate the Vulgate's "Blessed are those who hunger and thirst after righteousness" as paraphrase it almost beyond recognition:

> E senti dir: "Beati cui alluma
> tanto di grazia, che l'amor del gusto
> nel petto lor troppo disir non fuma,
> esurïendo sempre quanto è giusto!"
> (*Purg.* 24.151–54)

(And I heard say, "Blessed are they who are so illumined by grace that the love of taste kindles not too great desire in their breasts, and who hunger always so far as is just.")

All these encounters with the biblical text—in song, in visual art, and in the ritual process of the terraces—culminate in *Purgatorio* 29, where Dante presents an allegorical representation of the entire canon, from the alpha of Genesis to the omega of the Apocalypse. At the summit of the mountain, a flash of light from the east ushers in a procession of figures. The main part of the procession begins with a file of twenty-four "seniori" ("elders," v. 83) walking two by two. Behind them come four winged animals that escort a splendid griffin-drawn chariot. Following this ensemble is yet another file of elders: first a pair of old men, then a quartet of males who appear "of lowly aspect" (v. 142), and finally a single old man whose eyes are closed. Once all these figures take their places, the canto ends. The stage is set for the advent of Beatrice in *Purgatorio* 30.

Drawing on a rich store of imagery found first in the prophet Ezekiel and then in the Revelation to John, this elaborate, quasi-liturgical procession not only rehearses visionary moments in both Testaments but also gives us a vision of the Bible itself. For what Dante sees assembled before him is the Word of God made allegorical flesh. The twenty-four elders, recalling the "four and twenty ancients" of Apocalypse 4:4, represent the books of the Hebrew Bible as Jerome numbered them. The four winged creatures who come next in line are traditional symbols of the Gospels, and the company that follows upon the chariot gives us the rest of the New Testament: the Pauline Epistles and the Acts of the Apostles paired together, the four Catholic Epistles (Peter, James, John, and Jude) walking behind them, and at the end of the canonical procession, the "vecchio solo" (v. 143) who stands for the book of the Apocalypse.

Dante does not himself decode this Pageant of Revelation or make these attributions directly (aside from giving some strong iconographic clues). Instead, he cultivates the atmosphere of mystery and enigma characteristic of apocalyptic literature. Consequently, commentators since the fourteenth century have not been of one mind about how to interpret each and every member of the procession. The four men "of lowly aspect," for example, have been identified with the great doctors of the church—Augustine, Jerome, Ambrose, and Gregory the Great—and the single old man with his eyes shut has occasionally been glossed as Moses or Bernard of Clairvaux. Nonetheless, what has come to be the standard reading of the Pageant takes it as a presentation of the books of Old and New Testaments as they have been received within the church. While Dante's journey up the

mountain afforded him encounter after encounter with fragments of bibli-
cal language and imagery, that journey culminates in a vision of Scripture
as a unified whole—as God's *bibliotheca.*

The "mystical procession" of *Purgatorio* 29 suggests how for medieval
Christians the Bible was as much an event as a book. In its richness of detail
the Pageant incorporates something of the wide range of liturgical and
artistic media through which the sacred text was commonly transmitted
and received. Analogies are easy to find: the church's elaborate ceremonies,
liturgical processions, the pageantry devised for the newly proclaimed feast
of Corpus Christi, the cortège of the Grail, and early-fourteenth-century
allegorical pageants that Dante himself may have witnessed.[17] Commenta-
tors also point to the iconographic programs of specific churches in Ra-
venna, Anagni, and Rome that seem to bear some particular resemblance
to the *Purgatorio*'s procession of hieratic figures.[18]

In addition, the Pageant may also have links to such medieval liturgical
dramas as the *Ordo prophetarum*, attributed to St. Augustine and custom-
arily performed in the season of the Nativity. In the fourteenth-century
version of the rite described by Paolo Toschi, a procession began in the
choir and then moved out to the center of the nave.[19] There the gathered
congregation would sing a hymn of invitation, biding the prophets (from
Moses to Virgil and the Sibyl) to proclaim their own prophecy of Christ.
All these *profeti* were dressed in emblematic costume: Moses held the
tablets of the Law; Aaron wore the vestments of a high priest; and Eliz-
abeth, the mother of John the Baptist, was dressed in a white robe that
showed her to be "quasi pregnans." These figures would come to dramatic
life in brief scenarios, their particular role in salvation history articulated
through direct address or "annunciation" to the congregation. When the
procession finally reached the altar, the *Ordo* would culminate in a celebra-
tion of the Mass—a sacramental fulfillment of what the prophets had
foretold. We do not know if the poet ever witnessed such a production or
whether any of these various art forms inspired the Pageant directly. There
can be no question, however, that for Dante, as well as his contemporaries,
Scripture was embedded in a matrix of word and image, sound and gesture.

How Dante could make personal use of this complex Word to empower his
own speech, how he could "speak Scripture" as his own tongue, is nowhere

better seen than in his epistle to the Italian Cardinals. Written in May or June 1314, when a conclave was assembled at Carpentras with the charge to elect a successor to Pope Clement V, Dante's letter tries to persuade his six countrymen to end the papacy's "Babylonian Captivity" in France.[20] Dante promotes his cause first of all by writing in Latin, the language of the church as well as of the learned, and secondly by commanding the churchmen's immediate attention with his use of Scripture. Indeed, he opens with a quotation of the initial verse of the Lamentations of Jeremiah: "How doth the city sit solitary that was full of people! She is become as a widow that was great among the nations!" Dante goes on to establish a set of correspondences between Jeremiah's moment and his own, between biblical history and current events. Early-fourteenth-century Rome, therefore, is another Jerusalem, likewise widowed and abandoned. Just as the corruption of the ancient priesthood brought destruction to the chosen city of David, so the present hierarchy is responsible for the contemporary ruin.

Even as Dante establishes these "objective" correspondences, however, he is careful to work *himself* into the equation. Not only were the words of Lamentations 1:1 spoken by a prophet made worthy to speak by the command of the Holy Spirit, but they are also words that Dante himself, here using the first-person plural, is constrained to raise in his own time. Circumstances force him to echo the prophet's speech and, in effect, to share his identity. This association then gives him license to speak to the cardinals of his church as if they were the false priests who received the stinging rebuke of Jeremiah's Lamentations. Dante accuses them of neglecting to guide the "chariot of the Spouse of the Crucified." Instead, they preferred to turn a profit by selling doves in the temple, "where that which cannot be measured by price is made merchandise, to the hurt of them that come and go therein" (para. 4, p. 144). In a whirlwind of scriptural reference that gathers force through its appeal to both Testaments, the ark of the covenant becomes the chariot of the church, even as the Temple of Israel—whether in Jeremiah's day or later when Christ drove forth the money changers—is metamorphosed into the beleaguered Christian institution that the cardinals are now exploiting for their own gain.

In the opening paragraphs of this epistle, Dante uses the first-person plural to imply that he speaks for others who are less forthrightly "murmuring, or muttering, or thinking, or dreaming" (para. 8, p. 146) about these same concerns. But this inclusive "we" becomes a solitary "I," as the author reveals his awareness of how alone he is, how vulnerable to abrupt dismissal. Dante presents himself, therefore, as a voice perpetually crying in the wilderness: "one voice alone, one alone of filial piety, and that of a private individual" ("una sola vox, sola pia, et haec privata," para. 6, p. 145). He is also fully aware that he speaks to princes of the church as a layman, and thus as one whose words come not only from the farthest margins of power but from a suspect source, "ab infra, non de coelo"—from below and not from heaven (para. 9; p. 146).

Anticipating that he will be ignored because he is "no one," he shores up his authority by appeal to the Bible, by turning his private voice into biblical speech and his solitary identity into a "scriptural self." To begin with, he poses the obvious question—who is he who dares to speak in this way?—and then at once supplies and refutes the very Old Testament analogue the cardinals might well have in mind for him:

> Perchance in indignant rebuke you will ask: "And who is this man who, not fearing the sudden punishment of Uzzah, sets himself up to protect the Ark, tottering though it be?" . . . Nor does the presumption of Uzzah, which some may think should be laid to my charge, infect me, as though I had been rash in my utterance, with the taint of his guilt. For he gave heed to the Ark, I to the unruly oxen that are dragging it away into the wilderness.   (para. 5, pp. 144–45)

Here a biblical exemplum is proposed only to be firmly rejected. Dante imagines that the cardinals who receive this vilifying letter will compare him to Uzzah, who, according to the biblical account, met sudden death when he presumed to touch the sacred tabernacle: "Uzzah put forth his hand to the ark of God, and took hold of it: because the oxen kicked and made it lean aside. And the indignation of the Lord was enkindled against Uzzah, and he struck him for his rashness [super temeritate]: and he died there before the ark of God" (2 Kings [now 2 Sam.] 6:6–7). Dante refuses to accept this analogy, even if he does entertain the possibility that he will be called presumptuous. He has not, however, touched the holy ark of the church; he has only raised his hand in warning against those unruly "oxen" dragging it into the wilderness, away from its rightful destination in Jerusalem—or, rather, in Rome.

After Dante rejects the biblical likeness of Uzzah, he is free to assume others. He is not only a sheep of Christ's flock but also a would-be shepherd of the sheep. More importantly, he is another Paul, whose peculiar blend of boasting and humility in 1 Corinthians 15 provides the perfect model for Dante's own self-presentation here:

> Verily, I am one of the least of the sheep of the pasture of Jesus Christ; verily, I abuse no pastoral authority, seeing that I possess no riches. By the grace of God, therefore, I am what I am, and "the zeal of His house has eaten me up." For even from the mouths of babes and sucklings has been heard the truth well pleasing to God; and he who was born blind confessed the truth, which the Pharisees not only concealed, but in their malice even strove to pervert. These are the justification of my boldness.
>
> (para. 5, p. 144)

Like Paul, Dante may be not only the last of the apostles but also the least ("novissime autem omnium . . . sum minimus apostolorum," 1 Cor. 15:8–9). Nonetheless, also like Paul, he rejoices to be what by the grace of God he "is," an apostle whose ceaseless labor has not been in vain: "But by the grace of God, I am what I am; and his grace in me hath not been void, but I have labored more abundantly than all they: yet not I, but the grace of God with me" (1 Cor. 15:10).

Dante specifies the nature of this labor when, immediately after bringing a Pauline phrase into his own speech ("sed gratia Dei sum id quod sum," "but by the grace of God I am what I am"), he goes on to quote the Psalmist David: "zelus domus eius comedit me" ("the zeal of thy house hath eaten me up," Ps. 68 [69]: 10). These words occur in a sequence of verses in which the Psalmist describes his own marginality. Because of his zeal for the house of the Lord, he has borne the reproach of the community (v. 8), become a stranger and alien to his family (v. 9), indeed suffered the very same accusations that have been leveled by a rebellious Israel against God (v. 10). Dante's sparse quotation of the psalm evokes its larger thematic context with an eye to his own situation. Even if he stands outside the sphere of earthly power, being only "one voice alone, one alone of filial piety . . . a private individual," he is nonetheless a partner of righteousness. Like the Psalmist, he knows that he, too, is zealously *with* God.

If more of the psalm is relevant here than the single phrase "zelus domus eius comedit me," so too is the subsequent appearance of this text in a familiar New Testament narrative; recollection of one reference entails the memory of the other. The Evangelist John (2:13–25) describes how

Jesus cleansed the temple by overturning the tables of the money changers, chastising those who sold doves, saying "Take these things hence, and make not the house of my Father a house of traffic" (2:16). Seeing him perform this dramatic act, his followers immediately recalled the words of the Psalmist: "And his disciples remembered, that it was written: 'The zeal of thy house hath eaten me up' " (2:17). This New Testament use of the Old Testament text provides Dante with yet another validation for his own call to reform. For although the cardinals have married themselves to avarice, sold doves in the temple, and neglected their apostolic charge, Dante, who has no riches whatsoever, has been driven by true zeal for the Lord's people. As a result, he alone carries out God's mission, not only that of the prophets but that of Christ himself. Although a mere layman, *he* is defender of the faith.[21]

The "Scriptural speech" found in the epistle to the Italian Cardinals is also writ large throughout the *Commedia*. By piling up biblical phrases, together with the narratives in which they are embedded, Dante creates a biblical discourse that is virtually indistinguishable from his own speech. One thinks as well of St. Augustine's *Confessions*, whose sentences are often little more than biblical citation, allusion, and echo.[22] In either case, we see how someone immersed in a world of the Bible could be so imbued with its thought and language that to tell his own story, to argue his own case, meant retelling the Testaments—the old and new parchments, God's Word and his own.

CHAPTER 3

"John Is with Me"

In the opening sentence of *La poesia di Dante*, Benedetto Croce asks if there is any reason to judge Dante's poetry differently from that of others. Behind the question stands a challenge to any assumption that the *Commedia*'s alleged "divinity" confers upon it some kind of supraliterary status. Such notions mean nothing to Croce. Instead, what interests him is the artistic or "lyric" impulse of the poet that continually interrupts Dante's construction of a "romanzo teologico," overrides its structures with the revenge of the repressed, and finally unites Dante to other men of genius. If Croce acknowledges the poet's grandeur, therefore, he refuses to treat him as a unique case. He wants instead to see him (with Shakespeare and Goethe) no longer even as an individual but as an articulation of a "universal poetry" that resounds with the same quality in all great poets and artists. If Dante spoke divinely, it was because he spoke as a genius: "e Dante fu un Genio."[1]

Croce has not fared well in the annals of postwar American Dante criticism, which not only has repudiated his distinction between *poesia* and *non poesia* but by and large has taken the theological structures of the *Commedia* very seriously. Nonetheless, the very same question he posed at the outset of his work—the question whether Dante should be read and judged apart from other poets—has remained fundamental even for those whose answer is different from Croce's, and perhaps especially so for those for whom Dante is (to recall the Latin epitaph of Giovanni del Virgilio) "Theologus Dantes."

Many professional readers of the poem—beginning with Dante's own sons—have been made nervous by the poet's claims and have insisted that he was only speaking figuratively. Others have upheld the poem's essential connection to Scripture, even his assertions of something like "scripturality." Some have concentrated on the identity of the poet himself, specifically his kinship to the prophets of Israel[2] or to those biblical writers who openly use poetic form: the Psalmist, the author of the Song of Songs, and John the Evangelist, who was believed also to be the seer of the Apocalypse.[3] Still others have linked Dante to the medieval visionaries and mystics who claimed that heaven told them to "Write down what I tell you!"— twelfth-century figures like Joachim of Fiore and Hildegard of Bingen, or, closer to his own time, Marguerite Porete and Bridget of Sweden.[4]

In addition to discussion of the poet's identity as at least a quasi-biblical author, there has been interest in the way the Scripture informs the *Commedia*, both on the micro-level of its literary style and with regard to its overall composition.[5] Erich Auerbach, for instance, claimed that biblical typology or "figuralism"—"something real and historical which announces something else that is also real and historical"[6]—determines the whole structure of the poem. Likewise, in trying to account for the range of Dante's diction, its dramatic mixture of the lofty and the lowly, Auerbach pointed to the Scripture's *sermo humilis* as the poet's own model of writing.[7] And finally, there is Dante's epistle to Can Grande della Scala, with its breathtaking assertion that the *Commedia* is to be read according to the four "senses" of Scripture. Because only God could write according to this "allegory of the theologians," any claim of such fourfold exegesis by a human author is astounding, perhaps even blasphemous.[8] Could Dante possibly mean that his poem *was* the Bible?

The American Dante scholar perhaps still most influential in our own day, Charles Singleton, answered this question with a Yes and a No. For him, the *Commedia* is a human poem and not the Word of God. But because it is manifestly a *biblical* poem, whose author deliberately set out to "imitate God's way of writing,"[9] it may legitimately be treated as "scriptural"—as long as there are scare marks surrounding the assertion. Such sympathetic skepticism requires of the reader a kind of sophisticated naïveté. Dante's journey is "make-believe," but it demands that we treat it as if it were no less literal or historical than the Exodus from Egypt, and therefore as possessed of the Bible's other "senses" in full array. To do otherwise is to betray the poem's predominant mode of representation, even to rob it of its premise.

Following Singleton's direction, the reader of the *Commedia* becomes something like the religious believer who cannot accept the Bible's literal veracity yet is nonetheless able to give Scripture the benefit of the doubt. Disbelief is willingly suspended, and literary myth treated as if it were history. Indeed, what is certainly only "feigned history," to recall W. H. Auden's definition of fiction, is turned into something more substantial, until in effect it *becomes* substantial. As the author of *God: A Biography* put it recently, "The Christmas story didn't happen, in sum, and it need not be believed, but it still matters, and it still works."[10] By analogy, Singleton's readers allow Dante's poem to be the gospel truth. They understand, to quote the critic's most memorable formulation, that "the fiction of the *Divine Comedy* is that it is not fiction."[11] They acknowledge the fact of Dante's "make-believe," and then forget it. Although Singleton identified the poem's dominant strategy as its imitation of Scripture, his actual work with the *Commedia* was more exegetical than critical. He played almost exclusively by Dante's rules and, ignoring the "make-believe," stayed reverently within Dante's fictional universe.

Others coming after him have chosen to probe Dante's strategy itself. According to Robert Hollander, "Dante creates a fiction which he pretends to consider not to be literally fictitious, while at the same time contriving to share the knowledge with us that it is precisely fictional."[12] In *The Undivine Comedy*, Teodolinda Barolini takes a different tack and shows the extent to which that knowledge is *not* shared. She is interested in how Dante covers his traces, how he makes us believe that his words are the Word of the Lord.[13] The *Commedia*'s "likeness" to the Bible, therefore, is perhaps the poet's most sustained tour de force, his supreme fiction.

Somewhere in the far left of this playing field stands Harold Bloom. For him, Dante's pious admirers who consider the *Commedia* "another Scripture, a Newer Testament that supplements the canonical Christian Bible" have actually betrayed Dante. Except for the Psalms, Bloom's poet has no "pragmatic use" for Scripture whatsoever: "The *Comedy*, for all its learning, is not deeply involved with the Bible." Yet, when Bloom looks for a way to characterize the poet's sublime presumption, he inevitably resorts to the Bible: "His poem is a prophecy and takes on the function of a third Testament in no way subservient to the Old and the New." Unlike the theologian-Dante proposed by others, Bloom's sacred poet is akin to the Satan of *Paradise Lost*, "passionately ambitious and desperately willful."

Rather than toe any orthodox line, this Dante ignores the yoke of external authority and listens only to the dictates of his own imagination. He is "the author of the final testament," a "poem that prefers itself to the Bible." In other words, Dante himself writes the only "Scripture" he cares about.[14]

Few readers of the *Commedia* are likely to find Bloom's lively contribution to Dante studies adequate to their own experience of the text, if only because Bloom dispenses with most of the poem's content—its profound engagement not only with theology but with history and politics as well. Could it be that Dante's "achieved strangeness, his perpetual originality" were all that the poet really cared about? Nonetheless, this passion to "ruin the sacred truths" of Dante criticism creates an opportunity. Bloom's assertion, "The *Comedy*, for all its learning, is not deeply involved with the Bible," provokes an assessment of precisely what that involvement *is*. Did Dante write a latter-day Scripture, or a text that only imitates the Bible, or a poem that tries to supplant the Book it only pretends to supplement?

These questions are, in effect, raised at a particular moment in the poem when Dante stands face to face with an allegorical representation of the Scripture in *Purgatorio* 29, which we looked at briefly in the previous chapter, "Old and New Parchments." Elaborately staged two thirds of the way through the journey, this encounter with the Bible is a significant variation on what becomes a familiar scenario—a personal meeting between the character Dante and other writers.[15] While these moments are usually warm and valedictory, even a way for the poet to offer his authorial "acknowledgments," it is clear that Dante has another agenda in addition to the obvious. At the same time he delivers kudos, he invariably establishes the limits of those he meets, as well as his own superiority to them. He is always moving, quite literally, beyond.[16] However, by the time he reaches the summit of Mount Purgatory he finally meets his match. For there, in the Garden of Eden, he stands before the Book whose author is none other than God. He sees an allegorization of the entire canon, an unfolding "script" that in its very order reenacts the Bible's own temporal composition.

The complexity of this encounter requires of us a slow approach. As Dante and Matelda walk on opposite shores of Eden's Lethe, a bend in the river turns Dante toward the east. He faces in the direction from which Christ prophesied that the Son of Man would make his appearance at the end of time, "as lightning cometh out of the east and appeareth even into the west" (Matt. 24:27). With Eden's horizon thereby prepared for apocalypse, Matelda turns to Dante and commands him to look and listen: "Frate mio, guarda e ascolta" (v. 15). From that point on he falls into a silence that lasts for the rest of the canto, becomes the awed spectator of a *son et lumière* in which sights and sounds follow in rapid succession and with increasing clarity. Seven slowly moving candlesticks are the vanguard of an elaborate procession. Behind them a file begins with twenty-four old men ("seniori," v. 83) walking two by two, clothed in white, and garlanded with lilies. Four winged animals, their wings full of eyes, come next and serve as escort to a splendid griffin-drawn chariot. Alongside its right wheel, three maidens dance in a circle (v. 121); to the left, "quattro facean festa" ("four other ladies made festival," v. 130). Following behind the chariot and its retinue there appears another file of *seniori*, also dressed in white, but this time wearing crowns of roses that make them seem "tutti ardesser di sopra da' cigli" ("all aflame above their eyebrows," v. 150). At the head of this group Dante sees a pair walking side by side, then four men "of lowly aspect," and in last place a figure marching alone. Although his eyes are shut, this solitary has the "keen look" of someone caught up in a visionary trance. At the exact moment when the chariot is positioned directly across the river from Dante—the entire procession centered, therefore, on him—a thunderclap signals the completion of the scene, just as a lightning flash marked its beginning. All motion stops, and the canto comes to a close.

In this elaborate Pageant of Revelation, Dante does more than remind us of Scripture and tradition. He conjures up a vision of the Bible itself, his own version of what Bonaventure speaks of as the "length" of Scripture: "it begins with the commencement of the world and of time, in the beginning of Genesis, and extends to the end of the world and of time, namely, to the end of the Apocalypse."[17] In the file of elders, therefore, the Bible is spelled out, book by book. The twenty-four old men represent the books of the Hebrew Bible as Jerome numbered them in his "helmeted" prologue to Samuel and Kings.[18] The four winged creatures that succeed them, representing the Gospels, here surrounded by dancing personifications of the virtues, mark the succession from one Testament to the other. Following the griffin and his chariot, commonly associated by commentators with Christ and the church, two figures appear walking side by side who repre-

sent the Acts of the Apostles and the Pauline Epistles.[19] Behind them come
the four Catholic Epistles (Peter, James, John, Jude) and, at the end of the
canonical line, the entranced "vecchio solo" (v. 143) who signifies the Apoc-
alypse. With the whole "corpus" of Scripture thus spelled out, *Purgatorio*
29 comes to an end as Dante stands directly across from the griffin and his
chariot. Upon that chariot's stage Beatrice makes her dramatic entrance in
canto 30, appearing in the midst of the Pageant of Revelation as God's
particular word of revelation to Dante. In cantos 30–31, she calls him to
personal repentance; then in *Purgatorio* 32–33, with a sudden swing from
the individual to the universal, she affords him the *Commedia's* own ver-
sion of the biblical Apocalypse—a dark vision of history ending with the
enigmatic prophecy of a redeemer, the DXV (33.40–45).

It is customary to treat this stretch of cantos as highly traditional,
despite the many ways in which Dante seems to have assembled bits and
pieces of the past only to move off on his own.[20] Who else, after all, would
have dared to place his otherwise unknown earthly beloved at the very
heart of scriptural revelation, or shift so abruptly from his own particularity
to the vicissitudes of universal history? Who else would choose the Garden
of Eden to heighten our sense of the artfulness, perhaps even the "artifi-
ciality," of divine revelation? The emphasis on art is, in fact, striking. From
the moment Matelda tells Dante to look and listen, we, too, become
spectators of a theological masque, a drama framed by lightning and thun-
der, staged in discrete episodes, and marked by such phantasmagoric stage-
craft as moving candlesticks that seem to the observer like giant paint
brushes streaking the air with rainbows (29.73–78). In the company of a
Virgil who is "carca di stupor non meno" ("charged no less with amaze-
ment," v. 57), Dante is all eyes and ears, fixed on the spectacle that plays
before him—transfixed, that is, by the heavenly Creator's artistry. For it is
God who is the *metteur en scène* of this entire drama, even as he has been
author of the other special effects along the purgatorial way. From the
evening "dumb show" in the Valley of Princes (8:94–108), to the "visible
speech" (10.95) and "high fantasy" (17.25) encountered along the moun-
tainside, and, finally, to this allegorical *tableau vivant* at the summit of
the mountain, purgatory is an extended celebration of a God who is the
"miglior fabbro" (26.117), the always incomparably "better craftsman." In
Inferno 29–30 Dante exposed us to the demonic theatrics of the falsifiers;
now, in this corresponding moment in the *Purgatorio*, he focuses our

attention on divine artifice and inspired fiction. He celebrates God as impresario of the afterlife:

> Qual di pennel fu maestro o di stile
> che ritraesse l'ombre e ' tratti ch'ivi
> mirar farieno uno ingegno sottile?
> (*Purg.* 12.64–66)

(What master was he of brush or of pencil who drew the forms and lineaments which there would make every subtle genius wonder?)

At face value, Dante's praise of God's artistry is an act of humble piety, an admission that the Creator is without peer. Yet, as soon as we acknowledge that everything we behold comes from the brush or pencil of Dante himself, who else can we applaud for "così bel ciel com'io diviso" ("so fair a sky as I describe," 29.82) if not the "I" of the poet? It is Dante's subtle genius that brings us every form and lineament we see, his fiery paintbrush that streaks the imagined air with rainbows. Reading his lines, we inevitably stand in admiration of *his* handiwork. In *Purgatorio* 29, moreover, we admire that work by his explicit invitation. Although throughout the canto the pilgrim is rapt before the intricacies of the "mystical procession," our attention is several times drawn away from the allegorical vision to the voice of the poet—the poet who, rather than disappearing from the text so that we, too, may follow Matelda's command to watch and listen, reaches out from the narrative to include us in the drama of his own representational act. This shift in focus first occurs early on in the canto, just before the Pageant makes its grand entrance into Eden:

> O sacrosante Vergini, se fami,
> freddi o vigilie mai per voi soffersi
> cagion mi sprona ch'io mercé vi chiami.
> Or convien che Elicona per me versi,
> e Uranìe m'aiuti col suo coro
> forti cose a pensar mettere in versi.
> (*Purg.* 29.37–42)

(O most holy Virgins, if hunger, cold, or vigils I have ever endured for you, the occasion spurs me to claim my reward. Now it is meet that Helicon stream forth for me, and Urania aid me with her choir to put in verse things difficult to think.)

Purgatorio opened with a petition to the "sante Muse" in general and to Calliope in particular (1.7–12). But here the stakes are raised higher, as "sante" becomes "sacrosante" and the Muses become "Vergini." The rhetorical purpose of such moments, of course, is to signal a heightening of poetic material and to dramatize the poet's struggle to live up to it. Invocations typically prepare us to admire what the author is about to do—or, as in this case, to recall also what he has already done by way of preparation for this new moment.

Dante begins, therefore, by drawing attention to his poetic vocation and the rigors endured in its behalf. Leaving the merit of his poetry discretely unspoken, his claim to reward is the "hunger, cold, or vigils" he has suffered for the Muses. This brief catalogue of endurance clearly echoes St. Paul's lengthier "boasting" in 2 Corinthians 11:23–33, where he establishes his authority as an apostle by listing the many adversities he has endured: "In labour and painfulness, in much watching, in hunger and thirst, in fasting often, in cold and nakedness" (11:27). Paul's memory of past occasions when he gloried in infirmity then leads him in the following verses to mention "a certain man in Christ" who was enraptured to the third heaven of paradise, where he heard such ineffable words as are unlawful for anyone to utter (12:2–5). Although Paul says that of *this* man he will boast, and not of himself, tradition has never for a moment seriously doubted that he was speaking of himself.

Dante later takes on this Pauline identification in the opening of the *Paradiso* (1.73–75), where he charts his own ascent *in paradisum* with direct allusion to 2 Corinthians 12. Here in *Purgatorio*, however, his invocation to the Muses establishes literary credentials and gives just cause why the poet should be assisted in writing about "things difficult to think." And so, walking the fine line between weakness and strength that Paul also traverses in 2 Corinthians, Dante presents himself at once as supplicant and commander. While he may need Helicon's stream and Urania's celestial choir, he does not hesitate to specify "Or convien"—*now* is the time for his reward. Nor should we overlook the fact that the Pauline language he borrows here refers to sacrifices made for the gospel's sake, not those suffered in behalf of art. The hard work of writing "in versi" becomes the equivalent of the apostle's trials.

After this invocation, the Pageant itself is rendered more or less straightforwardly as something once beheld, with the often repeated claim "I saw" continuing to link Dante's narration to the eyewitness accounts of Ezekiel and John the Divine.[21] But again our absorption in the narrative is interrupted by Dante's once more drawing us to himself as poet. Describing the four living creatures that surround the griffin's chariot, Dante notes that each was "plumed with six wings, the plumes full of eyes." After briefly mentioning a resemblance between their myriad eyes and those of Ovid's Argus (*Met.* 1.625–27), he addresses the reader with a somewhat labored aside that nonetheless warrants close scrutiny:

> A descriver lor forme più non spargo
>   rime, lettor; ch'altra spesa mi strigne,
>   tanto ch'a questa non posso esser largo;
> ma leggi Ezechïel, che li dipigne
>   come li vide da la fredda parte
>   venir con vento e con nube e con igne;
> e quali i troverai ne le sue carte,
>   tali eran quivi, salvo ch'a le penne
>   Giovanni è meco e da lui si diparte.
>   (*Purg.* 29.97–105)

(To describe their forms, reader, I do not lay out more rhymes, for other spending constrains me so that I cannot be lavish in this but read Ezekiel who depicts them as he saw them come from the cold parts, with wind and cloud and fire; and such as you shall find them on his pages, such were they here, except that, as to the wings, John is with me, and differs from him.)

Here Dante the visionary becomes a commentator on his own text, as he points first to one source and then to another. It is a passage of such self-consciousness that some critics have taken it for an inexcusable act of pedantry and others as a prescient parody of the future commentary tradition itself.[22] The shift in tone, in any event, is oddly abrupt; suddenly we find ourselves shaken out of our absorption in the Pageant and embroiled with the composition of the poet's "sacred page." As Dante juggles his sources and negotiates a discrepancy between scriptural texts, he recalls not only the exegetical practice of the schools but also something of the academic tone of the Schoolmen.

In addition to establishing himself as a master of his *pagina sacra,* moreover, he specifically reminds us that he is a poet who must make hard choices about his words. "A descriver" opens this digression, which includes a witty word play on the decision to save rather than spend his rhymes. By way of economy, he refers us to other texts, first to Ezekiel's pages and then to John's, with Ovid's *Metamorphoses* not so very far in the background. Presumably by referring us to familiar sources he means to help us imagine the exact form of the "four living creatures" that surround the griffin's chariot. But if only for the moment, the effect is to preoccupy us more with his artistic choices than with the Pageant itself. The process of writing "in versi" takes center stage. Prophet's vision gives way to poet's shoptalk.

One looks in vain to Dante's biblical precursors for anything even remotely like this.[23] It is true that both Ezekiel and John are deeply involved with the Word of the Lord as *written* text. But in these biblical authors there is no emphasis on literary invention or on artistic choices to be made. Rather, Ezekiel is given a scroll containing "lamentations, and canticles, and woe," and then told to swallow it whole: "Son of man, eat all that thou shalt find: eat this book, and so speak to the children of Israel" (Ezek. 2:9–3:1). John the Divine also receives a divine command to eat a heavenly book (Apoc. 10:8–11), and he is charged more than ten times to write down what he beholds. Like Jeremiah, Daniel, and Habakkuk before him, therefore, John is told to take dictation: "Write, for these words are most faithful and true" (Apoc. 21:5).[24]

In none of these cases, however, is there interest in "literature." For even though biblical prophets customarily use language rich in image and metaphor, language full of rhetorical figures, they take no personal stock in their own styles, let alone in themselves as poets. Their texts are received from God, their words are trustworthy and true only because those words come from heaven. This self-effacement is not what we find in *Purgatorio* 29, where the eyewitness account of the visionary who simply reports what he sees gives way abruptly to the deliberations of a poet who invokes the Muses, courts the reader, ponders the spending of his rhymes, and openly weighs first one source and then another. To appreciate the full extent of this departure from the literary style of Scripture one has only to insert Dante's address to the reader into the pages of Ezekiel or John. The result would be an obvious paste-up, with no possible confusion as to which lines revealed the presence of a later hand.[25]

It is not Dante's difference from these biblical writers, however, that we are asked to consider in this brief passage; it is his similarity. When describing the winged creatures surrounding the griffin's chariot, for instance, he states that he is largely following Ezekiel's account: "che li dipigne / come li vide da la fredda parte / venir con vento e con nube e con igne" ("who depicts them as he saw them come from the cold parts, with wind and cloud and fire," vv. 100–102). Yet when it comes to a particular detail, he finds himself parting company with Ezekiel and standing instead in accord with John: "salvo ch'a le penne / Giovanni è meco e da lui si diparte" ("as to the wings, John is with me, and differs from him," vv. 104–5).

This choice between authorities might well seem a predictable one for any Christian writer to make. A special reliance on John's vision in Apocalypse 4 would indicate the greater authority of the New Testament in comparison with the Old. We find something similar in *Paradiso* 25, when Dante invokes both Isaiah and John on a particular point only to declare that it is nonetheless John who "assai vie più digesta . . . questa revelazione ci manifesta" ("makes manifest this revelation to us far more expressly," vv. 94, 96). There was also an exegetical tradition that equated the six wings of the living creatures with the six ages of human history. Whereas Ezekiel's vision of four wings suggests that he was able to see only as far as the fourth age, John's sight extended beyond the Incarnation's "fullness of time" to afford him knowledge of the sixth and final age.[26] Given this background, it might well stand to reason that when Dante admits to seeing six wings instead of four he is essentially proclaiming that, as a Christian, he sees beyond the prophets of Israel. In order to join his *Commedia* to the New Testament's fuller revelation, he must of necessity owe a special allegiance to John.

Except that what Dante actually says here is far more audacious. It is not "I am with John" but quite the contrary, "Giovanni è meco"—John is *with me*. This means that when it comes to the correct number of wings, the truth of the matter rests with his own eyewitness. He confirms John's vision on Patmos by squaring it with his own: final authority on the matter rests with him.

So too does the license to embellish and innovate. For when we look closely at Dante's actual borrowing from the Apocalypse, it becomes clear that he is not consistently "with John" at all. Nor is such an observation something we are allowed to miss. Quite the contrary, the poet makes a point of telling us to "read Ezekiel," and then to improve his vision with John's. Following that command, however, we note an extensive if subtle reworking of the Johannine text he is otherwise following. To begin with, while Dante's creatures are full of eyes only in their wings ("le penne piene d'occhi," *Purg.* 29.95), John's are twice said to be "full of eyes fore and behind . . . and round about and within they are full of eyes" (Apoc. 4:6, 8). Dante also crowns the creatures' heads with green garlands ("coronati ciascun di verde fronda," v. 93), and thereby adds his own imagistic touch to what is already a surfeit of inherited biblical imagery. Once we notice these obvious "departures" from John, moreover, others also come to light. Dante's white-robed elders are garlanded with lilies or roses, not with the familiar gold crowns of John's *seniores*; they also process together in stately movement rather than sitting stationary upon thrones (Apoc. 4:4). Furthermore, instead of chanting the songs that John reports as rising up from God's throne—the "Sanctus" (4:8) or the "Dignus es, domine" (4:11), both of which were incorporated into the liturgy of the church—Dante's elders sing original texts, which are, if strongly evocative of the style of both Scripture and liturgy, nonetheless written in Dante's distinctive amalgam of Latin and vernacular:

> Tutti cantavan: "*Benedicta* tue
>   ne le figlie d'Adamo, e benedette
>   sieno in etterno le bellezze tue!"
>   (*Purg.* 29.85–87)

(All were singing: "Blessed art thou among the daughters of Adam, and blessed forever be thy beauties.")

Who is the one proclaimed both as "*Benedicta*" (29.85) and as "*Benedictus*" (30.19)? In John's Apocalypse, the object of praise is God, "who was, and who is, and who is to come" (4:8). But in the *Purgatorio*, the woman who is said to be blessed among the daughters of Adam seems to be Dante's "private" beloved, Beatrice. Even the griffin, so confidently identified by the commentators as a "traditional" figure of Christ, on closer examination may well be Dante's own quite enigmatic invention.[27] One could go on. For all the many features that serve to ground the "mystical procession" in church culture, not to mention in the Scriptures themselves, the Pageant is, in fact, a new account. Dante repeatedly goes the Apocalypse one better.

This situation seems tailor-made for Harold Bloom, who indeed observes of the Pageant that, when Dante cites the authors of Scripture in *Purgatorio* 29, it is "not to rely on them but to get them out of his way."[28] On the whole, however, the particular audacity of "Giovanni è meco" has been ignored by the commentary tradition, has even on occasion been interpreted to mean exactly the opposite of what it actually says, so that the critic steps in to correct the slip of Dante's pen. According to the early-fifteenth-century commentator Serravalle, for instance, "John is with me" should be understood to mean the reverse: "excepto quod ad pennas Ioannes est mecum (ego teneo cum Ioanne)," "except when it comes to the wings, John is with me (I hold with John)."[29]

An exception to this flight from the audacious literal is Robert Hollander.[30] For him, "Giovanni è meco" asserts the primacy of the poet's own vision, his refusal to play the role of scribe or take his humble place at the margin of the scriptural canon. This is one of the several places, Hollander suggests, where we can see Dante having fun, even sharing a conspiratorial wink with his readers about the "comedy" of his whole enterprise: "That he could rear up this splendid edifice upon the brilliant and fictitious construction of a 'vision,' and then play with his own construction, is still another sign of his utter superiority as a maker of literature."[31]

I agree that "John is with me" is capable of provoking laughter, as it does routinely in the classroom. But I suspect that the laughs have less to do with Dante's "play with his own construction," or with any invitation to go backstage and look behind the *Commedia*'s stagecraft, than with the breezy way the poet makes his monumental claims. We smile because the authority he has so carefully constructed over the long course of the poem is here so casually presumed in what appears to be a throwaway line. The confidence is dazzling. Presumably, John is meant to be relieved that, when it comes to the number of the heavenly creatures' wings, it is *he* (rather than Ezekiel) who keeps company with Dante!

Another poet might have understood the wisdom of keeping such audacity under wraps. Yet in *Purgatorio* 29, where Dante Pilgrim stands face to face with Scripture, the poet seems to court the charge of presumption, not run away from it. Why else, when describing the griffin's chariot, should he remind us of Phaeton, that Ovidian overreacher who took hold of the sun's chariot and then destroyed himself through sheer temerity? The story is introduced into the canto when Dante, having contrasted the chariot with the inferior triumphal cars of ancient Rome, now compares it to

> quel del Sol che, svïando, fu combusto
>   per l'orazion de la Terra devota,
>   quando fu Giove arcanamente giusto.
>   (Purg. 29.118–20)

(that of the Sun which, going astray, was consumed at devout Earth's prayer, when Jove in his secrecy was just.)

This recollection of Phaeton's tragic fall—of going astray ("svïando"), of human powers unrestrained by a due sense of mortal limitation—reintroduces one of the poet's favorite cautionary tales precisely at a moment in the work when his own presumption has just been brought into the foreground with "Giovanni è meco."[32]

Nor is Phaeton the only warning encoded in the mystical procession. Later on in the Pageant (29.133–41), in the chariot's wake, the pilgrim sees a pair of elders "unlike in dress but alike in bearing." One of these is the Book of Acts, written by Luke, "who showed himself of the household of Hippocrates," and who radiates a solicitude for human well-being that one might expect to find in a great physician. The other elder, who "showed the contrary care," embodies the entire Pauline corpus. Seeing this latter figure, identified by an emblematic sword that is "sharp and shining," the poet registers an emotion new to the canto. Throughout the procession Dante Pilgrim has been in doubt, enraptured, deceived, full of wonder; but here for the first time he is afraid. The sight of Paul's Epistles frightens him: "mi fé paura" (v. 141). Commentators have long conjectured that Paul's eloquent severity is the reason for the pilgrim's fear. Unlike Luke's comfortable words, Paul's rouse and even wound the hearer. Beyond this general observation about the writings of the apostle, however, the figure's identifying sword suggests that a specific Pauline text may be relevant here. In the Epistle to the Hebrews (4:12–13) we read: "The word of God is living, and active, and sharper than any two-edged sword: piercing to the division of soul and spirit, of joints and marrow, and searching out the thoughts and intentions of the heart. And in his sight no creature is invisible: but all are open and laid bare to his eyes, to whom we must give a word of account." As author of this text, with its contrast between the penetrating power of God's Word ("sermo Dei") and the exposed impotence of "nobis sermo," Paul might well stand before Dante as a figure of the divine judgment on human speech. In the presence of Paul's two-edged sword, a human poet could easily find himself "nuda et aperta," cut to the quick and rendered silent, especially if the words he is shortly to speak in the *Paradiso* are a similitude of those "arcana verba" that Paul himself put off limits.

Once Phaeton and the Pauline Epistles have had their chastising effects, the final member of the procession appears: the book of the Apocalypse. The Pageant gives no sign of any Joachite "eternal gospel" bringing up the rear, no hint that the canon might yet be open to newer testaments. Instead, the march culminates in a book that ends with a solemn warning to anyone who would dare add another word: "I testify to every one that heareth the words of the prophecy of this book: If any man shall add to these things, God shall add unto him the plagues written in this book" (Apoc. 22:18). For *this* John to be "with" an ambitious fourteenth-century poet, therefore, would seem to require some explanation. But absolutely none is offered. Rather, Dante stands before the finished ranks of the biblical canon and prepares to join the end of the line.

"What shall we then say to these things?" (Rom. 8: 31). Viewed in one way, Dante is offering his poem only as a midrash on the biblical tradition, a fresh telling of God's story as it was entrusted to the church and presented anew in every era. Such a poem might well constitute the kind of prophecy that Albertus Magnus or Thomas Aquinas believed was still possible in Christian times—not the proclamation of any new revelation, but rather a call to take the old one seriously.[33] Viewed from the opposite point of view, however, the *Commedia* is a third testament meant to "fulfill" the promise of the other two. The Bible itself is of use, therefore, only when it is "with Dante." In this light, the Pageant's presentation of a closed canon is only a subterfuge to mask the extent of the poet's idiosyncrasy and invention— what Harold Bloom frequently refers to as Dante's "Gnosticism." Although the biblical procession moves in lock step from Genesis to Apocalypse, it has at its center Dante's utterly private revelation, Beatrice, whose mediator role in the plan of salvation can be found nowhere else in scripture or tradition.

Each of these diametrically opposed perspectives reveals only part of the picture, emphasizing either Dante's orthodoxy or his heterodox flights of fancy. But each serves to lessen a tension that the poem itself never releases—indeed, a tension that becomes ever more pronounced as the poet moves from purgatory into paradise. Neither "solution" captures Dante's extraordinary complexity or the constant boundary-crossing that characterizes both the *Commedia* and its author.[34] Dante manages simultaneously to be both the obedient scribe and the radically independent genius. He navigates between the fatal presumption of Phaeton and the loyal discipleship of Saint Paul, who not only warned about the censorious sword of the Spirit but also maintained that speaking boldly, "cum fiducia" (Eph. 6:19), was the way to proclaim the gospel's mystery.[35] Dante's interventions as poet-at-work remind us of the constructed, even fictional, nature of his vision; but his profound reliance on Scripture grounds that fiction in a Word that is finally not of his own making. As one who claims that John is "with" him, he may indeed be a theologian with a sense of humor. But he is always a comedian in earnest, whose stakes are no less high than the *mysterium evangelii* itself. He knows he is playing with sacred fire.

This "play," moreover, may well explain the curious mixture of prophetic vision and literary self-consciousness found in *Purgatorio* 29. Think of it like this. Dante could see that Ezekiel and John did not consider themselves to be poets in the self-conscious way that he did. Nonetheless, he could see that their texts demonstrated technical accomplishment, forming a sacred literature without profane rival. What, then, if someone who believed himself called to speak the Word of the Lord even as they did were to speak quite openly *as a poet*? What if poetry itself, far from being merely *infirma doctrina*, was actually a privileged mode of divine revelation?[36]

Later in the fourteenth century, there would be many others to champion the poet as theologian.[37] But at the time Dante was writing, the worth of poetry was very much under the Schoolmen's rigorous attack. How, then, might he fight back? He had the option, of course, to write yet another Latin prose treatise; or his reply could be a poem. He could answer the theologians' objections to mere literature by writing a "poema sacro" (*Par.* 25.1) that required exegesis and commanded belief. He would never abide the ancient dismissal of poets as liars. Rather, he would claim himself to be a scribe of God who felt the guiding pressure of God's hand and, like Ezekiel and John, wrote down all that he was allowed to behold. In doing so he would also openly reveal his status as a poet, would show himself drawing upon the vast treasury of his own words, holding himself accountable not only to the demands of heaven but to "lo fren de l'arte" ("the curb of art," *Purg.* 33.141). His detractors might wonder if such a coincidence of divine revelation and human artistry had ever occurred before. No doubt Virgil would come to mind, given the venerable traditions surrounding his unwitting prophecy of the birth of Christ in the Fourth Eclogue.[38] But what the pagan poet only dreamed of in Parnassus, Dante claims to have seen face-to-face. Jerome had once celebrated the Psalmist David as "our Simonides, Pindar, and Alcaeus, our Horace, our Catullus, and our Serenus all in one."[39] Now it was time to allow a visionary poet like himself, fully conscious of his literary métier, to take his place not only as our latter-day prophet—our David, our Ezekiel, our John, our Paul—but also as our latter-day *poeta sacro*—our Christian Virgil and Ovid—"all in one."

How, then, to portray an author of such monumental aspiration and sustained contradiction? Luca Signorelli's Dante, immortalized in the San Brizio Chapel of Orvieto Cathedral, shows him located securely within an architectural frame, fortified among his books, and (despite the pain etched into those hollowed cheeks) seated at his laurel-crowned ease. While there is some element of drama in the torque of Dante's body, as he turns his rapt attention from one text to another, the picture as a whole emphasizes the stability of his position. A more dynamic portrait of the artist, on the other hand, would render the ceaseless motion behind his apparent stasis. Perhaps only a moving picture would do, for then we would see him as he really is over the long course of the *Commedia*—less a scholar safely ensconced within his library and more an aerialist of the afterlife, a tightrope walker who negotiates the perilous high wire he has himself strung out between God's Book and his own poem. Part of the excitement of watching him make his high-flying moves is the realization that he is always performing without a net, as if inviting the disaster that never quite befalls him. But perhaps the most thrilling aspect of his artistry is the sustained *balance* of his entire act, the way his reckless daring is so artfully concealed. One simply cannot stop marveling at the sureness of his footing, the careful measure of each bold step forward, the confident way he holds on to the air.

CHAPTER 4

Self-Authenticating Artifact

The whole question of Dante's authority in the *Commedia*—where it comes from, how it is achieved—is currently as interesting to the poet's critics as it was in the fourteenth century; it is also increasingly problematic. This vexation may have to do with the general influence of late-twentieth-century critical theory, with its deep suspicion of "authors" and outright refusal of authority. Think, for instance, of Michel Foucault's rhetorical question, "What difference does it make who is speaking?"[1] More narrowly, critical vexation may be an inevitable reaction to the legacy of Charles Singleton, whose peculiar genius as a Dantista was to argue the poem's theological perspective from the inside, as if he were himself Dante, and thereby to double the already formidable power of the poet's authorial voice. In any case, having learned to read the *Commedia* under the spell of its assertions, many critics feel that the time has come to note how Dante's claim to truth is his own careful achievement, to see how his authority, both theological and poetic, is constructed.

For some this has meant an emphasis on rhetorical strategy, on how Dante makes (rather than receives from heaven) his identity as a writer.[2] For Harold Bloom, it has led to an outright celebration of this self-created authorial power. Bloom's Dante is "a ruthless visionary, passionately ambitious and desperately willful, whose poem triumphantly expresses his own unique personality"; he offers us "the supreme example of a wholly personal poem that persuades many of its readers to believe they are encountering ultimate truth."[3] Bloom represents an extreme point of view, but he is by no means alone in noting how Dante makes himself not only heard but also *believed*. No one argues that the emperor has no clothes, but a number of commentators find that much of what he wears turns out to be of his own fashioning—and not just the clothes but also the divine warrant for putting on the gorgeous apparel in the first place. Dante's constructed authority may well be his ultimate tour de force.

How is it, then, that he attains his peculiar power? When it comes to the ancient masters of poetry, he establishes his superiority on the basis of his theological vision and their pagan blindness: it is the Christian God, rather than the muse of Virgil and Ovid, who ultimately inspires him.[4] Vernacular poets get considerably shorter shrift. Either their pens do not follow closely behind Love's dictation, as Dante has Bonagiunta da Lucca claim in *Purgatorio* 24.58–60, or, as in the case of Guido Cavalcanti, they listen to the misleading voice of another kind of love and are judged accordingly.

Related to Dante's authorization of himself as poet of the *Commedia*, moreover, is the gradual unfolding of a call to divine prophecy hinted at from the very beginning of the poem but finally made explicit in *Paradiso* 17. There Cacciaguida, after disclosing Dante's future exile from Florence, charges him to write a full account of his journey, in effect commissioning him to write his great poem. Dante anticipates that the news he brings back will be bitter and hateful to many, for inevitably the messenger is blamed for bad news. But Cacciaguida concedes nothing to these fears. Dante must put all caution aside and tell the whole truth: "tutta tua visïon fa manifesta" (17.128). He must be as fearless as the prophets, as bold in his speech as the apostles:

> Coscïenza fusca
>   o de la propria o de l'altrui vergogna
>   pur sentirà la tua parola brusca.
> Ma nondimen, rimossa ogne menzogna,
>   tutta tua visïon fa manifesta;
>   e lascia pur grattar dov'è la rogna.
> Ché se la voce tua sarà molesta
>   nel primo gusto, vital nodrimento
>   lascerà poi, quando sarà digesta.
> Questo tuo grido farà come vento,
>   che le più alte cime più percuote;
>   e ciò non fa d'onor poco argomento.
>   (*Par.* 17.124–35)

(A conscience dark, either with its own or with another's shame, will indeed feel your speech to be harsh. But none the less, all falsehood set aside, make manifest all that you have seen; and then let them scratch where the itch is. For if at first taste your voice be grievous, yet shall it leave thereafter vital nourishment when digested. This cry of yours shall do as does the wind, which smites most upon the loftiest summits; and this shall be no little cause of honor.)

This charge to speak freely pulls no punches: if future readers of Dante's vision are made uncomfortable by what they find, "then let them scratch where the itch is"! But aside from the vernacular pungency of these words, Cacciaguida's charge is remarkable for its open appropriation of the biblical prophets.[5] Ezekiel, for example, is admonished to be bold as he confronts the children of Israel: "And thou, O Son of Man, fear not, fear not, neither be thou afraid of their words: for thou art among unbelievers and destroyers, and thou dwellest with scorpions. Fear not their words, neither be thou dismayed with their looks" (2:6). God also commands him to eat a heavenly book filled with "lamentations, and canticles, and woe" (2:9)—bitter words, but nonetheless good nourishment, "sweet as honey in his mouth" (3:3). Likewise Jeremiah: he must eat the Word of the Lord and speak it in his own words, no matter what the "assembly of jesters" makes of what he has to say: "I will make thee to this people as a strong wall of brass: and they shall fight against thee, and shall not prevail: for I am with thee to save thee, and to deliver thee, saith the Lord" (15:20). Nor in this rehearsal of Old Testament figures should we forget the witness of St. Paul, whose boldness in the face of opposition was a hallmark of his ministry.[6]

One might think that Cacciaguida's resonant call in *Paradiso* 17, and, indeed, all the subtler "callings" that precede it, would be enough to authorize the poem. But apparently Dante thought not, for over the course of several cantos in the heaven of the fixed stars, in *Paradiso* 24–27, he recruits the three apostles whom Jesus most favored—Peter, James, and John—and has each of them quite specifically command him to tell what he's been told, to reveal what he's seen.[7] Here types and shadows have their ending, for the three apostles of the Transfiguration (to whom Dante linked himself in *Purgatorio* 32.73–84) now appear in their own right. No longer figures of speech, they welcome Dante into their own blessed company and detain him for more than three cantos. The cumulative effect of this self-affirmation is almost breathtaking. No prophet or apostle in either Testament of Scripture was ever more fully commissioned; nor (I would venture) has any poet so daringly underwritten his own literary enterprise. "No one worked harder at becoming *auctor*," says A. J. Minnis, "not just a maker of verse but an authority."[8]

The Scripture underwrites this legitimization and, in the course of a heavily doctrinal theological examination, authorizes Dante's "sacred poem."[9] His elevation actually begins in *Paradiso* 22, when Beatrice and Dante ascend to the constellation of Gemini—the poet's birth sign—from whose "light impregnated with might power" he received "tutto, qual che si sia, il mio ingegno" ("all my genius, whatsoever it may be," v. 114). Looking down through eight concentric spheres of the universe to the tiny globe of earth fixed at its center, Dante smiles at how lowly ("vil," v. 135) our world appears. As the direction of his vision rises, moreover, so too does the poem's rhetorical pitch. Turning from Beatrice's yet-again-transfigured face, Dante has a visionary preview of the heavenly city he will enter in canto 30. He sees a meadow of light irradiated by the "rays of Christ" (23.72), beholds the Virgin Mary as a rose "in che 'l verbo divino / carne si fece" ("wherein the Divine Word became flesh," vv. 73–74), and surveys a mass of brilliant lilies that are in reality the glowing ranks of the Church Triumphant. It is as if Virgil's Elysian Fields had been grafted onto the Apocalypse of John the Divine and transformed into something still more lyric, more affective, more primal—in a word, something more Dantesque. With a sudden semantic shift that characterizes the poetics of *Paradiso* at large, Heaven's queen is celebrated first as a monarch in her court and then as a mother in the nursery. The blessed, therefore, are not only courtiers but also infants, who, after happily sucking their fill, stretch toward the mother they adore.[10] Flames become flowers, and flowers babies at the breast, as Dante offers his own ecstatic version of the "great supper of God" that John saw in Apocalypse 19:17. Beatrice hails this festivity at the opening of canto 24 as the Lamb's Supper: "la gran cena/del benedetto Agnello" (vv. 1–2). It is a celebration whose joy overflows all boundaries, as the blessed spin about like fiery comets ("a guisa di comete," v. 12), and as the poet's pen is forced to leap over a *gaudium* not even he can describe (vv. 25–27).

After setting the stage for such a festival, however, the poet changes the scene without warning, and what began as a joyous celestial banquet becomes without warning an academic examination. Addressing the soul of St. Peter, Beatrice asks Peter to "test" Dante—"tenta costui," v. 37—in order to determine his understanding of the three theological virtues, to demonstrate "s'elli ama bene e bene spera e crede" ("whether he loves rightly and rightly hopes and believes," v. 40). Her request signals a change in what is expected of him in this late stage in his journey. Below, in the heaven of the theologians, he had been a passive witness to the wisdom of his betters, to Aquinas, Bonaventure, and all the other *sapienti*. Now that he has been ushered into the *studium* of the upper reaches of paradise, however, he is displayed in the heavenly examination hall as if he were one of the City of God's brightest young lights, a prodigy ready to excel in a ritual of academic interrogation that would not have been afforded a layman on earth. In an extended simile (24.46–51) we are told that he is like a "bachelor" of arts on his way to a doctorate in theology—someone who does not presume to speak until the master proposes a question for *disputatio*; who "arms" himself with every conceivable "proof" and "reason" ahead of time; who makes ready to profess what he knows about the virtues to the three apostles who by tradition were understood to "figure" faith, hope, and love.[11]

Beatrice makes a point of saying that because these masters have their minds always fixed on God, they are fully aware of what their new pupil knows (24.40–44). Presumably, therefore, those who stand to be impressed by his display are the readers of this text, who no doubt need to be convinced that the outrageous claim to have seen God face-to-face while still in mortal flesh rests on the firm foundation of Christian doctrine. And so, on the very brink of his ascent "a l'ultima salute" ("to the final blessedness," 22.124), Dante demonstrates not only his erudition but the depth of his orthodoxy, his mastery of theology, his ease with the "disputations of the philosophers and the schools of the religious" (*Convivio* 2.12.7), and, most important of all, his deep knowledge of Scripture. Here we are light-years away from his befuddlement in earlier cantos over the nature of moon spots. Now Dante the Theologian has his day, and to the repeated acclaim of examiners who celebrate his success with a crescendo of professorial enthusiasm unknown in the academy this side of heaven. Each of his triumphant performances inspires a song of thanksgiving: "Dio laudamo" (24.113), "Santo, santo, santo!" (26.69), "Al Padre, al Figlio, a lo Spirito Santo . . . gloria!" (27.1–2). In the end, it seems as if the whole of paradise is beaming down upon him: "Ciò ch'io vedeva mi sembriava un riso/de l'universo" ("What I saw seemed to me a smile of the universe," 27.4).

Dante's enormous success has to do in large part with his quick recall of Scripture and recurrent appeal to its authority. To be sure, he also mentions "proofs physical and metaphysical" (24.134–35) and at least once refers to, without naming, one of the ancient masters now consigned to Limbo (26.38–39).[12] But on the whole, deference is given to the Bible, whose authority has no rival short of the direct knowledge of God enjoyed by the blessed in heaven. In this respect, the poet seems to be very much in line with the opening of the *Summa Theologiae*, where Aquinas maintains that all of sacred doctrine depends upon Scripture: "For our faith rests on the revelation made to the Prophets and Apostles who wrote the canonical books, not on a revelation, if such there be, made to any other teacher" (*ST* I–II, 1, 8, ad 2).[13]

This argument from the authority of the Bible is made throughout the first of the examinations, and in a variety of ways is designed to show how fully Dante knows the sacred text. When St. Peter asks him to define faith, for instance, he replies not only by giving the familiar formulation taken from the Epistle to the Hebrews (11:1), a work traditionally ascribed to St. Paul, but by echoing a reference to "carissimus frater noster Paulus" in one of Peter's own letters (2 Pet. 3:15):[14]

> Come 'l verace stilo
>   ne scrisse, padre, del tuo caro frate
>   che mise teco Roma nel buon filo,
> fede è sustanza di cose sperate
>   e argomento de le non parventi;
>   e questa pare a me sua quiditate.
>   (*Par.* 24.61–66)

(As the veracious pen of your dear brother wrote of it, who with you, father, put Rome on the good path, Faith is the substance of things hoped for and the evidence of things not seen; and this I take to be its quiddity.)

When next asked how it was that he came to know this virtue himself, Dante refers first to "La larga ploia / de lo Spirito Santo, ch'è diffusa / in su le vecchie e 'n su le nuove cuoia" ("The plenteous rain of the Holy Spirit which is poured over the old and over the new parchments," vv. 91–93).

Then he speaks of the individual textual "showers" that rained down upon him from the firmament of the entire biblical canon,

> per Moïsè, per profeti e per salmi,
>   per l'Evangelio e per voi che scriveste
>   poi che l'ardente Spirto vi fé almi.
>   (*Par.* 24.136–38)

(through Moses and the Prophets and the Psalms, through the Gospel, and through you who wrote when the fiery Spirit had made you holy.)

His indebtedness to Scripture shows, says Peter, that the Bible alone is "conclusive" for him, that its "syllogism" is so utterly compelling that any demonstration of truth by resort to philosophy is by comparison obtuse (vv. 94–96). Indeed, as Dante himself testifies, Scripture is "divina favella" ("divine discourse," v. 99) and "l'evangelica dottrina" ("the evangelic doctrine," v. 144); it is the single authority that "la mente mi sigilla / più volte" ("many times sets the seal upon my mind," vv. 143–44).

This repeated acknowledgment of Scripture's unique authority is also evident in the somewhat briefer examinations on hope and love. Again, Dante places himself openly under the aegis of biblical *auctores* and securely within the canonical tradition they constitute. At the same time, however, he makes a more covert move. For despite all his gestures toward orthodoxy, with their apparent disavowal of original thinking or departure from the norm, it is precisely here that Dante expands the sacred canon to include both himself and his poem. While likening himself to a bachelor of divinity intent on achieving a more advanced theological degree, he is actually reaching much higher—as high, that is, as the rank of the apostolic authors he joins in these cantos, "holy men of God who spoke, inspired by the Holy Spirit" (2 Pet. 1:21).

This ambitious bid for "scripturality" extends throughout these cantos of examination. It can perhaps best be seen, however, in *Paradiso* 25, where Dante comes before James, "il barone / per cui là giù si vicita Galizia" ("the Baron for whose sake, down below, folk visit Galicia," vv. 17–18). Dante's presentation of the saint emphasizes the courtly atmosphere of the City of God, as well as the themes of pilgrimage and martyrdom commonly associated with James. As with Peter and John, his status as a writer of biblical text is also brought to the fore, so that James the saint and "James" the text become one and the same. What the canto most openly brings into the foreground, however, is not so much the uniqueness of James as the singularity of Dante. It is his extraordinary pilgrimage from Egypt to Jerusalem (vv. 55–57) that we are asked to consider, his ascent to the *campus stellae* of his birth sign, Gemini, and, most strikingly, his unique possession of the virtue that James here epitomizes, "who did figure [hope] all those times when Jesus showed most favor to the three," vv. 32–33).

Whereas no special claims are made for Dante's exceptional faith or remarkable charity, all the stops are pulled for hope: "La Chiesa militante alcun figliuolo/non ha con più speranza" ("The Church Militant has not any child possessed of more hope," vv. 52–53). As if to "second" the immensity of this assertion—presented not as opinion but as a fact that is written indelibly in the mind of God (vv. 53–54)—Beatrice steps forward to protect Dante from the unbecoming charge of vainglory and boasting ("iattanza," v. 62). Because of the poet's superb control of his narrative throughout the *Commedia*, in which he is everywhere present but almost always concealed, it is easy to miss the cheek of this end run. But of course it is none other than Dante who makes all these moves himself—who decides what each of his characters will say, and when. Meanwhile, our attention is quite deliberately drawn to the common identity shared by Dante and James, each of whom is said to "figure" hope, either in the ranks of the Church Militant or within the Church Triumphant. The two have an "expertise" in common, and perhaps for this reason, when James asks Dante to say what hope is and how he came to know it personally, his reply is marked by the deep pleasure of performing well before someone likely to appreciate the effort. Marshaling his full resources before delivering his considered *responsio*, Dante is

> Come discente ch'a dottor seconda
> pronto e libente in quel ch'elli è esperto,
> perché la sua bontà si disasconda.
>
> (*Par.* 25.64–66)

(As the pupil who answers the teacher, ready and eager in that wherein he is expert, so that his worth may be disclosed.)

Then, with a blessed assurance in his own ability to hold forth on this particular subject, the ambitious *baccialier* proceeds to dazzle the learned doctors:

"Spene," diss' io, "è uno attender certo
  de la gloria futura, il qual produce
  grazia divina e precedente merto.
Da molte stelle mi vien questa luce;
  ma quei la distillò nel mio cor pria
  che fu sommo cantor del sommo duce.
'Sperino in te,' ne la sua tëodia
  dice, 'color che sanno il nome tuo':
  e chi nol sa, s'elli ha la fede mia?
Tu mi stillasti, con lo stillar suo,
  ne la pistola poi; sì ch'io son pieno,
  e in altrui vostra pioggia repluo."
                                    (*Par.* 25.67–78)

("Hope," I said, "is a sure expectation of future glory, which divine grace
produces and preceding merit. From many stars this light comes to me,
but first he instilled it into my heart who was the supreme singer of the
Supreme Leader. 'Let them hope in Thee who know Thy name,' he says
in his divine song [*tëodia*], and who knows it not if he have my faith? You
afterwards in your Epistle did instill it into me, together with his
instilling, so that I am full, and pour again your shower upon others.")

In this measured answer to the master of all who hope, Dante begins
by citing Peter Lombard's *Sententiarum* (3.26.1; *PL*, vol. 192, col. 811), a
School text that by the thirteenth-century had come to be regarded as
scarcely less authoritative than Scripture itself. "Hope is the sure expecta-
tion of future glory," he says, "which issues from God's grace and as a result
of human merit."[15] Hope is a virtue, in other words, to which both heaven
and earth have set a hand. Though initially a gift from God, it is a *habitus*
meant to be lived out, a virtue that grows with practice. Aquinas uses this
same text from the *Sententiarum* to argue that such "sure expectation" is the
legitimate hope of every Christian.[16] It is no presumption to trust that one's
future glory will consist in "the joyful possession of God."[17] Such certitude
does not preclude a possible fall into sin and a forfeiture of glory. Nor does
it mean that leading a life of virtue is merely an option for the person of
faith, for as Peter Lombard goes on to say in *Sententiarum* 3.26.1, "without
merits, to hope for something is not hope but presumption" ("sine meritis
aliquid sperare non spes sed praesumptio dici potest"). Nonetheless, one

may have a "certain expectation of future glory" simply because of God's omnipotence and mercy. These guarantee the gift of eternal life to the believer who will accept them: "To anyone having faith," Aquinas writes, "this omnipotence and mercy are certainties."[18]

In his reply to James, Dante catches the tone, as well as the rhetoric, of this Scholastic discourse. But as he goes on to speak more personally about how he learned to hope, he develops a "language of plenitude" that is replete with internal rhymes, repetitions, and doublings[19]—a richly poetic set of metaphors suggesting inspiration and influence, cooperation and mediation. Just as faith came through "The plenteous rain of the Holy Spirit which is poured out over the old and the new parchment" (*Par.* 24.91–92), so too hope rained down to him in an overflow of texts. Adapting what is essentially the cosmic model of divine influence first presented in *Paradiso* 2, he imagines a rain of filtered light, a shower of stars. This is, moreover, quite specifically a scriptural cosmos. Each author distills hope through writing, and each in turn instills hope within the reader. The succession of active verbs used to describe this dynamics of authorship ("vien," "distillò," "stillasti," "repluo") is rapid-fire. It bears out what A. J. Minnis has noted more generally in late-thirteenth-century exegesis: a new emphasis on the biblical writers as active agents rather than passive instruments, with each author recognized as having a distinctive style or genre, as well as his own personality.[20] Thus, we are told, David, "the supreme singer of the Supreme Leader" (*Par.* 25.72), wrote a personal "tëodia"; James, a "pistola."

And Dante? In the first canto of the *Commedia*, Virgil was warmly acclaimed as the source of Dante's poetic inspiration, as the fountainhead of speech (*Inferno* 1.79–80) and "honor and light" (v. 82) of other poets. By *Paradiso* 25, however, Dante is turning elsewhere to trace his descent, to account for his lineage, and to build his authority. Aligning himself with biblical writers, and placing himself at the end of a succession of testaments, he looks first ("pria") toward David and then ("poi") toward James; he is *their* star pupil. Following upon these past distillations of the Holy Spirit's downpour, moreover, he offers himself as one who can "re-rain" this collective scriptural dew on others—and can do so *now*. He is the custodian of hope's present tense, the author of the Spirit's present text. And so, with Virgil no longer in the picture—a pagan literary master who lives eternally in desire but quite explicitly without hope ("sanza speme vivemo in disio," *Inf.* 4.42)—he stages a move toward biblical authors who know God's name and sing God's song. His hopes rest in them.

It is not clear what overflow of *speranza* Dante received from the Epistle of James. Beatrice acclaims the saint as one who chronicled the bounty ("larghezza," *Par.* 25.29–30) of the heavenly basilica, which may well be a reference to James 1:17: "Every best gift, and every perfect gift, is from above, coming down from the Father of lights, with whom there is no change, nor shadow of alteration." Other passages also come to mind. According to the Epistle, those who remain faithful under persecution can hope for a crown of life (1:12); the poor of this world should expect a heavenly kingdom (2:5); those who suffer now must look to the future: "Be you therefore also patient, and strengthen your hearts: for the coming of the Lord is at hand" (5:8).

When it comes to the legacy of the Psalmist David, there is no question about the specific debt that Dante owes: it was the Ninth Psalm that first enabled him to have a "sure expectation of future glory." Dante himself quotes the psalm's eleventh verse in Italian (" 'Sperino in te' . . . 'color che sanno il nome tuo,' " *Par.* 25.73–74), and then hears it again sung by all the blessed, this time in Latin, at the end of the second exam ("*Sperent in te*," v. 98). This particular "tëodia," therefore, serves as the canto's "theme song," just as David, "the supreme singer of the Supreme Leader," is the forerunner of Dante's own literary hopes.

Much could be said about David as poet, as penitent sinner, as prophet, as a "model of compunction," indeed, as a model *tout court* for Dante.[21] Of interest here, however, is the specific "tëodia" cited (and twice sung) in *Paradiso* 25. Rather than simply offering a generic statement of confidence in God, such as one might find almost anywhere in the Psalter, Psalm 9 is striking in its particular relevance to Dante himself: it seems to describe both the existential situation of the exiled poet and the itinerary of the pilgrim in his journey from hell to heaven. Although the psalm itself is not a narrative, it can easily be read as a biblical story of deliverance that foreshadows and corroborates Dante's own. Quoted below are the most relevant verses, including the one that Dante cites twice (v. 11):

> 10 The Lord is become a refuge for the poor: a helper in due time in tribulation. 11 And let them trust in thee who know thy name: for thou hast

not forsaken them that seek thee, O Lord. 12 Sing ye, to the Lord, who dwelleth in Sion: declare his ways among the Gentiles: 13 For requiting their blood he hath remembered them: he hath not forgotten the cry of the poor. 14 Have mercy upon me, O Lord: see my humiliation which I suffer from my enemies. 15 Thou liftest me up from the gates of death, that I might declare all thy praises in the gates of the daughter of Sion. 16 I will rejoice in thy salvation: the Gentiles have stuck fast in the destruction which they prepared. Their foot hath been taken in the very snare which they prepared.

It takes no great leap of interpretation to see why this text should so appeal to Dante. Like David surrounded by his foes, the exiled poet of the *Commedia* is beset by enemies; Dante's foes have banished him from Florence, doomed him to wander throughout Italy, and impugned his honor with false accusations. This predicament, of course, is the state in which he writes his own vernacular "tëodia." It is the fate forecast for him throughout the poem, first in the veiled infernal predictions of Ciacco and Farinata and Ser Brunetto, then in the heaven of Mars through the painfully clear prophecy of Cacciaguida. But if, like David in the Psalm, he knows the sorrow of solitude, his appropriation of the text suggests that he too can hope to find in God a refuge for the oppressed ("refugium pauperi," Ps. 9:9), a rescue against all odds, someone who can lead him away from hell's gates to the portals of heaven. Nor will the injustices of the present day forever go unpunished. Those who persecute the righteous will fall down into a pit of their own making ("In laqueo isto," 9:15), into the infernal depths ("in infernum," 9:17). But he who sings the Lord's song knows the name of the one who will never forsake the oppressed. This divine vindicator, then, is the only one in whom to place ultimate hope: "Arise, O Lord: let not man prevail" ("Exsurge, Domine, non conferetur homo," 9:19).

Augustine's commentary on Psalm 9, which essentially becomes the *Glossa ordinaria* on it, offers the requisite Christological reading. He sees in the final call for God to arise, for instance, a prophecy of the Last Judgment, when Christ will separate the sheep from the goats and dispense universal justice. But the psalm also pertains to life now, as lived in history and before the end point when Christ will come to judge the living and the dead. Indeed, it is in his gloss on the verse that Dante twice cites—"Let them hope in Thee who know Thy name" (v. 11)—that Augustine suggests how

Christians should conduct themselves before the time of final reckoning, in an earthly city where the innocent continue to suffer and powerful men usually prevail. Those who wait on God, he says, will renounce the world and its riches, the enticement of "things that flow by in time's quick revolution, having nothing but 'will be' and 'has been'" ("in rebus quae temporis volubilitate praeterfluunt, nihil habentes nisi: 'erit' et 'fuit'").[22] Those who know the name of God will look beyond this temporal ebb and flow, beyond the flux of transient and perishable things: "Let them cease then to hope in and love things temporal and let them apply themselves to hope eternal" ("Desinant igitur sperare et deligere temporalia, et se ad aeternam spem conferant"). Or, as Aquinas decides in his consideration of whether the Christian should ever hope for the good things of this mortal life, "We should pray to God for no other favours apart from their subordination to eternal happiness. . . . To one who sets his heart upon something great, anything less is of minor importance" (*ST* II–II, 17, 2, resp. ad 2 and 3).

Although a move from time to eternity is the direction of the entire *Commedia*, most particularly it is the trajectory of the *Paradiso*. Thus, when James asks Dante to be specific about what his "sure expectation of future glory" consists in, Dante says that he hopes for nothing less than the resurrection of the body and the life everlasting. Once again, Scripture authorizes his reply:

> E io: "Le nove e le scritture antiche
>   pongon lo segno, ed esso lo mi addita,
>   de l'anime che Dio s'ha fatte amiche.
> Dice Isaia che ciascuna vestita
>   ne la sua terra fia di doppia vesta:
>   e la sua terra è questa dolce vita;
> e 'l tuo fratello assai vie più digesta,
>   là dove tratta de le bianche stole;
>   questa revelazion ci manifesta."
>   (*Par.* 25.88–96)

(And I, "The new and the old Scriptures set up the token of the souls
that God has made His friends, and this points it out to me. Isaiah says
that each one shall be clothed in his own land with a double garment,
and his own land is this sweet life; and your brother, where he treats of
the white robes, makes manifest this revelation to us far more expressly.")

In his initial definition of hope, Dante demonstrated his theological sophistication by quoting Peter Lombard's *Sententiarum.* When it comes now to stating what exactly he looks forward to, however, he leaves Scholasticism behind. Instead, his answer rains down, as it were, from a Book that reveals how mere mortals—like Abraham (James 2:23), Moses (Exod. 33:11), or the disciples of Jesus (John 15:14–15)—become the friends of God ("l'anime che Dio s'ha fatte amiche," v. 90). From the Old Testament, there is Isaiah's prophecy to the exiles of Israel that their great sorrow over the loss of Zion will be recompensed by an even greater restitution when they return home: "For your double confusion and shame, they shall praise their part: therefore they shall receive double in their land, everlasting joy shall be unto them" (Isa. 61:7). In the context of Christian doctrine, of course, the promise of *laetitia sempiterna* could not be equated with something as material as geographical territory: Israel's return to the Promised Land must mean something more "spiritual." And so the witness of the New Testament is brought to bear in order to suggest the anagogical sense of Isaiah's prophecy. From this perspective, the Promised Land is the heavenly *patria* that John beheld in his "more digested" ("più digesta," v. 94) vision in the Apocalypse: "After this I beheld a great multitude, which no man could number, of all nations and tribes, and peoples, and tongues, standing before the throne, and in sight of the Lamb, clothed with white robes [*amicti stolis albis*], and palms in their hands" (Apoc. 7:9).

The coordination of such disparate texts may appear merely arbitrary. But as Anna Chiavacci Leonardi has argued, what seems at first to be a bizarre juxtaposition of biblical sources is, in fact, quite traditional. In this case, interpretation depends on a "parallel" reading of Isaiah 61 and Apocalypse 7 that is at least as old as Gregory the Great's *Dialogues,* and as contemporary with Dante as one of Bonaventure's sermons on the Assumption of the Virgin Mary.[23] Accordingly, when Isaiah speaks of each Israelite being clothed in his own land, and then receiving a double portion as an inheritance, he is speaking allegorically about the glory of paradise— our hereditary homeland ("terra") in which eternal bliss will be enjoyed both in soul and in the resurrected body. What the Hebrew prophet foretold obscurely, John saw with greater clarity in the multitude of "white stoles" gathered around the Lamb's throne. Beyond the hope of paradise's *dolce vita* there is nothing more to look forward to. Therefore, as the testimony of David spills over into James, and as the prophecy of Isaiah "rains down" into the Apocalypse of St. John, their message is one and the same: "Let them hope in Thee who know Thy name."

But is it *only* in God's name that Dante places his hopes? Granted, the poet's open effort in *Paradiso* 24–27 is to cut his losses with the earthly city and look elsewhere for his future. At the same time, we note his attempt to define the *Commedia* as a form of *evangelica dottrina*, and to have it recognized as such by the authors of Scripture, who find in his words the same divine fire that illumined their own. Yet surely there is still another glory at stake and another name to claim—Dante's own as a poet. At first glance, the setting of these cantos does not seem propitious for any kind of literary apotheosis: an examination on the theological virtues is an unlikely place for Dante to make a particular case for his own poetry or, for that matter, for the enduring value of any human text. In *Paradiso* 26, after all, Adam warns about the ephemerality of all language. The "usage of mortals," he says, is as "fronda/in ramo, che sen va e altra vene" ("a leaf on a branch, which goes away and another comes," vv. 137–38). From this withering perspective both poets and their poetry would seem to be hopelessly caught up in time's quick revolution, lost in the wind. Unless, of course, a poet becomes a star, an author in God's textual firmament (like David and James), who discovers how to write himself into eternity: "The grass is withered, and the flower is fallen away. But the word of the Lord endureth forever" (1 Pet. 1:25).

Indeed, this transformation of ephemeral poetry into an enduring Word, of human writer into sacred author, is one way to view Dante's agenda at the very outset of *Paradiso* 25. In the course of the most intimate authorial aside in the entire poem, he freeze-frames his narrative, abruptly steps out of it, and speaks about himself and the work we are reading. Like Paul in 2 Corinthians 12:5–10—"For when I am weak, then I am powerful"—he turns his infirmities into the occasion of his glory:

> Se mai continga che 'l poema sacro
>   al quale ha posto mano e cielo e terra,
>   sì che m'ha fatto per molti anni macro,
> vinca la crudeltà che fuor mi serra
>   del bello ovile ov' io dormi' agnello,
>   nimico ai lupi che li danno guerra;
> con altra voce omai, con altro vello

ritornerò poeta, e in sul fonte
del mio battesmo prenderò 'l cappello;
però che ne la fede, che fa conte
  l'anime a Dio, quivi intra' io, e poi
  Pietro per lei sì mi girò la fronte.
                              (*Par.* 25.1–12)

(If ever it come to pass that the sacred poem to which heaven and earth
have so set hand that it has made me lean for many years should overcome
the cruelty which bars me from the fair sheepfold where I slept as a lamb,
an enemy to wolves which war on it, with changed voice now and with
changed fleece a poet will I return, and at the font of my baptism will I
take the crown; because there I entered into the Faith that makes souls
known to God; and afterward Peter, for its sake, thus encircled my brow.)

Earlier on, Dante could call his poem a "comedìa" (*Inf.* 16.128, 21.2), could
refer to the "twentieth canto of the first canzone" (20.2–3) or in the *Pur-
gatorio* speak of his "second cantica" (33.140). But now purely literary terms
are no longer adequate. Instead, he is the author of a "sacred poem" to
which both heaven and earth have set a hand. His work also belongs to
God.[24]

But who precisely is the human author of this "poema sacro"? In
Purgatorio 30.50 he is called "Dante" for the first and only time in the
Commedia—an authorial self-indulgence for which he feels the need to give
an account: "mi volse al suon del nome mio,/che di necessità qui si registra"
("I turned at the sound of my name, which of necessity is registered here,"
vv. 62–63).[25] An even bolder move is made in *Paradiso* 25, when for the first
time the author of the *Commedia* refers to himself as "poeta" (v. 8). In its
previous 29 appearances in the text, this title was reserved exclusively for
the masters of antiquity—Virgil first and foremost, "altissimo poeta" (*Inf.*
4.80), but also Homer, Ovid, Horace, Lucan, and Statius. Here at last
Dante assumes it for himself, thereby signaling, as Kevin Brownlee has
argued, that his own Italian language should enjoy equal status with Greek
and Latin, and he himself be accorded a position equal to his illustrious
predecessors.[26]

More than art is at stake, however, in this move to sacred poetry. Also
hanging in the balance is Dante's relation to God's truth, to "divina favella"
("divine discourse," *Par.* 24.99) and "l'evangelica dottrina" ("the evangelic

doctrine," 24.144)—a truth that shines within him, as he tells St. Peter, like a star in heaven. Unlike those authors he once celebrated in Limbo, whose collective wisdom he was so proud to augment in *Inferno* 4.97–102, he possesses "the Faith that makes souls known to God" (*Par.* 25.10–11). In recognition of this connection, he proclaims that were he to be crowned for his achievement as "poeta," it would have to be at the font of his own baptism, at the spiritual center of his own Florentine birthplace, in whose sacramental waters he was named as Christ's own for eternity.

The future-conditional tense of this entire passage—"Se mai con-tinga"—suggests that Dante thought it unlikely such a moment would ever occur. How could it, when Florence was a sheepfold fallen under the control of wolves, with its gates cruelly barred against him, the would-be shepherd of the flock? A lesser poet, a less fervent Christian, might lose faith and abandon hope. In both these capacities, however, he continues to trust in the value of what he and God have authored together. He has a sure expectation of heaven, unquestionably, but also of the *Commedia*'s own future glory, "il qual produce/grazia divina e precedente merto" ("which divine grace produces, and preceding merit," *Par.* 25.68–69). He hopes in paradise, but also in the *Paradiso*.

And so too, apparently, does St. Peter, who circles Dante's head three times with a coronet of light at the end of canto 24 (vv. 148–54) and once again at the start of canto 25 (vv. 10–12), and then tells him in canto 27, "apri la bocca,/e non asconder quel ch'io non ascondo" ("open your mouth and do not hide what I hide not," vv. 65–66). Poetry and prophecy, genius and apostle, man and text: all merge into a composite identity. So too does the crown that Peter inscribes around Dante's head. It is a token not only of the Peneian frond aspired to in *Paradiso* 1.22–36 but of that *corona iustitiae* that St. Paul expected for himself at his own resurrection, "which the Lord the just judge will render to me in that day" (2 Tim. 4:8). Why should Dante clamor for mortal accolades from Florence when heaven is so ready to honor him?

> così, benedicendomi cantando,
>> tre volte cinse me, sì com' io tacqui,
>> l'appostolico lume al cui comando
>> io avea detto: sì nel dir li piacqui!
>>> (*Par.* 24.151–54)

(so, singing benedictions on me, the apostolic light at whose bidding I had spoken encircled me three times when I was silent, so in my speech I pleased him.)

Is this the hubris of the chronic overreacher, with Dante (like Napoleon at the most solemn moment of his coronation) seizing the crown from the pope's hands and placing it securely on his own head? In the heaven of the fixed stars Dante rockets to his birth sign in Gemini, acknowledges the divine source of his genius, and places himself in the same constellation as David and James, Peter and John. It is a presumptuously soaring flight, and one that may recall another—Ovid's. At the end of his *Metamorphoses*, after defying the power of time's rude hand ever to erase his achievement, the master of shape changes and special effects places all his hopes in himself and the poem he has written:

parte tamen meliore mei super alta perennis
astra ferar, nomenque erit indelebile nostrum,
quaque patet domitis Romana potentia terris,
ore legar populi, perque omnia saecula fama,
siquid habent veri vatum praesagia, vivam.

(*Met.* 15.875–79)

(Still in my better part I shall be borne immortal far beyond the lofty stars and I shall have an undying name. Wherever Rome's power extends over the conquered world, I shall have mention on men's lips and, if the prophecies of bards have any truth, through all the ages shall I live in fame.)

With both poets, genius writes itself into heaven, seizes a crown, makes a bid for eternal stardom. But whereas Ovid's authority consists entirely in the grace and merit of his artifact—in the sheer brilliance of his poetic gift, in the fulfilled "prophecies of bards" who are primarily literary pundits—Dante has a far more complicated relationship both to his vocation as a writer and to his text. At the same time that he invents the terms of his own achievement in *Paradiso* 24–27—pulls all the strings, makes all the moves, supplies his own applause, co-opts the City of God—he also grounds his invention in a Christian discourse that finally is *not* of his own making. This means that the *Commedia* is infinitely more than "a purely personal gnosis," a "wholly personal poem," unless, like Bloom, one refuses to recognize a motivation for writing that goes beyond the author's own will, originality, and power. To do so, however, is to ignore much of the poem's enterprise and neglect the very premises of the poet's greatest daring. For Dante presents himself as someone with an assigned part to play, a tradition to pass on, a hope that transcends even his own ambitions. This is to say that he is bound by the very texts and authorities in whose constellation he presumes to orbit. And if bound by something larger than himself, then he is also judged, held accountable, even brought up short. In the end, he must acknowledge that he is left in silence by a God who ultimately retains the last word. He must confess the flickering of his power, the absence of fantasia: "A l'alta fantasia qui mancò possa" ("Here power failed the lofty phantasy," *Par.* 33.142). There are limits to what even the genius of Gemini can hope to write.

It is impossible when it comes to Dante and his work to insist on a tidy either/or. For how can we differentiate clearly between genius and apostle, *poeta* and *theologus*, when the *Commedia* never stops blurring such distinctions, when the poet himself never ceases to walk that very line between servanthood and self-service? In the previous chapter, "John Is with Me," we saw how this tightrope act is performed in *Purgatorio*'s Pageant of Revelation, where Dante's appeal to the authority of such biblical writers as Ezekiel and John turns out to be a declaration of his own *auctoritas*: "Giovanni è meco" (29.105). Now, in the course of *Paradiso*'s theological examination, he provides no less audacious a consideration of scriptural tradition and his individual talent. Thus, when St. James asks in canto 25 how he learned to hope, Dante's answer is a genealogy of authors and texts that culminates in himself. By catching the overflow of David and James, of the old parchments and the new, he gathers enough inspiration in his own vessel so that he can now "re-rain" their inspired Christian hope on others. Such a shower of light will inevitably be filtered through his particular medium, will come to us refracted through the extraordinary lens of the poet's genius. Just as surely this testament will be marked by his individual character and fate—his vulnerability to pride, wrath, and lust acknowledged on the terraces of purgatory; the indignity and suffering of his exile prophesied in the final canticle.

But what does Dante actually "shower" on his readers? If one takes seriously the theological burden of the *Commedia*, then the poet's "message" in *Paradiso* 25 is essentially what he received from Scripture: "And let them trust in thee who know thy name: for thou hast not forsaken them that seek thee, O Lord" (Ps. 9:11). The words of the poem, the fiction of the journey, may be his own invention, but the Word that inspires the vision is not. In this regard, at least, Dante is like the great Mendicant preachers of his day, who filtered an inherited theological legacy through their own vernacular, who, like St. Paul, delivered to others what they had themselves "received of the Lord" (1 Cor. 11:23). Any attempt to see the poet *only* in this light, however, ends up being as inadequate as is the notion of Dante as a Gnostic rapt at "purely personal" play within his own hall of mirrors. For he cannot be reduced to the status of a scribe who merely copies down an inspired text or a messenger who carries someone else's scroll. Rather, he is an *auctor* who writes with authority, self-proclaimed though it may be. Nor is there any hint of anticlimax about his position at the end of this authorial line. David wrote his "tëodia," James his "pistola," John his "alto preconio" (*Par.* 26.44)—and Dante his *Commedia.* He wants to shine in the Christian firmament as the brightest poet of the faith, the newest star.

This delicate balancing of public and private, of biblical revelation and his own invention, of truth and fiction is beautifully captured in a brief exchange between Dante and St. John at the close of *Paradiso* 25. In verses 112–14, where Beatrice first identifies the "beloved disciple" through narrative elements that are unique to the fourth Gospel—John's leaning on Jesus's breast at the Last Supper (13:23), Christ's charge from the cross to make Mary his own mother (19:26–27)—Dante begins to stare at his "living flame" with particular intensity. Neither Peter nor James inspired this kind of scrutiny, nor does John take to it kindly:

> Perché t'abbagli
> per veder cosa che qui non ha loco?
> In terra è terra il mio corpo, e saragli
>   tanto con li altri, che 'l numero nostro
>   con l'etterno proposito s'agguagli.
> Con le due stole nel beato chiostro
>   son le due luci sole che saliro;
>   e questo apporterai nel mondo vostro.
>   (*Par.* 25.122–29)

(Why do you dazzle yourself in order to see that which has here no place? On earth my body is earth, and there it shall be with the rest, until our number equals the eternal purpose. With the two robes in the blessed cloister are those two lights only which ascended; and this you shall carry back into your world.)

Dante stares at John with such determination because he wants to know whether pious tradition was right after all—whether instead of suffering death and burial like all the other disciples, "the one who Jesus loved" was assumed bodily into heaven. The final chapter of John's Gospel itself records the beginning of confusion on this score. After his resurrection, Jesus appears to his disciples on the shores of the sea of Tiberias and tells Peter that in his death he, too, would glorify God. Perhaps wondering if this awesome future would be shared by the other apostles, Peter asks specifically about John, "the beloved." Christ's response is sharp: "So I will have him to remain till I come, what is it to thee? Follow thou me" (21:22). Delivered in characteristically enigmatic Johannine style, this answer by no means settles the matter. The Evangelist goes on to add, with obvious annoyance over the persistence of the rumor: "This saying therefore went abroad among the brethren, that the disciple should not die. And Jesus did not say to him: 'He should not die'; but, 'So I will have him to remain till I come, what is that to thee?' " (21:23).[27]

In their discussion of these matters, both Augustine and Aquinas steer their way between Scripture and tradition, between what the Evangelist clearly sets forth in his Gospel ("And Jesus did not say to him: 'He should not die,'" 21:23) and what some credulous but faithful Christians have come to believe about his assumption. Dante, on the other hand, is not so constrained. For rather than constructing a response along the lines of theological *auctores*, who offer their readers a considered No that nonetheless allows the possibility of a Yes, Dante takes a position on this matter that is absolutely definitive. Why? He has information that neither Augustine nor Aquinas were privy to—the witness of the Evangelist whom he himself "heard" in the heaven of the fixed stars and who told him directly, in no uncertain terms, "In terra è terra il mio corpo, e saragli / tanto con li altri" ("On earth my body is earth, and there it shall be with the rest," *Par.* 25.124–25). Instead of a biblical proof text about John's body, the poet offers the saint's *ipssisima verba*![28] Dante's responsibility with regard to this information is also unambiguous. He is to set the record straight: "And this you shall carry back into your world," says John.

When Dante wrote the *Commedia* he no doubt searched the Scriptures, weighed received belief, opted for one authority over another, and came up with a response that suited both his convictions and his purposes. This might mean choosing Bonaventure over Aquinas, for instance, when it came to deciding whether unbaptized infants realized anything about their eternal loss; or siding with Dionysius the Areopagite over Gregory the Great when it came to the precise order of the angelic hierarchies. Very occasionally he sees things entirely according to his own lights, as when he parts company with orthodoxy and turns Limbo into the Elysian Fields. Nonetheless, for the most part he chooses between authorities.[29]

However it was that he actually made these decisions, they are never presented in the *Commedia* as deriving from Scripture or Reason (although neither of these pillars of authority are ever refuted). Rather, the poet gives us what he made up as if it were what he had received through experience, what he had seen with his own eyes, what had been revealed to him. Knowing that the argument from authority is weakest when based on human understanding but most forceful when based on what God has disclosed, he in effect has Scripture's authority merge with his own.

The question remains, however, why any reader should have faith in such an enterprise or take the "argument from authority" as compelling when it is made on the basis of a poet's disclosure. An analogous question about the authority of the Bible is in fact raised during the first theological examination, when St. Peter presses for clarity on the substance and the evidence of Dante's faith. Asked why he takes Scripture to be "divina favella" ("divine discourse," *Par.* 24.99), Dante answers with the stock reply of Christian apologetics. The argument was earlier delivered quite straightforwardly in *Convivio* 3.7.16: "the most basic foundation of our faith is the miracles performed by Him who was crucified for us . . . and those performed subsequently by the saints in His name." In *Paradiso* 24, however, Dante speaks more elliptically:

> La prova che 'l ver mi dischiude,
> son l'opere seguite, a che natura
> non scalda ferro mai né batte incude.
> (*Par.* 24.100–102)

(The proof which discloses the truth to me are the works that followed, for which nature never heats iron nor beat an anvil.)

The only proof of the Scripture's truth, in other words, is Scripture itself. Despite the venerability of this argument, Peter takes it to task as a kind of sophism. The miracles that supposedly substantiate the Bible are known to us only in its pages; the logic is circular. In his reply to this objection (vv. 106–12), Dante also draws heavily on tradition: the greatest miracle of all is that the gospel was accepted throughout the world without the benefit of miracles, that the incredible fact of the Incarnation was actually believed by so many, that the apostles of the gospel were not imposing but instead, as Augustine writes in *City of God* 22.5, "of obscure birth, of no importance, and of no learning."[30] Or, as Dante says to Peter, with a swipe at the state of the contemporary church, "tu intrasti povero e digiuno / in campo, a seminar la buona pianta / che fu già vite e ora è fatta pruno" ("you entered the field poor and hungry, to sow the good plant which was once a vine and is now become a thorn," vv. 109–11). Finally, what Dante takes to be the definitive proof of Scripture's truth is quite simply the fruit it bears: "La prova che 'l ver mi dischiude, son l'opere seguite," "the proof which discloses truth to me are the works that fol-lowed," 24.100–101). The truth of the Word is what it does, the works of love it produces.

Staying within the confines of the *Commedia*, we see the blessed cele-brate Dante's faith in God's Book, approve his mastery of theological dis-course and "evangelic doctrine," and hail the divine light shining through his own mortal words. To appropriate the words Dante himself uses to talk about his faith, "quest' è la favilla / che si dilata in fiamma poi vivace, / e come stella in cielo in me scintilla" ("this is the spark which then dilates to a living flame, and like a star in heaven shines within me," *Par.* 24.145–47). But why should anyone hold the *Commedia*'s "new parchment" to be a valid addition to the Scripture's texts, or consider a poet's speech to be in any sense "divine discourse"? To say that the text is true because it says it is—indeed, says it over and over again—is merely to beg the question. "The very thing itself which requires to be proved, and naught else, affirms [it] to you" (25.103–5): the logic once again is circular; one can never get outside the text to prove its truth. Unless, of course, one looks at the "works" that have followed from it, the fruit it has born—unless one looks, that is, at what has become of those readers who over the centuries have come to themselves thanks to its self-authenticated pages. At the outset of the *Paradiso*, the poet asks that his work might be the beginning of a great good: "Poca favilla gran fiamma seconda: / forse di retro a me con miglior voci / si pregherà" ("A great flame follows a little spark: perhaps, after me, prayer shall be offered with better voices," 1.34–35). The hermeneutic of suspicion might construe this hope that prayer be the result of reading the *Commedia* as nothing more than a disingenuous bid for fame, no less vainglorious than Ovid's *vivam*. But for the many who have found themselves transformed by Dante's words, the poet's wish has indeed been granted to him. The sparks have made a flame.

PART 2

Dante and Virgil

CHAPTER 5

Descendit ad inferos

Dante's *Inferno* seems at first glance to be largely a construct of classical poetry and Italian politics, a realm that lacks the *Commedia*'s overall rich allusiveness to Scripture. Not only are scriptural references comparatively scant, but the poet introduces no biblical paradigm such as we find at the outset of the other canticles—the Exodus in *Purgatorio* (2.46), the rapture of Paul to the third heaven in *Paradiso* (1.73–75). Instead, the *Inferno* is pervaded by Virgil's *Aeneid*, a poem Dante knows by heart, "tutta quanta" (*Inf.* 20.114), and that he identifies in his opening canto as the object of long study and great love. In particular, Aeneas's descent to the underworld serves as a model, not only for Dante Pilgrim—who, like "di Silvïo il parente, / corruttibile ancora, ad immortale / secolo andò, e fu sensibilmente" ("the father of Silvius went, while still mortal, to the immortal world, and was there in his bodily senses," *Inf.* 2.13–15)—but also for Dante the poet, who carefully traces the path of Virgil's deep and savage way in his own vernacular.

Yet it is also true that Dante's descent "to the immortal world" is inscribed within another journey to Hades: the descent of Christ into hell, his three-day sojourn among the dead, and his "harrowing" of all those who in ages past had longed for his coming. Virgil specifically refers to this event on several occasions in the first canticle: *Inferno* 4.52–63, 8.124–26, and 12.37–45. But it is recalled more indirectly whenever our attention is drawn to the ruined state of hell's "infrastructure," to its unhinged doorways, crumbled walls, and fallen bridges. Nor is it only the silent witness of architecture that brings Christ's descent to mind. For even in the year 1300, the demons are still haunted by the memory of a divine breaking and entering that took place centuries earlier. "Yesterday," recalls a devil in the Malebolgia, "più oltre cinqu' ore che quest' otta,/mille dugento con sessanta sei / anni compié che qui la via fu rotta" ("five hours later than now, completed one thousand two hundred sixty-six years since the road was broken here," 21.112–14). From clues like this one, delivered offhand but nonetheless lodged deep within infernal memory, we realize that Dante's own descent into hell extends from Good Friday afternoon to just before the dawn of Easter. Thus, he follows the underworld footsteps of Christ as well as Aeneas.

The trauma that *Inferno*'s demons cannot forget is the same event that the church began to confess around the mid–fourth century. Less than 100 years later, the clause "descendit ad inferos" was entered into the final version of the Apostles' Creed.[1] Yet, unlike the other articles of faith that pertain to the life of Christ ("he was conceived by the Holy Spirit, born of the Virgin Mary, suffered under Pontius Pilate, was crucified, died, and was buried"), the descent to hell lacks a narrative warrant in the Gospels, or any developed exposition elsewhere in the canon. Indeed, it is probably more accurate to speak of it as "scriptural" than as Scripture. Although hinted at by a number of New Testament texts, the harrowing itself is a theological fiction—a composite story constructed out of roughly twenty passages scattered throughout the Old Testament as well as the New.[2]

The Bible, therefore, provided the necessary elements for a narrative that it actually never told. It offered a cry in the darkness, a shattering of brass and iron, a triumphant Lord who freed those who were imprisoned in the shadow of death—but no harrowing. What the canon did not say outright, however, was supplied by a number of apocryphal texts.[3] The most important of these is undoubtedly the Gospel of Nicodemus, dating in Greek from the second century and then in Latin translation from the end of the fifth.[4] Because of the appeal of its vivid narrative, subsequently made available in many different vernacular versions, this "apocryphon" was soon absorbed into the church's biblical imagination. If never formally a canonical Scripture, its account of the harrowing virtually became gospel. And for good reason: it "discovered" for the faithful what was otherwise a missing moment in the sequence of Holy Week events stretching between the Passion and the Resurrection. It told a story that needed to be told.[5]

This extraordinarily theatrical narrative eventually became drama, first in the form of the quasi-liturgical *lauda* or *devozione* of Dante's day and then as an episode in the cycles of the more secular mystery plays.[6] But sacred theater was not the only means by which the descent of Christ was publicized in medieval culture. Visual representations of the harrowing abounded—in sculpture, carving, manuscript illumination, mosaic, and painting.[7] Despite some variation in composition and detail, the core iconography of the harrowing reproduces essentially the same picture. For instance, in the twelfth-century mosaic on the west vault of Venice's San Marco, a monumental figure of Christ commands the scene, holding the cross of his victory high above the wreckage of shattered hardware and sprung locks. Underfoot are the ruined gates of hell and the vanquished figure of Satan, who is shown splayed against the background darkness of a cavern or tomb. What primarily captures the viewer's attention, however, is the gesture on which the whole composition is centered. With a dramatic twist of his body, Christ grabs hold of Adam with a hand that still shows the imprint of his crucifixion, and pulls him up out of the grave and into his own glory. In vain, Satan clutches at Adam's foot, helpless against the redeemer in this tug-of-war. Eve and the other surrounding figures, who are in no way threatened by Satan's grasp, raise their hands toward Christ in what Otto Demus has called a "massed personification of entreaty."[8] Like Adam, they are hopeful that the redeemer will take them up.

By means of this single image, Christian iconographers were able to represent the theological complexity of Christ's redemption. Death and resurrection, defeat and victory, the intimate relationship of the New Adam to the Old, the incorporation of Israel into the New Dispensation, and the believer's own hope for deliverance—all these themes were brought together in a portrait of the savior doing the triumphant work of redemption.

What Dante made of the *descensus Christi* can best be seen against the background of theological traditions he was both working within and, in some instances, departing from. I say "traditions" because despite the fact that the medieval church accepted the harrowing as gospel—"Who, therefore, except an infidel, will deny that Christ was in hell?"[9]—there were different ways to understand what the event signified.[10] Both Clement of Alexandria and Origen, for instance, took the mysterious words in 1 Peter about Christ's preaching "to those spirits that were in prison" (4:1) to mean that the redeemer descended to hell in order to evangelize all of the dead—

the Jews first, certainly, but also the Gentiles. As a result, the harrowing entirely emptied hell of human souls. Augustine, on the other hand, held that the purpose of Christ's descent was neither to preach to the dead nor to give anyone a second chance for belief, but rather to conquer Satan and deprive him of his captives. Although Augustine thought it presumptuous to define precisely who these souls were, on the whole he did not hesitate to say. The redeemed were the faithful of Israel, who did not worship idols or give themselves over to "the empty pride of human praise and glory," or neglect to hope in a redeemer.[11] Therefore, redemption was only for the descendants of Abraham, who, as the Epistle to the Hebrews puts it, "died according to faith, not having received the promises, but beholding them afar off, and saluting them, and confessing that they are pilgrims and strangers on the earth" (11:13).

Yet Augustine understood the appeal of a more universal deliverance that might take into account the fact of pagan genius as well as pagan virtue:

> Especially will men rejoice for the sake of some who are intimately
> known to us by their literary labours, whose eloquence and talent we
> admire—not only the poets and orators who in many parts of their writ-
> ings have held up to contempt and ridicule these same false gods of the
> nations, and have even occasionally confessed the one true God . . . but
> also those who have uttered the same, not in poetry or rhetoric, but as
> philosophers.[12]

Still, even if it made compelling emotional sense to imagine such Gentiles among those whom Christ redeemed from hell, Augustine could not condone such wishful thinking. For here "the verdict of human feeling [is] different from that of the justice of God." To follow human feeling, in this case, would lead to heresy.[13]

Although Augustine's position in these matters by and large became the orthodoxy of the Western church, the descent of Christ to the dead remained subject to discussion throughout the Middle Ages.[14] Thomas Aquinas sorts through the entire tradition with his characteristic rigor in *Summa Theologiae* III, 52, 1–8, and offers a theological compendium against which we can judge both the orthodoxy and the novelty of Dante's presentation in the *Commedia*.[15] Aquinas begins by rehearsing the many reasons why Christ visited hell after his death: to deliver the faithful of Israel from the consequences of original sin, to overthrow Satan, to rescue the ancient Hebrews, and to demonstrate within the underworld the power he had previously shown on earth. He then goes on to distinguish between one kind of hell and another. In upper hell—variously spoken of as the "Limbo of the Fathers" and "Abraham's bosom"[16]—he places those whom the redeemer came to save: those who believed in the coming of a future savior, and who were faithful in their observation of Israel's law and "sacraments." Since he understands the religion of the Old Testament to be Christianity in the making, Aquinas characterizes the patriarchs and prophets as souls who in some profound sense were already believers in Christ: they were "joined to Christ's passion in faith vivified by love, which takes away sin" (III, 52, 6, resp.).

In contrast to this group, other souls were gathered in an adjacent but lower hell. Christ's descent meant nothing to them, except a renewed sense of their eternal desolation. For the redeemer descended to these dead (and here Aquinas quotes John Damascene) "not that he might convert the unbelieving or make believers out of them, but in order to put their incredulity to shame" (III, 52, 2 resp. ad 3). But who were these unbelievers? Aquinas distinguishes two sorts who lived before the age of grace. There are those who had no faith in Christ's passion; and those who, if they had faith, "had no likeness in charity to the suffering Christ" (3, 52, 6 resp.). In the first case, he seems to be referring to pagans who lived completely outside the world of the Old Testament law and prophets; in the other, to Jews who refused the faith of their ancestors and in so doing rejected the love of Christ. Therefore, while Jews might have been in one hell or the other, it would not have been so for the Gentiles. Their fate was to remain forever in the hell of the lost, with "no deliverance from the guilt of hell's punishment" (3, 52, 6 resp.).

Although in this treatment in the *Summa Theologiae* Aquinas insists on a stark contrast between the saved of Israel and the Gentile lost, elsewhere in his writings the status of the pagans appears in a more ambiguous and hopeful light. In one of his *Quaestiones disputatae*, the *De veritate*, for instance, he asks whether it is necessary to believe explicitly in Christ in order to be saved (quest. 14, art. 11). Although his answer turns out to be a qualified Yes, among the first "difficulties" he contends with is Dionysius's assertion that "many Gentiles were saved before the coming of Christ." Aquinas does not dispute the reliability of Dionysius on this point, but he worries about the implications. Is the explicit belief in the redeemer, made possible for Israel by the law and the prophets, not necessary for those who lived in another religious world altogether?

To answer this question, Aquinas distinguishes between different kinds of people—between leaders and common folk—and then identifies specific kinds of belief required of each group in successive historical ages. From the time of the Fall until the coming of Christ, the period at stake for those in hell at the time of the descent, it was necessary for the "leaders" of Israel to have explicit faith in the redeemer. Ordinary Israelites, however, needed to believe only implicitly: they could trust either in the faith of their spiritual leaders or in divine providence. But what about Gentiles before the coming of Christ, who for all their worldly wisdom had no "teachers of divine faith"—neither a law to interpret nor prophets to heed? His solution to this ancient dilemma was to regard all pagans, no matter how spiritually eminent they may have been, as "ordinary people." Therefore, at least until the advent of the age of grace, it was enough for the Gentiles to have only implicit trust in a redeemer that was simply a part of their belief in divine providence. Furthermore, he says, "it is likely that the mystery of our redemption was revealed to many Gentiles before Christ's coming, as is clear from the Sibylline prophecies" (14, 11, resp. ad 5).[17]

Many Gentiles? Aquinas does not name names, nor does he anywhere actually state that the "evacuees" from the Limbo of the Fathers included anyone other than Old Testament figures. Nonetheless, he leaves a door open to mystery, grants the possibility that among those distinguished ancients whom Augustine could not accept as the elect—not only the virtuous but those who are "intimately known to us by their literary labours, whose talents and eloquence we admire"—there might also have been some whom Christ rescued from hell.

The Aquinas of *De veritate* was not alone in this largesse, despite the degree to which Augustine's negative verdict on the matter predominated in the Western church. There were positive statements about the "faithfulness" of some pagans in Gregory the Great, Albertus Magnus, Bonaventure, and the early-fourteenth-century Florentine preacher Giordano da Pisa.[18] Peter Abelard went so far as to argue that in their exercise of reason, the great pagan philosophers had some foreknowledge of the Christian God. He maintained there was evidence of the Trinity, for example, in the writings of Plato, Cicero, and Macrobius, as well as in the oracles of the Sibyl.[19] Even Augustine, who otherwise took a hard line in such matters, was confident that at least the Sibyl was to be counted a member incorporate in the City of God. He also entertained the possibility that Plato was acquainted with the Bible, not only because of a concord between some of the philosopher's statements and those of Moses, but because it "seemed likely" that when Plato made his journey to Egypt he listened personally to the prophet Jeremiah (*City of God* 8.11).

Of all the Gentile candidates for sanctity, however, the foremost was Virgil, whose oracular Fourth Eclogue alone guaranteed him a stature comparable to that of the prophets of Israel:

> Ultima Cumaei venit iam carminis aetas;
> magnus ab integro saeclorum nascitur ordo.
> iam redit et Virgo, redeunt Saturnia regna;
> iam nova progenies caelo demittitur alto.
>
> (Eclogue IV, vv. 4–7)

> (Now is come the last age of the song of Cumae; the great line of the centuries begins anew. Now the Virgin returns, the reign of Saturn returns; now a new generation descends from heaven on high.)

According to Eusebius, Constantine first gave these lines the theological interpretation that shortly became commonplace: the virgin who returns is Mary; the child sent from the sky, Jesus.[20] The emperor held that Virgil had full knowledge of all these allegorical meanings, but given the pagan world he lived in chose to express himself only covertly. Most, however, believed that the poet spoke beyond his own understanding—spoke true words, but in ignorance of their meaning. This is the position Dante assumes in *Purgatorio* 21–22, where Statius describes how he was in part saved by the truth of the gospel as it "sounded" in the Eclogue's mysterious opening lines. Yet as the larger context of the *Commedia* proclaims, this consonance between Virgil and the New Testament could only be recognized by one who had already encountered the Christian message. The author of the Eclogue, on the other hand, was himself deaf to the good news hidden in his own text. Therefore Statius likens him to someone who carries a lantern in the darkness, but who holds it behind him, to show the way to those who come after: "che porta il lume dietro e sé non giova" (*Purg.* 22.68). Virgil's words were a lamp to other feet, a light to someone else's path. But to himself, they were as fugitive and obscure as messages spelled from the Sibyl's leaves: "horrendas canit ambages antroque remugit, / obscuris vera involens" ("dread enigmas and echoes from the cavern, wrapping truth in darkness," *Aeneid* 6.99–100).[21]

Dante's decision in the *Commedia* to put Virgil in upper hell, in Limbo, placed him at odds with all the theologians of his day. For everyone else, this shadowy realm of the afterlife—at least since the harrowing of hell—was the exclusive abode of souls innocent of every sin except the original one, that is, of infants who had died without baptism.[22] According to Aquinas, these newborn souls dwelled forever in a kind of oblivion, unaware of their loss of the beatific vision; according to Bonaventure, they lived in a state neither sad nor happy, yet were dimly aware of the bliss they were denied.[23] Apart from these subtle distinctions, however, there was common agreement on an essential point: after Christ's descent to hell, Limbo was the exclusive realm of infantile ignorance and innocence.

It should come as a surprise, therefore, that in *Inferno* 4 Dante shows no particular interest in these unbaptized babies. Rather, he draws our attention to one of the most extraordinary inventions of his poem: a population of mature, sophisticated pagan worthies who lived their lives before the coming of Christianity and therefore "non adorar debitamente a Dio" ("did not worship God aright," *Inf.* 4.38).[24] Virgil freely acknowledges the defect of faith, both in himself and in his companions. Because none of them ever crossed through the waters of baptism, the unique "porta de la fede" ("the portal of the faith," v. 36), they are all barred from salvation. But aside from this lack of faith, Virgil admits no other moral defect:

> Per tai difetti, non per altro rio,
>   semo perduti, e sol di tanto offesi
>   che sanza speme vivemo in disio.
>   (*Inf.* 4.40–42)[25]

(Because of these shortcomings, and for no other fault, we are lost, and only so far afflicted that without hope we live in longing.)

In all of this, Dante presents his contemporary readers with one theological impossibility after another—not only a Limbo thronged with illustrious adults, but also the notion that such adults might be stained only by original sin and not by any other *peccatum*.[26] These theological anomalies were noted by contemporary readers of the *Commedia* and came up whenever the poet's orthodoxy was discussed.[27]

In *Inferno* 4, Dante does not shrink from the surprise element of his theological invention; in fact, he underscores it by having his own name-sake within the poem be astonished at what he finds in Limbo—so many "gente di molto valore" ("people of great worth," v. 44) in a place where only unbaptized infants were supposed to be. Therefore, he presses Virgil about Christ's descent to hell: why were some of the dead taken up and others left behind? And might there be any currently dwelling in Limbo who one day would come to know salvation? He asks, "uscicci mai alcuno, o per suo merto / o per altrui, che poi fosse beato?" ("did ever anyone go forth from here, either by his own or another's merit, who afterwards was blessed?" vv. 49–50). By way of response, Virgil offers his personal memory of the *descensus Christi*:

> rispuose: "Io era nuovo in questo stato,
>   quando ci vidi venire un possente,
>   con segno di vittoria coronato.
> Trasseci l'ombra del primo parente,
>   d'Abèl suo figlio e quella di Noè,
>   di Moïsè legista e ubidente;
> Abraàm patrïarca e Davìd re,
>   Israèl con lo padre e co' suoi nati
>   e con Rachele, per cui tanto fé,
> e altri molti, e feceli beati.
>   E vo' che sappi che, dinanzi ad essi,
>   spiriti umani non eran salvati."
>
> (*Inf.* 4.52–63)

([he] replied: "I was new in this condition when I saw a Mighty One come here, crowned with a sign of victory. He took hence the shade of our first parent, Abel his son, and Noah, and Moses, obedient giver of laws, Abraham the patriarch and David the king, Israel with his father and his children and with Rachel, for whom he did so much, and many others; and He made them blessed. And I would have you know that before these no human souls were saved.")

Given all that might have been said, Virgil's answer here is oddly disappointing. He gives only the fully expected Old Testament names, divulges a piece of information that Dante would already have known—namely, that before the harrowing "no human souls were saved"—and sidesteps the vexed issue of whether any virtuous Gentiles were also taken up into glory.[28] Nor does he describe any of the harrowing's most dramatic moments, so richly savored in the Gospel of Nicodemus and subsequent theatrical representations: the shattering of the gates of hell, the demons' confusion, the wild joy of the patriarchs at their release. Instead, Virgil gives a bare account of the one moment in salvation history to which he was ever made privy. The only surprise is that, contrary to what we find in the Gospel of Nicodemus, the harrowing is described by someone who was *not* liberated by Christ. Virgil speaks as one left behind when others were taken up. He addresses himself to Christian history from the far shore of the abyss that separates the damned from those who are at rest in God: "between us and you, there is fixed a great chaos: so that they who would come from hence to you, cannot, nor from thence come hither" (Luke 16:26).

Joining "us and you" is Adam, whom Virgil rightly claims as "our first parent," and therefore as the common forefather of humanity. But from this common ancestry he and his companions inherit only original sin. Otherwise, they have no spiritual kinship with the people of Hebrew Scripture; they do not share the circumcision given to Abraham, or the covenant handed down to Moses, or the messianic expectation made known in the preaching of the prophets. Virgil can recite the essential Old Testament names and offer the appropriate epithets—"Moses, obedient giver of laws, Abraham the patriarch and David the king." In so doing, he can also point to the six ages of world history, as Augustine had calculated it, stretching from Adam in the beginning to Christ "in the fullness of time."[29] But neither this roster of biblical figures nor the time line on which they are arranged is relevant to his pagan circle. Nor are the Old Testament souls he names here anywhere to be found on Limbo's "enameled green." In contrast to Homer, Horace, Socrates, and Plato—the spirits seen walking decorously, speaking seldom but with great authority—none of the biblical figures Virgil mentions are any longer in hell. His scriptural roll call only serves to draw attention to their current absence.

Everything in this brief recollection heightens the poignancy of Virgil as a figure who stands outside looking in, like Moses on the edge of a Promised Land he would never enter. As a result, instead of the sense of jubilation, almost of comic relief, that so frequently characterizes the harrowing of hell in Christian tradition, Virgil's spare narrative of the event is suffused with a quiet sense of tragedy.[30] In the very place where patriarchs once rejoiced to behold their salvation, we find the bewildered sadness of someone who lived and died just before the "fullness of time."

Virgil's marginality—and the limits of his understanding of the harrowing—are again made apparent in *Inferno* 12.31–45. Standing above a river of blood filled with souls who in life "took to blood and plunder" ("che dier nel sangue e ne l'aver di piglio," v. 105), he catches sight of some rocky debris where once had stood a solid wall. Then he reflects on the event that effectively divides hell's sense of time into a before and an after:

> Or vo' che sappi che l'altra fïata
>   ch'i' discesi qua giù nel basso inferno,
>   questa roccia non era ancor cascata.
> Ma certo poco pria, se ben discerno,
>   che venisse colui che la gran preda
>   levò a Dite del cerchio superno,
> da tutte parti l'alta valle feda
>   tremò sì, ch'i' pensai che l'universo
>   sentisse amor, per lo qual è chi creda
> più volte il mondo in caòsso converso;
>   e in quel punto questa vecchia roccia,
>   qui e altrove, tal fece riverso.
>   (*Inf.* 12.34–45)

(Know then that the other time I came down here into the nether Hell this rock had not yet fallen. But certainly, if I reckon rightly, it was a little before He came who took from Dis the great spoil of the uppermost circle, that the deep foul valley trembled so on all sides that I thought the universe felt love, whereby, as some believe the world has many times been turned to chaos; and at that moment this ancient rock, here and elsewhere, made such downfall.)

Here Virgil reveals what the crucifixion's earthquake felt like inside hell, when all the foundations shook within the "deep foul valley." It was a moment when "the universe felt love" ("l'universo/sentisse amor," vv. 41–42).[31] But again his comprehension of this truth is only partial, and owes everything to Empedocles' philosophy rather than to any Christian notion of a universe governed by love. The "amor" he speaks of is part of an Empedoclean cycle of love and hate, order and chaos that occurs endlessly at random and to no particular purpose. Within such a scheme, birth and death have no inherent theological value, no "reason." All is simply, as Aquinas noted, a matter of chance: "[Empedocles] said nothing more than that it was naturally disposed to be so" ("nisi quia sic aptum natum est esse").[32] True, Virgil is not entirely identified with this position; it is only "as some believe" ("per lo qual è chi creda," v. 42). Nonetheless, his appeal to Empedocles' undirected ebb and flow suggests the limits of his understanding of the Christ event.[33] Virgil is able to entertain the possibility that in one moment the universe was shaken by love, but he does not see reality as grounded in that mystery, or know the Incarnation of Christ as the unique turning point in history. He felt hell tremble, and saw a "Mighty One" despoil the inferno of its booty; he still does not, however, comprehend what actually happened "in quel punto" (v. 44).

Virgil's personal reminiscences of the harrowing in *Inferno* 4 and 12 are occasions when he remembers how once he stood on the threshold of Christian revelation but could not cross over—the unique moment when he *almost* entered another spiritual world. But it is not only through these personal recollections that Dante brings the descent of Christ into the *Inferno* or uses the "comedy" of the harrowing to heighten our sense of Virgil's tragic loss. Toward these same ends the harrowing is also reenacted within the narrative, more or less subtly refigured. For instance, as Amilcare Iannucci has argued, Dante forges both a temporal and spatial correspondence between the *descensus Christi* and Beatrice's Good Friday descent to Limbo, the event that initiates Dante's liberation from the spiritual hold of the "selva oscura" and ultimately brings him to the City of God.[34] Each canticle offers, in fact, a reprise of her visitation to the underworld: it is mentioned by Virgil in the flashback of *Inferno* 2.52–120; by Beatrice in her reproof to Dante in *Purgatorio* 30.136–45; and then by Dante himself in the very last words he addresses to her, recalling how concern for his salvation impelled his lady momentarily to exchange heaven for hell:

> O donna in cui la mia speranza vige,
> e che soffristi per la mia salute
> in inferno lasciar le tue vestige . . .
> (*Par.* 31.79–81)

(O lady, in whom my hope is strong, and who for my salvation did endure to leave in Hell your footprints . . .)

By "harrowing" Dante, Beatrice also liberates Virgil, enabling him to travel away from Limbo as far as the Garden of Eden atop Mount Purgatory. But for Virgil, the exit is only temporary, his deliverance but a matter of a few days in eternity. After this respite he must once again return to a place "non tristo di martìri, / ma di tenebre solo, ove i lamenti / non suonan come guai, ma son sospiri" ("not sad with torments, but with darkness only, where the lamentations sound not as wailings, but as sighs," *Purg.* 7.28–30). In the end, the gates of hell prevail against him.

This sign of hell's power over Virgil is first dramatized in *Inferno* 8–9, as he and Dante stand before the barricaded city of Dis. Unable to pass within, Virgil is humiliated to be "denied the abodes of pain" by a horde of fallen angels who bar the gates against him. The situation openly recalls the devils' resistance to Christ recorded in the Gospel of Nicodemus, when "Hades said to his wicked servants, 'Close the cruel gates of brass, and lay on them the bars of iron, and bravely resist, that we who hold captivity may not be taken captive.'" Virgil himself likens this present moment to the one that Christ encountered more than a thousand years before:

> Questa lor tracotanza non è nova;
>   ché già l'usaro a men segreta porta,
>   la qual sanza serrame ancor si trova.
>   (*Inf.* 8.124–26)

(This insolence of theirs is nothing new, for they showed it once at a less secret gate, which still stands without a bolt.)

It may well be that such demonic insolence is nothing new, that it also greeted Christ when he stood outside an underworld bolted tight against his entry. But therein ends the similarity. Unlike the "Mighty One" who brooked no resistance, Virgil is all but undone by this inability to make hell listen to him:

> Li occhi a la terra e le ciglia avea rase
>   d'ogne baldanza, e dicea ne' sospiri:
>   "Chi m'ha negate le dolenti case!"
>   (*Inf.* 8.118–20)

(He had his eyes upon the ground, and his brows were shorn of all boldness, and he was saying with sighs, "Who has denied me the abodes of pain?")

His sense of desperation carries over into the beginning of the following canto, where the master of "fair speech" sputters in despair:

"Pur a noi converrà vincer la punga,"
   cominciò el, "se non . . . Tal ne s'offerse.
   Oh quanto tarda a me ch'altri qui giunga!"
                                         (*Inf.* 9.7–9)[35]

("Yet we must win this fight," he began, "or else . . . such did she offer herself to us! Oh, how long to me it seems till someone come!")

Ultimately someone does come, a messenger from heaven who gains immediate entrance with no effort at all: "Venne a la porta e con una verghetta/l'aperse, che non v'ebbe alcun ritegno" ("He came to the gate, and with a little wand he opened it, and there was no resistance," vv. 89–90). Once again the power of heaven prevails, and the gates of hell open by divine right. But this almost laughably easy entrance takes place only after a representative of the "Mighty One" passes over "l'orribil soglia" ("the terrible threshold," v. 92), which Virgil himself is powerless to cross.

Virgil's protracted embarrassment before the gates of Dis heightens the contrast between his own impotence in the face of demonic forces and Christ's triumph at the harrowing. Dante is not content, however, to leave it at that: he gives yet another reworking of the descent motif that suggests Virgil's deep vulnerability to evil. This disturbing view is disclosed early in canto 9, when Virgil and Dante are still stalled before the gates of Dis. Virgil says that despite this apparent setback, he is familiar with both the underworld's layout and its ways. Yet this attempt at reassurance does not settle the matter for Dante, who in effect asks if his guide really knows what he is talking about:

"In questo fondo de la trista conca
   discende mai alcun del primo grado,
   che sol per pena ha la speranza cionca?"
Questa question fec'io; e quei "Di rado
   incontra," mi rispuose, "che di noi
   faccia il cammino alcun per qual io vado.
Ver è ch'altra fïata qua giù fui,
   congiurato da quella Eritón cruda
   che richiamava l'ombre a' corpi sui.
Di poco era di me la carne nuda,

ch'ella mi fece intrar dentr' a quel muro,
per trarne un spirto del cerchio di Giuda.
Quell'è 'l più basso loco e 'l più oscuro,
e 'l più lontan dal ciel che tutto gira:
ben so 'l cammin: però ti fa sicuro."

(Inf. 9.16–30)

("Into this depth of the dismal hollow does any ever descend from the
first circle where the sole punishment is hope cut off?" I asked this
question; and he answered, "It seldom happens that any of us makes the
journey on which I go. It is true that once before I was down here,
conjured by that cruel Erichtho who was wont to call back shades into
their bodies. My flesh had been but short while divested of me, when she
made me enter within that wall to draw forth a spirit from the circle of
Judas. That is the lowest place, and the darkest, and farthest from the
heaven that encircles all. Well do I know the way, so reassure yourself.")

This bizarre story, with its recollection of yet another moment in Vir-
gil's early time in the afterlife, is meant to reassure Dante that his guide
knows how to descend even to hell's lowest depths. What is revealed, how-
ever, is anything but reassuring: the tidings that when Virgil was newly
among the dead, he was impressed into service by "cruel Erichtho," a de-
monic figure from the grotesque afterlife of Lucan's *Pharsalia* (6.507–830).
Erichtho, Lucan tells the reader, revived the soul of a Roman soldier recently
killed in battle in order to reveal "truth from the dead" ("certus discedat, ab
umbris / Quisquis vera petit duraeque oracula mortis / Fortis adit," 6.771–
73). The anecdote presents Virgil as someone who followed the command
of a witch and "harrowed" a soul placed by divine justice in the circle of
Judas. Virgil recalls the episode with a sense of pride, as if it demonstrated
his unique qualifications for the task Beatrice later called him to assume.
What it reveals, however, is the inversion of her request to give Dante safe
passage.[36] Whereas Beatrice, like Christ, visited hell to rescue a righteous
soul, Virgil did the exact opposite. He once acted at the behest of evil to
"redeem" a soul judged by God to deserve the circle of Giudecca.

These evocations of the harrowing, whether as the enduring memory of a
past event or as a narrative reworking of it, dramatize the pagan poet's

status as an informed outsider. We see his unwitting alienation from the one and only moment in salvation history he was able to witness, as well as from the Christian universe in which that moment has meaning.[37] But Virgil's condition is also brought home to us whenever Dante places him in the context of Scripture—whenever Virgil inadvertently speaks the language of the Bible (as he does in *Inferno* 8.43–45), or confronts a figure from biblical history, or is brought by means of poetic allusion into the gospel's world.[38] In every case, his partial or failed comprehension of the Christian realm foregrounds the peculiarly "Virgilian" quality of his own fate within the *Commedia*. For in Dante's poem he occasionally exemplifies that very quality of human ignorance that overshadows the *Aeneid* itself— the lack of understanding in the face of destiny that marks Dido, Aeneas, Palinurus, and Turnus as *nescius*. Every juxtaposition of Virgil and Christianity seems to exploit the tragedy of this "not knowing." The contact with grace sets him apart and puts him at a loss.

Such exposure is especially striking in *Inferno* 23, where Dante stages an encounter between the pagan poet and the Gospels that openly dramatizes his status as *nescius*. The encounter takes place in the circle of the hypocrites, in the context of that single sin against which Christ himself was most outspoken. Here is a world of "whitened sepulchres," of religious leaders who use the demeanor of piety as a cover-up. Thus, the damned are dressed as parodies of Cluny's monks, "Di fuor dorate son, sì ch'elli abbaglia; / ma dentro tutte piombo, e gravi tanto" ("so gilded outside that they dazzle, but within, all of lead," vv. 64–65). Those named in the canto are either contemporary Italian friars or the Pharisees and high priests that took counsel against Jesus and brought about his death. No one in the sixth *bolgia* can forget the catastrophe of that first Holy Week, because the bridge that once fully spanned its valley is now only a "ruina" (v. 137), yet another casualty of Christ's descent to hell and the earthquake that immediately preceded it. The reminders of the Passion are everywhere, as Dante himself discovers in the midst of an angry exchange:

> Io cominciai: "O frati, i vostri mali . . .";
>   ma più non dissi, ch'a l'occhio mi corse
>   un, crucifisso in terra con tre pali.
> Quando mi vide, tutto si distorse,
>   soffiando ne la barba con sospiri;
>   e 'l frate Catalan, ch'a ciò s'accorse,

mi disse: "Quel confitto che tu miri,
  consigliò i Farisei che convenia
  porre un uom per lo popolo a' martìri.
Attraversato è, nudo, ne la via,
  come tu vedi, ed è mestier ch'el senta
  qualunque passa, come pesa, pria.
E a tal modo il socero si stenta
  in questa fossa, e li altri dal concilio
  che fu per li Giudei mala sementa."
Allor vid'io maravigliar Virgilio
  sovra colui ch'era disteso in croce
  tanto vilmente ne l'etterno essilio.
      (*Inf.* 23.109–26)

(I began, "O Friars, your evil . . ."—but I said no more, for there caught
my eye one crucified on the ground with three stakes. When he saw me
he writhed all over, blowing in his beard with sighs; and Fra Catalano,
observing this, said to me, "That transfixed one you are gazing at
counseled the Pharisees that it was expedient to put one man to torture
for the people. He is stretched out naked across the way, as you see, and
needs must feel the weight of each that passes; and in like fashion is his
father-in-law racked in this ditch, and the others of that council which
was a seed of evil for the Jews." Then I saw Virgil wonder over him who
was thus outstretched, as on a cross, so vilely in the eternal exile.)

While most of the souls in the circle of the hypocrites walk in solemn
pain under the enormous weight of their leaden cloaks, those singled out
for greater torment are crucified naked on the ground. Quite literally in
harm's way, they are repeatedly crushed by the footsteps of those who
slowly walk over them. The one who particularly catches Dante's attention
is Caiaphas, high priest at the time of Christ's arrest, and here identified by
an allusion to the priest's own words, as recorded in John 11:50. The one
"crucified on the ground with three stakes," Dante is told, "counseled the
Pharisees that it was expedient to put one man to torture for the people."

Caiaphas formulates this strategy in John 11:45–53, after Christ raises
Lazarus from the dead. Frightened that news of the miracle would inspire
the multitude to become Christ's followers, and thereby provoke the Ro-
man authorities to "come, and take away our place and nation" (v. 48),
Caiaphas proposes to eliminate the miracle-worker under the cover of con-

cern for the greater good. His succinct solution to the problem of Jesus immediately becomes the officials' master plan: "it is expedient for you that one man should die for the people, and the whole nation perish not" ("expedit vobis ut unus moriatur homo pro populo, et non tota gens pereat," v. 50, cf. John 18:14). In hell these very words continue to haunt him, serving at once as his epitaph and as God's eternal judgment against him.

But as the Gospel also makes clear, Caiaphas spoke infinitely more than what he intended. He unwittingly delivered a true prophecy that in many ways transcended the theological insight of Christ's own disciples. As the Evangelist notes, Caiaphas's scheme—"that Jesus should die for the nation"—was to have universal, not to mention eternal, consequences. "And not only for the nation, but also to gather together in one the children of God, that were dispersed" (John 11:51–52). Therefore, Caiaphas unintentionally proclaimed the faith he wanted to destroy. Consequently, in Christian tradition he becomes an example of the "imperfect prophet" who does not comprehend the real import of what he prophesies. Aquinas, for example, contrasts the Psalmist David, who understood the meaning of the words he uttered *in spiritu*, with someone endowed only with a "prophetic instinct": "sometimes the person whose mind is moved to utter certain words knows not what the Holy Ghost means by them." Such, says Aquinas, "was the case with Caiaphas" (*ST* II-II, 173, 4 resp.).

In the course of this encounter, Dante is not the only one captivated by the sight of Caiaphas crucified. There is also the astonished Virgil, who for the one and only time in hell stands spellbound by what he sees. Rather than bring us inside the ancient poet's thoughts, however, Dante chooses instead simply to show him lost in wonder. In so doing he allows Virgil's "marvel" to open up a gap, a space for interpretation:

> Allor vid'io maravigliar Virgilio
>   sovra colui ch'era disteso in croce
>   tanto vilmente ne l'etterno essilio.
>   (*Inf.* 23.124–26)

(Then I saw Virgil wonder over him who was thus outstretched, as on a cross, so vilely in the eternal exile.)

Most critics have assumed that Virgil's amazement here arises from the sheer novelty of what he sees. For this is a torment and a group of sinners who were not yet in place when he made his earlier journey to lower hell—a new cast of characters, whose historical moment took place in Jerusalem not so very long after Virgil's death. Because that death was in 19 B.C.E., Caiaphas and his father-in-law Annas, as well as the rest of "that council, which was a seed of evil for the Jews," were all his near contemporaries, men who lived out their lives in another part of Virgil's own Roman Empire, "sotto 'l buon Augusto" ("under the good Augustus," *Inf.* 1.71). The difference between their moment and his, however, is that they were able to stand face-to-face with the Word made flesh, whereas he was not. No matter how disastrously they rejected the grace at their disposal, Providence nonetheless gave them the opportunity to make a choice about Christ. But not Virgil. As a late-fourteenth-century commentator recognized, the ancient poet's wonder before Caiaphas masks a renewed sense of sorrow for himself: "Virgil could be amazed at the error of one who, having Christ stand before him, did not recognize him as lord of heaven and earth, while at the same time regretting yet again that he had not lived in that time when he might have been able to know him."[39]

Moreover, in addition to his shock at what he sees before him, Virgil also has cause to wonder over what he hears—an uncanny echo of his own poetry in the quoted words of Caiaphas, "it was expedient to put one man to torture for the people" ("che convenia/porre un uom per lo popolo a' martìri," vv. 116–17).[40] The Virgilian text in question appears toward the end of *Aeneid* 5, where Aeneas and his men sail on to Italy and the new Roman destiny they are meant to establish. Worried at their prospects of making shore, Venus intercedes with Neptune. To comfort her, the god of the sea promises that he will allow the Trojans safe passage provided that something is given in exchange. One of the Trojans must be offered up as a sacrifice: "unum pro multis dabitur caput" ("one life shall be given for many," *Aen.* 5.815). None of the Trojans knows the bargain that Neptune has struck—not Palinurus, the one who is singled out for death, nor Aeneas, who mistakenly assumes that when his pilot disappears "amid the waves of night," it is because Palinurus was too trustful of the sea and wind ("o nimium caelo et pelago confise sereno," v. 870). Both are *nescius*, ignorant of the forces that control their lives. The god claims his prey, and fate works out its ineluctable purpose.

Despite vast differences of intention and moral character, Virgil and

Caiaphas are linked by the consonance of "expedit vobis ut unus moriatur homo pro populo" (John 11:50) and "unum pro multis dabitur caput" (*Aen.* 5.815). Dante also draws them together through the rhyme words that frame Virgil's astonishment over the crucified high priest: "concilio" (v. 122), "Virgilio" (v. 124), "essilio" (v. 126):

> "E a tal modo il socero si stenta
>   in questa fossa, e li altri dal *concilio*
>   che fu per li Giudei mala sementa."
> Allor vid'io maravigliar *Virgilio*
>   sovra colui ch'era disteso in croce
>   tanto vilmente ne l'etterno *essilio*.
>   (*Inf.* 23.121–26, emphasis added)

("and in like fashion is his father-in-law racked in this ditch, and the others of that *council* which was a seed of evil for the Jews." Then I saw *Virgil* wonder over him who was thus outstretched, as on a cross, so vilely in the eternal *exile*.)

To the careful reader who first notes the rhyme's pattern and then connects it to the larger story, there is a message only slightly concealed within these lines. The "concilio" (v. 122) of Hebrew priests and Pharisees shares with the pagan "Virgilio" (v. 124) the fate of an eternal "essilio" (v. 126). One "imperfect prophet" faces another, as if to underscore a point that the *Commedia* insists on repeatedly. It is not enough to prophesy in ignorance about the *unum pro multis*, no matter how truthful these words turn out to be. To be "knowing" in this regard is essential: one must know that the man sacrificed for others is also the lord of heaven and earth.

Dante makes this same point an issue later on, in the second canticle. In *Purgatorio* 20–22, he places Virgil within a dense network of biblical allusion that at least metaphorically brings him into contact with the life of Christ.[41] For instance, in *Purgatorio* 20, as Statius's completed purgation is marked by the singing of the *Gloria in excelsis Deo*, Virgil and Dante appear together "come i pastor che prima udir quel canto" ("like the shepherds who first heard that song," 20.140). Later, they are compared ("as Luke writes for us") to the two men whom Christ joins on the road to Emmaus: "sì come ne scrive Luca/che Cristo apparve a' due ch'erano in via,/già surto fuor de la sepulcral buca" ("as Luke writes for us that Christ, new-risen from the sepulchral cave, appeared to the two who were on the way," 21.7–9). Finally, as in Jerusalem the resurrected Christ said "Pax vobiscum" to his startled disciples (Luke 24:36), so here Statius addresses both Virgil and Dante with the vernacular equivalent of that biblical greeting: "O frati miei, Dio vi dea pace" ("O my brothers, may God give you peace," v. 13). To these formal words of welcome, Virgil makes what seems like an automatic (and appropriate) response:

> Noi ci volgemmo sùbiti, e *Virgilio*
> rendéli 'l cenno ch'a ciò si conface.
> Poi cominciò: "Nel beato *concilio*
> ti ponga in pace la verace corte
> che me rilega ne l'etterno *essilio*."
> (*Purg.* 21.14–18, emphasis added)

(We turned quickly and *Virgil* answered him with the greeting that is fitting thereto; then he began, "May the true *council* which binds me in eternal *exile* bring you in peace to the assembly of the blest.") (trans. modified)

However, no sooner does Virgil act as if fluent in the vocabulary of Christian ritual, "with the greeting that is fitting thereto," than he identifies himself as someone who ultimately does *not* speak the language of faith at all. The trio of rhyme words that framed his earlier wonder over the distended form of Caiaphas in *Inferno* 23 appear again, with the same message of exclusion and loss. "Virgilio" (v. 14) stands outside the possibility of heaven's blessed "concilio" (v. 16), separated from its hope by hell's eternal "essilio" (v. 18).

The reader has known that Virgil is barred from heaven since his self-disclosure in the opening canto of the poem (*Inf.* 1.124–26). It is far more poignant, however, to be reminded of his status as eternal outsider immediately after seeing him play so many parts in a drama of redemption that is finally not his own. The preceding sequence of biblical allusions, therefore, becomes painfully ironic. For Virgil is not, after all, *in via*, like Statius and Dante, or like the two individuals Christ spoke to on the road to Emmaus. Rather, he participates in salvation history for only the brief occasion of this journey, and even then, as he acknowledges to Statius, strictly on Beatrice's command:

Ond' io fui tratto fuor de l'ampia gola
    d'inferno per mostrarli, e mosterrolli
    oltre, quanto 'l potrà menar mia scola.
                    (*Purg.* 21.31–33)

(Wherefore I was brought forth from Hell's wide jaws to guide him, and I
will guide him onward as far as my school can lead him.)

The limitations of Virgil's "school" are the limits of Limbo, whose
fragile hemisphere of light is overwhelmed by the infernal darkness that
surrounds it on all sides. Nonetheless, the whole thrust of the encounter
with Statius is that Virgil's poetry, and perhaps even the flawed understand-
ing of his "school," can serve as genuine illumination for the reader who,
like Statius, is in a state of grace. Thus, when Virgil asks the Silver Age
Latin poet how he broke with paganism to become a believer, he is told (as
we saw above) that it was the result of reading the Fourth Eclogue. Without
the Eclogue's gloss, Statius says, Christian Scripture was unintelligible, a
sealed casket. But because of it—that is, because of the concordance found
between Virgil's mysterious words and those of the "new preachers"—
Statius discovered a door to understanding:

Tu dunque, che levato hai il coperchio
    che m'ascondeva quanto bene io dico,
    mentre che del salire avem soverchio.
                    (*Purg.* 22.94–96)[42]

(You, therefore, did lift for me the covering that was hiding from me the
great good that I tell of.)

Virgil rolled away the stone that blocked Statius in his ability to believe,
tore the "lid" off the gospel, and transformed an otherwise incomprehensi-
ble text into a "great good."

    This enlightenment could not, however, be the case for Virgil himself,
for he could only read the pagan words he actually wrote and not the
Christian meaning "uncovered" later. For this reason, and despite the gen-
erations of readers who have wanted to argue his fate otherwise, Dante
accords Virgil an altogether "Virgilian" destiny within the *Commedia*.[43] He
has the ancient poet return to the world of his own imagination, dispatch-
ing him in *Purgatorio* 30 to Limbo's Elysian Fields.

Virgil's return to the underworld, his descent back into a hell from which there is presumably no future exit, takes place at the very moment of Beatrice's arrival on the scene. In order to give this leave-taking its full due, Dante has the ancient poet disappear from the narrative precisely as a number of Virgilian texts are conjured up only to evaporate before our eyes.[44] The quotation of one Latin line from the *Aeneid* gives way to the translation of another line into the vernacular, before an echo of the Fourth Georgic completes the triad by reducing Virgil's presence in the text to a mere trace of the "lacrimae rerum" (*Aen.* 1.462)—the "tears of things" he wrote about with such eloquence. Thus, "Virgilio . . . Virgilio . . . Virgilio" (*Purg.* 30.49–51) dissolves into "pianger . . . piangere . . . pianger" (30.56–57). At the end of this sequence of Virgilian reminiscence, the ancient poet slips away between Dante's vernacular lines.

Dante begins this gradual fade-out by bringing into close proximity, even into rhyme, two completely different worlds of discourse: the language of the church and that of the *Aeneid*.

> Quali i beati al novissimo bando
> surgeran presti ognun di sua caverna,
> la revestita voce alleluiando,
> cotali in su la divina basterna
> si levar cento, *ad vocem tanti senis,*
> ministri e messaggier di vita etterna.
> Tutti dicean: "*Benedictus qui venis!*"
> e fior gittando e di sopra e dintorno,
> "*Manibus, oh, date lilïa plenis!*"
>
> (*Purg.* 30.13–21)

(As the blessed at the last Trump will rise ready each from his tomb, so upon the divine chariot, singing Hallelujah with reclad voice, *ad vocem tanti senis,* rose up a hundred ministers and messengers of life eternal, who all cried, "*Benedictus qui venis!*" and, scattering flowers up and around, "*Manibus, oh, date lilïa plenis!*")

Through the transforming power of simile, the biblical Pageant arrayed on the other shore of Lethe dissolves into a Last Judgment scene, with recollection of the dead rising up at the end of time as foretold by St. Paul in 1 Thessalonians 4:15: "For the Lord himself shall come down from heaven with commandment, and with the voice of an archangel, and with the trumpet of God: and the dead who are in Christ shall rise first." Dante hears two anthems rising up from this chorus of "alleluiando," both in Latin, and so easily juxtaposed that at first they might seem to say the very same thing. But rather than suggesting, as in *Purgatorio* 22, the harmony of Virgil and the Scripture "sounding" in one another, this particular rhyme is all about dissonance. The two Latin texts collide rather than rhyme.

The first—"Benedictus qui venis!"—draws upon both the Old Testament and the New, as well as upon the liturgy of the Mass. The precise scriptural quote, in the third-person singular, is "Benedictus qui venit," which comes originally from Psalm 117 (118):26, interpreted throughout the New Testament as a prophecy of Christ.[45] The phrase then appears in the Passion narratives of all four Gospels, as the crowds going up to Jerusalem hail Jesus as the "blessed one" David had foretold: "Hosanna. Blessed is he who cometh in the name of the Lord." Given the subsequent events of the Passion, this messianic salutation is charged with irony: the same crowd that blessed Jesus one minute called for his crucifixion the next. But in the larger gospel story, irony is ultimately overcome: the one who died on the cross was indeed blessed, his defeat transformed into victory by the power of his resurrection. And blessed too, the *Commedia* seems to say, are the other souls who come in the "name of the Lord," including Beatrice, the "you" who is specifically addressed here, and all those others who will also be "blessed" ("beati") when the last trumpet bids them "rise ready each from his tomb."

"Benedictus qui venis!" therefore, contains within its small compass the hope of the entire Christian Scripture, from the Psalmist David, to the evangelists, to St. Paul. But then Dante lifts out of *Aeneid* 6.883 the exclamation "Manibus, oh, date lilia plenis!" This exclamation—a direct quote save for that vernacular "oh"—appears toward the end of a long address spoken to Aeneas by his father. For almost 200 lines, Anchises has sung the praises of the souls who will go on to make Roman history, starting with Aeneas's as-yet-unborn son Silvius and stretching on to the emperor Augustus. This exhilarating roll call comes to an abrupt halt with the figure of the young Marcellus, adopted son and chosen heir of Augustus, who represents the future of the empire Anchises has just extolled. Aeneas wonders why the young man's eyes are downcast, his head garlanded with the premonitory shadow of death ("sed nox atra caput tristi circumvolant umbra," *Aen.* 6.866). Anchises then explains that, for all his promise, Marcellus is bound by the same "harsh bonds of fate" ("fata aspera rumpas," v. 882) that govern all human existence. In light of such blind and inexorable forces, therefore, all that he can do is scatter flowers of valediction, even if the gesture (by Anchises' own account) is ultimately futile:

> manibus date lilia plenis,
> purpureos spargam flores animamque nepotis
> his saltem accumulem donis et fungar inani
> munere.
>
> (*Aen.* 6.883–86)

(Give me lilies with full hand; let me scatter purple flowers; let me heap o'er my offspring's shade at least these gifts and fulfill an unavailing service.)

By citing "Manibus date lilia plenis" in the context of *Purgatorio* 30, the poet at once recalls the revered master's text and forces it to mean something else. As the company that surrounds Beatrice is "scattering flowers up and around" ("e fior gittando e di sopra e dintorno," v. 20), Anchises' lament for Marcellus is spoken in the context of an altogether different spiritual world. Rather than bewailing one whom "fate" demanded prematurely, the biblical "messengers of life eternal" now celebrate a Beatrice who also died while still in her youth, but who now comes onto the stage of the *Commedia* as "living proof" of the Resurrection's power. Instead of Anchises' "inani/munere," Dante gives us in the advent of Beatrice a sign of his faith in Christ's triumph.[46]

In order for Virgil's "Manibus date lilia plenis" to function meaningfully in Dante's new setting, therefore, it must be read over against what the author of the *Aeneid* himself wrote. And so, at the very moment when Virgil as a character disappears from the *Commedia*, Dante changes the black night and mournful shade of Marcellus into Beatrice's sunrise (30.22–27); turns the purple lilies called for by Anchises into flowers tossed by jubilant angelic hands; transforms an "unavailing service" performed in despair into an ecstatic affirmation that, as the Song of Songs says, love is as strong as death (8:6).

Readers will inevitably bring a complicated mixture of feelings to this subversion of the *Aeneid*'s "alta . . . tragedìa" (*Inf.* 20.113). Among them may be discomfort in the presence of such open Christian triumphalism, as well as uneasiness in the face of Dante's willful domination over the one poet he truly revered and could not have done without. Yet, for the *Commedia* to achieve its goals, "Benedictus qui venis!" must overwhelm "Manibus, oh, date lilia plenis!" and the *Aeneid* be sacrificed as an independent text. The temple of Apollo, or of "the unknown god" (Acts 17:23), is rebuilt as the "miro e angelico templo" ("wondrous and angelic temple," *Par.* 28.53) according to Dante's own design.

One might argue, of course, that this "takeover" is precisely what exegetes did with the Old Testament when they removed its "veil" (as Paul says in 2 Cor. 3) and insisted that it could only be read "aright" as an allegory of Christ. Indeed, as we have seen, Dante celebrates precisely this kind of "misreading" of Virgil in the Statius episode, where a Christological interpretation of the Fourth Eclogue substitutes for whatever it was that Virgil himself had in mind when he wrote "iam redit et Virgo, redeunt Saturnia regna." In *Purgatorio* 30, however, Dante plays a still more difficult hand. He demands nothing less than a full Christian re-vision of Virgil's poem, no sounding together but a pulling apart. No matter how heartfelt may have been his debt to the one he named "master" and "author" (*Inf.* 1.85), he insists on pouring his own new wine into old Virgilian skins, no doubt fully aware of what will be split open, even destroyed, in the process.

Or, to exchange one scriptural metaphor for another, we can say that the poet of the *Commedia* insists on harrowing the *Aeneid,* drawing it up into the biblical realm of his own imagination, "liberating" Virgil's poem from the confines of death, and breeding resurrection lilies out of funeral flowers. But even as he does so, Dante does not scruple to send its beloved author *sub umbras.* Whereas he himself descends triumphantly *ad inferos* and ascends to the stars, Virgil is reclaimed once again by the undertow of hell.

CHAPTER 6

Dido, Beatrice, and the Signs of Ancient Love

Even in a poem replete with significant encounters, Dante's meeting with Beatrice in *Purgatorio* 30 stands out as the most anticipated and the most spectacular. With her coming prepared for by a pageant of divine revelation that unfolds (biblical book by book) throughout canto 29, Beatrice appears within a "nuvola di fiori" ("cloud of flowers," 30.28) that is in reality a cloud of allusion: an intertextual mass that joins Latin to Italian, God's speech to poetic utterance, and epic to lyric. The acclamation of her arrival in the double cry of "Benedictus qui venis!" (30.19) and "Manibus, oh, date lilïa plenis!" (30.21)—a Christological salutation and a Virgilian lament—alerts us to the kind of juxtaposition carried on throughout the canto, as two worlds of discourse meet at an impasse to reveal the great gulf fixed between them. Among the many intertextual marvels of the passage, surely none is more extraordinary than the way Beatrice comes into focus precisely as Virgil departs; that is, the way her literal presence is conjured up by means of his literary erasure. As noted above in Chapter 5, "Descendit ad inferos," this passage from Virgilian quotation to translation to allusion, reflecting on a linguistic level the pagan poet's "passing away" from the narrative, is a tour de force even for Dante. My interest here is the rewrite at the center of the sequence: the translation of Dido's "adgnosco veteris vestigia flammae" ("I recognize the traces of the olden flame," *Aen.* 4.23) into the pilgrim's "conosco i segni de l'antica fiamma" ("I know the tokens of the ancient flame," *Purg.* 30.48). At the heart of his own epic venture, Dante depicts the romance Virgil could not allow, in a vernacular of redeemed *eros* utterly foreign to the Latin master and author:

Così dentro una nuvola di fiori
    che da le mani angeliche saliva
    e ricadeva in giù dentro e di fori,
sovra candido vel cinta d'uliva
    donna m'apparve, sotto verde manto
    vestita di color di fiamma viva.
E lo spirito mio, che già cotanto
    tempo era stato ch'a la sua presenza
    non era di stupor, tremando, affranto,
sanza de li occhi aver più conoscenza,
    per occulta virtù che da lei mosse,
    d'antico amor sentì la gran potenza.
Tosto che ne la vista mi percosse
    l'alta virtù che già m'avea trafitto
    prima ch'io fuor di püerizia fosse,
volsimi a la sinistra col respitto
    col quale il fantolin corre a la mamma
    quando ha paura o quando elli è afflitto,
per dicere a Virgilio: "Men che dramma
    di sangue m'è rimaso che non tremi:
    conosco i segni de l'antica fiamma."
                    (*Purg.* 30.28–48)

(So within a cloud of flowers, which rose from the angelic hands and fell
down again within and without, olive-crowned over a white veil a lady
appeared to me, clad, under a green mantle, with hue of living flame; and
my spirit, which now for so long a time trembling with awe in her
presence had not been overcome, without having more knowledge by the
eyes, through occult virtue that proceeded from her, felt old love's great
power. As soon as on my sight the lofty virtue smote that had already
pierced me before I was out of my boyhood, I turned to the left with the
confidence of a little child that runs to his mother when he is frightened
or in distress, to say to Virgil, "Not a drop of blood is left in me that does
not tremble: I know the tokens of the ancient flame.")

For the reader who comes to Dante, as the author seems to have
intended, with the whole of his poetic opera in mind, this purgatorial
entrance unmistakably recalls an earlier debut. In *Vita nuova* 2, when
Dante sees Beatrice for the first time, she also appears dressed in red and

cinctured becomingly ("Apparve vestita di nobilissimo colore, umile e onesto, sanguigno, cinta e ornata a la guisa che a la sua giovanissima etade si convenìa"). Her initial appearance also had a powerful effect on the viewer's spirit—three kinds of "spirito" are mentioned in rapid succession—so powerful, in fact, that he trembled "si fortemente" with an awareness of being in the presence of a power mightier than himself ("lo spirito de la vita . . . cominciò a tremare si fortemente . . . e tremando disse queste parole: 'Ecce deus fortior me, qui veniens dominabitur michi"). Nine years later, as we are told in the following chapter, a lady appeared to him in a dream, first emerging within a cloud of fire ("una nebula di colore di fuoco"), and then handling something mysterious that burns in her hands ("una cosa la quale ardesse tutta"). The fire turns out to be the dreamer's own heart.

Purgatorio 30 reprises this earlier material with a forthright repetition of detail and theme. And so Dante again finds himself confronted by a lady "vestita di color di fiamma viva" (v. 33), his spirit trembling in the presence of an old love, as he is shaken ("tremando," v. 36), overcome ("affranto," v. 36), stricken ("trafitto," v. 41), and pierced ("mi percosse," v. 40). The explicit mention of his own youth ("püerizia," v. 42) enforces what is, in fact, an unavoidable recollection of the opening of the *Vita nuova*. But more texts are recalled here than that first *libello*. The admission of verse 39, "d'antico amor sentì la gran potenza," virtually reproduces the initial line of the *canzone*, "Io sento sì d'Amor la gran possanza," while the portrait of a lover trembling in the presence of his beloved suggests the metaliterary "tutto tremante" of Lancelot, Paolo, and Dante Pilgrim in *Inferno* 5.136. The appearance of Beatrice, in other words, is the rehearsal of a career in poetry that stretches from the visions of boyhood ("püerizia") up to the poem's present; it is the reworking of a lifetime.

But if in these lines the poet offers us a retrospective, what claims our attention is the literal turnaround of the pilgrim. Wanting to share this recognition scene with Virgil, Dante says, "volsimi a la sinistra col respitto/col quale il fantolin corre a la mamma" ("I turned to the left with the confidence of a little child that runs to his mother," 30.43–44). Here for the second time in the *Purgatorio*, Dante has to turn if he wishes to see Virgil—the placement of the verb at the head of the line underscores the action. If Dante must turn, it is because there has been a reversal of the positions that the two figures have held relative to each other from the very outset of the poem. In the beginning, Dante followed Virgil, "per lo cammino alto e silvestro" ("along the deep and savage way," *Inf.* 2.142), and the pilgrim remained in that secondary position up through the fiery entrance into Eden.[1] Once in the Garden, however, the pilgrim steps in front of, and beyond, Virgil. We first become aware of this when Dante, after hearing Matelda's gracious "corollario" (*Purg.* 28.136) to the poets of pagan antiquity, turns around to catch the smiles of Statius and Virgil, both described specifically as standing *behind* him ("lo mi rivolsi 'n dietro allora tutto / a' miei poeti" ["I turned then right round to my poets"], vv. 145–46). Suddenly the last becomes first and the first last.

In *Purgatorio* 30, Dante's turn to the left—the direction of Virgil's lead throughout hell, rather than that of the rightward motion of purgatory[2]—seems at first as if it will introduce a similar exchange of smiles. Overwhelmed by the reappearance of his "antico amor," the pilgrim is reduced to the state of a "fantolin," a child who cannot speak but who nonetheless is driven to communicate his mixture of fear and excitement to the "mamma" who has shared everything along the way. Lacking speech of his own, therefore, he falls back on the parent text, the *Aeneid,* offering a vernacular version of his master's lines, "conosco i segni de l'antica fiamma" (*Purg.* 30.48). With this translation of Virgil's "adgnosco veteris vestigia flammae" (*Aen.* 4.23) offered at the moment of his own linguistic inadequacy, Dante bears witness to the truth of what he announced long ago: his indebtedness to "quella fonte/che spandi di parlar sì largo fiume" ("that fount which pours forth so broad a stream of speech," *Inf.* 1.79–80).

Commentators from the fourteenth century up to our own day have noted this reference to the *Aeneid* and taken it for what, on the surface of things, it obviously is: an act of homage to Virgil's "autorità" within the poem and a sign of Dante's confidence in his master. Certainly the context of what immediately follows verse 48, which Hermann Gmelin characterizes as a "jewel of Virgilian reminiscence,"[3] is valedictory, with pilgrim and reader alike acknowledging the loss of one who has been our guide from the start. Likewise, the rhyme words of verses 44, 46, 48—*mamma-dramma-fiamma*—recall the loving accolade of Statius in *Purgatorio* 21, where Dante allows another poet figure to give his own estimate of Virgil as a "mamma" worthy of great respect:

Al mio ardor fuor seme le faville,
   che mi scaldar, de la divina fiamma
   onde sono allumati più di mille;
de l'Eneïda dico, la qual mamma
   fummi, e fummi nutrice, poetando:
   sanz' essa non fermai peso di dramma.
                   (*Purg.* 21.94–99)

(The sparks which warmed me from the divine flame whereby more than a thousand have been kindled were the seeds of my poetic fire: I mean the *Aeneid*, which in poetry was both mother and nurse to me—without it I had achieved little of worth.)

Given the filial piety of the pilgrim's turn to his *mamma nutrice*, taken together with all the love for Virgil invoked from earlier moments in the poem, it does not seem too far-fetched to suggest that in *Purgatorio* 30 Dante confesses more than one "antico amor": love not only for the "alta virtù" of the lady standing veiled before him but also for the virtuosity of the master poet standing behind. Except, of course, that Virgil is no longer there to be turned to, being already vanished *sub umbras* in the manner of his Eurydice, his Turnus, and his Dido. In Virgil's absence we are left with only a textual trace, a translation of *Aeneid* 4.23 that serves to link Dante's love for Beatrice to Virgil's one full-blown romance. As soon as we recognize the allusion to Dido and Aeneas, however, our hermeneutic trouble begins. For what their story interjects into *Purgatorio* 30 is a reality antithetical to all that is gradually to be unveiled there: a tragic separation introduced into an essentially comic reunion.

When Dido tells her sister Anna that for the first time since the death of her husband, Sychaeus, she feels the old embers of erotic desire vital within her—"adgnosco veteris vestigia flammae"—she innocently uses an incendiary metaphor that will shortly come to describe her fate all too accurately.[4] By the end of *Aeneid* 1 the stratagems of Eros "furentem / incendat reginam atque ossibus implicet ignem" ("kindle the queen to madness and send flame into her very marrow," vv. 659–60). But it is over the course of Book 4 that we note how quickly the unseen fire destroys her, overriding her vow of chastity to the memory of her dead husband, melting her heart and her sense of restraint, eventually driving her in a frenzy around a city she can no longer rule: "ardet amans Dido traxitque per ossa furorem" ("Dido is on fire with love, and has drawn madness through her veins," 4.101). Pathetically disfigured by a passion she cannot control, she becomes yet another manifestation of the *furor* that Aeneas is called to stand steadfastly against. However victimized Dido may be both by the machinations of Venus and by the inflexible will of fate, she remains an obstruction in the path along which destiny is leading Aeneas—a human possibility he cannot afford to indulge. Along with so much else in the poem, she too must be sacrificed.

And so she is. By the end of *Aeneid* 4 the vestiges of love's ancient flame are made literal in the funeral pyre on which she is consumed, her dying words a curse of fire on Aeneas's head: "hauriat hunc oculis ignem crudelis ab alto/Dardanus et secum nostrae ferat omina mortis" ("Let the cruel Dardan's eyes drink in this fire from the deep, and carry with him the omen of my death!" 4.661–62). At the beginning of Book 5, as Aeneas stares ignorantly at the flames leaping above Carthage, the poet speaks darkly about "duri magno sed amore dolores/polluto notumque" ("cruel pangs when a great love is polluted," 5.5–6). In doing so he credits Dido with the capacity for great love, but what he emphasizes is the pollution, the "duri . . . dolores" that engulf her love and that endanger not only the individuals involved but the whole enterprise of civilization itself. Virgil may allow his *pius Aeneas* to look back at her pyre as his ships sail on to Italy—he may even allow Dido to cut him dead in the Mourning Fields of *Aeneid* 6.440–76—but for his hero the vestiges of old love are never to be rekindled. Certainly the future marriage with Lavinia that is decreed by fate has nothing whatever to do with passion; indeed, Virgil never even has the couple meet. However crucial the union may be to the future of Rome, Aeneas's joining himself to a woman of Latium is presented as nothing more fiery than the grafting of Troy onto native Italian stock. It is a procedure more georgic than erotic. What matters in the end is that the inevitable fury of *eros* be sublimated into *civitas*, and that the virtuous individual comply with the rigors of an impersonal destiny.

There is every reason to believe that Dante knew the whole of his *Aeneid*, even as he has Virgil himself say in *Inferno* 20.114. But it also true that he received the story of Dido filtered through a history of other readings and according to a process of interpretation that Barbara Bono has termed a "literary transvaluation."[5] There can be no doubt, for instance, that he knew the passage in the opening book of the *Confessions* where

Augustine laments the vanity of his youthful tears over the death of Dido "quia se occidit ab amore" ("because she killed herself for love"), "extinctam ferroque extrema secutam" ("killed herself by falling upon the sword," 1.13). The first of these phrases appears in translation in *Inferno* 5, where Dido is described by periphrasis as "colei che s'ancise amorosa, / e ruppe fede al cener di Sicheo" ("she who slew herself for love and broke faith to the ashes of Sichaeus," vv. 61–62). The second reference, to her sword, is recalled in one of the *Rime petrose*, "Così nel mio parlar voglio esser aspro" ("I Want to Be as Grating in My Words"), where the poet speaks of Love standing above him "con quella spada ond' elli ancise Dido" ("with that same sword he used to murder Dido," v. 36)—an identification with Dido's fate that presages the poet's assuming of her thirst for revenge at the end of the poem.

Dido's appearance in the infernal circle of the lustful—named in her honor "la schiera ov' è Dido" (*Inf.* 5.85)—suggests that Dante considered her a figure of *luxuria*, and in terms similar to those of the Virgilian allegorists Fulgentius and Bernardus Silvestris, the latter of whom speaks of her succinctly as "Dido id est libido." In *Convivio* 4.26, Dante describes the great pleasure ("tanto di piacere") she gave Aeneas, but nonetheless celebrates him as an exemplar of restraint who is able by sheer force of will to leave her delights "per seguire onesta e laudabile via e fruttuosa" ("to follow an honorable, praiseworthy, and beneficial course"). For Fulgentius, that "laudabile via" leads straight to Lavinia, whom he glosses as "labora via" ("the road of toil").[6] In a similar vein Dante will refer to Aeneas's Italian bride as standing at the origin of Rome's massive enterprise, when in *Paradiso* 6 he has Justinian recall the inaugural flight of the imperial eagle "dietro a l'antico che Lavinia tolse" ("behind the ancient who took Lavinia to wife," v. 3). By contrast, a few cantos further on, and in the sphere of Venus, Dido will twice be mentioned in her role as "other woman" (8.9 and 9.97–98), in both cases placed within the context of lust and the breaking of marriage vows: "noiando e a Sicheo e a Creusa" ("wronging both Sichaeus and Creusa," 9.98).[7]

We are meant to look back on all this Dido lore when Dante, trembling in the presence of Beatrice, turns to Virgil with a line his "dolcissimo patre" would be expected to recognize (and presumably to enjoy), despite its translation into Dante's illustrious vernacular: "conosco i segni de l'antica fiamma" (v. 48). Yet as the pilgrim soon discovers to his great sorrow, in all this looking backward there is in fact no one to look back to. Virgil is gone, and weeping for him is as pointless as the young Augustine's shedding of tears for Dido or Orpheus's crying three times for a Eurydice he will never see again. Thus, what first presents itself as a touching in-joke between poets, with Dante citing Virgil in order to describe the significance of his own experience, upon reflection becomes a sign of how little Virgil's poem can serve to guide Dante at this point in the journey—except, that is, by way of contrast. Looking back to the *Aeneid*, to Virgil, and to Dido, the pilgrim in fact sees nothing. Instead he is confronted by the radical translation of Virgilian "antico amor" who is now standing before him, who in her glorified body offers the antithesis of everything Virgil represented as the destiny of *eros*. At this moment in the poem Beatrice is none other than the "transvaluation" of Dido: a woman who, rather than obstructing her Aeneas from his heaven-destined course, enables him precisely to find his home—a city she will soon reveal as none other than "quella Roma onde Cristo è romano" ("that Rome whereof Christ is Roman," *Purg.* 32.102).

Nor is this the only revision of the Virgilian source. Once again, to recall *Aeneid* 4, Dido confesses that another man has rekindled the old flame of love, consecrated to the memory of her dead husband. Having realized the temptation to turn to him, she vows immediately (and vainly) to withstand it:

sed mihi vel tellus optem prius ima dehiscat
vel pater omnipotens adigat me fulmine ad umbras,
pallentis umbras Erebi noctemque profundam,
ante, Pudor, quam te violo aut tua iura resolvo.
> (*Aen.* 4.24–27)

(But rather, I would pray, may earth yawn for me to its depths, or may the Almighty Father hurl me with his bolt to the shades—the pale shades and abysmal night of Erebus—before, O Shame, I violate thee or break thy laws!)

Ironically, it is precisely isolation and shame that come to characterize the rest of her story, until death indeed releases her to "the pale shades and abysmal night of Erebus." There, in the Mourning Fields, she finds herself among "quos durus amor crudeli tabe peredit" ("those whom stern Love has consumed with cruel wasting," 6.442). When the now-impassioned Aeneas discovers her during his descent to the underworld, she is wandering among the shades of that tragic grove in the company of her first husband, Sychaeus, resolved to turn away from the tears of the man she once considered to be her second mate.

When the pilgrim delivers his own version of "adgnosco veteris vestigia flammae" in *Purgatorio* 30.48, a kinship is implied between himself and Virgil's *infelix Dido*. By this time in the poem we have become used to the gender reversals that so many of Dante's appropriations of the classics entail. But what comes unavoidably as a surprise here is the fact that when Dante-Dido feels the rekindled tokens of old passion, he does so in the presence of his *antico amor*, with the result that the reassignment of "roles" is almost vertiginous. For not only is Dante here playing Dido, and not only is Virgil serving as *soror Anna*, but Beatrice is at once Sychaeus *and* Aeneas, old flame and new. The Virgilian line that announces Dido's self-division, her pull between two loves, here signals nothing less than the pilgrim's return to unity.

This is not, however, to deny the fact of Dante's own resemblance to "Dido id est libido." A decade of unfaithfulness will preoccupy *Purgatorio* 30–31, as the pilgrim is charged specifically with having "ruppe fede al cener di [Beatrice]" ("broke[n] faith to the ashes of [Beatrice]," *Inf.* 5.62; cf. *Purg.* 30.121–32) and allowed the attraction of "pargoletta / o altra novità" ("young damsel or other novelty," *Purg.* 31.59–60) to lead him down diversionary paths. Beatrice will bring all the errors of the past to mind (something the poet Virgil never gives the wronged Sychaeus any opportunity to do), exacting Dante's contrition and claiming for her own purposes the tears just shed for the "dolcissimo patre." She does so, however, not in a shady grove of tragic lovers (the underworld's "pallentis umbras Erebi noctemque profundam," *Aen.* 4.26), but in an Edenic landscape, a "divina foresta spessa e viva" ("divine forest green and dense," *Purg.* 28.2). Indeed, it is difficult not to see the meeting of Dante and Beatrice after his recognition of "i segni de l'antica fiamma" as a comic replay of *Aeneid* 6, with the pilgrim playing the role of the penitent Aeneas, and Beatrice recast as the queen of Carthage. A single scenario, after all, is shared by the two pairs of lovers: within a shady grove, two lovers separated by the woman's death confront one another, and "talibus Aeneas ardentem et torva tuentem /

lenibat dictis animum lacrimasque ciebat" ("with such speech amid spring-
ing tears Aeneas would soothe the wrath of the fiery, fierce eyed queen,"
6.467–68). Except that in *Purgatorio*, of course, we are not in the Mourn-
ing Fields but in Eden. Nor will the tears of this new Aeneas cause the
woman he abandoned to abandon him. Beatrice turns herself toward him
rather than turning away, allowing him (after a moment of hard truth) to
cross the river Lethe and then to see her ardently holy eyes.

Moreover, when Beatrice first bids him to look up at her, he does so
willingly:

> Con men di resistenza si dibarba
>   robusto cerro, o vero al nostral vento
>   o vero a quel de la terra di Iarba
>   (*Purg.* 31.70–72)

(With less resistance is the sturdy oak uprooted, whether by wind of ours
or by that which blows from Iarbas' land.)

This reference to "la terra di Iarba" once again returns us to Dido. In
particular it summons up the violence of her passion in *Aeneid* 4 and, more
specifically still, returns us to an extended simile (vv. 441–49) in which her
fury is likened to a raging storm. In the face of her wrath, Aeneas stands like
a giant oak tree, able to withstand an almost unimaginable buffeting be-
cause its roots strike down to hell: "tantum radice in Tartara tendit" (v.
446). In *Purgatorio*, however, the storm represents a kind of liberation.
Virgil's stoic hero becomes a Christian pilgrim meant to be uprooted, to
yield before a feminine wind that overcomes him precisely in order that it—
that she—may raise him up. A Virgilian "no" becomes a Dantesque "yes."

In every case, therefore, Dante gives us a revision of Virgil's script that
transforms tragedy into romance, that turns the disclosure of darkness
visible into the unveiling of eternal light: "O isplendor di viva luce etterna"
("O splendor of living light eternal!" *Purg.* 31.139). And as if to heighten the
extent of this translation, he uses the same metaphor of flame that charac-
terizes *infelix Dido* throughout *Aeneid* 4 in order to describe the lady who
comes to him blessed and in the name of the Lord. It is, after all, the name
of Beatrice that lures the pilgrim into the measureless burning, "lo 'ncendio
sanza metro" (27.51), separating the terrace of lust from the Garden of
Eden. When he passes through that terrifying barrier and finally meets her,

she is, as noted above, "vestita di color di fiamma viva" ("clad . . . with hue of living flame," 30.33). Although she is veiled, he knows that she is his "antica fiamma" (30.48). But it is only when she uncovers her eyes to him in *Purgatorio* 31 that he actually sees the look "ond' Amor già ti trasse le sue armi" ("from which Love once shot his darts at you," v. 117). The personification of Amor inevitably reminds us of *Aeneid* 1.695–722, that is, of Cupid and his arrows lodged "in grembo a Dido" ("in Dido's lap," *Par.* 8.9) and kindling a passion that eventually kills her. Yet what we are shown in *Purgatorio* is another possibility of love altogether; and so, using the conventions of amatory literature to a different end, Dante allows his smitten pilgrim to luxuriate in the fiery glance of his celestially "Roman" (not Carthaginian) beloved: "Mille disiri più che fiamma caldi / strinsermi li occhi a li occhi rilucenti" ("A thousand desires hotter than flame held my eyes on the shining eyes," *Purg.* 31.118–19).[8]

It is significant that when he stands before her in this way, transfixed by passion and face to face, it is not she alone he sees, but the image of the griffin reflected in her eyes. Because of the mediatorial status that allows Beatrice to be both herself and a revelation that transcends her, Dante will take the stock romance convention of the lover's rapturous gaze and use it throughout the *Paradiso* as the means by which the pilgrim is transfigured from glory to glory. When he is at first blinded by her fire, Beatrice says by way of comfort that if she burns with flames of love beyond what he has known on earth—"s'io ti fiammeggio nel caldo d'amore / di là dal modo che' n terra si vede" (5.1–2)—the "kindling" of her love is none other than the eternal light of heaven. Every other fire that draws him away has been a seduction from that primal source; or to quote Beatrice directly, "non è se non di quella alcun vestigio, / mal conosciuto, che quivi traluce" ("it is naught save some vestige of [eternal] light, ill-recognized, which therein shines through," 5.11–12). In a poem that develops its symmetries so carefully, it is probably not by chance that here we should have a woman enflaming "nel caldo d'amore," talking about the vestige of love, and carrying on an extended discussion of free will and broken vows—all in the *fifth* canto of the *Paradiso*, a universe away from *Inferno* 5, where Francesca, Dido, and their common "schiera" ("troop," v. 85) whirl in a vortex of passion, going nowhere.

Nor may it be arbitrary (to return once again to the translation of

Dido's "adgnosco veteris vestigia flammae" in *Purgatorio* 30.48) that Dante renders the Virgilian *vestigia*, "traces," as *segni*, "tokens." At first glance the decision to depart from the obvious choice of the Italian *vestigio*—meaning the tracing of a roadway, or an imprint, marking, or footprint—seems very strange, especially when elsewhere in the line Dante's vernacular stays so close to the Latin: "adgnosco" becomes "conosco" and "flammae," "fiamma." It may even appear perverse when we consider how the most memorable use of *vestigio* in the *Commedia*, in *Paradiso* 31.81, specifically entails Dante's recollection of how his "antico amor" was willing (as he says) "in inferno lasciar le tue vestige"—a leaving of footprints in Hell that refers to the meeting of Beatrice with Virgil in Limbo. Presumably in the context of *Purgatorio* 30, as the appearance of Beatrice signals Virgil's departure, it would make marvelous poetic sense to have one vestige recall another.

Unless, of course, the concern of the poet at this juncture in the narrative is to assert a discontinuity between Virgil's poem and his own, to underscore a parting of ways. To be sure, this is generally the effect of introducing Dido's story into the text only to refute and rewrite it in the figure of his own relationship with Beatrice. The whole import of their love is that *eros* does not necessarily lead to madness and death; it can also lead to God. But more particularly, I wonder if Dante's obviously deliberate decision not to translate Virgil's "vestigia" literally may suggest a subtle polemical move on his part: a disavowal of the master's poetic authority at the very moment when the pilgrim turns around to Virgil with the poignant and affectionate offering of one of his own lines. In other words, Dante's imitation of *Aeneid* 4.23—his giving Virgil credit for that poem's extensive influence on the formation of his own imagination—may amount as well to a gesture of refusal. The poet gives Virgil the compliment of imitation, and then gives both him and Dido away.

What I want to suggest is that for Dante the word *vestigia* may have been fraught with associations that made its use unacceptable in *Purgatorio* 30, a canto in which the poet is taking stock of Virgil by taking leave of him. To begin with, there is the celebrated use of the word at the conclusion of the *Thebiad*, where Statius, after roundly congratulating himself on the achievement of his twelve-year (and twelve-book) labor, makes it clear in the end that he considers himself a disciple of an epic master. Addressing his own poem, he says: "vive, precor; nec tu divinam Aeneida tempta. / sed longe sequere et vestigia semper adora" ("O live, I pray! nor rival the divine *Aeneid*, but follow afar and ever venerate its footsteps," 12.816–17).

A similar use of the word to describe a precursor's superiority (and a latecomer's wisdom in following behind) is found in the rather different context of *Convivio* 4.7, where Dante explores the degree to which nobility of spirit is or is not a matter of inheritance. At one point in the discussion he wants to persuade the reader that the vilest of persons are those who inherit from their forebears a legacy of righteousness, but who then willfully depart from it. To illustrate, he conjures up a hypothetical landscape that, *mutatis mutandis*, works its way into the opening canto of the *Inferno*. (Indeed, the passage is full of vocabulary that will carry massive freight over the course of the *Commedia*.) Imagine, the author of the *Convivio* asks, a field full of obstacles—stones, hedges, timber, a ditch—and then envision a path going through it. Imagine this same field blanketed with snow so deep that no vestige of the path remains to be seen ("sì che d'alcuno sentiero vestigio non si vede," 4.7.7). A man appears on the trackless scene and wants to pass over to a house located on the other side:

> E per sua industria, cioè per accorgimento e per bontade d'ingegno, solo da sé guidato, per lo diritto cammino si va là dove intende, lasciando le *vestigie* de li suoi passi diretro da sé. Viene un altro appresso costui, e vuole a questa magione andare, e non li è mestiere se non seguire li *vestigi* lasciati; e, per suo difetto, lo cammino che altri sanza scorta ha saputo tenere, questo scorto erra, e tortisce per li pruni e per le ruine, e a la parte dove dee non va. Quale di costoro si dee dicere valente? Rispondo: quegli chè andò dinanzi. Questo altro come si chiamerà? Rispondo: vilissimo.
> (*Convivio* 4.7.7–8, emphasis mine)

(Through his own resourcefulness, that is, through observation and good native intelligence, with no one but himself for a guide, he reaches his destination by the direct path, leaving behind him the *marks* of his footprints. Someone else comes along after him making for the same house who need do no more than follow the *marks* already made. But through his own fault, he strays from the path marked out by the other person who knew how to keep to it without anyone to guide him; pursuing his way torturously through the thorn bushes and debris, he ends up in the wrong place. Which of these is to be deemed a person of worth? My reply is the one who went first. How is the other to be described? Utterly base.)

The primary point of Dante's example is disdain for anyone who has inherited a virtuous course of life "dal padre o d'alcuno suo maggiore" ("from a good father or other ancestor," 4.7.9) and who then fails to walk in those parental paths of righteousness; who refuses to be "ben camminato" ("well guided," 4.7.8). As Statius says in the closing lines of the *Thebaid*, one is to venerate the predecessor and "longe sequere et vestigia semper adora." What the *Convivio* specifically lauds in such a forefather is his ability "through the goodness of genius, guided solely by himself," to navigate the perilous but blank field on his own; it celebrates the footprints ("vestigi") he has left behind for others to follow after him. Nor does the exemplum lack a scriptural warrant. No less an authority than Solomon commands the man who has been blessed in having such a worthy ancestor: "Non trapasserai li termini antichi che puosero li padri tuoi" ("You shall not overstep the ancient bounds set by your fathers," *Convivio* 4.7.9; cf. Prov. 22:28, "Ne transgrediaris terminos antiquos, Quos posuerunt patres tui," "Pass not beyond the ancient bounds which thy fathers have set").

Later on in the *Convivio* (4.24), when Dante is exploring those virtues appropriate to adolescence, he will return to this advice and to these metaphors. For instance, the adolescent who enters the wood of error of this life would not know how to keep to the good path were it not for the elders who can point it out to him ("così l'adolescente, che entra ne la selva erronea di questa vita, non saprebbe tenere lo buono cammino, se da li suoi maggiori non li fosse mostrato," 4.24.12). Likewise, it is to be expected that the son will fix his attention on his father's footsteps ("mirare a le vestigie de li paterni piedi," 4.24.15) more than on those of any other superior. Once again, the injunction has scriptural authority, this time not only from Solomon ("Audi, figlio mio, l'ammaestramento del tuo padre," 4.24.14; cf. Prov. 1:8, "Audi, fili mi, disciplinam patris tui," "My son, hear the instruction of thy father"), but also from St. Paul ("Figliuoli, obedite a li vostri padri per tutte cose, per ciò che questo vuole Iddio," 4.24.17; cf. Col. 3:20, "Filii, obedite parentibus per omnia: hoc enim placitum est in Domino," "Children, obey your parents in all things: For this is well pleasing to the Lord").

Given that Dante took this emphasis on filial piety into the *Commedia*—not to mention the perilous landscape, the lost pathway, and the venerable guide—it is intriguing to consider the snowy field of *Convivio* 4.7 as the blank page of the poem that was to be, and to imagine the Virgil of the *Aeneid* as the worthy predecessor who, full of the goodness of genius and "solo da sé guidato," left behind him poetic vestiges for the pilgrim to follow. Nor is the association entirely fanciful. *Inferno* 23 closes with Dante following in the footprints of Virgil's beloved feet ("dietro a le poste de le care piante," v. 148), and the next canto presents us with a field that is likened to a parchment on which the hoarfrost pens a snowy text ("in su la terra assempra/l'imagine di sua sorella bianca," 24.4–5), only to have its writing ("la sua penna") erased by the sun's rays. In *Purgatorio* 22, finally, Dante follows the steps of Virgil and Statius, listening attentively to the "sermoni" of the classical poets, "ch'a poetar mi davano intelletto" ("which gave me understanding in poetry," v. 129).

I want neither to read the *Convivio* retrospectively in the light of the *Commedia* nor to force any connection between its parable of moral path-marking and the *Thebaid*'s acknowledgment of literary indebtedness. What I am suggesting, however, is that in Dante's lexicon the word *vestigio* seems very much to be tied to the notion of authority, and tied specifically to the authority of one who, by moral rectitude and the goodness of literary genius, left footprints to follow—or to walk away from. For the author of the *Convivio*, the good son follows the good father; he does not transgress the "termios antiquos." But while the *Commedia* would seem in so many obvious ways to replicate this scenario—having the "dolcissimo patre" res-cue Dante from the wood of error and then lead him every step of the way to the "selva antica" of Eden—it is also manifestly the case that Virgil's power both to rescue and to guide comes to him ultimately from another Father, from the God whom the ancient poet does not know (*Inf.* 1.131). Virgil is the forerunner called to lead the pilgrim through the wilderness; but as the itinerary of the journey periodically makes plain, in *Inferno* as well as in *Purgatorio*, he is not "solo da sé guidato." He comes at the will of heaven.

While the facts of Virgil's situation are presented as a given from the opening of the poem, their hard truth is brought home in *Purgatorio* 30. For it is there that Dante, who covers the literary field of this canto with so many traces of the master, shows unmistakably that Virgil's adored foot-prints are ultimately *not* the ones to follow. To venerate them by following in their path would be, in fact, to lose the "vera via" and circle back to hell. Instead, the vestiges to keep track of are the ones Beatrice left behind her in Limbo, summoning Virgil out of the kingdom of death and starting the pilgrim on a journey of desire that leads him not only beyond the author of the *Aeneid* but also beyond Beatrice herself to God.

A question remains, however, as to why Dante should have chosen to translate Virgil's *vestigia* as *segni*. The latter word occurs 53 times over the course of the *Commedia*, 30 of which are in the *Paradiso*. Its first appearance, moreover, is in the mouth of Virgil when he describes the harrowing of hell by one who was "con segno di vittoria coronato" ("crowned with sign of victory," *Inf.* 4.54). This use of *segno* to refer to the cross, as commentators from the fourteenth century on have taken it to do, occurs again at the beginning of the *Purgatorio*, where the angelic boatman who delivered his cargo of souls to the shores of purgatory "fece il segno lor di santa croce" ("made the sign of holy cross upon them," 2.49) and sent them on their way. And so we will find it used once more in *Paradiso* 14.101, describing the "venerabil segno" inscribed within the sphere of Mars. Dante will also speak of the ensign of the imperial eagle as a "sacrosanto segno" (*Par.* 6.32; cf. 6.82 and 100), as "[il] segno/che fè i Romani al mondo reverendi" ("the sign which made the Romans reverend to the world," *Par.* 19.101–2). In either case, however, *segno* is a privileged word, pointing the reader to two of the poem's major icons and to the heart of its thematic preoccupations.

In addition to these two major examples, which do not in themselves elucidate the substitution of "segni" for "vestigia" in *Purgatorio* 30.48, Dante will also employ the word to indicate the goal of an action, a destination, the "target" of desire; in short, the terminus of something that stands beyond. Thus in *Paradiso* 1.124–26 Beatrice tells the pilgrim that his ascent to the Empyrean is empowered by divine providence,

> e ora lì, come a sito decreto,
>   cen porta la virtù di quella corda
>   che ciò che scocca drizza in segno lieto.

(and thither now, as to a place decreed, the virtue of that bowstring bears us on, which aims at a joyful target whatsoever it shoots.)

Segno as ontological target—the end point God has chosen for humanity—also appears in *Paradiso* 8.105, while in 11.119–20 it will specifically describe the right course of St. Peter's bark, the church, on the high sea of history ("la barca/di Pietro in alto mar per dritto segno"). To be sure, the word is used in *Paradiso* to express not only human destiny but also human limits: the "segno d'i mortal" ("mark of mortals," 15.42), "lo segno del nostro intelletto" ("the mark of our intellect," 15.45), and, most importantly, "il trapassar del segno" ("the overpassing of the bound," 26.117). But even so, where *segno* signifies limitation, it also signifies hope. For as Dante learns at the outset of his journey to paradise, God condescends to the human condition "per far segno" (4.38), to communicate an ineffable reality either through scriptural metaphor—"e piedi e mano/attribuisce a Dio e altro intende" ("and attributes hands and feet to God, having other meaning," 4.44–45)—or through the celestial semiotics that appear for a moment only to disappear once they have been comprehended. As the pilgrim tells St. James in *Paradiso* 25.88–89, the written Word of God is the source of his hope, for "le nove e le scritture antiche/pongon lo segno," the new and old Scriptures hold out the sign, or token, of what lies behind them.

Within the drama of the *Commedia*, of course, the paradigmatic *segno* is Beatrice. In *Purgatorio* 30, after the pilgrim recognizes in her presence "i segni de l'antica fiamma," she withholds herself from him until he recognizes the extent to which formerly he had turned away from those *segni*. Drawing out the map of his misreading, she reminds him that from his youth on she had directed him toward the right goal ("in dritta parte," v. 123); that even when she died, she sent him inspirations ("ispirazion," v. 133) and dreams ("in sogno," v. 134) and other indications of the true way ("e altrimenti/lo rivocai," vv. 134–35). After he confesses his past enthrallment—the false signs ("cose fallaci," 31.56) that had obscured the mystery of her "carne sepolta" ("buried flesh," 31.48), she enables him to drink of the river Lethe and then see her as she is. Reading her aright remains a difficulty, however, for he must learn how to be drawn in by "l'antica rete" ("the old net," 32.6) of her smile without at the same time being fixated by it; he must learn to "use" his beloved (in Augustinian terms) rather than to enjoy her.[9]

Dante comes to this proper understanding of her significance gradually over the course of the *Paradiso*. It is to the "sign" of her face that he will continually turn his gaze, as if pulled by her beauty to the mark of his greater desire ("al segno di maggior disio," 3.126), and therefore to a reality that lies beyond her. By the end of the journey, the gaze of Beatrice will bring him to the gathered company of heaven, who in look and love are all directed on one mark ("viso e amore avea tutto ad un segno," 31.27). It is there, in the full view of her fellow citizens, that Dante turns to share the experience of "quella Roma onde Cristo è romano." But what he discovers then is that she is no longer beside him; instead she has reclaimed her eternal place in the divine community and, after a parting smile, "si tornò a l'etterna fontana" ("turned again to the eternal fountain," 31.93). Neither disappearing like Virgil nor turning away like Dido from the disconsolate Aeneas, Beatrice focuses her attention where Dante will soon turn his—"tutto ad un segno."

The unique sign to which all heaven is drawn is the God who lies beyond even Dante's powers of signification. Yet, given the incarnational theology that informs the poem, perhaps it is not off the mark to trace a line between the "segni de l'antica fiamma" that Dante experienced as early as the *Vita nuova* and the vision of "la nostra effige" ("our image," *Par.* 33.131) that rivets the pilgrim's attention in the end. Such a connection between human *eros* and the divine love is unimaginable for Virgil, who could give Dante a tragic line but never its transfigured (and comic) meaning; who could present Dido's loss, but not the discovery of a Beatrice. And so, looking back to the world of the *Aeneid* with a vestige of his master's poetry, and finding nothing there, the pilgrim turns instead to the resurrected presence standing before him, as to a sign of the love that moves the sun and the other stars. At the moment when one dispensation passes away and another makes its living claims, the poet of *Purgatorio* 30 shows us that Cupid is not the only god at work in human passion, nor death the last word on *antico amor*.

PART 3

Dante and Ovid

CHAPTER 7

The Metamorphosis of Ovid

Unlike those poets who conceal their debts to the past, Dante makes his literary forebears required reading. From the opening canto of his *Commedia* he keeps us in company with Virgil, whom the pilgrim recognizes in no uncertain terms as "lo mio maestro e 'l mio autore" ("my master and my author," *Inf.* 1.85). Virgil receives the lion's share of the poet's gratitude, but others are soon given their due as well, literary virtuosos gathered in the first circle of the inferno, where they walk freely within a softly illumined landscape that is unmistakably modeled on the Elysian Fields of *Aeneid* 6. Distinguished among all the dead by virtue of their "onrata nominanza" ("honored fame," *Inf.* 4.76), the august company of Homer, Horace, Ovid, Lucan, and Virgil presents us at the outset with the resources without which the *Commedia* would be, quite literally, unimaginable.

Then, having acknowledged these luminaries, he does something more: he places himself among them. Shortly after his arrival in Limbo, as the pilgrim watches these lords of highest song confer together, he finds suddenly that they are smiling at him, signaling for him to join their ranks, so that, as the narrator recalls, "io fui sesto tra cotanto senno" ("I was sixth amid so much wisdom," *Inf.* 4.102). Dante's staging of his own literary debut, counting himself a member of their exalted circle, might well seem outrageous in that the only work Dante could claim in the year 1300, the fictional date of this encounter, is his *Vita nuova*. Be that as it may, in Limbo Dante revels in his classification as an "honorary pagan," apparently sharing with his ancient masters the superlative status of most lofty poet— "altissimo poeta" (v. 80)—and engaging them in earnest conversation. We are not told what that talk was about, but there is every reason to fantasize that it would have concerned poetry, and perhaps even the work which the prematurely celebrated ephebe would go on to write in their collective shadow.

This is one way of viewing Dante's sojourn in the groves of the pagan academy—warm and valedictory, the dramatization of an author's "acknowledgments." But however courteous Dante's loving encounter with classical poetry may be, there is no escaping the fact that the meeting is set in the first circle of hell, within a small oasis of light surrounded on all sides by the darkness of an eternity without hope. However much Dante may learn from the "bella scola" of pagan antiquity about the art of making poetry, the structure of the *Commedia* makes clear that a great gulf stretches between him and them. Full of "honor" though the ancients may be (as has often been remarked, the word *onor* and its derivatives occur with almost obsessive frequency in *Inferno* 4), these "great shades" are devoid of grace, their light ultimately overcome by darkness. For this reason, despite Dante's strong attraction to them—despite the intense exaltation of spirit he experiences even in recollecting his time in Limbo (vv. 119–20)—these are masters who must be left behind. Not that they will ever be discarded as poetic sources, even in the most sublime reaches of paradise. Nonetheless, taken strictly on its own terms, their legacy for the Christian poet is a dead letter, cut off from the radiance and joy that constitute Dante's ultimate vision. Compared to the "altissimo canto" (v. 95) of pagan antiquity, the poet of the *Commedia* has (or so he would have the reader understand) an infinitely higher song to sing.

Most readers experience the poignancy of this judgment on antiquity in terms of the figure of Virgil: the pilgrim's guide through hell and purgatory; the virtuous pagan whose poetry has saved others, though not himself; the noble Roman whose exclusion from a drama of redemption in which he plays so many important parts amply warrants Robert Hollander's characterization of him as the figure of tragedy inscribed within Dante's comedy.[1] Yet within the *Commedia* there is another literary progenitor, second in importance and in frequency of allusion only to Virgil, but for whom, on the contrary, we are asked to feel no particular attachment. Nor, despite the accumulated evidence of his literary presence, do we even seem expected to notice him very much. Scarcely less problematic than the master Dante loved so deeply yet consigned to hell is the master he did not seem to love at all. This is the poet whom Dante will name only once after the group embrace of Limbo, and then for the sole purpose of telling him to keep silent in the face of Dante's greater achievement. I am referring, of course, to Ovid, about whom Dante will say in that notoriously Ovidian 25th canto of the *Inferno*, "io non lo 'nvidio" ("I envy him not," v. 99)—a boast that not only conceals a profound imitation of the author of the *Metamorphoses* but also makes a point of negating the connection between them. "Io non lo 'nvidio," claims our poet, or, to state the matter as plainly as the text, *io non Ovidio*—I am not Ovid; I am better![2]

Why, in the *Commedia*, should Dante routinely conceal, and occasionally (as in this one case) openly disparage, a poet about whom he speaks elsewhere with respect? In the *De vulgari eloquentia* (2.6.7) Dante identifies Ovid as one of the *regulatos* (or standard-makers) of succeeding writers. In the *Convivio* Dante acknowledges him not only as one who provides a model for poetic allegory (2.1.3) but as the author of a pagan corroboration of Genesis 1 (4.15.8), who also offered suitable ethical exempla to illustrate the virtues of old age (4.27.17, 19). It is largely on the basis of this pre-*Commedia* reverence that Ettore Paratore characterizes Dante's Ovid as an author whose work (but most especially whose *Metamorphoses*) offered Dante "a providential teaching not much inferior in degree to that of the *Aeneid*."[3]

So again, why should we come later to the *Commedia* and find Dante's relationship to this paragon to be so fraught, so hide-and-seek, and even, as Teodolinda Barolini has shown, so gratuitously downgraded?[4] After all, Dante was writing at the end of what has been called the *aetas Ovidiana*, when the *Metamorphoses* in particular was regarded not only as an invaluable repository of ancient myth but also as a source of philosophical, scientific, and moral insight. Why should Dante borrow as freely as his contemporaries from the Ovidian banquet and then bite the hand that feeds him?

The answer may lie in the possibility that Dante's Ovid is two distinct figures; or, rather, that Dante perceived Ovid one way before writing the *Commedia* and then in another way in his great poem. What we might call the "authoritative" Ovid seems to have prevailed from the *Vita nuova* through the unfinished *Convivio*. This is the figure who, at least since Arnulf of Orleans in the twelfth century, was allegorized beyond literal recognition into a sage and serious poet; whom Pierre Bersuire would turn into an *Ovidius moralizatus* full of lofty ethical instruction; whom Paratore characterizes as having offered Dante a prolonged meditation on "l'azione miracolosa del supremo potere moderatore e arbitrio della vita del cosmo" ("the miraculous action of the supreme governing power and will of the life of the cosmos").[5]

But when we come to the great poem that would claim Dante's attention for the latter portion of his life, another view of Ovid seems to be at work. It is as if in the mysterious period between the *Convivio* and the *Commedia*, when Dante seems to have been discovering the significance of Virgil as his "master and author," he was also parting company from Ovid as "maestro," albeit certainly not as "autore." Cutting through two centuries of ameliorating allegorization, he seems to have read the *Metamorphoses* for itself, *in littera*. What he largely found there was not some quasi-biblical writer almost as authoritative as Virgil, as Paratore would have it, but a curator of the fallen world in all its hideous permutations: a pagan master who would provide not a meditation on the cosmic power of providence but a sustained nightmare of rage, rape, and human loss. In Ovid, Dante discovered powerful images for the horrific inversions of *Inferno* and failed analogies for the redeemed reality he intended to intimate in the other canticles. The poet of changes would offer him, in other words, a richly detailed picture of a world without grace from which he might draw his own varied portraits of damnation, or against which he could suggest another order of things entirely.[6]

In addition to discovering in the *Metamorphoses* a treasury of nightmares, Dante also may have found in Ovid's frequent references—whether in addresses to the reader, in the frequent celebrations of his own enterprise and achievement, or in what Karl Galinsky refers to (by way of contrast with Virgil) as the "greater egocentricity of his narrative"[7]—the portrait of an artist as genius that at once drew and repelled him. This double response to the vocational persona of Ovid—Dante's recognition of the urge to establish oneself by sheer force of stylistic brilliance and his attempted correction of that Ovidian urge in himself—is perhaps most apparent in *Inferno* 25, when Ovid is called up from the hidden depths of the text to be named on its surface. The moment is unique in the *Commedia*, the only time after Limbo when Dante expressly mentions Ovid. Unmistakably imitating the *Metamorphoses* even as he tells the Latin maestro to be silent, disparaging Ovid's story of Arethusa while he appropriates Ovid's account of Salamacis,[8] Dante fills over 90 lines with a spectacle of "mutare e trasmutare" ("change and transmute," v. 43) that has no apparent point beyond its own descriptive (that is, Ovidian) achievement. At the end of the canto the poet pulls himself up short and confesses that his pen has run away with him (25.143–44); at the beginning of the next canto, moreover, he acknowledges that before it is too late he must rein in the powers of his own genius lest they lead him where virtue does not guide (*Inf.* 26.21–24). That all of this should take place in the circle of the thieves and on the brink of the false counselors suggests that Dante knew not only what he was taking from the silenced master but also what he must leave behind.

The explicit conjuration of Ovid as a model presents the Latin poet both as a poetic persona that Dante could assume at will and as a persona to be abandoned. What I am suggesting, then, is that the figure of Ovid serves Dante as a cautionary tale, as a countertype to his identity as poet, just as Ovid's own Phaeton and Icarus function throughout the *Commedia* as countertypes of the pilgrim.[9] This is to say that the author of the *Metamorphoses*, with his penchant for privileging technique over meaning and for running in bravura circles around the linear trajectory of Virgil's *Aeneid*, offered Dante an idea of poetic vocation to reject. To be sure, Ovid could give Dante the materials of myth and a brilliance of technical manipulation not easily rivaled; but Ovid could not in himself offer a model for the Christian mythmaker. His *carmen* ("song") was too inextricably linked to error, and his unfettered genius (as Ovid himself proclaims in the *Tristia*) shipwrecked his career.

Such an assessment was by no means a foregone conclusion for a poet of Dante's time. No less a precursor than Brunetto Latini closes his *Tesoretto* by discovering "ovidio maggiore" (v. 2359) at the end of a series of allegorical mentors (Nature, Philosophy, Virtue, Love) and then attributing his return to the *vera via* to the intervention of Ovid's artistry:

Ma ovidio per arte
mi diede maestria,
si ch'io trovai la via
ond' io mi traffugai;
(*Il tesoretto*, vv. 2390–93)

(But Ovid through artistry
Gave me the mastery,
So that I found the way
From which I had strayed.)

Such a choice proved to be unthinkable for Dante, and not only because he was at pains to distance himself from Latini's vernacular allegory, of which he otherwise made such good use. More importantly, the departure from Latini in this case highlights Dante's election of one poetic mentor over another; that is, his choice of a Virgilian poetic vocation over an Ovidian poetic career.

We do not, of course, have any indication from the poet of the *Commedia* that he thought explicitly in these terms. We have only the great prominence of Virgil, the virtual concealment of Ovid, and the gradual development of a constructed identity—"Dante Poet." I am suggesting that Dante saw in the author of the *Metamorphoses* a foil not only for Virgil but also for himself. Dante was a poet with a destined journey to undertake, a *vera via* to travel. Ovid, on the other hand, was a poet happily going nowhere, a poet reveling in the momentary marvelous and refusing the epic mode with its assumptions of overarching significance and "call." Indeed, Ovid's joy is to sing a *perpetuum carmen* for the sheer sake of singing, or more precisely, for the sake of enhancing the glory of the singer—the "diffuse authorial self" who is the central figure of the *Metamorphoses*, if that work can be said to have one.[10] I would argue that Dante recognized Ovid's refusal to follow in Virgil's footsteps or to pursue any direction other than that of his own imaginative freedom. Instead of an *iter durum* and a destined hero's transforming struggle, he saw that Ovid celebrates himself and his own sustained tour de force, and that he relishes the tale because of the telling. His achievement was style, and style both made and was the man: *homo rhetoricus*. What matter that some master of rhetoric like Quintilian would later find him wanting in comparison to Virgil, taking him to task for a lack of seriousness, an unseemly enthrallment with his own gifts, an unwillingness to discipline his talents rather than indulge them?[11] No matter at all, if he could achieve his own purpose in breaking with Virgilian tradition to do something utterly new, something that would guarantee for its author an immortality that belongs neither to gods nor to emperors nor to Rome itself, but only to poets. As Ovid says in the closing lines of the *Metamorphoses*,

> Iamque opus exegi, quod nec Iovis ira nec ignis
> nec poterit ferrum nec edax abolere vetustas.
> cum volet, illa dies, quae nil nisi corporis huius

ius habet, incerti spatium mihi finiat aevi:
parte tamen meliore mei super alta perennis
astra ferar, nomenque erit indelebile nostrum,
quaque patet domitis Romana potentia terris,
ore legar populi, perque omnia saecula fama,
siquid habent veri vatum praesagia, vivam.

(15.871–79)

(And now my work is done, which neither the wrath of Jove, nor fire, nor sword, nor the gnawing tooth of time shall ever be able to undo. When it will, let that day come which has no power save over this mortal frame, and end the span of uncertain years. Still in my better part I shall be borne immortal far beyond the lofty stars and I shall have an undying name. Wherever Rome's power extends over the conquered world, I shall have mention on men's lips, and, if the prophecies of bards have any truth, throughout all the ages I shall live in fame.)

It should come as no surprise that Ovid saves the final word of his *Metamorphoses* for himself: "vivam" ("I shall live"). Flying in the face of all the mutability he records, the poet stakes his hope for eternity on his own undying fame.

Taking Ovid at his word, and thereby rescuing him from the interpretive transformations of the allegorists, Giovanni del Virgilio was to argue in 1322–23, only a year after the death of his friend Dante, that the *causa finalis* of the *Metamorphoses* was not its alleged ethical teaching but rather the perpetuation of the poet himself "ut ipse famam perpetuam acquireret ("in order that he himself might acquire perpetual fame").[12]

From the constructed perspective of the *Commedia*, this hope in perpetual fame is whistling in the wind at best or the world of the *Inferno* at worst. Indeed, the desire to make oneself eternal—to live on in a treasure of one's own making—is quite explicitly celebrated by Dante within the sterile landscape of the sodomites. There, in *Inferno* 15, he turns the apparent prizewinner into a loser, in an act of aggression not only against the dear, kind, paternal image of Brunetto Latini but against the venerable equation of art with immortality.

Even so, there can be no question that Dante knew for himself Ovid's expressed desire. "In nova fert animus" ("Into [the] new my mind is bent"), the opening words of the *Metamorphoses*, might just as well serve as an epigraph for the *Commedia*. It is also clear that Dante set out to exorcise this impulse over the long course of the poem, most overtly through characters encountered by the pilgrim (such as Latini and Ulysses) but also by means of mythological countertypes whose failed journeys are continuously juxtaposed with the guided navigation of both pilgrim and poet. Ulysses, Phaeton, Icarus: these are the figures who haunt the poet not only with their presumption but also with the possibility of death by fire or by drowning. They are also the examples used by Ovid in the *Tristia* to dramatize his own sorry exilic state, as he struggles to keep his wit afloat against the thunderbolts of an august "Jupiter" following the shipwreck (*naufragium*) of his career. Ovid seems to provide Dante with a cautionary figure, in other words, both before and after his fall. Ovid is pride and its disastrous effects; the self-congratulatory genius and the broken exile.

According to what the Middle Ages knew of Ovid's biography (which was learned not from any classical vita but only from a culling of the poet's own self-revelations), Ovid's exile from Rome was the central event of his life, with much of his writing—the *Metamorphoses* most significantly but also the *Remedia* and the *Fasti*—taken to be an extended act of reparation, a bid to go home. Both Giovanni del Virgilio and Boccaccio entertain a story that ultimately the poet's pen was mightier than the emperor's decree, enabling him finally to return to Rome (although ironically to die of suffocation at the hands of the crowds eager to welcome him back).[13] For most commentators, however, Ovid came to his sorrowful death while still in exile, thereby providing them with yet another sign of Fortune's sway over even the most brilliant of men.

We can only conjecture what Dante made of this history, but certainly it is not difficult to imagine that he saw there the outlines of his own story, both as an exile who found himself "brought to different ports and inlets and shores by the dry wind that blows from wretched poverty" (*Convivio* 1.3) and as a poet who might conceivably return to the city that had exiled him with his masterwork as his passport. Of this hope he writes at the beginning of *Paradiso* 25, where he speaks in his own authorial voice about the possibility of going home:

> Se mai continga che 'l poema sacro
>   al quale ha posto mano e cielo e terra,
>   sì che m'ha fatto per molti anni macro,

vinca la crudeltà che fuor mi serra
　　del bello ovile ov' io dormi' agnello,
　　nimico ai lupi che li danno guerra;
con altra voce omai, con altro vello
　　ritornerò poeta, e in sul fonte
　　del mio battesmo prenderò 'l cappello;
però che ne la fede, che fa conte
　　l'anime a Dio, quivi intra' io.
　　　　　　　　　　　　(*Par.* 25.1–11)

(If ever it come to pass that the sacred poem to which heaven and earth
have so set hand that it has made me lean for many years should
overcome the cruelty which bars me from the fair sheepfold where I slept
as a lamb, an enemy to the wolves which war on it, with changed voice
now and with changed fleece a poet will I return, and at the font of my
baptism will I take the crown; because there I entered into the Faith that
makes souls known to God.)

Dante offers this address to the reader immediately after the pilgrim's
examination on faith and just before he is questioned on hope. For the brief
moment of these four *terzine*, he steps outside the fictional framework of
his pilgrim's journey in the year 1300 to speak instead about his own situa-
tion "now," banished from the city where he "slept as a lamb" and writing
his sacred poem. While willing to admit the ravages of time and experi-
ence, he shows neither self-pity nor remorse. He is a defender of the sheep,
an enemy of wolves, and more than willing to wage war against them. Nor
does he betray any modesty about the nature or dimension of his gift: he is,
like Homer and Virgil and Ovid before him, a *poeta*. There is no lack of
faith or hope in the literary enterprise of the *Commedia* itself. But in con-
trast to Ovid's defiant longing at the close of the *Metamorphoses*—"perque
omnia saecula fama,/siquid habent veri vatum praesagia, vivam" ("if the
prophecies of bards have any truth, throughout the ages I shall live in
fame," 15.878–79)—Dante's ultimate wish in this passage from *Paradiso* 25
is for the poem he has labored over to be considered "sacred" and therefore
only partly of his doing; for it to be grounded, as poetry, in the "faith that
makes souls known to God." What matters is that the laurel crown he cov-
ets should find its significance at the font of his baptism, and nowhere else.
　　Like the poet of the *Metamorphoses*, Dante is confident about the

durability of his enterprise but claims throughout the poem that neither his "alto ingegno" nor its achievement is entirely his own. Likewise, as we see in these lines from *Paradiso* 25, he shares with all fellow exiles a sense of profound loss. But at least in the *Commedia*, the solace of outrage and the consolation of an active martyrdom replace Ovidian self-pity. There is no writing of a *liber exulis* to placate the authorities, no sense of a diminished voice half-heartedly making the old bid for fame. Dante has, after all, something other than his misfortune to bear witness to. Despite the ongoing palinode of the *Commedia* with respect to his own earlier writings, there is nothing in the end for him to regret. He will even come to envision his exile as an exodus. Although constituting only a party of one, he claims nonetheless a fair sheepfold to serve, and to serve precisely by means of the literary shepherd's only weapon—*poetando*.

We have every reason to assume that the main source of Dante's pastoral imagery in *Paradiso* 25 is Scripture, for both Testaments identify the good shepherd precisely as the one willing to lay down his life for the sheep. But it is tempting to wonder if Dante might also have had a specific Ovidian text in mind—*Tristia* 1.6—in which Ovid draws upon a similar fund of imagery in order to dramatize the circumstances of his exile. In that poem he assumes the stance of an outraged Ulysses, expressing gratitude for a wife who has been nothing less to him than a faithful Penelope; that is, who has protected him from being stripped bare in Rome "by those who have attacked the timbers of my wreckage" ("naufragii tabulas qui petiere mei," v. 8). The passage then continues as follows:

> utque rapax stimulante fame cupidusque cruoris
> incustoditum captat ovile lupus,
> aut ut edax vultur corpus circumspicit ecquod
> sub nulla positum cernere possit humo,
> sic mea nescio quis, rebus male fidus acerbis
> in bona venturus, si paterere, fuit.
>   (*Tristia* 1.6.9–14)

(As the wolf ravening under the goad of hunger and eager for blood strives to catch the sheepfold unguarded, or as the hungry vulture peers about for the possible sight of some unburied corpse, so there was one, treacherous in my bitter fortune, who, hadst thou suffered it, would have come into my wealth.)

Because she has come to his rescue, Ovid offers his wife whatever a failing poetic voice can do to memorialize her heroism: "quantumcumque tamen praeconia nostra valebunt,/carminibus vives tempus in omne meis" ("so far as my praise has power, thou shalt live for all time in my song," vv. 35–36). As does Dante in his address to the reader in *Paradiso* 25, Ovid presents an imperiled sheepfold ("incustoditum . . . ovile"), a predatory wolf ("rapax . . . lupus"), and a sense of having been singled out as victim. And yet the point of any such comparison has to be a more fundamental contrast between the two poets, for the scale of Ovid's drama (and the light in which we are asked to see him) is so strikingly different. While Dante envisions himself as defender of the threatened sheepfold, it is Ovid's wife who plays the analogous role in the *Tristia*. Except, of course, that in fending off the circling wolves, she is not protecting commune or community; she is guarding the poet's wealth. For this bravery Ovid will celebrate her as best he can. But the bravado that ends the *Metamorphoses* and that occasionally resurfaces (with pathetic qualification) elsewhere in the *Tristia* is absent here.[14] The exile bemoans his ill fortune and gives thanks for the diminished thing that remains to him. On the other hand, Dante, while acknowledging that suffering has changed both "fleece" and voice, admits no loss whatsoever. Locked out of Florence, he becomes a voice crying in the wilderness, strengthened by exile and daring to boast of a "sacred poem" to which both heaven and earth have set hand.[15]

Given all that I have argued thus far, it might be expected that this essay would close with lines clearly drawn and Dante's Ovid neatly disposed of, both in his pride and in his fall. And yet, of course, the *Commedia* itself invariably refuses the neat solution. Once Virgil departs from the narrative at the end of the *Purgatorio*, taking with him what heretofore has been the poem's primary literary subtext, none other than the *Metamorphoses* becomes the major classical presence throughout the *Paradiso*. What is more, the Ovidian persona, the writer as Ovid, becomes a kind of model for Dante—the poet of the new and unprecedented, of *trasumanare* (*Par.* 1.70). That such a "metamorphosis" should occur in the final canticle is in keeping with the larger risks the poet undertakes there. Unlike his biblical prototype St. Paul, who kept silent about his rapture to the third heaven, Dante dares in this final section of the poem to speak of an ineffable reality about which the apostle himself said it was unlawful to utter a word (2 Cor.

12:4). By his own admission, he is sailing yet uncharted literary waters—
"L'acqua ch'io prendo già mai non si corse" (*Par.* 2.7)—and therefore
undertaking a venture at once utterly new and very dangerous. Surely for
this reason Dante is concerned especially in the opening canto of *Paradiso*
to invoke the powers of divine inspiration, to be made worthy of the vision
he begs to tell. Until this point he had relied upon the Muses to aid him,
but now he turns himself to the higher authority, to "buono Appollo," with
a request that he be made like St. Paul before him, a vessel of God's election
("fammi del tuo valor sì fatto vaso," v. 14). Dante prays:

> Entra nel petto mio, e spira tue
>   sì come quando Marsïa traesti
>   de la vagina de le membra sue.
> O divina virtù, se mi ti presti
>   tanto che l'ombra del beato regno
>   segnata nel mio capo io manifesti,
> vedra'mi al piè del tuo diletto legno
>   venire, e coronarmi de le foglie
>   che la materia e tu mi farai degno.
>   (*Par.* 1.19–27)

(Enter into my breast and breathe there as when you drew Marsyas from
the sheath of his limbs. O divine Power, if you do so lend yourself to me
that I may show forth the image of the blessed realm which is imprinted
in my mind, you shall see me come to [the feet of] your beloved tree and
crown me with those leaves of which the matter and you shall make me
worthy.)

The Ovidian tale Dante alludes to here is told in the sixth book of the
Metamorphoses (vv. 383–91), in association with other stories of human
insubordination and divine punishment. In the first of them, the tale of
Arachne (6.1–145), a master weaver of narrative tapestry dares to rival and
surpass the gods in such storytelling. In the case of the satyr Marsyas, a
musician challenges Apollo to a musical duel and is judged by the Muses to
be the loser. But unlike the Arachne story, with its lengthy descriptions of
two contending tapestries, the tale of Marsyas says nothing whatsoever
about the nature of the artistic endeavor, the skill of his playing. Instead,
the poet's interest is centered exclusively on loss. In what may well be the
most gruesome moment in the *Metamorphoses,* Ovid gives us Marsyas as he

is flayed alive, crying out to Apollo, "quid me mihi detrahis?" ("Why do you tear me from myself?"):

> clamanti cutis est summos direpta per artus,
> nec quicquam nisi vulnus erat; cruor undique manat,
> detectique patent nervi, trepidaeque sine ulla
> pelle micant venae; salientia viscera possis
> et perlucentes numerare in pectore fibras.
>
> (*Met.* 6.387–91)

(As he screams, his skin is stripped off the surface of his body, and he is all one wound: blood flows down on every side, the sinews lie bare, his veins throb and quiver with no skin to cover them: you could count the entrails as they palpitate, and the vitals showing clearly in his breast.)

It would be easy to assimilate Dante's reference to this horrific flaying if it were found somewhere in the *Inferno* and in that context used to suggest a sinner's *contrapasso*. Then the fate of this Ovidian overreacher might serve as a warning: abandon hope all ye who follow in the footsteps of Marsyas and dare to duel with God. But in the first canto of *Paradiso*, whatever are we to make of Dante's identification of himself with Ovid's doomed artist, and how understand Dante's plea to God, named here as "Apollo," to "enter into my breast and breathe there as when you drew Marsyas from the sheath of his limbs"?

Centuries of commentary have taken refuge in allegory, seeing in Dante's request a prayer to be delivered from the sins of ignorance, hardness of heart, arrogance, and presumption—all that the Christian poet needs to be liberated from if he is to be crowned at the foot of the cross, that tree more beloved of God than the laurel. With the Ovidian reference viewed in this way, we can see Dante asking that the Marsyas in him be drawn out, laid bare, even martyred, in order that God may fill him with the same life-giving breath that brought forth the Creation in the beginning. How else to become the vessel of poetic election, first emptied in order to be filled to overflowing with an "image of the blessed kingdom"? How else to become poet of the beatific vision?

But if we also allow Marsyas to serve as an image of the master of the *Metamorphoses*, then what we see here is Dante's coming to terms with Ovid as poet by dramatically turning him inside out through a violent act of poetic revision. In identifying himself with Marsyas, Dante can acknowledge not only the overreacher's impulse to take on Virgil and best him at *poetando*, but also the urge to throw down the gauntlet before the good Apollo—to create a new heaven and a new earth, and do so in a vernacular language that is to be created canto by canto, a language that even heaven's angels will be heard to sing in the end.[16]

No example less radical than this terrible flaying will suffice to suggest the radical transformation of identity that Dante's conversion as poet must entail, or the danger that he knows he runs in writing as he does. He invites a dreadful punishment and claims it, like the cross, to be a sign of glory and deliverance. At the outset of the final canticle, then, the horrific death of Marsyas is metamorphosed before the reader's eyes to serve as a figure of Dante's own conversion: the profane genius is transformed into the "sacred poet." In a move as breathtaking as anything else in the *Commedia*, the poet of the *Paradiso* presents himself as a new Ovid, delivered from the sheath of his limbs and born again—as Dante.

CHAPTER 8

Watching Matelda

After Dante passes through the purifying flames that encircle purgatory's terrace of lust, he enters a pastoral world that extends luxuriantly across the level summit of the mountain. Midway through canto 28 he will learn that the place is Eden, the "paradiso voluptatis" of Genesis 2. This identification, taken together with other recollections of Adam and Eve, force us to be mindful of the Garden's biblical subtext. But it is also true that Dante's "divina foresta" (*Purg.* 28.2) grows out of pagan literary soil quite as much as it does out of Scripture. Surveying its "campagna santa" ("holy plain," v. 118), one inevitably thinks of the *locus amoenus* ("pleasant place") celebrated in classical poetry from Homer on, or of the vernacular "pleasance" of medieval romance and love lyric.[1] Indeed, the *Commedia* rehearses all the time-honored elements of the traditional scene: dense shade, a clear brook, a grassy bank, a meadow full of flowers, a gentle breeze, mellifluous bird-song—in short, the requisite "charms" of the same ideal landscape that delighted Theocritus even as it did the authors of the *Romance of the Rose*.

Appearing suddenly on the far shore of a narrow river that runs through this "selva antica" ("ancient wood," v. 23), a river soon to be identified as Lethe, Dante sees "una donna soletta" ("a lady all alone," v. 40), who dances upon this ecphrastic stage like a nymph from ancient pastoral. Such a likeness is, in fact, made explicit in the following canto, where the lady appears "come ninfe che si givan sole / per le salvatiche ombre" ("like nymphs who used to wend alone through the woodland shades," 29.4–5). A solitary figure, gathering flowers and singing a song the pilgrim cannot understand: the sheer wonder of the maiden's apparition drives away the claims of every other reality ("disvia / per maraviglia tutto altro pensare,"

28.38–39). But if the pilgrim is immediately overwhelmed, he is by no means rendered speechless; in fact, he addresses her with some familiarity and in language that evokes countless courtly love poems, as well as his own speech in the *Vita nuova*:

> Deh, bella donna, che a' raggi d'amore
> ti scaldi, s'i'vo' credere a' sembianti
> che soglion esser testimon del core.
> *(Purg.* 28.43–45)

(Pray, fair lady, who do warm yourself at love's beams, if I may believe outward looks which are wont to be testimony of the heart.)[2]

Recognizing the condition (if not the identity) of this genius loci, he observes how the lady's entire being is radiant with the signs of *amor*. But if he is able to discern the testimony of her heart simply by reading the unmistakable "sembianti" of a woman in love—if he knows fire when he sees it—the fact remains that the object of her affection is unknown to him. He can read her face, but cannot interpret what he sees written there. And so, with the crystal stream of Lethe still separating them, he asks her to come closer—not so he can see her better but so he can hear what she is singing ("tanto ch'io possa intender che tu canti," v. 48). He longs to understand the text of her song, which presumably will name the love that so enthralls her.

Despite our knowledge that this place is Eden, and therefore beyond the vicissitudes of all other earthly landscapes, the extent to which the Garden is a secular (not to say pagan) literary construct poses certain problems. The use of Golden Age conventions inevitably introduces the notion of a paradise that is bound to be lost. The Arcadias of literature can never entirely conceal their death's head, nor does pastoral ever exclude a foreboding of its own evanescence or destruction. To be sure, such mortal realities have been expelled from Eden, along with Adam and Eve. But because they are implicitly inscribed within the literary landscape, it is impossible not to experience them as somehow present here, if only in our collective experience as readers.

Hardly less problematic is Dante's appropriation of the *locus amoenus* as a setting not only for Eden but also for romance. The "donna soletta," whom the pilgrim sees warming herself with love's beams, may well recall the chaste Astrea or Eve before the Fall, as has been suggested by astute commentators on these cantos.[3] But we are quite as likely to make other postlapsarian associations that are equally supported by the canto's intertextual range, if not by the context of Eden. This is to say that the profane literary components that Dante incorporates within his divine forest carry with them certain expectations as to what the "dolce gioco" ("sweet sport," 28.96) of such a bower will turn out to be. After all, the charms of its landscape—from shade to birdsong to meadows of flowers—are the very same delights that have inspired the erotic dalliance of other literary gardens where the rays of love warm in ways quite different from those intended for Eden. Such bowers of bliss can also be woods of trial and error; indeed, they usually are. Thus, while it seems clear that the poem sets up a contrast between the pilgrim's imperiled confusion in the dark wood of its first canto and his secure plunge here into Eden's "selva antica,"[4] it is also true that the reader is likely to bring some degree of prurient expectation into this forest's "ombra perpetüa" ("perpetual shade," *Purg.* 28.32).

If we find this double message implicit in the topoi Dante uses to construct his Eden, so too is it suggested by the selection of particular words in the pilgrim's address to Matelda. There is, for instance, his choice of the verb *disviare*—meaning to drive away, put off course, lead astray—in order to describe the initial shock of Matelda's appearance as "cosa che disvia / per maraviglia tutto altro pensare" ("a thing that for wonder drives away every other thought," vv. 38–39).[5] Because the pilgrim has completed his purgation and is free to follow his pleasure, the reader knows that this must be an innocent use of the word. And yet "disvia" is not without its shadows; in fact, its employment elsewhere in the poem is most often negative, as when Marco Lombardo says in *Purgatorio* 16, "se 'l mondo presente disvia, / in voi è la cagione, in voi si cheggia" ("if the present world goes astray, in you is the cause, in you let it be sought," vv. 82–83), or when the poet of *Paradiso* bids the "milizia del ciel" ("soldiery of Heaven") to pray for "tutti svïati dietro al malo essemplo" ("those who have gone astray . . . following the ill example," *Par.* 18.124, 126).

More alarming still is the extent to which Dante uses an altogether profane poem by Guido Cavalcanti to serve as an extended subtext for the pilgrim's encounter with Matelda.[6] The ballad "In un boschetto trova' pasturella" ("In a Little Grove I Found a Shepherdess") tells, in the first person, of a man who comes upon a woman of surpassing beauty, singing as though she were in love ("cantava come fosse 'nnamorata," v. 7), and walking through a forest all alone ("che sola sola per lo bosco gia," v. 12). The man who meets her decides immediately that he wants to take joy ("gio' pigliare," v. 18) from the shepherdess, who just as instantly responds to his request by leading him deeper into the woods, where he "seemed to see the god of love" ("che 'l die d'amore mi parea vedere," v. 26). This witty *pastorella*, an Italian version of what was originally a Provençal genre, plays with and against the more elevated conventions of courtly love. Its "lady" is neither noble nor inaccessible; indeed, when asked for an embrace, she offers a great deal more—"di tutto piacere" ("everything pleasant"). The extraordinary extent to which Dante has recalled Cavalcanti's work in *Purgatorio* 28, making use of verses from each of its stanzas and incorporating numerous elements of its style, argues that its frank eroticism is somehow meant to be perceived within Dante's "divina foresta." Once again, of course, we are meant to recognize that Eden offers a different kind of grove from Cavalcanti's and understand that Matelda's rays of love are of another order entirely. The pilgrim is not astray in the "selva antica," nor does an amorous Matelda divert him "in boschetto." Nonetheless, the intertextual power of Cavalcanti's ballad is such as to keep us mindful not only of the ease with which an earthly paradise can be lost but also of how it can be profaned. The recognition of the lyric subtext is unsettling.

Underwriting Dante's composition of Eden at an even deeper level than Cavalcanti, however, is the premier authority on the Golden Age and the absolute master of woodland romance and seduction—the poet Ovid.[7] In keeping with the practice of concealing Ovid throughout the *Commedia*, no mention is made of his name when Matelda speaks of those who "anticamente poetaro/l'età de l'oro e suo stato felice" ("in olden times sang of the Age of Gold and its happy state," *Purg.* 28. 139–40), despite the fact that his account in *Metamorphoses* 1.89–112 provides the very details of the paradise to which she draws our attention. Nor does Dante follow the example of Brunetto Latini's allegorical *Il tesoretto*, whose eponymous "pilgrim," at the end of his journey, enters "un bel prato / fiorito d'ogni lato" ("a beautiful meadow flowering on every side," vv. 2201–2) only to come upon the richly clad person of "ovidio maggiore" (v. 2359). This is an Ovid who teaches Brunetto the knowledge of love ("e lo bene e lo male") and then liberates him from the momentary paralysis that follows this instruction:

Ma ovidio per arte
mi diede maestria,
si ch'io trovai la via
ond' io mi traffugai;
(*Il tesoretto*, vv. 2390–93)

(But Ovid through artistry
Gave me the mastery,
So that I found the way
From which I had strayed.)[8]

At this point Brunetto takes leave of the ancient poet, after being put back by him on "la via/ond' io mi traffugai" ("the way from which I had strayed"). Thanks to Ovid he returns devoutly to God and the saints, vowing to confess his sins to the appropriate friars, and thus to bring his "libretto" to a quick conclusion.

The *Commedia* chooses quite another way to situate Ovid in Eden's "bel prato." Neither invoking him by name nor making him a character, Dante presents him nonetheless by means that are all the more striking for being indirect. By making two references to the *Metamorphoses* and one to the *Heroides*—references that occur in rapid succession within the short course of nine *terzine* (vv. 49–75)—the pilgrim attempts to bring Matelda into focus through the poetry of "ovidio maggiore." We come gradually to see her, therefore, not so much through Dante's own eyes as through Ovid's; she is conjured before us as a composite figment of *his* pagan imagination. In part this procedure is of a piece with the *Commedia*'s extensive play with intertextuality: this suite of three allusions shows how Ovid gave Dante a cast of characters and scores of plot lines out of which to build his own poem. Yet to trace the Ovidian allusions to their sources is, in fact, to discover how programmatically they *mis*represent the reality celebrated in *Purgatorio* 28. What Ovid can do is help us see what Matelda and her world look like or seem to be; he cannot, on the other hand, tell us what they *are*.

The first of these allusions appears as part of the pilgrim's initial approach to Matelda ("Deh, bella donna . . . ," vv. 43–51). Speaking across Lethe, which flows "bruna / sotto l'ombra perpetüa" ("dark under the perpetual shade," vv. 31–32), he asks her to come closer so that he can understand what she is singing. Then he says,

> Tu mi fai rimembrar dove e qual era
>   Proserpina nel tempo che perdette
>   la madre lei, ed ella primavera.
> (*Purg.* 28.49–51)

(You make me recall where and what Proserpine was at the time her mother lost her, and she the spring.)

The "where" ("dove") to be recalled here is at once a specific text (*Met.* 5.385–401) and the *locus amoenus* that it describes. But as is so often the case in Dante's intertextuality, the larger context of the allusion is worth reconstructing.

After telling the story of Perseus and Medusa, Ovid turns in the fifth book of the *Metamorphoses* to the arrival of Athena on Mount Helicon, home of the Muses and site of the spring struck open by Pegasus's hoof. At first the goddess admires only the sacred waters of this new fountain, but then her attention is drawn to the larger beauties of the place: "silvarum locus circumspicit antiquarum/antraque et innumeris distinctas floribus herbas" ("then [she] looked round on the ancient woods, the grottoes, and the grass, spangled with countless flowers," vv. 265–66). When the peace of Helicon is disturbed by the chatter of nine magpies, "imitantes omnia picae" ("which can imitate any sound they please," v. 299), the Muses tell Athena about the birds' origin: how the daughters of King Pierus once challenged the Muses to a duel of voices and artistry (v. 310); how their song celebrated the challenge of the Titans and in so doing falsely slandered the Olympian deities; how they were answered by Calliope in her song about Ceres—a portion of which Dante will "remember" in *Purgatorio* 28—and how, finally, the Pierides were judged by the nymphs of Helicon to be the weaker singers. Having lost the contest, they were transformed into magpies, so that "Nunc quoque in alitibus facundia prisca remansit/raucaque garrulitas studiumque inmane loquendi" ("even now in their feathered form their old-time gift of speech remains, their hoarse garrulity, their boundless passion for talk," vv. 677–78). With this retribution *Metamorphoses* 5 comes to a conclusion; the next book goes on to tell the story of Arachne (6.1–144), yet another artistic overreacher.

Availing himself of all these poetic resources—the setting of a mountaintop *silva antiqua*, the development of narrative within narrative, and a sustained reflection on the consequences of artistic arrogance—Dante joins himself in *Purgatorio* 28 to a specific point in Ovid's text. It comes toward the beginning of Calliope's song, when Ceres' daughter, Proserpina, is described in the midst of a green and pleasant Sicilian landscape remarkably similar to the Muses' own Helicon, as well as to the Eden of Mount Purgatory:

Haud procul Hennaeis lacus est a moenibus altae,
nomine Pergus, aquae: non illo plura Caystros
carmina cycnorum labentibus audit in undis.
silva coronat aquas cingens latus omne suisque
frondibus ut velo Phoebeos submovet ictus;
frigora dant rami, tyrios humus umida flores:
perpetuum ver est. quo dum Proserpina luco
ludit et aut violas aut candida lilia carpit,
dumque puellari studio calathosque sinumque
inplet et aequales certat superare legendo,
paene simul visa est dilectaque raptaque Diti:
usque adeo est properatus amor.

(Met. 5.385–96)

(Not far from Henna's walls there is a deep pool of water, Pergus by name. Not Caÿster on its gliding waters hears more songs of swans than does this pool. A wood crowns the heights around its waters on every side, and with its foliage as with an awning keeps off the sun's hot rays. The branches afford a pleasing coolness, and the well-watered ground bears bright-coloured flowers. There spring is everlasting. Within this grove Proserpina was playing, and gathering violets or white lilies. And while with girlish eagerness she was filling her basket and her bosom, and striving to surpass her mates in gathering, almost in one act did Pluto see and love and carry her away: so precipitate was his love.)

Numerous elements of this Ovidian scene are transposed to *Purgatorio* 28. In addition to the stock charms of the ideal landscape—a woody hilltop, cool shade, water, birdsong, colorful flowers—Dante's bower shares with Ovid's an eternal spring (cf. "qui primavera sempre," *Purg.* 28.143, and "perpetuum ver est," *Met.* 5.391). Further, Dante borrows Ovid's technique of description by negative comparison. For example, the device in Ovid's "non illo plura Caystros/carmina cycnorum labentibus audit in undis" ("Not Caÿster on its gliding waters hears more songs of swans than does this pool," *Met.* 5.386–87) is also evident in this passage from *Purgatorio*:

> Tutte l'acque che son di qua più monde,
> parrieno avere in sé mistura alcuna
> verso di quella, che nulla nasconde.
> *(Purg.* 28.28–30)

(All the waters which here are purest would seem to have some defilement in them, compared with that, which conceals nothing.)

The primary point of Dante's Ovidian remembrance, however, is even more specific. It pertains not only to an atmospheric "where" but also to a particular "when," to a "tempo" when the love-struck god of the underworld first caught sight of Ceres' virgin daughter. Watching Matelda rejoice, as she gathers her flowers and sings her song, the pilgrim recalls the fatal moment when Pluto saw Proserpina—the moment just *before* he delighted in her and carried her away. What the Ovidian subtext highlights, moreover, is the rush of events that proceed from that single look, as Pluto's vision at one and the same time provoked him to delight *and* to rape: "paene simul visa est dilectaque raptaque Diti" (*Met.* 5.395). After this collapse of cause and effect into one line, Ovid sweeps his narrative along, with the terrified Proserpina, her garment torn and her flowers scattered, vainly crying out for her mother as she is abducted to Dis. Alluding to this sequence of events, Dante suggests the aftermath of Pluto's vision in fewer than two lines when he says that Matelda recalls to the pilgrim that other maiden, "nel tempo che perdette/la madre lei, ed ella primavera" ("at the time her mother lost her, and she the spring," *Purg.* 28.50–51). With the verb "perdette" brought to the foreground not only by its placement in rhyme position but by being made to describe both Ceres' loss of her daughter and Proserpina's loss of the spring, Dante gives us in miniature the fate of innocence in Ovid's world.

The effect of the pilgrim's remembrance is to import a set of tragic expectations into Eden's "onesto riso e dolce gioco" ("honest joy and sweet sport," v. 96). It suggests that from Dante's vision of Matelda, delight—and also rape—will follow. And yet, of course, instead of *visa-dilecta-rapta*, what we find is that Dante, the "Pluto" of *Purgatorio* 28, heeds Ceres' counsel that maidens should be wooed and not raped ("roganda,/non rapienda," *Met.* 5.415–16), while Eden's "Proserpina" actively invites his gaze instead of defending herself against it. For following immediately upon the allusion to *Metamorphoses* 5, Matelda is said to have drawn closer to the shore of Lethe in answer to the pilgrim's bidding. Though her eyes at first avoid direct contact, "non altrimenti/che vergine che li occhi onesti avvalli" ("like a virgin that lowers her modest eyes," *Purg.* 28.56–57), she soon looks at Dante face to face. At this range he can all but make out her song "co' suoi intendimenti." But rather than allowing it to gloss his experience, he turns from the largely *stilnovist* atmosphere of the encounter to offer another Ovidian reference. As above, it is an allusion to a moment just *before* disaster strikes, disconcertingly invoked in a regained paradise that constantly refutes the reader's expectations of a happiness about to be dashed:

> Non credo che splendesse tanto lume
>   sotto le ciglia a Venere, trafitta
>   dal figlio fuor di tutto suo costume.
>   (*Purg.* 28.64–66)

(I do not believe that so great a light shone forth under the eyelids of Venus, transfixed by her son against all his custom.)

Having already likened Matelda to the innocent Proserpina, Dante now compares her to Venus, the same goddess of love who infected Pluto with lust precisely in order that he might undo the maiden's virginity. The reference this time is to *Metamorphoses* 10, and once again the larger context of the specific allusion is of interest. After recounting the loss of Eurydice at the outset of the book, Ovid tells us that Orpheus took refuge on the summit of a hill that spread out into a wide plain green with luxuriant grass ("Collis erat collemque super planissima campi / area, quam viridem faciebant graminis herbae," vv. 86–87). To protect himself from the heat of the sun, he strikes his lyre and brings into being a grove of 26 different species of trees—a tour de force designed not only to reveal the power of Orpheus but to demonstrate Ovid's ingenuity in outdoing the more restrained Virgilian *locus amoenus*.[9]

Within the dense grove his music has brought forth, Orpheus then invokes the Muses to help him sing the songs of boys beloved of the gods and "inconcessisque puellas/ignibus attonitas meruisse libidine poenam" ("maidens inflamed by unnatural love and paying the penalty of their lust," vv. 153–54). Toward the end of his recital, after singing about the birth of Adonis from the incestuous union of Myrrha and her father, he tells how one day Venus was accidentally grazed by the arrow of her son Cupid; how, being captivated by the appearance of the singularly beautiful Adonis, she was then consumed by the same passion customarily inflicted on others. Once "natum" ("wounded," v. 527), the goddess forsakes her customary haunts, preferring Adonis even to heaven ("caelo praefertur Adonis," v. 532) and dallying with him in the shade of a poplar tree, whose "torum caespes" ("grassy turf," v. 556) conjures up yet another pleasant grove. Cradling his head in her lap, Venus warns her beloved against the dangers of wild beasts that roam through the forest that surrounds their bower. But with an irony typical of Ovid, the goddess's warning turns out to presage the death of Adonis, who shortly thereafter is gored by the tusk of a wild boar. Venus discovers his body in a pool of blood, and vowing that cruel fate should not have the last word, she transforms his blood into a red anemone as a consolation for her loss. Her claim is that the blossom will be a "monimenta . . . / semper" (vv. 725–26). Yet as Ovid reminds his readers immediately at the close of Orpheus's song, the anemone is a notoriously fragile blossom, "namque male haerentem et nimia levitate caducum / excutiunt idem, qui praestant nomina, venti" ("for the winds from which it takes its name shake off the flower so delicately clinging and doomed too easily to fall," vv. 738–39). The flower's *semper* is at best only seasonal.

Whereas Dante's first Ovidian recollection portrays Matelda as a maiden about to be carried off to Hades, this second speaks of her as "traffita" (*Purg.* 28.65), transfixed, by a passion that, for all its incandescence, cannot forestall death. As she walks toward the pilgrim across a carpet of red and yellow flowers, "in su i vermigli e in su i gialli" (v. 55), his remembrance of these two passages from the *Metamorphoses* brings to mind the loss of eternal spring and the ephemeral reality of flowers "doomed too easily to fall." To be sure, the Edenic context resists these literary associations, which are as incongruous here as the sound of a dirge played at a wedding. But as if deliberately to heighten this incongruity, Dante adds yet another recollection of Ovidian discord and loss. As Matelda smiles radiantly on the other side of Lethe, arranging in her hands flowers that bloom in this earth "sanza seme" ("without seed," v. 69), the pilgrim sees her configured yet a third time in the framework of Ovid's poetry:

> Tre passi ci facea il fiume lontani;
>   ma Elesponto, là 've passò Serse,
>   ancora freno a tutti orgogli umani,
> più odio da Leandro non sofferse
>   per mareggiare intra Sesto e Abido,
>   che quel da me perch' allor non s'aperse.
> (Purg. 28.70–75)

(The river kept us three paces apart, but Hellespont where Xerxes passed it—ever a curb on all human pride—did not suffer more hatred from Leander for its swelling waters between Sestos and Abydos than that from me because it did not open then.)

As with the other allusions, this similitude in its comparison of Matelda and Dante to Hero and Leander imports the tumult of eros (not to say tragedy) into the innocence of the Garden. Dante's source for the story is most likely the exchange of letters between the doomed lovers of *Heroides* 18 and 19. It is Leander who writes first, telling Hero that he must wait out the storm that makes impossible his nightly swim to Sestos. Knowing that he risks her anger, he asks her to be patient and says that he sends the letter in lieu of himself ("interea pro me pernoctet epistula tecum," 18.217). Hero, on the other hand, cannot rest ("non patienter amo," 19.4); she is consumed both by jealousy ("quis enim securus amavit?" "for who that loved was ever free from care?" 19.109) and by erotic desire ("ponuntur medio cur mea membra toro?" "why must I lay my limbs in the mid space of my couch?" 19.158). Her epistle's strategy is to lure him, raging storm or no, into the sea—and to her bed: "Quod timeas, non est! auso Venus ipsa favebit, / sternet et aequoreas aequore nata vias" ("There is naught for you to fear! Venus's self will smile upon your venture; child of the sea, the paths of the sea she will make smooth," 19.159–60). The letter ends with a hope that the waves will soon be broken and peace be near. Given the epistolary format of the *Heroides*, Ovid can say no more than this. He must rely on his readers to remember that the woman's prayers (and Venus's protection) are all in vain. Leander soon drowns in the same raging Hellespont that also claims Hero's body in the end.

For a third time, then, Dante asks us to recall another romantic disaster and to anticipate another Fall. With his appropriation of this tale from the *Heroides*, however, he has left behind the world of the *Metamorphoses* and the consolations it extends occasionally to the gods. For while every year Proserpina may regain her mother (and the world the spring), and while Venus may comfort herself with the transformation of Adonis's blood into a flower's *monimenta semper*, Hero and Leander are mortals whose love leads them tragically (and only) to death. Separated forever, they seem proof that many waters can, in fact, quench love.

Charles Singleton, in confronting this suite of glaringly inappropriate Ovidian similitudes—superimposed as they are upon the profane subtext of Cavalcanti's *pastorella*—has suggested that Dante is inviting the reader to "recognize a familiar focus for one kind of allegory." Since Matelda is neither a ravished Proserpina nor a lovestruck Venus, nor the purged pilgrim a Pluto or a Leander possessed by sensual passion, Singleton says the poem is "doing its calculated work"; that is, its subtexts and similes (like the lush eroticism of the Song of Songs) force the reader to recognize that what seems to be, cannot be. We must look beyond the literal level of the text for the allegorical meaning hidden within it. Discarding the Ovidian erotic surrounding Matelda's appearance as if it were so much chaff, therefore, Singleton argues that we are meant instead to go to the canto's kernel of significance. What looks like the beginning of romance or seduction is a false appearance designed to make us read more spiritually. Rather than as some Leander longing for his carnal lover, the pilgrim should be seen as one who desires what Matelda "figures" in the *Commedia*: "that innocence and rectitude which Adam once had here in Eden."[10]

An approach of this kind simplifies our reading of the canto by reducing the complexity of Ovidian reference to an allegorical strategy. The allusions form an elaborate sign indicating that "since the literal may not be, we [must] look beyond, for other meaning."[11] Unfortunately, by treating the poem in this way we forfeit the richer poetic experience that Matelda's elaborate appearance seems quite deliberately to provoke. To take Dante's intertextuality more seriously by taking it more literally is not to argue that the pilgrim has succumbed to an erotic compulsion in keeping with Ovid's poetic universe and thereby earned himself another round on the terrace of lust. It is, rather, to see that in addition to whatever allegorical significance may be present here, the poem is also doing its "calculated

work" precisely on the *literary* level, by providing us in this complex inter-
textual moment with a sustained reflection on the nature of literature, the
poetic imagination, and the ancient master of *ars amatoria.*

As we observe the pilgrim watching Matelda, we are shown how his
mind is flooded with all that has been dreamed "in Parnaso." What he
remembers—about gardens, and women, and the men who are drawn to
them by the warmth of love's beams—comes to him (as to us) filtered
through a variety of literary texts. Indeed, as we observed above, *Purgatorio*
28 functions almost as a retrospective on poetry from ancient times until
Dante's own present. But it is also evident that Matelda is brought quite
specifically into focus within the lens of *Ovid's* art. As each of the Ovidian
identities projected upon her proves not only inadequate but also false, the
cumulative effect is to discredit their source. Indeed, it is almost as if, in the
course of Dante's misprision of Matelda, Ovid comes to be identified with
the postlapsarian imagination itself. The pilgrim's reliance on Ovid's com-
posite witness of loss seems to expose that poet's vision as a distortion of
this Edenic reality, an erroneous set of experiences and expectations from
which the pilgrim is being delivered. His climb up the mountain is, in fact,
a liberation from such an inheritance, so that by the end of his ascent his
will ("arbitrio") once again can be made like Adam's in creation, "libero,
dritto e sano" ("free, upright, and whole," 27.140). For him no longer to be
conformed to the sins of this world, however, does not mean that his mind
is instantly renewed, nor a lifetime of reading forgotten. The springs of
Parnassus are not purified so easily. And so, standing on the shore of Lethe
but not yet washed in its flood, he sees Matelda not as she is but as earth's
memory might represent her, as she might be construed within the litera-
ture of a fallen creation—as Ovid might see her.

It is surely striking that, after introducing us to Matelda by means of
three Ovidian projections upon her—that is, after having introduced her in
terms of what she is *not*—Dante finally should have his "donna soletta"
come into her own by means of an altogether different order of intertextual
reference. Breaking through the literary framework of the pilgrim's percep-
tion, she reveals herself with a smile—and with a Scripture:

> "Voi siete nuovi, e forse perch' io rido,"
>   cominciò ella, "in questo luogo eletto
>   a l'umana natura per suo nido,

maravigliando tienvi alcun sospetto;
  ma luce rende il salmo *Delectasti*,
  che puote disnebbiar vostro intelletto.
E tu che se' dinanzi e mi pregasti,
  dì s'altro vuoli udir; ch'i' venni presta
  ad ogne tua question tanto che basti."
                    (*Purg.* 28.76–84)

("You are newcomers," she began, "and, perhaps, why I am smiling in this place chosen for nest of the human race some doubt holds you wondering; but the psalm *Delectasti* gives light that may dispel the cloud from your minds. And you that are in front, and did entreat me, say if you would hear more, for I have come ready to all your questions till you are satisfied.")

Matelda recognizes newcomers ("nuovi") when she sees them, and greets the strangers with a smile they will later return, at the close of the canto, when she links this "luogo eletto" to the dreams of ancient poets. She has, of course, been smiling throughout her encounter with the pilgrim; but her smile contrasts with the troubled associations her amorous appearance has inadvertently inspired him to make. This contrast between who she is and how he has perceived her, between the nature of her Garden and that of the Ovidian bowers he has recalled, is elucidated throughout the rest of the canto as we are led to see the extent to which secular literature has, in fact, *not* prepared him for this experience. But from the very outset of her response to Dante, and in order to satisfy all his questions about her, Matelda must rewrite the scenario in which she has been (mis)placed. And so, in order to lift the darkness of the pilgrim's mind, the clouded understanding that he shares with "quelli ch'anticamente poetaro" (v. 139), she offers all three poets—Virgil, Statius, and Dante—the light of interpretation. She teaches them how to "read" her.

To begin, she identifies the *locus amoenus* in which they stand as the Garden of Eden, lest they be held by "alcun sospetto" ("some doubt," v. 79) as to why she is smiling in the midst of what might otherwise be taken as a stage set for Ovidian disaster. It is true, of course, that this primordial bower sustained the cataclysm of a Fall, as *Purgatorio* 32 will soon recall. But even as the griffin is seen there to renew the life of humanity's "pianta dispogliata" ("tree stripped," 32.38), and in so doing to proclaim the restoration of paradise lost, so here Matelda's smile looks beyond the loss of Adam and Eve to the renewal brought about by Christ. She smiles with knowledge that "goes beyond tragedy to a sort of Christian romance."[12]

Romance, moreover, is precisely what is being redefined in *Purgatorio* 28. Having been perceived by the pilgrim as a woman warmed by *amor*'s beams, as a "donna innamorata" (29.1), Matelda chooses now to disclose the truth not only about the Garden but about her love. From the beginning of his approach, the pilgrim has wanted to understand ("intender," 28.48) what she is singing, to catch the meanings ("intendimenti," v. 60) of her "dolce suono" ("sweet sound," v. 59), and in so doing to learn how or with whom she is enamored. At last she makes her revelation. Rather than giving her song to him directly, however, she provides him with a biblical gloss: "ma luce rende il salmo *Delectasti*,/che puote disnebbiar vostro intelletto" (vv. 80–81). *Delectasti* is offered as a satisfaction to the *stilnovist* suitor who first entreated her, and a "salmo" reveals her song. Citing not the *incipit* of Psalm 91 but the word that opens its fifth (and most familiar) verse, Matelda in effect reorients the pilgrim away from Ovid's poetry by referring him instead to a biblical text:

> 1 A Psalm. A Song for the Sabbath. 2 It is good to give praise to the Lord: and to sing to thy name, O Most High. 3 To shew forth thy mercy in the morning, and thy truth in the night: 4 Upon an instrument of ten strings, upon the psaltery: with a canticle upon the harp. 5 For thou hast given me, O Lord, a delight in thy doings: and in the works of thy hands I shall rejoice. 6 O Lord, how great are thy works! Thy thoughts are exceeding deep. 7 The senseless man shall not know nor will the fool understand these things. 8 When the wicked shall spring up as grass: and all the workers of iniquity shall appear: that they may perish for ever and ever. 9 But thou, O Lord, art most high for evermore. 10 For behold thy enemies, O Lord for behold thy enemies shall perish: and all the workers of iniquity shall be scattered. 11 But my horn shall be exalted like that of the unicorn: and my old age in plentiful mercy. 12 My eye also hath looked down upon my enemies: and my ear shall hear of the downfall of the malignant that rise up against me. 13 The just man shall flourish like the palm tree: he shall grow up like the cedar of Libanus. 14 They that are planted in the house of the Lord shall flourish in the courts of the house of our God. 15 They shall still increase in a fruitful old age: and shall be well treated. 16 That they may shew that the Lord is righteous and there is no iniquity in him.

We are told in Genesis 2:15 that God placed Adam in Eden's "paradiso voluptatis" with a task: "ut operaretur, et custodiret ilium" ("to dress it, and to keep it"). Through Matelda's citation of this sabbatical psalm, Dante in effect suggests what that prelapsarian "work" might have been. He gives us the figure of an unfallen Eve, passing through the Garden "cantando e scegliendo fior da fiore" ("singing and culling flower from flower," *Purg.* 28.41), engaged in a labor of love that utterly fulfills her. Her gathering (*deligo, deligere*) is none other than her delight (*delecto, delectare*).[13] Here work and play come together in a single act of pleasure, for to tend this Garden means to be possessed of a passionate delight in the being of the Creator, whose attributes—*misericordia, veritas, cognitationes profundae*—are all made known in the works of his hand. The luxuriant bounty of Eden is what Matelda will go on to describe for the rest of the canto, in details that (as noted above) take us back quite specifically to Ovid's account of the Golden Age. But by using the gloss of the psalm at the outset of her guided tour, Dante makes it clear that the importance of his earthly paradise lies less in its appearances ("sembianti," v. 44) than in its meaning ("intendimenti," v. 60); that is, lies less in its status as the premier *locus amoenus* than in its testimony to the Creator. While Dante's ancient predecessors celebrated the material extravagance of an earth that once gave everything for nothing, the song that his Matelda sings renders thanks to the Giver of the gifts.

Nor (to follow the suggestion of the psalm) are those divine gifts to be understood only in terms of the landscape. For the works of God's hand over which Matelda's "salmo" rejoices also include the possibility of the just man ("iustus," Ps. 91:13), represented for us in *Purgatorio* 28 both by the newly purged pilgrim and by Statius. As it does to all the redeemed who have worked their way to the summit of the mountain, Eden offers them eternal spring and abundant beauty. But the same Creator who planted the Garden here at the antipodes, and made it attainable only after death, also enables humanity to know an inner or spiritual paradise, a "garden" wherein the just man flourishes like the palm tree and increases like the cedars of Lebanon. According to the psalm, this state can be enjoyed even in our fallen world, where sinners spring up like grass ("sicut foenum," v. 8) and the enemies of God seem to triumph. What it extends, moreover, is the earnest of a still-greater hope: not only that the just will survive in the midst of adversity, but that they shall be planted forever "in domo Domini" (v.

14), where they may continue to grow and always bear fruit ("Adhuc multi-
plicabuntur in senecta uberi et bene patientes erunt," v. 15). God grants to
the just a paradise within, in the "poco tempo" (*Purg.* 32.100) of the present
time, as well as extending the promise of a fuller life *in paradisum* for
eternity. Thus, insofar as the *Delectasti* of Psalm 91 not only encodes Ma-
telda's delight but reaches out beyond the boundaries of Eden, it reveals a
way to live joyfully even in a fallen world, provided that one is aware, as the
foolish ("vir insipiens," v. 7) and stupid ("stultus," v. 8) are not, how
extensively the creation bears witness to the Creator. In the immediate
context of the Garden, Matelda's Scripture suggests the perspective of
prelapsarian humanity, whereby merely to see a field of flowers is to be in
love with God and to sing his praises. But just as surely, it implies the
possibility of recovering something of that Edenic perspective here and
now; that is, in the reader's own world.

   This same double focus is also to be found in medieval exegetical use of
Psalm 91. Singleton has drawn our attention to Abelard's *Expositio in hexae-
meron*, which in its reflection on the sixth day of creation reminds its
readers that despite the loss of Eden, the beauties of this life—be they song
or sight or smell—are still capable of inspiring love for and praise of the
Creator, "juxta quod eum Psalmista dicit: 'Delectasti me, Domine, in
factura tua, et in operibus manuum tuarum exsultabo'" ("even as the
Psalmist says, addressing Him: 'Delectasti . . . ,'").[14] Whether or not Dante
knew Abelard's commentary, with its significant "proof text" taken from
Psalm 91:5, is uncertain. We can be sure, however, that he was familiar with
Bonaventure's *Itinerarium mentis in Deum* (*The Mind's Road to God*),
which employs Matelda's *Delectasti* to even greater rhetorical advantage. At
the conclusion of his first chapter, after telling his readers that they must
mount from visible reality to that which is purely spiritual and immutable,
Bonaventure asks them to consider the "sevenfold condition" of all crea-
tures. He proposes a contemplation that takes in the full range of being,
until the creation in its totality yields universal testimony to the power,
wisdom, and goodness of God. Unless, of course, the one who surveys the
"things that are made" does not have eyes that see, or ears to hear, or a
tongue to praise, or an intelligence to understand; unless, that is, the one
who contemplates is a fool. Having given this proviso, Bonaventure ends
the chapter with a homiletic charge to the reader:

Open your eyes, therefore, attend with your ears, open your lips, and apply your heart, in order that you may see your God in all creatures, may hear Him, praise Him, love and adore Him, magnify Him and honor Him, lest the whole world rise against you. For on this account the whole world will fight against the unwise [Prov. 5:21]; but to the wise there will be matter for pride, who with the Prophet can say, "Thou hast delighted me, O Lord, in thy doings: and in the works of thy hand I shall rejoice exceedingly" [Ps. 91:5]. "How great are thy works, O Lord, thou hast made all things in wisdom; the earth is filled with thy riches" [Ps. 103:24].[15]

"Ut in omnibus creaturis Deum tuum videas, audias, laudes, diligas colas, magnifices et honores." With this string of joyful imperatives, Bonaventure bids his audience to dispel the cloud from their minds (to recall Matelda's "disnebbiar," *Purg.* 28.81): "that you may see your God in all creatures, may hear Him, praise Him, love and adore Him, magnify and honor Him." He asks them to live in the world as Adam and Eve must once have lived in the Garden, in love with the one in whom all things consist.[16]

In *Purgatorio* 28, we see Matelda warm herself with the beams of love. Mistaken by the pilgrim for a succession of Ovidian heroes, she is in reality the embodiment of an altogether different kind of romance—one that Dante will continue to explore in the 30th canto, as our attention passes on to Beatrice and the poem continues its purgation of poetry. But quite as important as realizing what Matelda is not is the recognition of what she is: no "pastorella" dallying in the meadow of male fantasy but a psalmist in her own right, whose *carmen perpetuum* (unlike Ovid's) is a celebration of a divine beloved; whose work is to make songs ("psallere," Ps. 91:2) for God: "In decachordo, psalterio, / Cum cantico, in cithara" (Ps. 91:4). Like the Edenic birds, which never ceased to practice their art ("lasciasser d'operare ogne lor arte," *Purg.* 28.15),

> ma con piena letizia l'ore prime,
>   cantando, ricevieno intra le foglie,
>   che tenevan bordone a le sue rime,
>   (*Purg.* 28.16–18)

(but singing . . . greeted the morning hours with full joy among the leaves, which kept such burden to their rhymes),

Matelda expresses her delight in the Maker's *opera* by joining her voice to that of nature, by practicing her own art. Through what amounts to the "mixed media" of dance and song and lyric, she makes her creaturely response to the Creator precisely through artistic creation.[17] In so doing, she not only suggests what Adam and Eve might have done before the Fall but also presents us with the possibility that music and lyric—the work of human art—can continue to serve as a form of worship.

If this is indeed the case, then there could be no more fitting gloss to her vocation in the Garden than the text of Psalm 91, epitomized in the single verb she cites, *Delectasti*. For what we find in the Scripture she alludes to is a raison d'être for the psalmist's own art, a miniature *ars poetica* that underwrites the offering of praise "cum cantico, in cithara"; that underwrites, in fact, the enterprise of Dante's own "poema sacro" (*Par.* 25.1). In every case—be it Matelda's undisclosed song, David's psalm, or the poet's hundredfold "canto"—what we are being asked to consider, as distinct from the works of "quelli ch'anticamente poetaro," is the possibility of a "scripture" so unexampled in literature that Dante must invent a word to name it: "tëodia" (*Par.* 25.73).

While *Delectasti* is a scriptural word, the notion of text as delectation is by no means foreign to the *Commedia*'s sustained reflection on the power of all writing, its own included. Nancy Vickers has shown convincingly how in the poem's lexicon the verb *dilettare* and its adjectival cognate *diletto* are associated, at two strategic moments, not only with the act of reading but with aesthetic seduction.[18] In *Inferno* 5, Paolo and Francesca read the story of Lancelot and Guinevere, and without "alcun sospetto" ("any doubt," v. 129)—a phrase Dante repeats only once, in *Purgatorio* 28.79— they take delight in it: "Noi leggiavamo un giorno per diletto" ("One day we read for pleasure," *Inf.* 5.127). The result is disaster: the literature of romance plays into their passion and leads them "ad una morte" ("to one death," v. 106). In *Purgatorio* 10, however, we find an altogether different scenario. As the pilgrim enters the first terrace of purgatory, his attention is caught by a series of bas-reliefs that are intended to be read, left to right, as if they were a serial text. Immediately overwhelmed by their verisimilitude, the pilgrim is enraptured by the "scripts" he sees portrayed there. The word used in summary to describe the pleasure taken in these images is the Italian equivalent of the Vulgate's *delectare*: "Mentr' io mi dilettava di guardare," "While I was taking delight in gazing on the images," vv. 97–98).

Between these two readings of "per diletto," there is a great gulf. In one reading, delectation leads to damnation, while in the other, the delight of reading is the stimulus to praise and transformation. The pilgrim's pleasure in God's handiwork on the terrace increases his love for the divine artist, and as Vickers notes, "by encouraging the penitent to continue his laborious ascent, it advances him toward revelation."[19] It is this latter delight that we find echoed in David's psalm and Matelda's song—two examples of *tëodia*—both of which rejoice in the Book of Nature for the sake of its Creator, the "author" or "craftsman" (*Purg.* 10.99) whose handiwork even the birds praise, night and day.[20]

Given the degree to which Ovid's literary world is shown from the perspective of Eden to form a "selva oscura" of misfired allusions and tragic romance—indeed, to be an anti-*tëodia*—it might be tempting to identify the ancient poet with those mists Matelda refers to when she says to the pilgrim, "purgherò la nebbia che ti fiede" ("I will clear away the mist that offends you," *Purg.* 28.90); that is, to see him as a nightmare to be left behind in Lethe, or at last awakened from once the Scripture has made its clarion call. But this is only partly the case, because in the economy of Dante's poetics of conversion, whatever is rejected is usually first subsumed and then transformed in the *Commedia*'s ongoing metamorphosis of pagan literature. This becomes abundantly clear in the *Paradiso*, where Ovid largely replaces Virgil as dominant Latin subtext. But it can also be observed at the climax of the poem's second canticle. For even as Dante asks us to turn away from the fates of Proserpina, Venus, and Hero in order to turn not only to Matelda but also to Beatrice, it happens that we are not meant to abandon Ovid after all. Instead we are asked to imagine his poetic legacy anew. In *Purgatorio* 30, when the pilgrim's "antico amor" (v. 39) is about to reveal herself to him from the other side of Lethe—in the moment just before their reunion—the poet likens Beatrice's appearance to a misty sunrise:

> la faccia del sol nascere ombrata,
>   sì che per temperanza di vapori
>   l'occhio la sostenea lunga fiata.
>   (*Purg.* 30.25–27)

> (the face of the sun rise shaded, so that through the tempering of vapors the eye sustained it for a long while.)

It is at this moment, perhaps, that we remember the "where" and "when" of Ovid's Proserpina, how every year in the spring she leaves the darkness of Dis to rejoin her mother Ceres in order to restore spring to the earth "ut sol, qui tectus aquosis / nubibus ante fuit, victis et nubibus exit" ("like the sun which, long concealed behind dark and misty clouds, disperses the clouds and reveals his face," *Met.* 5.570–71). In the judgment of the *Commedia*, Ovid may provide a pagan mist meant to be tempered; but from start to finish Ovid sustains the eye and in that way reveals the sun.

CHAPTER 9

Transfiguring the Text

When Matelda concludes her introduction to Eden in *Purgatorio* 28, she offers Virgil and Statius a gracious "corollary" to her speech. It is a garland of praise meant to increase the poets' joy as they discover the original home of human happiness. It is also a respectful recognition of the truth within their dreaming.

> Quelli ch'anticamente poetaro
>   l'età de l'oro e suo stato felice,
>   forse in Parnaso esto loco sognaro.
> Qui fu innocente l'umana radice;
>   qui primavera sempre e ogne frutto;
>   nettare è questo di che ciascun dice.
>   (*Purg.* 28.139–44)

(They who in olden times sang of the Age of Gold and its happy state perhaps in Parnassus dreamed of this place. Here the root of mankind was innocent; here is always spring, and every fruit; this is the nectar of which each tells.)

Hearing these words of praise for *caro-poetaro-sognaro* (to highlight the rhyme words of vv. 137, 139, 141), a smile passes between the two ancient poets that spans the abyss between the paganism of the one and the Christian faith of the other. No doubt we are to experience their reciprocal pleasure here as a continuation of what they shared earlier in *Purgatorio* 22, where Statius confessed how Virgil's Fourth Eclogue, with its description of the Golden Age returned by the birth of a divine child, enabled him to believe the apostolic teachings about Christ's incarnation—a pagan text (*mirabile dictu!*) shedding its unintended light on the otherwise inscrutable pages of Sacred Scripture.

Now, in canto 28, the two ancients (described by Dante as "miei poeti") enjoy a second and related windfall. For what Matelda offers them in her corollary is an affirmation of yet another pagan insight. She tells them that those who fantasized about a Golden Age at the root of human history were, in fact, dreaming the truth. Hearing this news, Virgil and Statius must feel as if they had awakened from the sleep of literature to find the myths and metaphors of olden times to be reality. They learn that their "sogno" is as substantial as the *terra firma* on which they stand, smiling in wonder and delight at the divine comedy of poetic inspiration. Albeit only "in Parnaso," the ancients were able to discern the dim outlines of Eden's paradise.

Among the ancient dreamers, "quelli ch'anticamente poetaro," Virgil himself is surely to be numbered. Although his Fourth Eclogue sang of the return of the Golden Age rather than of its beginning, he nonetheless evoked the happy state that was enjoyed in the "primo tempo umano" (*Purg.* 22.71). But the one poet who deserves Matelda's corollary more than any other is Ovid, whose *Metamorphoses* offered the fullest classical account of the "età de l'oro." Indeed, in his description of the first world's constant spring, its rivers of nectar, and its unblemished human innocence, we find the Latin "undersong" that hums within Matelda's vernacular speech.[1] Virgil and Statius smile in recognition: so Ovid was right after all!

"Forse," "perhaps." Matelda's reluctance to identify the Golden Age completely with Eden warns us against too close an association of the *scriptura paganorum* with the Christian Scriptures. For as even Statius makes clear in his glowing encomium to Virgil, the pagan poets dreamed only for the benefit of those who would come after them; they themselves did not see the truth of what they wrote. Nor were they privy to the prophetic or allegorical significance that renders their texts so efficacious for readers like Statius or Dante, who encounter them in the golden age of grace. Only for Christians does the *Metamorphoses* yield what Ettore Paratore claims to be its primary value for Dante, that is, its value as "the story of humanity from its origin until its providential 'end' in Caesar, and therefore as a reprise, in a minor tone, of the *Aeneid*."[2]

The poet whose work Paratore characterizes here in such lofty terms is very much an Ovid *in bono*. But the *Commedia* affords another perspective on the master of the *Metamorphoses,* a view of him not as a quasi-biblical writer in the same class as Virgil (albeit "nel tono minore") but as a curator of postlapsarian misery whose elegant exploration of distorted shape and lost identity presents us with a poetic model *not* to be followed. I have suggested elsewhere that *Inferno* 24–26 proposes just such a warning in its contrast between Dante's dalliance with Ovidian metamorphosis and his call to a poetics of conversion, a "redeemed rhetoric" in which verbal genius (*ingegno*) finds its motive and sanction in the service of another's Word.[3] In "Watching Matelda" I argued that Ovid's massive presence in *Purgatorio* 28 requires a radical rereading, even a deliberate misinterpretation of the Ovidian sources, if Ovid's text is to yield its "nectar" of truth. Ovid may well have had a true dream of the Golden Age, but at least within Eden the poet of the *Purgatorio* is at pains to remind us of the great divide between pagan metamorphosis and Christian transformation.

A heightened sense of this discontinuity is presented in the penultimate canto of the *Purgatorio,* where, in the course of nineteen lines (32.64–82), Dante gives us a dramatic juxtaposition in two adjacent similes. The first one plunges us into the world of Ovidian dreaming, with its recollection of the lethal slumber of Argus; the other, recalling a moment in the biblical story of the Transfiguration, rouses us from sleep with a shock of evangelical awakening. As well as offering one of the *Commedia's* most striking intertextual shifts, this dynamic contrast takes place at an important narrative transition during Dante's sojourn in Eden. It is a passage whose complexity requires a careful approach.

Earlier in *Purgatorio* 32, the same pageant that brought Dante face to face with Beatrice suddenly turns his attention elsewhere. Wheeling around to the right, the "mystical procession" moves through a landscape described as deserted, "l'alta selva vòta" (v. 31). It is a wood at once magnificent to behold and empty of mortal life—a paradise lost to humankind. When the murmur of "Adamo" breaks the silence, Dante finds himself standing before a leafless tree that seems starkly out of place in this otherwise verdant garden. The tree is despoiled, "dispogliata" (v. 38), as if to emphasize the violence of the primordial act of disobedience that ruined its lush beauty. But Dante also calls it "vedova" ("widowed," v. 50) to suggest another aspect of its loss: the tree was bereft of its spouse even as it was ravaged and despoiled. This "pianta" is, of course, *the* tree, not only the Tree of Knowledge from the biblical Eden (Gen. 2:17)—"whose mortal taste / Brought death into the world, and all our woe" (to recall the opening of Milton's *Paradise Lost*)—but also the arboreal symbol of the human race itself, both lofty in creation and desolate because of Adam's fall.[4]

With the procession stalled before this manifestation of sin and its wages, the reader seems invited to attend a wake, a mournful remembrance of things both distantly past and all too present. Yet what unfolds before our eyes is a very different kind of ceremony—not a funeral at all but a re-marriage or renewal of vows. In a *tableau vivant* of Pauline typology—"For as in Adam all die, so in Christ shall all be made alive" (1 Cor. 15:22)—the griffin, symbolizing Christ, yokes the crossbar of his chariot to the trunk of the barren tree. In so doing, he joins the wood of redemption to that of per-dition, and thereby brings about a spectacular metamorphosis: "s'innovò la pianta,/che prima avea la ramora sì sole" ("the tree was renewed that first had its branches so bare," vv. 59–60). This transformation of death into life is described as a sudden arrival of spring, as if it were part of spring's annual rebirth. In reality, however, it represents a kind of temporal event altogether different from anything in the natural cycle of the seasons—one that is not "in time's covenant." For in this sudden blossoming at the touch of the griffin's crossbar Dante gives us an image of the supernatural intervention of the divine in human affairs. In it we see the restoration of Adam's family tree through Christ's incarnation, death, and resurrection. We see, in other words, all that the Pageant of Revelation has borne witness to and that the griffin symbolically represents. Expressed in the language of rebirth ("si rinovella," "s'innovò"), the transformation of Eden's barren tree into full life gives us the great paradigm of Christian metamorphosis.

Except for the pilgrim, everyone who witnesses the griffin's allegorical reenactment of the story of grace responds to it by singing a hymn. Presum-ably, this music is some kind of Te Deum intended to celebrate the redemp-tion brought about by Christ, the "second Adam." Yet Dante describes it by resort to three negative statements; he can speak of it only in terms of what it is not: "Io non lo 'ntesi, né qui non si canta . . . né la nota soffersi tutta quanta" ("I did not understand the hymn, and it is not sung here . . . nor did I bear to hear the music to the end," 32.61–63). Overwhelmed by an art he cannot "bear to hear," he loses consciousness and falls asleep.

Sleep in itself is nothing new in the second canticle: at roughly nine-canto intervals throughout the *Purgatorio*, Dante demonstrates the vulner-ability of human flesh, the "something of Adam" ("quel d'Adamo," 9.10), that requires him to rest. Three times he falls asleep at night and dreams until he awakens with the dawn. In all three dreams—of the eagle (canto 9), of the Siren (canto 19), and of Leah (canto 27)—he receives an allegorical vision that bears either on what has just taken place or on what is about to happen. Given the regularity of this pattern, the change in canto 32 is striking. Here Dante falls asleep not at night but in the middle of the morning; his sleep results not from his having a natural, mortal body but from hearing too much supernatural music; and, most importantly, he has no dream whatsoever.[5] Instead, while the dreamless pilgrim sleeps, the poet has a memory of Argus, and with it a worry about his own representational task—the impossibility of describing his oblivion.

One might take this latter preoccupation as an anticipation of the *Paradiso*, where the poet repeatedly offers a "confessione d'impotenza,"[6] confiding that such transcendent subject matter defies the powers of his memory and art. One thinks of the opening of the canticle, for instance, where Dante states that he neither knows how nor is able to describe the vision he has had: "ridire/né sa né può" (*Par.* 1.5–6). In that same opening canto we also find the poem's most famous ineffability topos: "Trasumanar significar *per verba* / non si poria" ("The passing beyond humanity may not be set forth in words," vv. 70–71). These disclaimers of linguistic adequacy continue to mount as the poem moves toward its conclusion. Yet the particular interest of *Purgatorio* 32.64–69 has less to do with the poet's overwhelm than with the consequences of Argus's lethal slumber:

> S'io potessi ritrar come assonnaro
>   li occhi spietati udendo di Siringa,
>   li occhi a cui pur vegghiar costò sì caro;
> come pintor che con essempro pinga,
>   disegnerei com' io m'addormentai;
>   ma qual vuol sia che l'assonnar ben finga.
>   (*Purg.* 32.64–69)

(If I could portray how the pitiless eyes sank to slumber, hearing of Syrinx, the eyes whose long vigil cost so dear, like a painter who paints from a model I would picture how I fell asleep; but whoso would, let him be one that can depict slumber well.)

The moment referred to here occurs in Ovid's long saga of Io (*Met.* 1.588–746). After Jupiter has sent Mercury to free the maiden-turned-heifer from the control of Argus, Mercury discovers both guardian and ward in the midst of a richly verdant setting. Disguised as a shepherd, Mercury tries to lull the hundred-eyed Argus with the music of his reed pipe. When music alone is not enough, he turns to story and tells a tale that takes place in yet another "Edenic" setting on Arcadia's cool mountain slopes. He tells how the chaste nymph Syrinx, fleeing Pan's lust, was at the last moment preserved in her chastity by being transformed into a clump of hollow marsh reeds. Gathering those reeds in a bundle at his breast, Pan then finds some consolation in his loss: by sighing into the hollow reeds, he accidentally discovers that he can make music from the "remains" of Syrinx. Delighted by his invention and captivated by the strange music made from his melancholy ("arte nova vocisque deum dulcedine captum," v. 709), he turns the bundle of reeds that once was Syrinx into the ranks of what will come to be called the "Pan pipe." He transforms the nymph he could not possess into an instrument he can play at will. Before Mercury can actually finish this tale, however, Argus falls asleep. The god straight-away severs his drowsing head and consigns the unsuspecting sleeper into a night from which there is no waking: "Arge, iaces, quodque in tot lumina lumen habebas,/exstinctum est, centumque oculos nox occupat una" ("Argus, thou liest low; the light which thou hadst within thy many fires is all put out; and one darkness fills thy hundred eyes," vv. 720–21).

This multilayered episode from the *Metamorphoses* gives us more than another ringing of the changes on the theme of transformation. Mercury's story of Syrinx inevitably heightens our awareness of the power of storytelling itself. So too does the tale that Mercury uses to ensnare Argus, the account of how the reed pipe came into being and how Syrinx was "lost" in Pan's music. Both stories have a basic point in common: the captivating powers of art to charm, distract, disarm, and destroy.[7] If readers of *Purgatorio* 32 do what these embedded allusions to the *Metamorphoses* implicitly ask—that is, if we superimpose Ovid's Argus upon the sleeping form of Dante—the fit between the two turns out to be largely a matter of appearances. This is not to deny some genuine external similarities between these accounts: a densely lush setting, a stream, music, a consciousness overcome by words and music. Otherwise, we are once again put into the contradictory situation noted in *Purgatorio* 28, where none of the Ovidian allusions can do more than superficial justice to Matelda or to Eden; or again in *Purgatorio* 30, where the evocation of Virgil's world of tragic loss simply does not ring true in the midst of the *Commedia*'s vindication of life over death. Dante is no more like Argus captivated by Mercury's song than Matelda is like Proserpina at the moment of her abduction to the underworld, or than Beatrice is Marcellus's double. Rather than suggesting continuity between Dante and Ovid, this suite of negated analogies heightens the contrast between them, draws attention to the rift between the "selva oscura" of classical poetry and the *Commedia*'s "paradise regained." Therefore, as Dante falls safely asleep in Eden, surrounded by the singing of heavenly voices, the recollections of Argus and Syrinx bring us back to the world of deformation and loss that the cantos of Eden have otherwise kept outside the purifying wall of fire. They conjure up a world where the god betrays, the unwitting sleeper becomes his victim, and story lulls the listener into death.[8]

From the nightmare of this Ovidian frame of reference, Dante suddenly wakes at the sound of a single word—"arise!"—which takes the reader out of the *Metamorphoses* and into the New Testament:

> Però trascorro a quando mi svegliai,
>   e dico ch'un splendor mi squarciò 'l velo
>   del sonno, e un chiamar: "Surgi: che fai?"
>   (*Purg.* 32.70–72)

> (I pass on, therefore, to when I awoke, and tell that a splendor rent the veil of my sleep, and a call, "Arise, what are you doing?")

After describing his falling asleep by a reference to the fatal slumber of Argus, Dante comes to his senses at the call of Scripture. For in the phrase "un splendor mi squarciò 'l velo / del sonno" ("a splendor rent the veil of my sleep")—juxtaposed as it is with the command to arise ("Surgi")—what do we find but clear traces of biblical terminology, and with them an evocation of the climactic events of Christ's life from Good Friday to Easter? On the one hand, there is a literal recollection of that moment in the Passion when the veil of the temple was rent in two (Matt. 27:51, Mark 15:38, Luke 23:45); on the other, a verb in the imperative (*surgi*) that is itself emblematic of resurrection. In a single tercet, then, we pass out of the nightmare of Argus's blinding and death to enter another realm of allusion altogether. Ovidian metamorphosis gives way to Christian transfiguration:

Quali a veder de' fioretti del melo
    che del suo pome li angeli fa ghiotti
    e perpetuë nozze fa nel cielo,
Pietro e Giovanni e Iacopo condotti
    e vinti, ritornaro a la parola
    da la qual furon maggior sonni rotti,
e videro scemata loro scuola
    così di Moïsè come d'Elia,
    e al maestro suo cangiata stola;
tal torna' io.

(Purg. 32.73–82)

(As when brought to see some of the blossoms of the apple tree that makes the angels greedy of its fruit and holds perpetual wedding feasts in Heaven, Peter and John and James were overpowered, and came to themselves again at the word by which deeper slumbers were broken, and saw their company diminished alike by Moses and Elias, and their Master's raiment changed, so I came to myself.)

This densely allusive simile begins with the cry to rise up and give account ("Surgi: che fai?"); it ends with Dante's coming to consciousness, expressed in a verb (*tornare*) that recalls numerous other reorientations of his, from the first "mi ritrovai" of the *Commedia*'s prologue scene (*Inf.* 1.2) to this moment at the summit of purgatory ("tal torna' io"). Through a sudden shift in metaphor, the garden paradise in which Dante falls asleep is no longer the pagan grove where Argus met his death; rather, the appropriate intertextual setting is the summit of the biblical Mount Tabor. As Ovid's Arcady dissolves, Christ's Mount of Transfiguration takes center stage.[9]

This crucial moment in gospel history is recorded in all three synoptic Gospels—Matt. 17:1–13, Mark 9:2–9, and Luke 9:28–36—but it is Matthew's version, quoted here (17:1–9), that gives the fullest account:

> 1 And after six days Jesus taketh unto himself Peter and James and John his brother, and bringeth them up into a high mountain apart: 2 And he was transfigured before them. And his face did shine as the sun: and his garments became white as snow. 3 And behold there appeared to them Moses and Elias talking with him. 4 And Peter answering said to Jesus: Lord it is good for us to be here: if thou wilt, let us make three tabernacles, one for thee, and one for Moses, and one for Elias. 5 And as he was yet

speaking, behold a bright cloud overshadowed them. And lo a voice out of the cloud, saying: This is my beloved Son, in whom I am well pleased: hear ye him. 6 And the disciples hearing, fell upon their face, and were very much afraid. 7 And Jesus came and touched them: and said to them: Arise, and fear not. 8 And they lifting up their eyes, saw no one, but only Jesus. 9 And as they came down the mountain, Jesus charged them: Tell the vision to no man, till the Son of Man be risen from the dead.

Whereas allusion to Argus was only superficially relevant to Dante—was even a misrepresentation of his actual situation in Eden—the Transfiguration story offers a far more accurate gloss. Just as on Mount Tabor Peter, John, and James were overcome by an unexpected foretaste of glory, until Christ restored them to their senses with the command to arise, "Surgite" (Matt. 17:7), so too on the summit of Mount Purgatory was Dante overcome by a preview of heaven's music—until the sound of the same word, "Surgi" (32.72), here spoken by Matelda, brings him back to his senses.

The Transfiguration story is not the only Scripture text at play in this simile. Dante's blossoming apple tree and perpetual wedding feast link his text first to the "apple tree among the trees of the wood" of Song of Songs 2:3 and then to the "marriage supper of the Lamb" of Apocalypse 19:9.[10] Likewise, when the poet glosses "surgi," "arise," as "la parola / da la qual furon maggior sonni rotti" ("the word by which deeper slumbers were broken" (vv. 77–78), he recalls numerous occasions in the Gospels when Christ used this same word both to resurrect the dead and to heal. The widow's son at Nain (Luke 7:14) and the daughter of the ruler of the synagogue (Mark 5:41, Luke 8:54) were both raised from the dead by the command "arise"; the cripple of Luke 5:24 and the leper of Luke 17:19 were made whole by the same word. According to the book of Acts, moreover, Peter raised up Dorcas from the dead by saying, "Tabitha, surge" (Acts 9:40).

In an almost dizzying show of Dante's debt to Scripture and tradition, therefore, the Transfiguration simile weaves together texts gathered from the entire canon. It forms a layered mass of biblical allusion that joins Testament to Testament, Eden to Apocalypse, and thereby offers the whole sweep of scriptural revelation as a complex analogy to Dante's own experience and identity. Indeed, what is most at stake here is not what happened to Dante at this given moment in the narrative but *who* it is that he is meant to wake up and become—an apostle like Peter, James, and John.

But how is he to be like them? The Transfiguration simile compares Dante quite specifically to the inner circle of the disciples at the moment of their awakening:

> e videro scemata loro scuola
>   così di Moïsè come d'Elia,
>   e al maestro suo cangiata stola;
> tal torna' io.
>
> (*Purg.* 32.79–82)

(and they saw their company diminished alike by Moses and Elias, and their Master's raiment changed, so I came to myself.)

Yet this waking up is not where the biblical story ends. For once the disciples behold Jesus in his unadorned humanity—all alone, without the bright cloud of glory—he charges them to keep everything they have seen and heard a secret: "Tell the vision to no man," Jesus says, "till the Son of Man be risen from the dead" (Matt. 17:9). Having received this charge, they follow their master down the mountain and into Jerusalem, to begin what will be the final chapter of his mortal life.

In the sequence of gospel events, vision leads to action. This move provides the traditional exegete of the Transfiguration with his final homiletic point, the call "to take on the historical task."[11] In a sermon on this text, for instance, Augustine understands the disciples' waking up from sleep to be symbolic of their spiritual rebirth: "When therefore they fell to the ground, they signified for us that we die. . . . When the Lord truly raised them up, it signified the resurrection." He concludes his sermon as follows:

> Come down, to labour in the earth; in the earth to serve, to be despised and crucified in the earth. The Life came down, that He might be slain; the Bread came down, that He might hunger; the Way came down, that He might be wearied in the way; the Fountain came down, that He might thirst; and dost thou refuse to labour? "Seek not thy own." Have charity, preach the truth; so shalt thou come to eternity, where thou shalt find security.[12]

Christ explicitly told his disciples *not* to reveal their vision on the mountain to anyone, "till the Son of Man be risen from the dead" (Matt. 17:9). In the aftermath of the resurrection, however, Augustine is free to command that they take up their cross, follow their master, and "preach the truth." Silence must now give way to speech. And so it does as well in the Second Epistle of Peter (1:16–21), where Peter uses his personal experience of the Transfiguration to guarantee the truth of his own words, the divine origin of everything he has to say:

> 16 For we have not by following artful fables made known to you the power and presence of our Lord Jesus Christ; but we were eyewitnesses of his greatness. 17 For he received from God the Father, honour and glory: this voice coming down to him from the excellent glory: "This is my beloved Son, in whom I am well pleased: hear ye him." 18 And this voice we heard brought from heaven, when we were with him on the holy mount. 19 And we have the more firm prophetical word: whereunto you do well to attend, as to a light that shineth in a dark place, until the day dawn, and the daystar arise in your hearts: 20 Understanding this first, that no prophecy of Scripture is made by private interpretation. 21 For prophecy came not by the will of man at any time: but holy men of God spoke, inspired by the Holy Ghost.

In *Purgatorio* 32, Dante more or less openly appropriates all these ramifications of the Transfiguration story for himself. When he comes to his senses in Eden's version of Mount Tabor, his first concern is to find the one who has been the Christ-event for him: he asks Matelda, "Ov' è Beatrice?" ("Where is Beatrice?" 32.85). Dante finds Beatrice sitting alone on the bare ground, bereft of the griffin and his "company" ("compagnia," v. 88). Then he becomes like the disciples when they, too, recovered their wits and found the scene on Tabor drastically changed: "And they lifting up their eyes, saw no one, but only Jesus" (Matt. 17:18). When Beatrice speaks to Dante, however, it is not as Christ did when he commanded his disciples, "Tell the vision to no man, till the Son of Man be risen from the dead" (Matt. 17:9). Rather, just as Augustine charged his listeners to "come down" from the Transfiguration and openly preach its truth, so she tells Dante to proclaim what he is about to behold: "Ritornato di là, fa che tu scrive" ("what you see, mind that you write it when you have returned yonder," 32.105). Or, as she says again in the final canto of the *Purgatorio*,

> Tu nota; e sì come da me son porte,
>   così queste parole segna a' vivi
>   del viver ch'è un correre a la morte.

E aggi a mente, quando tu le scrivi,
  di non celar qual hai vista.
            (*Purg.* 33.52–56)

(Do you note, and even as these words are uttered by me, so teach them
to those who live the life that is a race to death; and have in mind, when
you write them, not to hide what you have seen.)

Beatrice's command to take up the pen and write has its own scriptural
resonance: it recalls the common charge to Moses and the prophets of
Israel—Isaiah, Jeremiah, Ezekiel—all of whom received some version of the
Word of the Lord as it also came to Habakkuk: "Write the vision and make
it plain upon tables" (Hab. 2:2). Given the intensely apocalyptic context of
these concluding cantos of *Purgatorio*, however, it is most likely John the
Divine we are meant to recall, and especially the commission given to him
before his vision of Dragon, Whore, and Giant: "Write therefore the things
which thou hast seen, and which are, and which must be done hereafter."[13]

The question remains, of course, why anyone should listen to Dante or
believe that what he eventually wrote down is that "more firm prophetical
word" (2 Pet. 1:19) earlier given to the visionaries of the Old and New
Testaments. Once again, the Transfiguration simile suggests the poet's an-
swer. In the gospel account, the disciples hear the voice of God say, "This is
my beloved Son, in whom I am well pleased: hear ye him." With these
words ringing in their ears they fall to the ground, terrified at the sound of
divine speech. Then Jesus tells them to arise and fear not. When they come
to their senses, it is Jesus alone, not Moses and Elias, who confronts them.
Christian exegesis had no doubt about what the disappearance of these
venerable figures signified. As Augustine said in his Transfiguration ser-
mon, "After the resurrection, what is the Law to thee? what Prophecy?
Therefore neither Moses nor Elias is seen. He only remaineth to thee, 'who
in the beginning was the Word, and the Word was with God, and the Word
was God.' "[14] The Law and the Prophets, in other words, had found their
fulfillment in Christ.

"E videro scemata loro scuola" (*Purg.* 32.79): in calling attention to the
moment in the Transfiguration narrative when authority is implicitly trans-
ferred from old to new, Dante's choice of vocabulary suggests that there is
another succession, another change in voices to be listened to. Comparing
himself to the disciples in the instance when they came to their wits and

found Moses and Elias gone—"e videro scemata loro scuola / così di Moïsè come d'Elia"—he brings together two words, *scemata* and *scuola*, that appear together in only one other place in the poem, which also provides an analogous context. In *Inferno* 4, as the pilgrim is led into Dante's version of the Elysian Fields by the one whom he has acknowledged from the first to be his master and author, he encounters Virgil's "bella scola," the august company of Homer, Lucan, Horace, and Ovid. To this group of five, all sharing the superlative "altissimo poeta," he adds himself as sixth, rejoicing in his status as "de la loro schiera" (v. 101). Then the momentum of the journey once again carries him off, and "la sesta compagnia in due si scema" ("the company of six diminishes to two," v. 148).

With the sole exception of its use in *Purgatorio* 32.79, where "scuola" describes the Old Testament precursors of Christ, the word Singleton translates as "company" always denotes what is pagan or in some sense defective—teaching that must be superseded if the pilgrim is to attain the end of his journey. And so we have Limbo's "bella scola" of pagan poetry in *Inferno* 4.94; the limited Virgilian "scola" of *Purgatorio* 21.33; the faulty, perhaps philosophic "scuola" of *Purgatorio* 33.85; and the equivocal teaching of "le vostre scole" that Beatrice denounces in *Paradiso* 29.70. Each of these "schools" represents a partial truth. But as the long course of the poem gives us abundant opportunity to observe, every pre-Christian forerunner, every school of philosophy or genre of poetry, is at most a *praeparatio evangelii*. Like Moses and the prophets, Virgil and Ovid have a place in the curriculum—provided that they are read retrospectively, in light of that life-giving reality which Christ both is and represents. But here too a distinction must be made regarding Ovid. As Kevin Brownlee notes, "salvation does not result from reading the *Metamorphoses*: it is not a salvific text as are the *Aeneid* and the Fourth Eclogue which converted the redeemed Statius."[15]

When Dante brings the Transfiguration story into the extended simile of *Purgatorio* 32, he is primarily making an association between himself and the apostles, not between himself and Christ. Nor does he forge any explicit connection between the departure of Moses and Elias, representing the "Old" Testament, and his own sustained attempt in the *Commedia* to supplant the "bella scola" of ancient poets. Much is left unspoken, hidden between the lines. Still, the ultimate effect of his massive turn to Scripture at the end of the second canticle is to authorize his speech in the "sacred poem," to make the *Commedia* not only one poetic word among others but an utterance that is—as it was later called—"divine." Subtext upon subtext constructs this legitimization, helps Dante to maintain (like Peter himself in his epistle) that he is of the apostles' school, telling *their* truth, offering his readers no "artificial fables" devised by mere poets. To this end, not even Virgil or Ovid could offer this kind of legitimacy. Only Scripture and its divinely inspired authors enable the poet of the *Commedia* to claim for himself at least an echo of what the thunder said on Mount Tabor: "ipsum audite," "hear ye him."

PART 4

Dante and the Saints

CHAPTER 10

Divide and Conquer:
Augustine in the *Commedia*

One of the many surprises in the *Commedia* is the virtual absence of the figure of Augustine. He appears only briefly at the end of the *Paradiso* to take his eternal place in the heavenly rose, directly below the Saints Francis and Benedict (32.35); but while Benedict is encountered at length in the sphere of Saturn (canto 22) and Francis is praised for almost an entire canto by no less an authority than Thomas Aquinas (canto 11), the Bishop of Hippo is merely glimpsed in passing, in the eleventh hour of the poem's penultimate canto. He neither speaks nor is spoken about. It is almost as if, despite his choice seating in paradise, he had been judged to be some minor citizen of the City of God rather than the theologian who described it at such imposing length.

This minimal presentation in the *Commedia* is not what Dante's other works might have led one to expect.[1] At the outset of the *Convivio*, for instance, it is to the Augustine of the *Confessions* that Dante appeals when he seeks a warrant for speaking about the course of his life as moving "di [non] buono in buono, e di buono in migliore, e di migliore in ottimo" ("from not good to good, and from good to better, and from better to best," 1.2)—a curriculum vitae from bad to best that foreshadows the tripartite itinerary of the *Commedia*. In his epistle to Can Grande della Scala, Dante uses Augustine to authorize another kind of boldness: should readers demur at the poet's claims to have been taken up into paradise (as was Paul), let them turn to Augustine's *De quantitate anime* and no longer begrudge Dante the experience ("et non invidebunt").[2] In *Monarchia*, moreover, Dante cites only Augustine by name in referring to those who, although coming after Scripture, nonetheless write with something of its divine inspiration ("Sunt etiam Scripture doctorum, Augustini et aliorum, quos a Spiritu Sancto adiutos," 3.3). Indeed, as Dante's impassioned epistle to the Italian cardinals also argues, the church is bereft of genuine spiritual guidance in following the Bible's teaching precisely because it has thrown Augustine away ("iacet Augustinus abiectus," para. 7).

Yet disposing of Augustine is precisely what the poet himself seems to have done in the *Commedia*. Why this should be true has been the subject of speculation among the relative few who have taken the matter seriously. Some have argued that Dante simply failed to see the importance of Augustine; others have conjectured that Aquinas's Aristotelian bias blinded Dante to the contributions of a Christian Platonist; and at least one has contended that the dictates of a poet's imagination freed Dante from having to account for anyone's presence or absence.[3] It is far more likely, however, that Augustine's eclipse in the *Commedia* has to do with politics—with the political polemic that drives the *City of God* in direct opposition to many of Dante's own convictions. Augustine negated pagan Rome, discredited Virgil, and refused the idea of temporal beatitude as a legitimate human "end." It was his authoritative nay-saying that Dante had to contravene in his own bid to underwrite not only a renewed Roman Empire but a vision of redeemed political life on earth.[4]

But how does one take on so estimable an opponent? Though perhaps too venerable to be confronted directly (much less damned to *Inferno* 34, like Brutus and Cassius, as a traitor to Caesar), Augustine might nonetheless be countered by two strategies. On the one hand, Dante could co-opt his opponent, as he does perhaps most flagrantly in *Convivio* 4.4 and *Monarchia* 2.5, where—without the slightest nod to the real gist of his source—he rewrites Augustine's vilification of the Romans' "greed for praise" (*City of God* 5.12) and turns it into an encomium of the Romans as God's chosen people. On the other hand, he could try to silence the opposition by ignoring it, that is, by writing the person of Augustine out of the narrative of the *Commedia*. This seems at first glance to be exactly what Dante did. The saint who by anyone's estimation should merit at least a canto in the *Paradiso* becomes instead a mere face in the crowd, a name barely mentioned.[5]

What critics have gradually come to recognize, however, is that although Augustine is all but excluded from the narrative surface of the poem, he functions as an extensive, even an informing presence within the text itself. Late in the last century, Edward Moore ended his brief discussion of the two writers by acknowledging that he found himself, despite the paucity of direct Augustinian references in Dante's work, "continually coming on fresh points of resemblance," even though the possible mediation of Aquinas or Bonaventure made it difficult to decide at times exactly who was Dante's primary source.[6] In the last two decades, Moore's intuition of resemblance has moved closer to actual points of identification. To John Freccero in particular goes the credit for having dug deeply into the text of the *Commedia* and come up with buried treasure—not the vague, atmospheric Augustinianism that one might find in almost any medieval work, but examples of concrete linguistic indebtedness that betoken a profound intertextual relation. In several influential essays, he has stressed Dante's deep reliance on the *Confessions*; along with Francis X. Newman and Marguerite Mills Chiarenza, he has also explored the relation between the three modes of vision delineated in Augustine's *De genesi ad litteram* and both the structure and the poetics of the *Commedia*'s three canticles.[7] More recently still, Ronald Martinez, Giuseppe Mazzotta, and Jeffrey Schnapp have each drawn attention to Dante's polemical reading of the *City of God*.[8] All three have explored his vision of history as a radical reworking of both Virgil and Augustine and commented on his creation of a new notion of the earthly city to supplant the quite different constructions of Rome in his two Latin forebears.

What has not yet been noted, however, is the placement of this revision at the center of the *Commedia*. For what we find undergirding *Purgatorio* 13–17 is Augustine's meditation on Cain and Abel taken out of the anti-Roman polemic of *City of God* 15 and translated into Dante's own political vernacular. It is in *Purgatorio* 15, moreover, that Augustine is introduced to us through an unattributed but unmistakable paraphrase of *City of God* 15.5, a text whose description of the *civitas Dei* Dante puts in the mouth of none other than Virgil, the *poeta nobilissimus* whose vision of Rome he so maligned. Thus, although Dante deprives us of the extended Augustinian appearance we might well have expected in paradise, he not only brings Augustine to the surface textually at the heart of the poem but does so through the mediation of Virgil. The maneuver constitutes one of Dante's most outrageous acts of ideological revision, revealing yet another dimension of his will to power over his "authorities"—that is to say, the politics of his poetics.

The Augustine that Dante reinvents in *Purgatorio* 13–17 is not the monastic rule maker glimpsed below Francis and Benedict in the heavenly rose. Rather, he is the great theologian of history, theorist of the earthly city, and, more specifically still, the author of the *City of God.* Halfway through that work, in the fifteenth book of his *magnum opus et arduum,* Augustine takes up the historical development of two branches of humanity, two cities, "one made up of those who live according to men, the other of those who live according to God" (15.1). Here he moves from Eden into history, passing through the "common door of mortality opened up in Adam" to enter the realm of Cain and Abel (15.21). As Adam's offspring, the brothers inherit a common legacy of sin; they are both made from the same condemned lump ("ex eadem oritur quae originaliter est tota damnata," 15.1). But that is where the resemblance ends, for Augustine spins out the ramifications of his work's magisterial either/or precisely in terms of the differences between the two. Cain, the firstborn, represents the flesh; he is what Paul refers to as the "old man," absorbed in things earthly and therefore blind to things divine. By contrast, Abel is the second-born, the "new man" of spiritual regeneration; he is what Paul speaks of as the "vessel of mercy for honor" (Rom. 9.22–23). This antithesis enables Augustine to understand the mystery of God's choice of the younger over the elder in Genesis 4. God received Abel's offering with favor because it was "divided" properly, because Abel had discerned the difference between the goods of the earth and the God who gave them. Cain failed to find favor because— while giving something of his own to God—he gave himself to himself ("dans aliquid suum, sibi autem se ipsum," 15.7). He used God to enjoy the world, losing himself in secondary goods even as he abandoned the source of all goodness.

These familiar Augustinian themes achieve a civic focus in book 15, where Cain is shown to be writ large in the earthly city he founded. The *civitas terrena* refers not so much to any actual urban place as to the "worldly mind" itself. Augustine sees it as the social manifestation of the same love of self (*amor sui*) that caused the expulsion of the rebel angels from paradise and of Adam and Eve from Eden. Like mortality, the spirit of the earthly city is the sinful birthright of Cain and Abel. But whereas Cain builds his life on its premises, treating it not only as his home but as his god, Abel defines himself as an alien sojourner within enemy territory. He lives in the *civitas terrena* as a pilgrim passing through, praying for its peace, perhaps, but always knowing that his citizenship is not on earth but in heaven.

Resorting to a common typology, Augustine sees Christ the Good Shepherd foreshadowed in Abel, the first keeper of sheep: "pastor ovium hominum, quem pastor ovium pecorum praefigurabat Abel" (15.7; see also 18.51).[9] Yet, far more important to the larger purpose of Augustine's polemic is another kind of typology altogether: a blood link between Rome and the city of Cain, both founded on fratricide. Just as Cain murdered his brother out of envy and wrath before making the *civitas terrena* his refuge, so Romulus, overcome by envy, killed Remus and established what became the seat of empire. The Roman imago reflects Cain's archetype (15.5). In each case, in the words Augustine quotes from Lucan's *De bello civili* (1.95), "fraterno primi maduerunt sanguine muri" ("the rising walls of the city were wetted with a brother's blood").

What distinguishes Romulus's crime (and the *civitas terrena* throughout its history) is the refusal of human partnership. To maintain his sovereignty, Romulus eliminated what would have compromised his power: the threat of diminishment by a living partner ("vivo consorte"). Augustine considers this murder Rome's foundational event, the establishment of that *libido dominandi* which in time would make the city not only master of the world but victim of its own might. By refusing partnership, Romulus was choosing what was to become Rome's dead end—its fate to divide and conquer even itself.

Augustine finds no escape from this death wish in Roman history. While he concedes that the city has had its civic heroes and its share of martyrs, he strenuously qualifies their achievement: Roman virtue is at best the sublimation of Roman vice, a higher version of the self-adulation that is the city's "greed for praise and passion for glory" (5.12). Even though the *civitas terrena* can merely refine its concupiscence, however, humanity is not left without an alternative. There is leaven at work within the lump, among those who live on earth looking toward heaven as their standard and whose living therefore reflects the polity of God's kingdom. As an antidote to the cities of Cain and Romulus, Augustine offers the ethos of Abel—the ethos of community itself. Experienced here in part but known fully only in the city that is above and free, this community is a common-wealth "ubi sit non amor propriae ac privatae quodam modo voluntatis sed communi eodemque inmutabili bono gaudens atque ex multis unum cor faciens, id est perfecte concors oboedientia caritatis" ("where there is no love of a will that is personal or, as we may say, private, but a love that rejoices in a good that is at once shared by all and unchanging, a love that makes 'one heart' out of many, a love that is the whole-hearted and harmonious obedience of mutual affection," 15.3).

What makes this *oboedientia caritatis* possible is the right priority of love. Abel chose God, not himself, as his good; in so doing, he fixed on the only object of desire that others can share without rivalry or fear of loss. Not only can they share such a love, they can actually increase it by doing so. Less can become more, and living partnership can be, not a compromise of power, but a source:

> Nullo enim modo fit minor accedente seu permanente consorte possessio bonitatis, immo possessio bonitas, quam tanto latius quanto concordius individua sociorum possidet caritas. Non habebit denique istam posses-sionem qui eam noluerit habere communem; et tanto eam reperiet am-pliorem quanto amplius ibi potuerit amare consortem. (*City of God* 15.5)

> (A man's possession of goodness is in no way diminished by the arrival, or the continuance, of a sharer in it; indeed, goodness is a possession enjoyed more widely by the united affection of partners in that possession in proportion to the harmony that exists among them. In fact, anyone who refuses to enjoy this possession in partnership will not enjoy it at all; and he will find that he possesses it in ampler measure in proportion to his ability to love his partner in it.)

By converting the very notion of possession from the exclusive to the corporate, Augustine turns a cause of strife into the source of concord; he shows how one heart can be made out of many. What he also does, of course, is stand the values of the earthly city upside down. Pointing past the obsession with lesser goods that characterizes the children of Cain, he upholds the "possessio bonitatis" as itself the highest good. It alone is the source of real power, power that is not lessened with sharing but that indeed must be shared to be possessed at all. The prizing of this love of goodness above everything else makes concord instead of antagonism, abundance instead of want—and all because the end of such desire is divine and thus infinite. To share true love is in fact to multiply it. This discovery makes it possible to imagine a new order of *civitas* entirely, one in which partnership, the concept that pervades this text, is not only possible but necessary. *Consortio* constitutes the kingdom. This, says Augustine, is what Abel bore witness to, what Cain could not bear, and what Romulus never knew: "the united affection of partners in possession."

The passage just quoted from the *City of God*, together with the extended analysis of the *civitas terrena* that surrounds it, underwrites the central cantos of the *Purgatorio*. It is there, on the terraces of envy and wrath in cantos 13–17, that Dante gives his own account of how former citizens of Cain's city become fellow travelers with Abel. *Amor sui* having been formally renounced on the terrace of pride (cantos 10–12), Dante turns to explore the social dimensions of regeneration, the means of transforming *civitas* itself. What one finds in these cantos are pilgrims preparing themselves for life in the city of God, for partnership in goodness, by learning to reject the values Augustine associates with the earthly city.

The terraces accomplish this change of citizenship through a program of positive and negative exempla not unlike those in the *City of God*, whose stark contrast between the two cities Augustine sustains from start to finish, implicitly asking his readers to choose between them. On every terrace Dante opposes exempla of virtue to those of vice, as if to dramatize within the history of the earthly city, both biblical and pagan, the perennial choice of one *civitas* or another. His exempla of virtue, which mark the beginning of each stage of purgation, act as "cords of the whip drawn from love" to urge the penitents on toward the expiation of the contrary sin (13.39). Exempla of vice, in contrast, function as sin's "curb" at the end of the process (13.40).

On the terraces of envy and wrath, Cain is the paradigmatic curb to *invidia*, while a New Testament version of Abel is the final spur to mercy. Thus the envious hear a voice crying out, "Anciderammi qualunque m'apprende" ("Everyone that finds me shall slay me," 14.133). The cry is a translation of the one Cain utters in Genesis 4:14 ("omnis igitur qui invenerit me, occidet me"), after he realizes his status as a fugitive and before he builds himself a city of refuge ("et aedificavit civitatem," 4:17). Later on, in canto 15, standing in chiastic relation to Cain on the terrace of wrath— standing, that is, as the last spur to virtue rather than as the first curb to vice—is a vision of Stephen, "primus martyr pro nomine Christi," who offers a New Testament fulfillment of his prototype Abel, "in martyrio primus." Portrayed at the moment of his death at the hands of an angry Jerusalem mob, Stephen sinks down to the earth but keeps his eyes turned upward to the gates of heaven ("ma de li occhi facea sempre al ciel porte," *Purg.* 15.111), asking God to pardon his persecutors. In a reenactment of Christ's forgiveness on the cross, he answers their stones ("pietre," v. 107) with prayers for divine mercy ("pietà," v. 114). The entire scene (vv. 106–14) is not only a reprise of the biblical account of Acts 7 but a miniature of the conflict Augustine develops at length: a picture of the earthly city hurling itself in wrath against the city of God but finding its hatred answered by love. The mob's cry to kill—"Martira, martira!" (v. 108)—coupled with the martyr's plea for "pietà" presents both the impulse to destroy the good that forever haunts the city of Cain and the transcendence of that hatred through the act of forgiveness that Augustine identifies as the mark of the city of God in pilgrimage. Murder here becomes martyrdom, for Stephen as for Abel before him.

This turn from one notion of *civitas* to another, presented in the *Purgatorio* by the progress from Cain to Abel-Stephen, is dramatized further on these terraces through a series of encounters and interventions. When the pilgrim first approaches a company of the envious in *Purgatorio* 13, for instance, he asks whether any soul among them is Italian ("s'anima e qui tra voi che sia latina," v. 92). Posing the question in the present tense, he provokes a response that gently takes him to task for failing to realize the change of identity entailed in purgation:

> O frate mio, ciascuna è cittadina
> d'una vera città; ma tu vuo' dire
> che vivesse in Italia peregrina.
> (*Purg.* 13.94–96)

(O my brother, each one here is a citizen of a true city: but you mean one that lived in Italy while a pilgrim.)

Sapia, the soul who speaks here, uses the same distinctions Augustine deploys in *City of God* 15; she also makes a crucial shift in tense to bring home her point. Is anyone on the terrace of envy an Italian? The answer is both yes and no. She *is* ("è") a citizen of heaven's true city who once *lived* ("vivesse") in Italy; yet even then she lived "in Italia peregrina." Whether she is alive or dead, her citizenship—like Abel's and like Paul's in Philippians 3.20—is in heaven: "in caelis est."

But is it? Sapia goes on to describe herself as once belonging to Siena ("Io fui sanese," v. 106) but now, as a pilgrim, reforming the sinful disposition that formerly led her to rejoice in the defeat of her fellow citizens. Yet at the end of the canto, her request to Dante that he restore her name among the Sienese concludes with her defamation of her people as "gente vana" ("vain fools," v. 151), whose future embarrassment she seems to enjoy predicting. A citizen of the true city, she continues nonetheless to bear the imprint of the *civitas terrena*—and for the poet's purpose. Unlike Augustine, who maintains his either/or without portraying the process of conversion between one *civitas* and another, Dante shows Cain's power lingering even over those penitents who have thrown in their lot with Abel. He depicts the blur of civic allegiances rather than their neat separation, demonstrating to the reader that Augustine's two cities are intermingled in individuals as well as in history. The status of the soul in purgatory reflects the confused, "in process" state of the living.

A similar confusion of attachments can be seen in the next canto, where yet another of the envious, Guido del Duca, distances himself from his native Romagna in a prolonged jeremiad against its degeneracy and at the same time demonstrates the region's hold over him by the sheer weight of his loathing. The Italy he denounces may well be on its way to becoming a wasteland; but it is also true that to some extent he is still astray in its dark wood, losing sight of the "true city" to which he belongs and toward which he moves in penance. Nonetheless, Guido knows what ails the earthly community of which he himself is still too much a part. He knows that what envy first unleashed from hell is the same refusal to share that Augustine saw as the curse pursuing Cain and Romulus. "O human race," Guido asks, "why do you set your hearts where there must be exclusion of partnership?" ("o gente umana, perché poni 'l core / là 'v' è mestier di consorte divieto?" 14.86–87). After this encounter—and with the word *consorte* in the air—Dante first hears Cain's cry ("Anciderammi qualunque m'apprende") and then learns from Virgil what to make of it. The "hard bit" of Cain's example, the wages of envy, is meant to keep humanity within bounds and out of Satan's trap. Instead, however, "you" take the bait, fall into the hands of the adversary, and pass beyond the help of curb or spur. Addressing Dante as "voi"—a plural broad enough to include the whole of humanity from Cain's day until the present of the *Commedia*—Virgil closes the canto by describing the misplaced sense of direction that all but defines what Augustine means by the *civitas terrena*:

> Chiamavi 'l cielo e'ntorno vi si gira,
>   mostrandovi le sue bellezze etterne,
>   e l'occhio vostro pur a terra mira;
> onde vi batte chi tutto discerne.
>   (*Purg.* 14.148–51)

(The heavens call to you and circle about you, displaying to you their eternal splendors, and your eyes gaze only on the earth: wherefore He smites you who sees all.)

So ends canto 14, with the reader's attention drawn down to the earth. But what happens from the very beginning of *Purgatorio* 15 is an abrupt volte-face that has readers suddenly looking up to discover not only the heavens but an altogether different civic reality. The first lines call attention to the play of the sun bringing evening to the Southern Hemisphere and midnight to the Northern (15.1–6). In part this opening is the poet's device for conveying the passage of time in purgatory, as the pilgrim completes the cure of envy and moves on to confront the terrace of wrath. More important, it is Dante's subtle way of suggesting the joyful realities of reciprocity and harmony—between endings and beginnings, evening and midnight, north and south, there and here. These reciprocities are to be found even in the laws of physics (as in the equality of the angles of incidence and reflection referred to in the simile of vv. 16–21), but they are utterly foreign to the earthly city just recalled in *Purgatorio* 14.

With the setting of this new thematic, then, readers are prepared for the dazzling arrival of one who will in effect give harmonious reciprocity a local habitation and a name: an angel sent from the "family of heaven" (15.29) who erases from Dante's brow the "P" symbolizing the *peccatum*, or sin, of *invidia* and invites him to ascend higher, toward the same celestial light from which the angel has descended. Thus introduced to the city of God in action, but still mindful of the conversation of the previous canto, Dante asks Virgil to unravel a knot in the discourse of Guido del Duca: "What did the spirit of Romagna mean when he spoke of 'exclusion' and 'partnership'?" ("'divieto' e 'consorte' menzionando?" 15.44–45). Coming to the heart of the matter in these two remembered words—words that echo Augustine's indictment of envy as the refusal of partnership—Dante has Virgil respond by diagnosing an earthly problem and then pointing to its solution in the kingdom of heaven:

Perché s'appuntano i vostri disiri
dove per compagnia parte si scema,
invidia move il mantaco a' sospiri.
Ma se l'amor de la spera suprema
torcesse in suso il disiderio vostro,
non vi sarebbe al petto quella tema;
ché, per quanti si dice più lì "nostro,"
tanto possiede più di ben ciascuno
e più di caritate arde in quel chiostro.

(*Purg.* 15.49–57)

(Because your desires are centered there where the portion is lessened by partnership, envy moves the bellows to your sighs. But if the love of the highest sphere turned upwards your desire, that fear would not be at your heart. For there, the more they are who say "ours," the more of good does each possess, and the more of charity burns in that cloister.)

In the earthly city desire almost always aims at what is peripheral, where division always means less and never more. But this occurs because the "highest sphere" is not allowed to hold sway in human affairs. If our longings were aligned with that sphere, however, another world would exist. Division of possessions would mean their growth, and the more of us who shared, who said "ours" ("nostro"), the more each of us ("ciascuno") would hold. With the rhyme words of verses 53, 55, and 57—*vostro-nostro-chiostro*—Virgil presents the unfolding of "yours" into "ours" that we will find in paradise; in three tercets he takes readers from earth to heaven. But with a "fleshly" mind still oriented to the realm where "the portion is lessened by partnership," Dante cannot understand how a "good" ("un ben," v. 61) can possibly be distributed so that many possessors are richer than a few. Virgil is therefore prompted to initiate him further into the economy of heaven, whereby "that infinite and ineffable Good" who is God speeds with love toward rational creation and reaches toward it (so to speak) as light. Material possessions or temporal sovereignty may dwindle with division, but light (like love) grows. Giving always means gaining, at least if the recipient can reflect what has been given and thereby increase the glow. Or, as the climactic tercet of the sequence insists, the distribution of God's gifts means more—"più," "più," "più"—for all:

> E quanta gente più là sù s'intende,
>   più v'è da bene amare, e più vi s'ama,
>   e come specchio l'uno a l'altro rende.
>
> (*Purg.* 15.73–75)

(The more souls there are that are enamored there above, the more there are for loving well, and the more love is there, and like a mirror one reflects to the other.)

If the bitter rancor of *Purgatorio* 14 recalls the hell of the earthly city, what readers find here is a proleptic glimpse of a paradise bounded only by love and light. No wonder that at the end of this exposition Virgil refers Dante to Beatrice for more enlightenment on the "highest sphere"—or for direct experience rather than description (vv. 76–78). Virgil's words in fact anticipate Beatrice's discourse in the *Paradiso*. Yet the voice that actually resounds in his account of heaven belongs to none other than Augustine, that is, to the previously quoted passage in the *City of God* where the commonwealth of Abel, characterized by the joy of partnership, is set against the invidious cities of the fratricides Cain and Romulus:

> Nullo enim modo fit minor accedente seu permanente consorte possessio bonitatis, immo possessio bonitas, quam tanto latius quanto concordius individua sociorum possidet caritas. Non habebit denique istam possessionem qui eam noluerit habere communem; et tanto eam reperiet ampliorem quanto amplius ibi potuerit amare consortem.
>
> (*City of God* 15.5)

(A man's possession of goodness is in no way diminished by the arrival, or the continuance, of a sharer in it; indeed, goodness is a possession enjoyed more widely by the united affection of partners in that possession in proportion to the harmony that exists among them. In fact, anyone who refuses to enjoy this possession in partnership will not enjoy it at all; and he will find that he possesses it in ampler measure in proportion to his ability to love his partner in it.)

The earliest fourteenth-century commentators first mentioned Dante's indebtedness to this Augustinian text, and their successors have continued to cite the passage as the primary doctrinal source for Virgil's lines.[10] Indeed, the connections between the two are so clear that the passage from *City of God* 15.5 seems more a subtext than a source. Not only does Dante appropriate Augustine's analysis (and not of these particular lines alone but, as we have seen, of the larger discussion of book 15), he also closely translates Augustine's Latin vocabulary into his own Italian: "consortio" becomes "consorte," "bonitas" "bene," "possessio" "possiede," and "communio" "compagnia."

Merely to note the borrowing, however, is to acknowledge a debt but miss its implication; it is, in fact, to miss an ingenious (perhaps even outrageous) authorial maneuver. For whatever is one to make of Dante's decision to give this Augustinian glimpse into the city of God—in fact the poem's first view of paradise—to Virgil, a pagan poet banished forever from the *civitas Dei* precisely because he lived in the time of what he himself calls "the false and lying gods" (*Inf.* 1.72)? That this phrase, "falsi e bugiardi," obviously echoes Augustine's dismissal of the "falsi et fallaces" deities of Roman religion[11]—the deities, that is, of Virgil's religion—only reinforces the irony of the transposition in *Purgatorio* 15, where the enemy speaks the accuser's lines. For Dante has given Augustine's description of the economy of heaven to the writer against whom Augustine more or less openly waxed polemical: the chief poet of the *civitas terrena* of Romulus, whose characterization of Rome as an "empire without boundary" (*Aen.* 1.279) was for Augustine nothing less than a celebration of a blasphemy, the mendacity of a venerable liar: "mendax vates erat." All the more dangerous for being revered, Virgil was for Augustine the paradigmatic "gentile," a purveyor of pagan delusion against whom the *City of God* (even from its preface) raises its massive contra.[12]

Nor is the bizarre phenomenon of an Augustinian Virgil limited to this single passage in the fifteenth canto. In *Purgatorio* 17, the central canto of the *Commedia*, Virgil's discourse on the moral basis of purgatory (vv. 94–105), as well as his exposition of the ordering of love according to a threefold division (vv. 106–39), is deeply indebted to passages in *City of God* 15.22 and *Christian Doctrine* 1.27.[13] Likewise, his description in the same canto of the soul's search for a good "wherein the mind may find rest" ("nel qual si queti l'animo," 17.128) seems clearly to allude to the opening of the *Confessions* and the portrayal of the restless heart searching for its resting place ("inquietum est cor nostrum, donec requiescat in te").

If indeed, as this concentration of subtexts and allusions suggests, Dante chose to present Augustine's teachings at the heart of the *Commedia* by placing them all in Virgil's mouth, bizarre conflations result. On the one hand, this transposition creates something like a patristic Virgil: a doctor of the church he cannot join, he can at least discern the towers of the true city, from which he is nonetheless in eternal exile, as he himself tells Statius in *Purgatorio* 21.18. On the other hand, it also offers us the possibility of a Virgilian Augustine—that is, an Augustine who is allowed to function both as architect of the city of God and as master of rightly ordered love but who has been delivered from the errors of his anti-imperial ways. Dante adopts Augustine's indictment of the *civitas terrena* and applies it, as we have seen, all along the terraces of envy and wrath. But there is no reference to Romulus or to the bloodstained walls of his city. Instead, the lust for domination Dante denounces is shown to drive the city-states of Italy; it has nothing whatsoever to do with Rome. On the contrary, Rome offers the pilgrims of purgatory example after example of virtue as well as of vice; its pagan history has the heuristic value of Scripture. Here again Dante tacitly rejects what Augustine does in *City of God* 5, where the portraits of the Roman worthies are said to demonstrate at best but a flawed and shadowy likeness of real civic virtues.[14]

Dante's reinvention of Augustine entails, therefore, a major correction of the theologian's political vision—a Roman revision. In addition to rehabilitating Virgil, moreover, Dante works toward a similar end through another figure on the terrace of wrath, one whose dialogue with the pilgrim flies in the face of Augustine's teaching. For while the Bishop of Hippo rejects the notion of a political solution to the "exclusion of partnership"— and rejects as well any idea of a beatitude constituted in and of the earthly city—Marco Lombardo (and with him, the author of the *Monarchia*) embraces the temporal order, discusses its redemption, and even (*pace* Augustine) calls its redeemer "Rome." Bracketed by what we might well regard as the "orthodox" Augustinian discourse of cantos 15 and 17 (orthodoxy voiced by Virgil!), *Purgatorio* 16 presents us with a vision of Rome's place in history antithetical in the spirit to the *City of God*:

> Soleva Roma, che'l buon mondo feo,
>   due soli aver, che l'una e l'altra strada
>   facean vedere, e del mondo e di Deo.
>   (*Purg.* 16.106–8)

(Rome, which made the world good, was wont to have two suns, which made visible both the one road and the other, that of the world and that of God.)

Though rich in Augustinian analysis, Marco's extended speech turns Augustine's ideology of the earthly city against the saint.[15] Dante redeems Romulus by transforming him from a descendant of Cain into a figure for Abel. He changes a symbol of civic self-destruction into one that promises earthly beatitude, a Rome from whose ramparts one might well discern the towers of the true city ("la vera cittade," 16.96). Later in the *Purgatorio* Dante even goes so far as to have Beatrice identify the "highest sphere" of the Empyrean as none other than "that Rome where Christ is Roman" (32.102); in *Paradiso* 32.119 he goes so far as to celebrate Mary as "Augusta."

Although this harmonization of Augustine and Virgil is carried out at considerable expense to the integrity of both, the taking of such liberties seems never to have worried Dante. On the contrary, the drive of the poem is itself a kind of *libido dominandi*, a domination of the past (whether pagan or Christian) to render a new account—to render, that is, *Dante's* account. What is especially intriguing about the achievement of this *discordia concors* in the *Purgatorio*, however, is that it should find its focus in the fifteenth canto, the same structural moment at which in the other two canticles the pilgrim encounters a father figure he is meant either to reject or to emulate. In *Inferno* 15, he meets a classicized Ser Brunetto Latini, whose humanism represents a road not to be taken and whose reflections on politics and literature recall the greed for praise and passion for glory that Augustine denounces in the heroes of Rome. At the other pole of eternity, in *Paradiso* 15–17, Dante's great-great-grandfather Cacciaguida hails his arrival in the heaven of Mars with Latin words ("O sanguis meus," 15.28) that echo Anchises' injunction to Julius Caesar (*Aeneid* 6.835) and that here become a Christian salute as well as an imperial one.[16] In Cacciaguida, as opposed to Brunetto, the poet finds his ideal citizen of the earthly city: a soul passionately devoted to civic life, appreciative of its joys, but under no delusions about either its permanence or its ultimacy. "Your affairs all have their death" (*Paradiso* 16.79), he tells the pilgrim, as if to correct Virgil's Jovian prophecy of an earthly empire without end; but he does not echo Augustine's refusal of empire's providential mission.

Purgatorio 15 apparently breaks this pattern of father-son encounters by failing to stage any such meeting. Unless the pattern is fulfilled in some other way, one perhaps more suited to the fleeting and provisional "visions" that appear for an instructional moment all along the terraces of purgatory and then are gone. In a poem careful of its own symmetries, of the structural repetitions that signal a development, it would be unusual if the deliberately analogous father-son episodes of the *Inferno* and the *Paradiso* should lack a middle term. I suggest that what we find in *Purgatorio* 15 is a third parallel, a remarkable composite of paternal acceptance, rejection, and transposition that offers us a hybrid father suitable to the transitory "in between" space of purgatory—a father who "appears" only to disappear (like all the other "non falsi errori," 15.117) when he has been understood. At once Roman and Catholic, he is a father who offers the pilgrim his first understanding of heaven (which Virgil alone should not be able to do), without separating that eternal hope from the vocation of earthly empire building (which Augustine himself would refuse to consider).

At the heart of the *Commedia*, then, Dante gives us the architect of the *City of God* speaking through the poet of the *Aeneid.* Disarming the Bishop of Hippo of his anti-Roman artillery simply by ignoring it, Dante lays the basis in his own work for an Augustinian vision of a redeemed secular order that does not require the fratricidal Romulus as its foil. He establishes a partnership with the goals of the earthly city that Augustine largely excluded from the *City of God,* so that pilgrimage within the *civitas terrena* becomes less a passing through alien territory than a crusade on the world's behalf. Having in different ways corrected his ancient masters on the true calling of the city and its citizens, this Italian son makes peace with his Latin fathers by reconceiving them in his own terms. From their constructions of the earthly city he proposes a third Rome of his own imagining; from pagan epic and sacred history he invents a "sacred poem" to which both Virgil and Augustine have contributed. Seer of the earthly city and visionary of the city of God, he reconciles the opposition between his authorities by transcending them in himself—Christian Virgil and *alter Augustinus.*

CHAPTER II

Augustine, Dante, and the
Dialectic of Ineffability

From the outset of the *Paradiso* Dante makes it clear that his pilgrim is modeled on St. Paul, that "man in Christ" who was "caught up into paradise and heard such unspeakable words which it is not lawful for a man to utter" (2 Cor. 12:4). According to St. Augustine, perhaps the most influential interpreter of this rapture, Paul's experience was nothing less than unmediated contact with the ineffable God—verbal beatitude.[1] For one extraordinary "moment" of eternity the apostle was taken out of the diachronic body of our speech and enabled, along with the blessed, to understand God's language—a language so unutterably beyond our own that Augustine will refer to it paradoxically as silence.[2] Dante claims this same translation into the divine ineffability in his poem's third canticle. But if St. Paul serves as the prototype for the voyager *in paradisum*, what are we to make of the poet who writes 33 cantos of *terza rima* about an experience that is not only beyond expression but also unlawful for anyone to speak of? This apparent divergence from the Pauline tradition may account for the fact that the anxiety of the *Commedia*, which heretofore has been located in the pilgrim, shifts suddenly to the poet. Dante is openly aware that in this "ultimo lavoro" (*Par.* 1.13)—his final and highest endeavor—he travels uncharted territory: "L'acqua ch'io prendo già mai non si corse" (*Par.* 2.7). While the Chosen Vessel made the same ultimate journey, *his* itinerary remained a closed book. Nor is the danger of the enterprise risked by the poet alone; the reader, too, is forewarned that the voyage "in pelago" (*Par.* 2.5) is perilous and not to be undertaken lightly.

Certainly much of this uneasiness has to do with the fact that once the final apocalyptic cantos of the *Purgatorio* are behind us, Dante's mimesis of

Scripture seems to be complete. There remains only the ominous warning that ends John's Apocalypse, a warning understood to mark the definitive closing of the canon: "For I testify, unto every man that heareth the words of this book, If any man shall add unto these things, God shall add unto him the plagues of this book" (Rev. 22:18). By beginning the *Paradiso* precisely where the Bible itself leaves off, Dante stands to "add" to a revelation that has already had its last word. Even though heaven has put its hand to the sacred poem, may not the poet's act be (to appropriate Adam's phrase for the original sin) a "trapassar del segno" (*Par.* 26.117), a trespass of the boundary set between human speech and the divine reality?

Dante defends himself against these charges at the opening of the *Paradiso* when he states that what the poem will actually say is at several removes from the ineffable. For although the pilgrim saw God *in speciem*, that vision of beatitude can be represented to us only in the lightning flash (*fulgore*) that shatters the final canto and with it the entire poem:

> Nel ciel che più de la sua luce prende
>   fu' io, e vidi cose che ridire
>   né sa né può chi di là sù discende;
> perché appressando sé al suo disire,
>   nostro intelletto si profonda tanto,
>   che dietro la memoria non può ire.
> (Par. 1.4–9)

(I have been in the heaven that most receives of His light, and have seen things which whoso descends from there has neither the knowledge nor power to relate, because, as it draws near to its desire, our intellect enters so deep that memory cannot go back upon the track.)

What this journey "si profonda tanto" means for the *Paradiso*, as Dante's gloss in the epistle to Can Grande further makes plain, is that the poem articulates the struggle of language to speak the little that memory can recall. It is the copy of a copy of an ineffable Original: "knowledge he has not, because he has forgotten; power he has not, because even if he remembers and retains it thereafter, nevertheless speech fails him."[3] Therefore, when the pilgrim finally ends his journey in God, the poem has already reached its end. The only way the poet can speak the ineffable words he once heard is in the silence that reigns once the "alta fantasia" of his poetry concedes its defeat.

Yet if the poet's final silence acknowledges the gap between our words and the Word of God, Dante's poem is nonetheless a *resonant* failure. It may well be only a shadow of the blessed kingdom (1.23), a little spark (1.34), the stuttering of a mute (10.25), not substantial enough even to be called "little" (33.123). But these disclaimers are all, in fact, claims of a relationship that obtains between human speech and God's full silence, between this poem and its ineffable subject.[4] Dante could do this because, having inherited a Christian notion of language that Marcia Colish has felicitously called "redeemed rhetoric," he believed in the power of the divine Word to "dwell" in human speech, to reveal the inexpressible God through the finite medium of words in time and space. This is not to say that the ineffable words were thought susceptible to any literal translation. Rather, mortal words could function as a call to vision, as a preparation (as Augustine said of the writing of St. Ambrose) "ad audiendum silentium narrationis eius, et videndum invisibilem formam eius" ("to hear the silence of his discourse, and to see his invisible form").[5]

While such claims were routinely made for Scripture, they could also be extended to other texts outside the biblical canon. However, what constitutes Dante's originality, not to mention his daring, is his appropriation of such claims for his own poem. Not only does the *Commedia* share with the Bible its allegorical and anagogical significance, it also purports to reveal the ineffable God in a similar way. Thus in *Paradiso* 4, when Beatrice explains the appearance of the blessed throughout the material spheres of the Ptolemaic universe, the poet gives us a glimpse into the procedure of his fiction. Whether the heavenly spirits show themselves to the pilgrim as lights, or the poem describes them to us in words, configurations of any kind exist only provisionally, "per far segno." They make signs for a reality that completely transcends our time- and space-bound *ingegno*:

> Per questo la Scrittura condescende
>   a vostra facultate, e piedi e mano
>   attribuisce a Dio e altro intende.
>   (*Par.* 4.43–45)

(For this reason Scripture condescends to your capacity, and attributes hands and feet to God, having other meaning.)

The primary correspondence here is between the heavenly "script" the pilgrim sees as he ascends the heavenly spheres and the figurative language of the Bible, both of which are accommodations of pure spirit to our "fleshly mind." But as John Freccero has suggested, this analogy is relevant not only to what Dante saw then, in the heavens, but to what he writes now, on the page: "that is, heaven's condescension to the pilgrim is matched by the poet's condescension to us."[6]

If we push this kinship of accommodation further and say that Dante intends us to read the *Paradiso* as if it were an extended biblical anthropomorphism, then two conclusions may be drawn. The first is that the canticle's claim to truth does not lie in any supposed mimetic correspondence between its language and the ineffable "other"; rather, the poem itself is a metaphor whose meaning wholly transcends its literal terms. Second, the poem is a metaphor of a certain kind, for when the Holy Spirit speaks in Scripture of God's hands or feet—when, that is, the Spirit uses glaringly inappropriate language—it is precisely to remind us that there is finally no human speech adequate to the divine reality. Thus for Augustine words that do not "work" on a literal level are a sign that God is more fully expressed in our awed silence than in anything our voices can sound. Such language calls the reader to go beyond the letter of *every* text. If read aright, therefore, metaphor introduces an analogy between our speech and God's Word that will of necessity force the reader to see the insufficiency of language. To speak of the "strong right arm" of God is to expose the fiction of metaphor. Words about the ineffable sabotage their own literal meaning in order to draw attention to what cannot be spelled in letters at all, but can only be attended to and longed for.

In *Paradiso* I Dante gives us a statement of the way the poem's metaphoric structure will function on behalf of the ineffable:

> Trasumanar significar *per verba*
>   non si poria; però l'essemplo basti
>   a cui esperïenza grazia serba.
>   (*Par.* 1.70–72)

(The passing beyond humanity may not be set forth *per verba*: therefore let the example suffice any for whom grace reserves the experience.)

This *terzina* offers us one of the first of the *Paradiso*'s many ineffability topoi. It is a straightforward declaration that what the poet is about to tell us cannot be put into words. Given this basic limit, the most he can do is bear witness with the poem's mute *essemplo*, thereby pointing the reader to a beatitude he can neither remember nor describe.

If we look more closely at the movement within these three lines, however, we may discover the peculiar tension of this poem—the poetic counterplot within Dante's visionary orthodoxy. In the initial *trasumanare* he gives us a word of his own devising, a verb created to express the inexpressible transcendence of our life and language: "to pass beyond humanity."[7] Juxtaposed to it at the end of verse 70 is a Latin phrase, *per verba*, which, as Denis Donoghue has suggested, is an allusion both to St. Paul's rapture into the *arcana verba* of the third heaven (2 Cor. 12:2–4) and to the "Latin" exegetical tradition of Augustine and Aquinas that grew up around it.[8] Placed between Dante's neologism (*trasumanare*) and this evocation of the language of heaven (*per verba*) is *significare*, literally "to mean" or "to describe," denoting the semiotic activity of human language itself: the making of signs. As long as this line is read as a completed whole— "trasumanar significar *per verba*"—it offers us a dramatic display of verbal ingenuity and confidence. A variety of linguistic stops are pulled to assert the transcendence of humanity in words—the sheer power of *significare*. And yet, of course, the line does *not* stand grammatically on its own. The force of Dante's syntax pulls us on to what follows immediately upon it: the Promethean impulse within fallen language is brought up short by the stern reality of "non si poria." What we find in the assertion and negation of these two lines, therefore, is a miniature of the poetic strategy of the entire canticle. For what the *Paradiso* offers with one hand it resolutely withdraws with the other; what it speaks cannot be set forth in words.

Yet, as we know from the third line, the *terzina* does not leave us at a stalemate, any more than the poem's contradictions render it meaningless and vain. Although it abjures any claim to render the ineffable in its final silence, it nonetheless presents us with the *essemplo* of one who heard the unspeakable words. Moreover, it also extends a promise of the same beatitude "a cui esperïenza grazia serba," to any for whom grace reserves the experience. Viewed linguistically, this experience is nothing other than the eschatological end toward which the whole verbal creation groans in travail—the translation of words into Word. Thus, what the last line of the *terzina* brings is the possibility of *trasumanare*—glimpsed in the first line, denied in the second, and now acknowledged as a reality that cannot be signified. Rather, transcendence rests hidden in the implication of grace; it is a truth spoken between the lines until in eternity God's Word is "all in all." In this way, then, the canticle's "passing beyond humanity" is a passage from the poet's language to his silence, but a silence that is far more eloquent than anything his words actually can say. What we see in *Paradiso* 1.70–72, therefore, is a dialectic of ineffability that moves from the claims of language, to a recognition of its limits, to the intimation of a transcendent, unrepresentable reality. In *Paradiso* 23.61–63 Dante describes the move as a "jump" into silence:

> e così, figurando il paradiso,
>   convien saltar lo sacrato poema,
>   come chi trova suo cammin riciso.

> (and so, depicting paradise, the sacred poem must needs make a leap, even as one who finds his way cut off.)

Although this dialectic of ineffability is characteristic of all speech about the numinous, there are nonetheless some literary works in which it is focal. Stanley Fish has characterized these as "self-consuming artifacts," and traced their ancestry back to Plato and then through St. Augustine to the Christian West. While not once mentioning Dante, his thesis is of great relevance to the *Paradiso*, certainly the most spectacular "self-consuming artifact" in all of literature. Fish shows how the dialectic arises out of a desire to communicate the ineffable, not for purposes of speculation but rather to the end of conversion: to lead the reader-respondent into a direct experience of the ineffable. Although the dialectic uses "outer" words, they are considered to be only the instruments or vehicles of "inner" truth. As Plotinus says in the *Enneads* (6.9.4), this truth is " 'Not to be told; not to be written': in our writing and telling we are but urging toward it; out of discussion we call to vision; to those desiring to see, we point the way; our teaching is of the road and of the travelling." Because the ineffable is "not to be told; not to be written," the language of the dialectic must more or less openly disavow itself, forcing the reader to look not only beyond words but also beyond the diachronic world in which we (apparently) exist. Using the example of the *Phaedrus*, Fish describes the experience of reading such a work as a mimetic reenactment of the Platonic ladder, with each successive "rung" rejected even as it is negotiated, until finally the whole structure is thrown over, leaving the reader with him- or herself—and with whatever enlightenment has grown with the climb. Thus the strategy of such work is to emphasize the partial, transitory, inadequate nature of language, and in so doing to call the reader to that higher ("intellectual") vision that can be realized only in silence. Language fulfills its purpose only by acknowledging its own inadequacy. Or, as Fish puts it, "A self-consuming artifact signifies most successfully when it fails, when it points away from itself to something its forms cannot capture."[9]

While Fish discusses St. Augustine, the great Christianizer of this Platonic tradition, he does not refer to the most remarkable example of the "anti-aesthetic" in the Augustinian corpus, the Ostia "vision" of *Confessions* 9.10. It provides an important precedent, perhaps even an actual model, for the dialectic of the *Paradiso*: a struggle to speak about an experience of the ineffable and at the same time to dissolve that speech into silence.[10] The episode virtually concludes the autobiographical portion of the work and opens on a day close to Monica's death, as she and Augustine find themselves discussing what the joy of the blessed will be.[11] Their conversation begins in the outer or corporeal words of normal discourse (what Augustine will speak of in *Confessions* 13.15 as "syllabis temporum"), and proceeds by analogy to find some correlative on earth or in the material heavens by which to imagine the bliss which "eye has not seen, nor ear heard, nor mind conceived." When no such likeness can be found, they discover themselves undergoing a gradual interiorization of their speech—"interius cogitando et loquendo et mirando"—until they transcend even their inner selves and are translated into eternity, "the place of everlasting plenty, where you feed Israel forever with the food of truth." There, where God is "all in all," they "speak" and "gasp after" the divine Word to such an extent that with the longing of their whole being they momentarily "reach out and touch" him. This contact lasts only for the duration of a heartbeat, before they once again fall back into their bodies. Augustine describes this reentry in linguistic terms as a fall from the infinite synchronicity of God's silence to the "noise" ("strepitus") of our diachronic speech, "where each word has a beginning and an end—far, far different from your Word, O Lord, Who abides in Himself forever, yet never grows old and gives life to all things."

After an unspecified interval, the pair then attempts to reconstruct their experience of *trasumanare* in the outer words of mortality. The reconstruction will first track their now-lost rapture in language and then try to erase its own linguistic traces:

> Dicebamus ergo: "si cui sileat tumultus carnis, sileat phantasiae terrae et aquarum et aeris, sileant et poli et ipsa sibi anima sileat, et transeat se non se cogitando, sileant somnia et imaginariae revelationes, omnis lingua et omne signum et quidquid transeundo fit si cui sileat omnino—quoniam si quis audiat, dicunt haec omnia: Non ipsa nos fecimus, sed fecit nos qui manet in aeternum:—his dictis si iam taceant, quoniam erexerunt aurem in eum, qui fecit ea, et loquatur ipse solus non per ea, sed per se ipsum, ut audiamus verbum eius, non per linguam carnis neque per vocem angeli nec per sonitum nubis nec per aenigma similitudinis, sed ipsum, quem in his amamus, ipsum sine his audiamus, sicut nunc extendimus nos et rapida cogitatione attingimus aeternam sapientiam super omnia manentem, si continuetur hoc et subtrahantur aliae visiones longe inparis generis, et haec una rapiat et absorbeat et recondat in interiora gaudia spectatorem suum, ut talis sit sempiterna vita, quale fuit hoc momentum intelligentiae, cui suspiravimus, nonne hoc est: Intra in gaudium domini tui? et istud quando? an cum omnes resurgimus, sed non omnes inmutabimur?"

(We said therefore: If to any man the tumults of the flesh be silenced, if the fancies of the earth, and waters, and air be silenced also; if the poles of heaven be silent also: if the very soul be silent to herself, and by not thinking upon self surmount self; if all dreams and imaginary revelations be silenced, every tongue, and every sign, if whatsoever is transient be silent to any one—since if any man could hearken unto them, all these say to him, We created not ourselves, but he that remains for all eternity; if then, having uttered this, they also be then silent, (as having raised our ear unto him that made them) and if he speak alone; not by them but by himself, that we may hear his own word; not pronounced by any tongue of flesh, nor by the voice of the angels, nor by the sound of thunder, nor in the dark riddle of a resemblance; but that we may hear him whom we love in these creatures, himself without these (like as we two now strained up ourselves unto it, and in swift thought arrived upon a touch of that eternal Wisdom, which is over all):—could this exaltation of spirit have ever continued, and all other visions of a far other kind been quite taken away, and that this one exaltation should ravish us, and swallow us up, and so wrap up their beholder among these more inward joys, as that his life might be forever like to this very moment of understanding which we now sighed after: were not this as much as Enter into thy Master's joy?

But when shall that be? Shall it be when we shall all rise again, though all
shall not be changed?)   (trans. Watts)

Most of the attention accorded this passage (and, indeed, the entire
episode) has concerned its mixture of Christianity and Neoplatonism.
More remarkable than the simultaneous presence of two "worlds of dis-
course," however, is the fact that discourse itself is under attack. Language
is both the exorcist and the demon cast out. Because the processes of
writing and erasure are essentially one process here, our response is un-
avoidably double. Is this a "self-consuming artifact," or an example of the
same impulse that tried at Babel to take heaven by storm? For in this liter-
ary tour de force, remarkable in even so practiced a Ciceronian as Augus-
tine, we are confronted by nothing less than a massive self-contradiction: a
periodic sentence of 183 intricately woven words, whose express purpose is
to dissolve language into the silence it repeatedly invokes. Furthermore, it
is a sentence that, for all its density and weight, is given the most tentative
rhetorical construction: launched by a surmise ("si cui," "If to any man"), it
continues in supposition until closing, open-ended, in a question: "though
all shall not be changed?" It is as if, despite its great verbal bulk, the
sentence were trying very hard not to be on the page at all.

Closely following the itinerary of the earlier conversation-vision shared
with Monica, Augustine moves through the hierarchy of Creation, sum-
moning forth each successive mode of revelation only to reduce each one to
silence, even those that God has used to reveal himself in a glass darkly:
"linguam carnis . . . vocem angeli . . . sonitum nubis . . . aenigma similitu-
dinis." With its rejection of "every tongue, and every sign," the sentence is
ultimately bound to reject itself. This it does, but only in order to signal
the unmediated experience of the ineffable that Augustine and Monica
"touched" in their rapture, "that we may hear his own word . . . that we may
hear him whom we love."

"That we may hear his own word": the ultimate experience of *trasu-
manare* is situated at the central stillpoint of the sentence, the final goal not
only of this account but of every verbal excursion into the *via negationis*.
Moreover, by placing the beatific "sound" of God's "silent narration" at the
center of a linear progression—a diachronic imitation of the eternal Now of
God—Augustine also forces us to realize that this is not an end that the
sentence can hope to attain in the "body" of our speech. All these words

can do is reach after what they themselves cannot touch. Yet, as the continuing course of the sentence demonstrates, this acknowledgment of the limits of language can at the same time serve to point beyond them. For if we cannot now either hear or speak the Word in his ineffability, we can at least look forward, even as the sentence moves us forward in time and space, to the apocalyptic transformation of our speech. We can look forward, that is, to the moment, the twinkling of an eye, when the divine Word "enraptures" and "absorbs" and "hides away" our mortal language in the resurrection of the flesh. Therefore, by concluding with a citation of 1 Corinthians 15—St. Paul's great discourse on the *parousia* at the end of time—Augustine leaves the sentence open to its own future transformation. He awaits the resurrection of human words in the eternity of God's *ineffabilia verba*.

Augustine does not end the episode, however, looking toward the eschatological experience that grace reserves for the blessed. Instead he goes on to announce that the text we have just read—and presumably not only this sentence but the entire story of the rapture—is just a facsimile: "dicebam talia, etsi non isto modo et his verbis" ("and thus I spoke, but not in this manner or in these words"). In this sudden switch to the first-person singular, our attention is moved from the visionary rapture of Augustine and Monica at Ostia ("Dicebamus ergo") to the solitary act of writing about it ten years later. Our attention shifts to the *ego* who writes in this manner and in these words about an encounter with the ineffable that leaves all words and rhetoric behind. That we should be told at the end of the account that what we have read is a version or a paraphrase of the "vision," but not the actual journey *in id ipsum*, should come as no surprise. Yet while we know that the "syllables inscribed in time" cannot speak God's eternal Word, the consummate skill of the rhetorician is such that we are always in danger of forgetting it. We are in danger, that is, of mistaking the language of the episode for the truth that can only be heard when what is written or told passes away into silence. Augustine's authorial "confession" at the end of the episode prevents the reader's inevitable seduction by the pyrotechnics of his performance. He breaks his own spell. Instead of allowing us to marvel, let alone mistake his tour de force for an adequate description of the experience grace reserves for the silence of eternity, he forces us to take the story of his rapture as only the next best thing. It is a consolation prize in the absence of the ineffable, pointing away from itself to "something" its forms cannot capture.

We have already seen how Dante makes this same discrediting gesture at the very beginning of the *Paradiso*, when he says that his vision of beatitude can be neither recalled nor expressed as it actually was—hidden, "si profonda tanto," in God's ineffability—but can only be represented indirectly, in the condescension of intellectual vision to our senses. Or, as he says of Plato in the epistle to Can Grande, the flight to the literally inexpressible can only be taken "per assumptionem metaphorismorum" ("through the insinuation of metaphor," para. 29). I have also characterized this metaphoric nature of the final canticle as dialectical, as moving through 33 cantos of assertion and negation, of writing and erasure, until the reader is left (like Augustine and Monica) with no mortal words to hold on to, but only the divine Word to reach out and long for.[12] But if the inexpressible *fulgore* that concludes the *Commedia* also marks the destruction of the poem's metaphor—a discarding of the "ladder" that reader and poet have climbed in their ascent to the outer limits of language—it is nonetheless a destruction for which the entire poem has carefully prepared. Like Augustine's periodic sentence in the Ostia episode, the language of the *Paradiso* is busy with its own elimination, with the conversion of speech into silence. In both instances we see the peculiar role that virtuosity plays in the dialectic of ineffability. The highly self-conscious brilliance of such words demands to be used up in the act of reading. Their most spectacular effects are to be seen in their demise.[13]

How the *Paradiso* gradually writes itself out of existence and into silence is suggested most dramatically in the so-called "anti-images" of the *Paradiso*, such as the cross of Mars (*Par.* 14) and the eagle of Jupiter (*Par.* 18–20)—configurations of light that remain visible only long enough to be comprehended, and then fade indistinguishably into their meaning. But if this is true of specific metaphors such as these, it is also true of the entire canticle, which constantly replaces its images and fictions, one after another, not in hopes of ever describing the ineffable, but rather to exhaust the possibility of expression. Following the dialectical movement suggested above, the poem everywhere silences itself, but only after each negated assertion of likeness has enlarged our notion of what *cannot* be imagined.

In the sphere of the Sun, for instance, where the doctors of the church appear as lights singing and dancing in two concentric circles, the poet bids us imagine what he saw by means of an extraordinarily extended analogy:

> Imagini, chi bene intender cupe
>   quel ch' i' or vidi—e ritegna l'image,
>   mentre ch'io dico, come ferma rupe—,
> quindici stelle che 'n diverse plage
>   lo cielo avvivan di tanto sereno
>   che soperchia de l'aere ogne compage;
> imagini quel carro a cu' il seno
>   basta del nostro cielo e notte e giorno,
>   sì ch'al volger del temo non vien meno;
> imagini la bocca di quel corno
>   che si comincia in punta de lo stelo
>   a cui la prima rota va dintorno,
> aver fatto di sé due segni in cielo,
>   qual fece la figliuola di Minoi
>   allora che sentì di morte il gelo;
> e l'un ne l'altro aver li raggi suoi,
>   e amendue girarsi per maniera
>   che l'uno andasse al primo e l'altro al poi.
>
> (Par. 13.1–18)

(Let him imagine, who would rightly grasp what I now beheld (and, let him hold the image firm as a rock), fifteen stars which in different regions vivify the heaven with such brightness that it overcomes every thickness of the air; let him imagine that Wain for which the bosom of our heaven suffices night and day so that with the turning of the pole it does not disappear; let him imagine the mouth of the Horn which begins at the end of the axle on which the first wheel revolves—all to have made of themselves two signs in the heavens like that which the daughter of Minos made when she felt the chill of death; and one to have its rays within the other, and both to revolve in such manner that one should go first and the other after.)

The opening imperative, "imagini," is repeated at the head of the third and fourth *terzine*. It is an emphatic command that not only etches in mind "come ferma rupe" the image inscribed on the page but also heightens our awareness of the poet's activity: the making of metaphor "mentre ch'io dico." What Dante gives us to retain is a totally fictional heaven in which several actual constellations are selected and rearranged in the shape of a double Ariadne's crown: an astronomical neologism! With the repetition of "imagini" and the painstakingly elaborate composition of the image, the passage all but coerces our recognition of its achievement—an eighteen-line demonstration of the poet's ingenuity and of the power of verbal *trasumanare*. Yet as soon as the analogy has been made, the reader who was first told to hold onto it ("ritegna l'image") is now ordered to let it fall away. For what has been obediently kept in mind is not, after all, the "truth":

> e avrà quasi l'ombra de la vera
>   costellazione e de la doppia danza
>   che circulava il punto dov' io era
> poi ch'è tanto di là da nostra usanza,
>   quanto di là dal mover de la Chiana
>   si move il ciel che tutti li altri avanza.
>
>   (*Par.* 13.19–24)

(and you will have as it were a shadow of the true constellation, and of the double dance, which was circling round the point where I was; for it is as far beyond our experience as the motion of the heaven that outspeeds all the rest is beyond the motion of the Chiana.)

The effect of these lines is to undermine the entire preceding *imago*. Yet if the poet rejects his analogy as only a shadow of the truth, it is a shadow nonetheless. Nor is the power of analogy itself entirely denied. While the dancing circles of light may be "tanto di là da nostra usanza," Dante conveys this fact through another likeness, a comparison of the preternatural speed of the Primum Mobile with the notoriously sluggish course of the river Chiana. Although this comparison argues a dissimilitude between earth and heaven, there is nonetheless something of a likeness. The poet is not contrasting movement with stasis, but two vastly different kinds of movement. Before we can take this as an apparent (if tenuous) endorsement of the passing beyond humanity in words, however, we must remember that here Dante is claiming to speak not of the ineffable directly but only of different kinds of metaphor. He is comparing heaven's "son et lumière" with his own imaginative fireworks; that is, he is comparing two accommodations to "nostra usanza." Therefore, no matter how remote from our experience may be the "vera costellazione" in the sphere of the Sun—no matter how far beyond even this dazzling demonstration of imaginative vision—it is still only a condescension, a translation of silence into sounds and shapes and shadows. The vision will utterly dissolve once the pilgrim has assimilated its "point." Throughout the canticle, Dante gives us a layering of images with no discernible Ur-text beneath them. The ineffable Source is discovered only in the poem's failure and dissolution, in its passage from speech to silence.

This passing away of the text is nowhere more poignant than in the first of four ineffability topoi that punctuate the final canto:

> Da quinci innanzi il mio veder fu maggio
> che 'l parlar mostra, ch'a tal vista cede,
> e cede la memoria a tanto oltraggio.
> Qual è colüi che sognando vede,
> che dopo 'l sogno la passione impressa
> rimane, e l'altro a la mente non riede,
> cotal son io, ché quasi tutta cessa
> mia visïone, e ancor mi distilla
> nel core il dolce che nacque da essa.
> Così la neve al sol si disigilla;
> così al vento ne le foglie levi
> si perdea la sentenza di Sibilla.
>   (Par. 33.55–66)

(Thenceforward my vision was greater than speech can show, which fails at such a sight, and at such excess memory fails. As is he who dreaming sees, and after the dream the passion remains imprinted and the rest returns not to the mind; such am I, for my vision almost wholly fades away, yet does the sweetness that was born of it still drop within my heart. Thus is the snow unsealed by the sun; thus in the mind, on the light leaves, the Sibyl's oracle was lost.)

The contrast Dante sets up at the beginning of the passage is between the growing perfection of the pilgrim's ability to see ("veder") and the proportional decline of the poet's speech ("parlar"), a decline accentuated by the rapid repetition of "cede . . . cede" in verses 56–57. Charles Singleton has noted that this confession of failure at the end of the canticle returns us to the opening disclaimer of *Paradiso* 1.4–9, where memory and language were first said to be overwhelmed by their "subject."[14] Between that threshold admission and this, the poem has almost completed its magnificent circle. Yet any notion of completion runs the risk of falsifying the particularity of this ending. Despite the perfection of its symmetry, the poem demands that we take it as incomplete, stopped in its tracks "a tanto oltraggio" ("at such excess"). The "excess" here is God's infinite and eternal Light, "lo raggio / de l'alta luce che da sé è vera" ("the beam of the lofty Light which in itself is true," vv. 53–54), refracted throughout the canticle in myriad condescensions to our mortality, but now seen by the pilgrim "da sé," as it truly is. Considered linguistically, however, that Light is the silence of God's Word, defying the powers of all human speech but even now drawing the faltering words of the poet into its totality.

Be this as it may, it is the poet's renewed sense of separation from his experience, and of the profound distance of his words from the Word, that predominates in the three following *terzine*. He begins with the simile of a man who wakes from a dream to find that it has vanished, leaving only an emotional imprint behind: "la passione impressa." While this feeling testifies that "something" has been seen, the dream itself—what is simply called "l'altro"—does not return to mind. Dante then proceeds to apply this simile about "someone" ("Qual è colüi") quite specifically to himself ("cotal son io"). Just as the dream is almost entirely obliterated, so is the heavenly vision "quasi tutta cessa." What remains, like the faint recollection of emotion, is merely a distillate: "e ancor mi distilla / nel core il dolce che nacque da essa." At first glance the second of these two figures seems largely to repeat (and personalize) the first. Yet in the juxtaposition of these two "remnants" there is a movement from the palpable, direct "impressa" to the more subtle transformation of vapor and liquid. There is a movement, that is, toward dematerialization.

This process continues in the next and final *terzina*, where we turn from "impressa" and "distilla" to a still further stage of dematerialization: "Così la neve al sol si disigilla." For the first time in this short series the "original" departs without so much as a token of its reality or an intangible sweetness born in the heart. The snow simply evaporates into the sunshine without leaving a trace. Like the word "impressa," "disigilla" suggests the whole enterprise of artistic creation and signification—except that instead of conferring shape and form (cf. "sigillare," *Par.* 7.69), "*disigilla*" points to dissolution, to the evaporation or un-signing of language—the imperceptible dissolve into the "oltraggio" of God's ineffability.

The inherent melancholy of these metaphors about the loss of metaphor is accentuated by the "si perdea" of the final simile, an allusion to the *Aeneid* and to the Sibyl's oracular text scattered irretrievably in the wind: "così al vento ne le foglie levi / si perdea la sentenza di Sibilla." At the end of Virgil's account of this "deconstruction," we read that those who saw the inspired lines flutter word by word into oblivion walked away from the experience in disgust: "inconsulti abeunt sedemque odere Sibyllae" ("uncounselled, men depart, and loathe the Sibyl's seat," *Aen.* 3.452). There is, however, no such rancor in Dante. If in this eloquent declaration of defeat the poet foreshadows the death and dissolution of his own text, he does so only from the perspective of mortal language, knowing at once the desire to pass beyond humanity and the utter impossibility of doing so *per verba*. But once again, as with the *terzina* of *Par.* 1.70–72, he does not leave us at a dead end. Rather, with a subtle allusion to the dispersal of the Sibyl's "sentenza," he points us (beginning in v. 85) to the transcendent third term of the dialectic. He gestures toward the beatific vision that grace alone holds in reserve, to a moment when scattered "syllables inscribed in time" will be gathered into one ineffable Word, bound by love into the silence of God's Book:

> Nel suo profondo vidi che s'interna,
>   legato con amore in un volume,
>   ciò che per l'universo si squaderna.
>   (*Par.* 33.85–87)

(In its depth I saw ingathered, bound by love in one single volume, that which is dispersed in leaves throughout the universe.)

By his own repeated witness, Dante can give us no selected readings from this divine Text. All he can do is heighten our longing for it so that no mortal words, not even those of his own "sacrato poema," will fully satisfy. In thereby leaving the reader unfulfilled, the *Paradiso*'s "self-consuming artifact" actually fulfills its destiny, leading us away from the sound of our own speech to a reality that escapes language altogether. In this way Dante's failure makes good his promise to Can Grande, for as the poem scatters its words into the collection of the divine "volume," the *Commedia* indeed ends in God himself—"in ipso Deo terminatur tractatus"—and not in any human words about him.

CHAPTER 12

"By Gradual Scale Sublimed": Dante and the Contemplatives

So from the root
Springs lighter the green stalk, from thence the leaves
More airy, last the bright consummate flower
Spirits odorous breathes: flowers and their fruit
Man's nourishment, by gradual scale sublimed.

—*Paradise Lost* 5.479–84

From beginning to end, Dante's *Paradiso* unfolds within the context of monasticism. At the outset the first of the blessed whom the pilgrim meets is Piccarda Donati, whose breaking of her cloistral vow under family pressure does not prevent her from initiating Dante into the rule of the heavenly kingdom: "E'n la sua volontade è nostra pace" ("in His will is our peace," 3.85). At the conclusion of the journey, he joins up with St. Bernard, whose great abbey at Clairvaux was at best a shadowy preface of the divine community, which the saint enables Dante also to enter. Despite the earthly differences between failed nun and illustrious abbot, both of these monastics share with the pilgrim the great legacy of organized religious life and the fulfillment of its gift to the larger church on earth: they teach him to know God. It is fitting, therefore, that two cantos of this final portion of the *Commedia* are specifically devoted to exploring the fruits of the contemplative life, and that at the heart of this exploration the pilgrim should come upon the founder of Western monasticism himself, St. Benedict of Nursia.

In *Paradiso* 22, Dante meets St. Benedict within the sphere of Saturn, the seventh heaven of the Ptolemaic universe, where those of the blessed who practiced monastic contemplation share with him a measure of their far greater vision. These spirits live out their beatitude beyond the dimensions of time and space: they appear in this sphere only as an extraordinary condescension to the pilgrim's mortality, a condescension "per far segno / de la celestïal" (4.38–39), as a sign of the heavenly reality that lies entirely beyond signification. The different "identity" of each sphere is significant, however, for it is through these fictive or metaphorical appearances that we begin to understand the different ways and degrees by which the blessed "sentir più e men l'etterno spiro" ("feel more and less the divine breath," 4.36). Thus, those who in cantos 21 and 22 momentarily take their place in Saturn have prepared for their eternal experience of God in the Empyrean by following the influence of the "cold planet" while still on earth. Its influence led them not to melancholia but to contemplation: they gave themselves (to quote the Postillatore Cassinese) "to the contemplative life in hermitage and in religious solitude . . . living in silence and in chastity."[1] Dante's high esteem for the vocation of Rachel is suggested not only by the inevitable association of Saturn with a paradisiacal Golden Age but by its celestial position above the six lower spheres and all the versions of the active life they represent.

Our entry into this sphere is marked by a striking disruption of the poem's narrative procedure. From the first canto of *Paradiso* onward, the pilgrim moved from one planetary sphere to another, from one power of vision to yet deeper sight into the heart of things. Dante makes these transitions by looking into the face of Beatrice, finding her eyes or smile even more beautiful than he found them before. In this repeated discovery he discovers himself translated "a claritate in claritatem," from glory to glory (2 Cor. 3:18), into new intensities of light and sound.[2] But at the entrance to the sphere of Saturn in canto 21, this pattern is suddenly broken: Beatrice does not smile, and the "dolce sinfonia di paradiso" (21.59) is silent. This absence, however, suggests a presence so full that were Dante actually to be shown its "face" in Beatrice's smile, he would become, she says, like Semele when she beheld Jove in his divinity and was immediately turned to ash.[3] The degree to which the contemplatives know God, therefore, is magnitudes beyond the capacity of the blessed encountered in the spheres below, a reality that the pilgrim can learn for himself only gradually. To this end Beatrice urges him to make mirrors of his eyes and in the act of "speculation" to practice the discipline of the contemplative life (21.16–18). What he comes to reflect, and hence to reflect upon, is the central visionary image of Saturn:

> di color d'oro in che raggio traluce
>   vid'io uno scaleo eretto in suso
>   tanto, che nol seguiva la mia luce.

Vidi anche per li gradi scender giuso
   tanti splendor, ch'io pensai ch'ogne lume
   che par nel ciel, quindi fosse diffuso.
E come, per lo natural costume,
   le pole insieme, al cominciar del giorno,
   si movono a scaldar le fredde piume;
poi altre vanno via sanza ritorno,
   altre rivolgon sé onde son mosse,
   e altre roteando fan soggiorno;
tal modo parve me che quivi fosse
   in quello sfavillar che 'nsieme venne,
   sì come in certo grado si percosse.

(Par. 21.28–42)

(I saw, of the color of gold on which a sunbeam is shining, a ladder rising up so high that my sight might not follow it. I saw, moreover, so many splendors descending along the steps, that I thought every light, which appears in heaven, had been poured down from it. And, as by their natural custom, the daws move about together, at the beginning of the day, to warm their cold feathers, then some fly away not to return, some wheel round [from where] they had started, while others wheeling make a stay; such movements, it seemed to me, were in that sparkling, which came in a throng, as soon as it smote upon a certain step.)

Saturn is named here by periphrasis as the crystal "che 'l vocabol porta, / cerchiando il mondo, del suo caro duce / sotto cui giacque ogne malizia morta" ("which bears the name, circling round the world, of its beloved leader beneath whom every wickedness lay dead," 21.25–27). This evocation of the Golden Age, renowned both for mortal innocence and for the radical simplicity of its lifestyle, introduces a number of antitheses that are developed throughout *Paradiso* 21–22: then versus now, austere beginnings versus subsequent decadence, founders versus descendants.

The souls in Saturn reveal themselves to Dante by means of a formation of lights similar to the Cross of Mars or the Eagle of Jupiter. In this case there is a ladder, shining like a sunbeam on gold. This *scaleo* is both ancient and venerable. It no doubt originates in Jacob's spectacular dream at Bethel (Gen. 28:12–13) of a ladder culminating in God's presence, with angels ascending and descending along its rungs. Elsewhere in Scripture,

Jacob finds Wisdom at the apex of the ladder, who "showed him the king-
dom of God and gave to him knowledge of the holy ones" (Wisdom 10:10).
For this reason, no doubt, Boethius's Lady Philosophy is adorned with the
very same emblem, showing the "gradus ab inferiore ad superius" that
Wisdom prompts her aspirants to climb.[4] At least since the *Rule of St.
Benedict*, moreover, the ladder had been specifically identified with con-
templation as a way of humility:

> Wherefore, brethren . . . must we set up a ladder by our ascending actions
> like unto that which Jacob saw in his vision, whereby angels appeared to
> him ascending and descending. By that descent and ascent we must
> surely understand nothing else but this, that we descend by self-
> exaltation and ascend by humility. And the ladder is our work in the
> world, which for the humble heart does the Lord to heaven raise up.[5]

Peter Damian also has the *scala* in mind when in *Dominus vobiscum* he
praises the hermit's life as a "golden way" by which to ascend to one's true
home in heaven: "Tu via aurea, quae homines reducis ad patriam" (in *PL*,
vol. 145, col. 248).

Dante glosses this received emblem of the contemplative life with a
simile: he asks us to imagine the blessed spirits on the ladder as if they were
a flock of jackdaws "al cominciar del giorno" (21.35). In early dawn the
birds rise together as a flock; but then as the day grows warm, they fly off in
their different directions. A more exotic bird might well have been chosen
for the simile, but Dante opts instead for the lowly jackdaw, as if to
reinforce the emphasis on humble simplicity throughout these cantos. The
commentary tradition takes this figure to represent the various paths fol-
lowed by the great contemplative monastics, some of whom never left the
cloister, others of whom moved out to work actively in the world, while still
a third group left and then returned "[from where] they had started." Such
an interpretation accords with readings of Jacob's vision at Bethel offered
by Peter Damian, Bernard, and Bonaventure.[6]

Whether or not the simile presses for such an interpretation, Dante's
does not celebrate the contemplative life at the expense of the active. As
dramatized in the life stories of those he meets in the heaven of Saturn—
Peter Damian and Benedict—a commitment to prayer and solitude is by
no means alien to a concern for the world. Rather, the contemplative
makes a contribution to the church's mission that extends quite beyond any

monastic enclosure. And not only to the church: Dante's representative contemplatives are also builders of the larger society.

To exemplify this point, the first of the spirits to "condescend" to Dante personifies just such a richness of calling. Descending to the bottom step of the golden ladder, much as Cacciaguida made his way to the foot of the cross in *Paradiso* 15.20, is the soul of Peter Damian (d. 1072). As abbot of the Benedictine Camaldolese monastery at Fonte Avellana, he reorganized his community so as to combine the ideals of hermit and monk, solitude and community. In doing so, he claimed to be following the "mind" of St. Benedict, who respected the eremitical life while rejecting it for himself. At the behest of Pope Stephen IX in 1057, and much against his will, Peter left Fonte Avellana to become first bishop and then cardinal. He dedicated himself not only to the reform of monasticism and a return to the ideals of the primitive church, but also to a renewal of relations between papacy and empire. To this end, he functioned as a diplomat between the curia of Pope Gregory VII and the imperial court of Henry III. In addition, moreover, he produced a wide range of writing that won him a reputation as a Latin stylist: letters, sermons, saints' lives, treatises, and minor works of both poetry and prose. The latter include epigrams, prayers, hymns, liturgical offices, and *carmina sacra*. Among the poems that might have warranted his inclusion in *Paradiso* 21 is his "Hymnus de gloria paradisi," as well as an homage to St. Benedict that celebrates him as one of the stars of heaven—a fire brightening God's "aurora aurea."[7] After his varied activities in the world, he set aside the various honors previously given him and returned to the life of a common monk at Fonte Avellana, coming home to roost like one of the jackdaws in Dante's simile.

Dante's Peter Damian reveals only a fraction of this story in *Paradiso* 21. Speaking of life in his beloved hermitage, he says that he was "content in contemplative thoughts" (v. 117)—a phrase that both in alliteration and syntax ("*con*tento ne' pensier *con*templativi") suggests the happy enclosure of the monastic life itself. Like the apostles Peter and Paul, he lived simply, with olive oil his only seasoning. Like them, too, he was barefoot and lean, learning in heat and frost alike to become "firm" (v. 114)—an allusion, no doubt, to the rooted ideal of the Benedictine *votum stabilitatis*. In the midst of this recollection, however, his thoughts turn abruptly from then to now, from the Fonte Avellana he remembers to the infinitely diminished reality Dante himself might have encountered. The same cloister that used to render souls to God "fertilemente" (v. 119) has become a wasteland. The monastic garden is now rank and deserted, its paradise of prayer and work become yet another version of paradise lost.

In Peter Damian's jeremiad we find the kind of invective characteristic of the saint's *Liber gomorrhianus*, in which he speaks vehemently about the abuses of his own day. Therefore, Dante does not use the eleventh-century monk to wax nostalgic about a purity that never was, for even in Peter Damian's time the curial hat continually passed from bad to worse ("di male in peggio si travasa," v. 126). Yet if the church was corrupt in Peter Damian's era, which was itself already fallen away from that of Peter and Paul, how much greater is the apostasy of the "moderni pastori," Dante's contemporaries. In some of the broadest humor to be found in the *Commedia*, the successors of the "lean and barefoot" disciples of Christ almost beggar description:

> Venne Cefàs e venne il gran vasello
> de lo Spirito Santo, magri e scalzi,
> prendendo il cibo da qualunque ostello.
> Or voglion quinci e quindi chi rincalzi
> li moderni pastori e chi li meni,
> tanto son gravi, e chi di rietro li alzi.
> Cuopron d'i manti loro i palafreni,
> sì che due bestie van sott' una pelle:
> oh pazïenza che tanto sostieni!
> (*Par.* 21.127–35)

(Cephas came, and the great vessel of the Holy Spirit came, lean and barefoot, taking their food at whatsoever inn. Now the modern pastors require one to prop them up on this side and one on that, and one to lead them, so heavy are they, and one to hold up their train behind. They cover their palfreys with their mantles, so that two beasts go under one hide. O patience that do endure so much!)

It has been suggested that this grotesque portrait of tottering excess, of a hierarchy in the saddle but sorely in need of propping up, gives us (however indirectly) Dante's own ideal of the virtuous prelate: "a man mature in ascetic practices, rich in apostolic zeal, wholly dedicated to his spiritual mission, and disdainful of honors and worldly comfort—a Peter Damian, for instance, or a Bonaventure."[8] Yet the overwhelming impression left by the passage itself is completely negative. Damian etches in vitriol a church hierarchy become "the beast."

These angry words shatter the silence of the sphere with what the poet identifies as "un grido di sì alto suono, / che non potrebbe qui assomigliarsi" ("a cry of such deep sound that nothing here could be likened to it," 21.140–41). Beatrice interprets this uproar as a righteous call for "la vendetta"—an unspecified act of divine vengeance. Against this tumultuous background, she turns Dante's attention in the following canto to the "hundred little spheres of light" (22.28–29) swarming on the ladder, and in particular to the brightest of them all. Attentive, the pilgrim "was standing as one who within himself represses the urge of desire, who does not make bold to ask, he so fears to go too far" (vv. 25–27). The situation seems to recall the sixth chapter of the *Rule*, "De taciturnitate," where Benedict writes, "it becomes the master to speak and teach, but it is fitting for the disciple to be silent and to listen."[9] This association might seem merely fanciful but for the fact that the *magister* who breaks through Dante's reserve at this point in the text is none other than the author of the *Rule*! Benedict goes on to tell Dante of his origins and identity, which the pilgrim had hesitated to ask about outright:

> Quel monte a cui Cassino è ne la costa
> fu frequentato già in su la cima
> da la gente ingannata e mal disposta;
> e quel son io che sù vi portai prima
> lo nome di colui che 'n terra addusse
> la verità che tanto ci soblima;
> e tanta grazia sopra me relusse,
> ch'io ritrassi le ville circunstanti
> da l'empio cólto che 'l mondo sedusse.
> Questi altri fuochi tutti contemplanti
> uomini fuoro, accesi di quel caldo
> che fa nascere i fiori e' frutti santi.
> Qui è Maccario, qui è Romoaldo,
> qui son li frati miei che dentro ai chiostri
> fermar li piedi e tennero il cor saldo.
>
>   (*Par.* 22.37–51)

(That mountain on whose slope Cassino lies was of old frequented on its summit by the folk deceived and perverse, and I am he that bore up there

His name who brought to earth that truth which so uplifts us; and such grace shone upon me that I drew away the surrounding towns from the impious worship that seduced the world. These other fires were all contemplative men, kindled by that warmth which gives birth to holy flowers and fruits. Here is Macarius, here is Romualdus, here are my brethren who stayed their feet within the cloisters and kept a steadfast heart.)

These biographical details of Benedict's life (c. 480–c. 543) come from Gregory the Great's second *Dialogue*: Benedict's foundation of a community on the summit of Monte Cassino, his supplanting of local paganism, and his eventual winning over the hearts of the country people round about. The speech also ends with a characteristic invocation of the *votum stabilitatis* in the mention of brothers who "stayed their feet within the cloisters." But what is perhaps most interesting in the poet's handling of these lines is his incorporation of images and metaphors from the earlier canto, the cumulative effect of which is to generate a common lexicon for the sphere of Saturn. We notice this first of all in the submerged figure of the ladder when Benedict speaks of himself as the one who first brought *up* to Monte Cassino the name of Christ, who brought *down* to earth "that truth which so *uplifts* us" (vv. 40–42). There is also the continued play on the opposition of cold and hot. The sphere of Saturn, the "cold planet," with its presumably icy austerities, is nonetheless populated by souls described as fires "accesi di quel caldo / che fa nascere i fiori e' frutti santi" ("kindled by that warmth which gives birth to holy flowers and fruits," vv. 47–48). This complex of imagery in turn recalls Peter Damian's assertion in canto 21 that the cloister's heats and frosts yield a spiritual harvest "fertilemente" (v. 119).

The "ardor" (v. 54) of Benedict's self-disclosure causes Dante to expand in confidence "come 'l sol fa la rosa quando aperta / tanto divien quant' ell' ha di possanza" ("just like the sun that makes the rose expand / and reach the fullest flowering that it can," vv. 56–57, trans. Mandelbaum). This "full-blown" simile grows, as metaphor, out of the "warmth that gives birth to holy flowers and fruits" cited just a few lines before. Its point, moreover, is to prepare us for the question that is to flower next: not the pilgrim's wordless question about who Benedict once was—the unspoken query that launched their dialogue—but the clear inquiry about who he is, what he looks like, now. "Ch'io / ti veggia con imagine scoverta" ("May I behold you, not veiled by light, but directly," vv. 59–60).

Throughout the third canticle, Dante has been content to see the blessed *in maschera*, within their veil of light; now, however, he asks to see one of his heavenly interlocutors as he essentially is, without the masquerade. This anomaly all but forces us to ask why the sphere of Saturn should be the occasion for this request and St. Benedict the one singled out. The answer lies, I think, in Dante's understanding of the contemplative life as a formal, "regularized" preparation for the beatific vision: for the sight of God *facie ad faciem*, face to face. Thus far in the *Commedia*—indeed, even from the time of the *Vita nuova*—Dante's yearning for such vision has been focused on Beatrice and been mediated through her. It is in her unveiled face that he first sees the "splendor of the living light eternal" (*Purg.* 31.139), and by means of her reflected radiance that he rises through the heavens to the Empyrean. She represents human love transfigured; she reveals how eros can be redeemed—can even become a means of ascent to God. On the other hand, Benedict, the father of Western monasticism, represents a radically different route to the same destination, one in which eros, rather than becoming transcendent, is itself transcended altogether. Yet in the pilgrim's longing to see Benedict "con imagine scoverta," as in his earlier longing to see Beatrice unveiled, we find juxtaposed two ways by which to know God—the affirmation of a creaturely mediator and the negation of such mediation. The juxtaposition of Beatrice and Benedict here may ultimately suggest a convergence of what these two souls represent. In any event, Francesco da Buti's fourteenth-century commentary on this moment is especially apt: "[The] contemplatives ponder the high things of God, contemplating the creature and thereby ascending to contemplate the Creator; and because the human soul is made in God's likeness, therefore the contemplatives have the desire to see the essence of the human soul more than that of any other created thing. Thus the poet has it that such thoughts come to him in this place."[10] One thinks as well of St. Augustine's conjecture, at the close of the *City of God*, that the blessed will see God *facie ad faciem* precisely by looking into one another's faces.[11]

When Benedict turns in answer to the pilgrim, it is to acknowledge both the profundity of what Dante has asked and its impossibility of granting his request at this turning of the celestial stair.

Ond' elli: "Frate, il tuo alto disio
  s'adempierà in su l'ultima spera,
  ove s'adempion tutti li altri e 'l mio.
Ivi è perfetta, matura e intera
  ciascuna disïanza; in quella sola
  è ogne parte là ove sempr' era,
perché non è in loco e non s'impola;
  e nostra scala infino ad essa varca,
  onde così dal viso ti s'invola.
Infin là sù la vide il patriarca
  Iacobbe porger la superna parte,
  quando li apparve d'angeli sì carca."
                              (*Par.* 22.61–72)

(Whereon he, "Brother, your high desire shall be fulfilled up in the last sphere, where are fulfilled all others and my own. There every desire is perfect, mature, and whole. In that alone is every part there where it always was, for it is not in space, nor has it poles; and our ladder reaches up to it, wherefore it steals itself from your sight. All the way thither the patriarch Jacob saw it stretch its upper part, when it appeared to him so laden with Angels.")

The reply is straightforward enough. Saturn, the mediation of all heavenly metaphors, the ladder of vision itself—all these must be transcended before Dante is able to see the saint's *imagine scoverta*. Such a vision is reserved for those who are in the presence of God, in the last and ineffable sphere—the *Emperio*—whose name is ingeniously encoded here within the verbs of fulfillment: "s'adempierà" (v. 62), "s'adempion" (v. 63). It is in the Empyrean, in fact, that Benedict will be seen without a veiling of light (*Par.* 32.35), seated between Francis and Augustine in that heavenly cloister where Christ himself is the abbot (*Purg.* 26.129).

While Benedict's language encourages us to imagine the vision of the Empyrean primarily as something to climb toward, it also presents the satisfaction of the "high desire" as a state to grow into. Thus he speaks here of the completion of a growth process, a ripening. Thus beatitude is "perfetta, matura, e intera," and the spiritual flowers born in the monastery are intimations of that eternal rose into whose petals Beatrice will lead him in *Paradiso* 30. Likewise, the pilgrim's request to see Benedict unveiled, in his glorified flesh, is the shadowy forecast of the sight to which he will wholly give himself at the very end of the poem, when he sees the three circles of the Blessed Trinity, with "la nostra effige" (33.131), our human image, incarnate at the center.

It is not, however, with talk of what remains to be seen at the top of the stairway, of the fruition of "high desire," that Benedict leaves Dante. Rather, he shifts abruptly from the supernal heights of Jacob's ladder, "laden with angels," to the earthly neglect of its bottommost, earthly rung:

> Ma, per salirla, mo nessun diparte
> da terra i piedi, e la regola mia
> rimasa è per danno de le carte.
> Le mura che solieno esser badia
> fatte sono spelonche, e le cocolle
> sacca son piene di farina ria.
> Ma grave usura tanto non si tolle
> contra 'l piacer di Dio, quanto quel frutto
> che fa il cor de' monaci sì folle;
> ché quantunque la Chiesa guarda, tutto
> è de la gente che per Dio dimanda;
> non di parenti né d'altro più brutto.
> La carne d'i mortali è tanto blanda,
> che giù non basta buon cominciamento
> dal nascer de la quercia al far la ghianda.
> Pier cominciò sanz' oro e sanz' argento,
> e io con orazione e con digiuno,
> e Francesco umilmente il suo convento;
> e se guardi 'l principio di ciascuno,
> poscia riguardi là dov' è trascorso,
> tu vederai del bianco fatto bruno.
> Veramente Iordan vòlto retrorso
> più fu, e 'l mar fuggir, quando Dio volse
> mirabile a veder che qui 'l soccorso.
>
> (*Par.* 22.73–96)

(But no one now lifts his foot from earth to ascend it, and my Rule remains for waste of paper. The walls, which used to be an abbey, have become dens, and the cowls are sacks full of rotten meal. But heavy usury is not exacted so counter to God's pleasure as that fruit which makes the hearts of monks so mad; for whatsoever the Church has in keeping is all for the folk that ask it in God's name, not for kindred, or for other filthier thing. The flesh of mortals is so soft that on earth a good beginning does not last from the springing of the oak to the bearing of the acorn. Peter began his fellowship without gold or silver, and I mine with prayer and fasting, and Francis his with humility; and if you look at the beginning of each, and then look again whither it has strayed, you will see the white changed to dark. Nevertheless, Jordan driven back, and the sea fleeing when God willed, were sights more wondrous than the succor here.)

Benedict's final words bring us back to the *vendetta* with which this canto opened: the call for a miracle of biblical proportions, a *soccorso* that will destroy, cleanse, and deliver. Yet there is more here than the repetition of a prophecy. There is also what has come by now to be the familiar structure of the speech itself: the contrast between then and now, between apostolate and apostasy. This contrast was drawn most immediately in canto 21, in Peter Damian's bitter comparison of St. Peter and St. Paul with "li moderni pastori" (v. 131). Earlier, it was writ large in the heaven of the Sun, where praise for Francis and Dominic changed suddenly into denunciation of those who now bear their names. Its most dramatic instance, moreover, is still to come in *Paradiso* 27, where the rapturous joy of the blessed turns to bitter mourning, as St. Peter cries out against the pollution of his office by the current pope, Boniface VIII:

> Quelli ch'usurpa in terra il luogo mio,
>   il luogo mio, il luogo mio che vaca
>   ne la presenza del Figliuol di Dio,
> fatt' ha del cimitero mio cloaca
>   del sangue e de la puzza; onde 'l perverso
>   che cadde di qua sù, là giù si placa.
>
>   (*Par.* 27.22–27)

(He that usurps on earth my place, my place, my place, which in the sight of the Son of God is empty, has made of my tomb a sewer of blood and filth, so that the apostate who fell from here above takes comfort there below.)

Noteworthy in Benedict's speech is the presence of those same images employed earlier in canto 22 to evoke the glory of the contemplative life. There is the ladder, of course, now become functionless from sheer disuse. There is also that cluster of metaphors suggesting growth and maturation. The spiritual "granary" of the abbey has become the den of thieves; its harvest is spoiled and the fruit of monastic life degenerated into a mad lust for money or power "ne d'altro più brutto" ("or for other filthier thing," v. 84). Benedict sees the full-blown hope of contemplation—a white rose, fully opened to the sun—become something cankered, darkened with corruption, turned brown from white ("del bianco fatto bruno," v. 93). Surveying the present scene, he sees only *fleurs du mal.*

Nonetheless, despite the anger of these lines and their very dim view of the church on earth, Benedict's parting word does not convey despair; rather, he speaks of hope, of *soccorso.* Having left the pilgrim with that promise, therefore, he is able to depart from him (and from the sphere of Saturn) altogether.

> Così mi disse, e indi si raccolse
>   al suo collegio, e 'l collegio si strinse;
>   poi, come turbo, in sù tutto s'avvolse.
>   (*Par.* 22.97–99)

(Thus he spoke to me, then drew back to his company, and the company closed together; then like a whirlwind all were gathered upward.)

The word that Singleton twice translates here as "company"—*collegio*—can refer to any group bound together by a common function or identity. But Dante's use of it earlier in the *Commedia* has a more specific and monastic connotation. In *Inferno* 23, for instance, the Jovial Friars welcome Virgil and Dante "al collegio / de l'ipocriti tristi" ("to the assembly of the sad hypocrites," vv. 91–92). Then in *Purgatorio* 26, Guido Guinizelli speaks of paradise itself as "[il] chiostro / nel quale è Cristo abate del collegio" ("the cloister in which Christ is abbot of the brotherhood," vv. 128–29). From all that we have learned in the sphere of Saturn, moreover, both of these eternal dimensions of *collegio*—the infernal and the heavenly—are possibilities afforded by the monastic life on earth. In this specific context, however—in the gathering of the contemplatives around Benedict—we are reminded specifically of what the prologue to the *Rule of St. Benedict* calls an "expanded heart" ("dilatato corde"), one that "runs with the unspeakable sweetness of love in the way of God's commandments" ("via mandatorum Dei"). The goal of that love is to persevere, "so that, by never abandoning his rule, but persevering in his teaching in the monastery until death . . . we may deserve to be partakers of his kingdom."[12]

It is into the heart of that kingdom—into the Empyrean, which stands, so to speak, at the "top" of the ladder—that Benedict vanishes from sight. When he goes, all that remains for Dante to hold onto is the ladder itself, and with this contemplative *scaleo*, the hope of his own heavenly ascent. In this way, the pilgrim finds himself in the position of the prophet Elisha, who watches Elijah rise into heaven in a whirlwind, "per turbinem in caelum" (2 Kings 2:11; cf. "come turbo," v. 99). This biblical reference, with its provocative suggestion of a prophetic identity to be taken on, may not be the only text at play here. There is also, perhaps, an incident that Gregory describes at the end of his second *Dialogue*:

> [On the day Benedict died] two monks, one of them at the monastery, the other some distance away, received the very same revelation. They both saw a magnificent road covered with rich carpeting and glittering with thousands of lights. From his monastery it stretched eastward in a straight line until it reached up into heaven. And there in the brightness stood a man of majestic appearance, who asked them, "Do you know who passed this way?" "No," they replied. "This," he told them, "is the road taken by blessed Benedict, the Lord's beloved, when he went to heaven."[13]

In *Paradiso* 22, the "majestic one" who appears at the departure of Benedict is Beatrice, whom the poet addresses in this monastic context, and without any sense of incongruity, as "la dolce donna," "my sweet lady" (v. 100). Nor does this novice mistress waste any words in addressing him:

> La dolce donna dietro a lor mi pinse
> con un sol cenno su per quella scala,
> sì sua virtù la mia natura vinse;
> né mai qua giù dove si monta e cala
> naturalmente, fu sì ratto moto
> ch' agguagliar si potesse a la mia ala.
> S'io torni mai, lettore, a quel divoto
> trïunfo per lo quale io piango spesso
> le mie peccata e'l petto mi percuoto.
> (*Par.* 22.100–108)

(My sweet lady, with only a sign, thrust me up after them by that ladder, so did her power overcome my nature; nor ever here below, where we mount and descend by nature's law, was motion so swift as might match my flight. So may I return, reader, to that devout triumph for the sake of which I often bewail my sins and beat my breast.)

So the episode ends. The pilgrim follows rapidly in the wake of the contemplatives, not yet to the Empyrean itself, but to the next rung of the celestial ladder, to the heaven of the fixed stars. From that vantage Dante will look down through the concentric spheres of the universe and see our world as a small and paltry thing. Thus Benedict saw it, says Gregory, gathered into a single ray of light.[14] Most poignant, however, is the poet's brief address to the reader, which places Benedict's ladder and all it represents outside the sphere of the fiction and into that world in which the poet writes and the reader reads—the world in which we live. "So may I return, reader, to the devout triumph for the sake of which I often bewail my sins and beat my breast." The poet's words are explicitly about himself, about his hope to return after death to the reality of which this poem can be but the dark glass of a similitude. But as we have known from the very first line of *Inferno*—"nel mezzo del cammin di nostra vita"—the fiction of his experience is also an invitation to discover the truth of our own journey. Dante gives the reader a ladder to climb, a *scaleo d'oro* whose canto-by-canto intention, to quote the poet's epistle to Can Grande, is "to remove those living in a state of misery, and to bring them to a state of happiness" (para. 15).[15] In the end, the poem is itself a rule that blossoms with observance, an ascent of the imagination "by gradual scale sublimed."

PART 5

Dante and the World

CHAPTER 13

Crossing Over: Dante and Pilgrimage

Among the many contributions made by cultural anthropologists to the study of religion, few have proved as useful as the notion of liminality. The term itself, deriving from *limen,* the Latin for "threshold," comes from Arnold van Gennep's pioneering *Les rites de passage* (1908). In his study of tribal rituals that mark transitions "from group to group or from one social situation to the next,"[1] van Gennep identified three successive but distinct stages: a *separation* from the everyday world, an entrance into ritual time and space called the "margin" or *limen,* and a *reaggregation* into mundane existence. A half-century later Victor Turner seized upon the middle term of this sequence as the very heart of the ritual process. But whereas van Gennep conceived of a finite moment within the processive form of traditional rites of passage, Turner saw more extensive, even revolutionary, implications. He likened his discovery of liminality to a pebble tossed into a pool; its widening circles drew him beyond the small, preindustrial societies with which he had been initially concerned, leading him to consider the place of "margins" or "thresholds" in global civilizations such as our own. He came to think, in fact, that the notion of liminality was applicable to "all phases of decisive cultural change, in which previous orderings of thought and behavior are subject to revision and criticism, when hitherto unprecedented modes of ordering relations between ideas and people become possible and desirable."[2] Instead of a delimited stage in the ritual of preindustrial societies, he found a "potentiality" at play in our own world.

But at play where? Turner suggested that liminal moments throughout Western history have given birth to a variety of "margins": utopias, new philosophical systems, political programs, even scientific hypotheses. He also saw in Christian monasticism an effort to turn the ritual threshold into a way of life, that is, into "a very long threshold, a corridor, almost, or a tunnel."[3] However, the form of liminality that finally claimed his interest was not the stabilized margin represented by monastic enclosure but rather the ancient and enduring phenomenon of pilgrimage. For Catholic Christians throughout the ages, he argued, the journey to and from a sacred place offered the laity the great liminal experience of the religious life: "While monastic contemplatives and mystics could daily make interior salvific journeys, those in the world had to exteriorize theirs in the infrequent adventure of pilgrimage."[4]

Victor and Edith Turner explore the ways in which the pilgrim's "adventure" resembles many elements of the traditional rite of passage (separation, *limen*, and reaggregation) in the introduction to *Image and Pilgrimage* (1978).[5] The journey begins with an act of separation, as the pilgrim leaves not only the familiar geography of home but the structures and priorities of mundane life. Gradually, the markers of class and status loosen their hold, as a more egalitarian *communitas* develops between fellow travelers that are all on their way to a common spiritual destination. Daily life itself is increasingly spiritualized, transformed by the reality of those *sacra*, or sacred things, that are revealed to the pilgrim in the holy places and expounded through various kinds of instruction and exhortation. Physical discomfort, even actual ordeal, is also part of this extended initiation, for the way of a Christian pilgrim is inevitably a *via crucis*. Indeed, suffering has its intended purpose in this experience, either as a purgation of the "old" self or as the birth pangs associated with the emergence of a "new," more authentic person. Whereas reaching the sacred site at first seems like the primary goal of the journey, what gradually emerges in importance is the pilgrim's new and deeper level of existence. What really matters is the crossing of a spiritual rather than a physical threshold; the "end" of the journey is a renewed heart and mind. Finally, once the pilgrimage is completed, the rounds of daily life resume within the familiar structures of home. However, things are not the same as they were before the journey. Like the wise men in T. S. Eliot's "Journey of the Magi," the pilgrim is "no longer at ease here, in the old dispensation." Encounter with the sacred has destabilized the structures of secular life and altered the status quo; it has opened the windows of perception onto something new.

Working from this generic model of pilgrimage, the Turners go on to identify four main types—prototypical, archaic, medieval, and modern. In subsequent chapters, he analyzes several contemporary instances of each, including pilgrimages to sites ranging from St. Patrick's Purgatory in Lough Derg, Ireland, to Lourdes in France, to a number of sites in Mexico. We may fruitfully bring the anthropologist's analysis to bear on what is perhaps the most important literary pilgrimage in all of Christian tradition, a sacred journey undertaken precisely as a liminal experience of transformation— the one Dante describes in the pages of his *Commedia*. There are, of course, other notable literary treatments of pilgrims and pilgrimages that reflect different aspects of this "liminoid phenomenon": other poems, such as Chaucer's *Canterbury Tales*, Tasso's *Gerusalemme Liberata*, and the first book of Spenser's *Faerie Queene*, or such prose works as Petrarch's "familiar letters" on fourteenth-century pilgrims or the descriptions of holy sites in the anonymous medieval *Mirabilia urbis Romae*. None of these works, however, even approaches the depth or the extent of Dante's reflections on pilgrimage; nor does any yield the poet's insights into the fundamental place of Christian ritual in the experience of liminal transformation. In other words, while cultural anthropology offers the reader of Dante a lens through which to see anew the entire enterprise of the *Commedia*—and most especially that of the poem's own middle space, the *Purgatorio*—the *Commedia* in its turn brings the notion of liminality to life.

I want to argue that Dante conceives of the whole of his poem as a pilgrimage text written "for the reason that the pilgrim's staff is brought back wreathed with palm" (*Purg.* 33.77–78), that is, it was written both to testify to a process already completed and to inspire others to undertake the same. On one level, the *Commedia* presents Dante's experience as an actual itinerary through real (if otherworldly) space, not as a dream vision from which the poet wakes up into reality. Yet this allegorical work is also an *itinerarium mentis*, the journey of a soul from death to life; or as Beatrice puts it toward the end of the poem, from the bondage of earth's Egypt to Jerusalem's *beata vita* (*Par.* 25.55–56). In the fiction of the poem, Dante is rescued from the "dark wood" of spiritual malaise and led through the three realms of the afterlife by a series of divinely appointed guides. Separated from the mundane world of Florence, he crosses over one boundary after another; in so doing, he learns the mysteries of hell, purgatory, and paradise, and is transformed by what he sees. Toward the end of this progress he is told to make his entire vision known to the world: "tutta tua visïon fa manifesta" (*Par.* 17.128). The *Commedia* itself, therefore, is to be memory's witness, the memoir of the poet's crossing over "al divino da l'umano, / a l'etterno dal tempo . . . / e di Fiorenza in popol giusto e sano" ("to the divine from the human, to the eternal from time . . . and from Florence to a people just and sane," 31.37–39).

Yet at the same time that Dante makes this singular claim, he is also at pains to underscore a common ground between his unique itinerary through the afterlife and those sacred journeys undertaken, at home or abroad, by other Christians. For this reason, he invokes the particulars of pilgrimage—what the Turners call the laity's "great liminal experience of the religious life"—in order to join his voyage to those taken by so many of his contemporaries to Jerusalem, Rome, or Compostela.[6] He does this in the first place by setting his Holy Week journey in 1300, during the Jubilee "holy year" promulgated by Pope Boniface VIII, when Christians making a pilgrimage to the sacred sites of Rome were offered the same spiritual benefits of a pilgrimage to Jerusalem ("not only a full and copious, but the most full pardon of all their sins").[7] Because the Holy Land was no longer in Christian hands, and in any case stood at too great a distance for most people to visit, the popular response to Boniface's offer of plenary indulgence was enormous. The resulting influx of people into Rome, estimated variously between two hundred thousand and two million,[8] is explicitly recalled at one point in the *Commedia*, in a context rich in irony. When in *Inferno* 18 the poet looks down into a ditch that is packed with panders and seducers, he notes that the damned are crowded together in a single passageway but nonetheless move past one another in opposite directions. Despite the presumed difference between the ditches of hell and the pilgrim-thronged streets of Christian Rome, this two-way flow of traffic reminds Dante (as no doubt it would have reminded many a contemporary reader) of efforts made at crowd control during the holy year:

> come i Roman per l'essercito molto,
> > l'anno del giubileo, su per lo ponte
> > hanno a passar la gente modo colto,
> che da l'un lato tutti hanno la fronte
> > verso 'l castello e vanno a Santo Pietro,
> > da l'altra sponda vanno verso 'l monte.
> > > > > (*Inf.* 18.28–33)

(thus the Romans, because of the great throng, in the year of the Jubilee, have taken measures for the people to pass over the bridge, so that on one side all face toward the Castle and go on to St. Peter's and on the other they go on toward the Mount.)[9]

If this is the *Commedia*'s one explicit recollection of the holy year, it is by no means the only remembrance of Roman pilgrimage. When Dante enters the Empyrean, for instance, he is as wonder-struck as some northern "barbarian" first setting foot in Rome, seeing the Lateran rise up, and agog at the architectural wonders of the city ("Roma e l'ardüa sua opra," *Par.* 31.34). Taking in the City of God, he is

quasi peregrin che si ricrea
    nel tempio del suo voto riguardando,
    e spera già ridir com' ello stea,
                    (*Par.* 31.43–45)

(like a pilgrim who is refreshed within the temple of his vow as he looks around, and already hopes to tell again how it was.)

When subsequently he finds himself in the presence of St. Bernard, more-over, he is as amazed as any visitor to the chapel in St. Peter's that is consecrated to the Veronica Veil. Standing "face to face" with the imprint of Christ's features, he is

Qual è colui che forse di Croazia
    viene a veder la Veronica nostra,
    che per l'antica fame non sen sazia,
ma dice nel pensier, fin che si mostra:
    "Segnor mio Iesù Cristo, Dio verace,
    or fu sì fatta la sembianza vostra?"
tal era io.
                    (*Par.* 31.103–9)

(As is he who comes perchance from Croatia to look on our Veronica, and whose old hunger is not sated, but says in thought so long as it is shown, "My Lord Jesus Christ, true God, was then your semblance like to this?" such was I.)

While the whole of the *Commedia* can be said to represent a pilgrimage from the city of man to the city of God, it is quite specifically in the

Purgatorio that the poet undertakes his major exploration of liminality. There are a number of reasons why this should be the case. In the first place, in contrast to the eternal states of beatitude or damnation, purgatory is a temporal realm, governed by time and characterized by process and change. Standing betwixt and between the eternal, it presents the Catholic imagination with a more open middle term, a threshold to be traversed after death by those who, while not in a state of mortal sin, are still not ready to receive the beatific vision.[10] What they require is a period of transformation, a *limen*, which may extend for centuries—a "margin" for renewal in the afterlife.

In addition to being temporal, purgatory is also a temporary realm coterminous with the age of grace. "Born" after the resurrection of Christ— born, that is, as one of the first fruits of redemption—it will also pass away at the time of the Last Judgment, when purgation finds its ultimate purpose and fulfillment in beatitude. For this reason purgatory is (to recall Turner's understanding of the *limen*) more a phase or a process than a state; for this reason, too, its residents are only sojourners. Assisted by the suffrages of those who are still alive in the Church Militant—the faithful who keep fasts, make prayer, give alms, and most especially have masses offered up—the penitents make their expiation in hope rather than despair. For although the souls endure pains that are not unlike those of hell, they can look forward to an eventual release from their misery. The Church Suffering will end as the Church Triumphant.

Jacques Le Goff counts the mid–thirteenth century as the "birth" of purgatory and the Jubilee year of 1300 as its theological and social triumph; he also celebrates Dante for giving purgatory its "noblest representation," that is, for making "an enduring selection from among the possible and at times competing images whose choice the Church, while affirming the essence of the dogma, left to the sensibility and imagination of individual Christians."[11] Without doubt the poet did indeed take full advantage of this imaginative liberty. In the first place, he resolved the vexed whereabouts of the *locus purgatorius* as nobody else before him had. He brought purgatory up from the horrors of the underworld, turned it into a sevenstory mountain at the antipodes from Jerusalem, and placed it in the bright light of day. He also crowned it with Eden, the " 'luogo eletto / a l'umana natura per suo nido" ("place chosen for nest of the human race," *Purg.*

28.77–78). With geography ultimately made the handmaiden to theology, Dante showed the site of penance to border Eden rather than hell, thus suggesting that penitence properly culminates in the restoration of innocence and joy.[12] The end of the purgatorial pilgrimage, therefore, is that the soul should be as guiltless as Adam and Eve before the Fall.

Yet the proximity of suffering to bliss did not turn purgatory itself into a paradise of earthly delight. Pain was necessary, both in "working off" unexpiated sin and in making restitution to God. The proud, therefore, double over under the burden of heavy weights, the envious have their eyes sewn shut, gluttons become skeletal ghosts, and the lustful walk a "burning road" (26.28). Such pain is never torture; rather, suffering is the inevitable component of a spiritual maturation whereby the human worm struggles to become the angelic butterfly: "noi siam vermi / nati a formar l'angelica farfalla," 10.124–25).

Dante's break with tradition in this regard does not so much set him apart from the refined reflections of the Scholastic theologians as it distances him from the image-makers of popular religion, his precursors in theological mythopoeia. Their representation of purgatory as a torture chamber, indistinguishable from hell except in the time limit to its horrors, continued to predominate for centuries, as in the nightmare Shakespeare could still conjure up in *Hamlet* (1.5.9–22):

> I am thy father's spirit, doom'd for a certain term to walk the night,
>> And for the day confin'd to fast in fires,
>> Till the foul crimes done in my days of nature
>> Are burnt and purg'd away. But that I am forbid
>> To tell the secrets of my prison-house,
>> I could a tale unfold whose lightest word
>> Would harrow up thy soul, freeze thy young blood,
>> Make thy two eyes, like stars, start from their spheres,
>> Thy knotted and combined locks to part,
>> And each particular hair to stand on end,
>> Like quills upon the fretful porpentine.
>> But this eternal blazon must not be
>> To ears of flesh and blood.

In Dante's hands, the "prison-house" becomes a spiritual clinic in which the penitent's broken bones come eventually to heal. "Non attender la forma del martire: / pensa la succession," "Heed not the form of the pain," the poet tells the reader on the first terrace of the mountain; "think what follows" (10.109–10). Contrition and joy go hand in hand.

Dante also turned purgatory into a spiritual school where souls become wise and learn beatitude systematically. Instead of a determinate prison sentence, however, the penitents endure the hard labor of instruction only as long as is necessary: they "graduate," so to speak, precisely when they are ready to do so. We see this transitional moment twice in the canticle, once for Statius in *Purgatorio* 20 and once for Dante himself, in canto 27. After climbing the mountain over the course of three days, thereby symbolically expiating all seven of the deadly sins, Dante stands at last on the threshold of Eden, ready for the new life. Virgil says to him:

> Non aspettar mio dir più né mio cenno;
>   libero, dritto e sano è tuo arbitrio,
>   e fallo fora non fare a suo senno:
> per ch'io te sovra te corono e mitrio.
>
> (*Purg.* 27.139–42)

(No longer expect word or sign from me. Free, upright, and whole is your will, and it would be wrong not to act according to its pleasure; wherefore I crown and mitre you over yourself.)

Most importantly for our purposes, however, Dante transformed the middle term of the afterlife into an extended threshold between earth and heaven, a "margin" where souls could move from one order of being to another, until in time they are reborn in God. Indeed, among the poet's most valuable contributions to Catholic theology was his explicit cultivation of that dimension of liminality which, if inherent in any notion of purgatory, nonetheless remained undeveloped in earlier (not to mention later) representations. What he portrayed in the central canticle of his poem was exactly what the church's teaching on penitence had long needed as a theological redress—a sense of health and excitement to be found in the refining fire, of exhilaration over new discoveries awaiting the broken and contrite heart. For in Dante's vision the point of purgatory was not so much to "serve time" in a place of temporal suffering as it was to enter a process of transformation, to become someone new. In short, the poet took what was popularly imagined as an upper chamber of hell and turned it into an extended passage to heaven. His purgatory is the *limen* of the afterlife, a threshold crossing in which (to quote the Turners again) "previous orderings of thought and behavior are subject to revision and criticism, when hitherto unprecedented modes of ordering relations between ideas and people become possible and desirable."

In Dante's purgatory this process of revision, the discovery of a new way of ordering reality, is the result not only of God's grace but also of human prayer. In this regard, of course, the *Commedia* simply reflects what the church had long taught: within the communion of saints, the intercessory prayers of the faithful on earth could lighten the trials of the dead. This belief is demonstrated throughout the *Purgatorio* whenever the souls either ask to be remembered by relatives and friends or recall the suffrages made in their behalf: prayers, fasts, almsgiving, votive masses. "I sought peace with God on the brink of my life," says one of the envious, "and my debt would not yet be reduced by penitence, had not Pier Pettinaio remembered me in his holy prayers, who in his charity did grieve for me" (13.124–29). The souls also approach Dante himself for intercessions, as when Arnaut Daniel calls out from the fires on the terrace of lust and asks to be remembered in his pain, "*sovenha vos a temps de ma dolor!*" (26.147). At least once, moreover, the poet himself makes an authorial request for prayer, bidding his audience to turn their reading of the *Commedia* into an extended suffrage for the souls in purgatory. In *Purgatorio* 11, after reporting that the penitents on the terrace of pride pray for those who remain behind on earth, the poet asks his readers,

> Se di là sempre ben per noi si dice,
>   di qua che dire e far per lor si puote
>   da quei c'hanno al voler buona radice?
> Ben si de'loro atar lavar le note
>   che portar quinci, sì che, mondi e lievi,
>   possano uscire a le stellate ruote.
>
> (*Purg.* 11.31–36)

(If there they always ask good for us, what can here be said or done, by those who have their will rooted in good? Truly we ought to help them wash away the stains they have borne thence, so that pure and light they may go forth to the starry wheels.)

While Dante inherited a traditional belief in the efficacy of prayer for the faithful departed, he was in other respects quite innovative. For in addition to the economy of intercession, he imagined another connection between the Church Militant on earth and the Church Suffering in purgatory: he transferred to the *limen* of the afterlife those ritual aids to spiritual formation and transformation that are characteristic of ordinary Catholic Christianity. In his hands, therefore, purgatory became a worshipping community, with prayer and praise shown to constitute the souls' penance quite as much as the mechanics of their pain. The Scholastic theologians who effectively "invented" purgatory said nothing about any liturgical practice taking place within the *ignis purgatorius.* Nor did the preaching friars and other popularizers, who, if they exhorted the living to acts of piety on behalf of the dead, did not represent the souls themselves as engaged in ritual process. Likewise the medieval visionaries of the afterlife, who imagined all kinds of purgatorial suffering, never depicted what Dante shows on every level of the mountain: the singing of hymns, the recitation of the Our Father and other prayers, the echo of the Beatitudes. Here as well the poet discovered his own way. In *his* purgatory, the penitents worship their way into holiness.

To signify the importance of liturgy both as the medium for penance and as the agent of personal transformation, Dante filled the 33 cantos of *Purgatorio* with liturgical song, prayer, ceremony, and drama. Thus, although his penitents work out their salvation through physical suffering and ordeal, their participation in Christian worship is what renews and reorders them. While Dante invents some of these rites for the poem, they are not without precedent. When he first approaches the "holy mountain," for instance, he enacts a kind of Asperges Me by washing his face and girding himself with a rush (1.94–105, 121–29). Likewise, upon completing his journey he is immersed in two Edenic rivers, and emerges from their sacramental bath "puro e disposto a salire a le stelle" ("pure and ready to rise to the stars," 33.145). Liturgical invention, however, is not the norm; rather, the souls in purgatory sing their way up the mountain in familiar songs that are taken from the daily action of the Mass and the Divine Office: the Miserere and the Agnus Dei, the Salve Regina and Te Deum Laudamus, and most especially, the Psalms.[13] They meditate on Scripture formerly ignored and say the prayers and chant the hymns for which they once had little time.

This reliance on the texts and rituals of the Church Militant is put in the foreground at the outset of the canticle, when Dante hears new arrivals to purgatory chanting the words of Psalm 113 (114):

> "*In exitu Israel de Aegypto*"
>   cantavan tutti insieme ad una voce
>   con quanto di quel salmo è poscia scripto.
>   (*Purg.* 2.46–48)

("*In exitu Israel de Aegypto*" all of them were singing together with one voice, with the rest of that psalm as it is written.)

By immediately drawing attention to this unison performance, the poet alerts us to the great difference between hell and purgatory. Whereas the damned knew nothing about corporate song, the redeemed here unite "ad una voce," finding their private speech become the corporate word of Scripture. The particular choice of this psalm is also telling, for in keeping with venerable allegorical interpretation, "In exitu Israel de Aegypto" invokes both the Old Testament's Exodus and the New Testament's redemption in Christ—the two salvation events that underwrite Dante's entire journey in the *Commedia*. The psalm also has its place in the ancient baptismal liturgy of Easter Eve, where Israel's passing through the Red Sea is conflated with the sacrament of Christian initiation.[14] Dante draws a connection, therefore, between two spiritual rites of passage: just as on earth the newly baptized cross over into the Body of Christ, so the souls in purgatory also move *in exitu*, out of sin's dominion, and across the threshold of their sanctification. As on earth so in purgatory, the redeemed become pilgrims *in via*.

In *Purgatorio* Dante structures our experience of this crossing in three quite distinct stages. Each one is given its own location on the mountain; each also explores a distinctive moment of spiritual transformation that correlates quite remarkably with the stages of van Gennep's rites of passage. The first, commonly identified by contemporary Dante critics as "ante-purgatory," corresponds to the initial phase of separation. Located at the base of the holy mountain and standing outside the gates of purgatory proper, a kind of limbo is presented by the poet for all those not yet ready to begin their ascent, who must first "ripen" in preparation. These include a number of categories: excommunicates (who remain here 30 years

for every year outside the church), the spiritually slothful, those who re-
pented only *in articulo mortis*, and souls whose lives were preoccupied with
worldly rather than spiritual matters. What characterizes everyone is a deep
attachment to what has been so suddenly or so incompletely left behind in
the world. Therefore, they point to their mortal wounds or describe the
circumstances of their deaths. They are preoccupied with their bodies, the
places they once lived, and with all that brought them to their mortal end:

> Siena mi fé, disfecemi Maremma:
> salsi colui che 'nnanellata pria
> disposando m'avea con la sua gemma.
>
> (*Purg.* 5.134–36)

(Siena made me, Maremma unmade me, as he knows who with his ring
had plighted me to him in wedlock.)

Yet in the midst of preoccupations over how they conducted or ended
their lives on earth, these souls are even now finding another existence, a
new self. Thus the late repentant who died violent deaths are "cantando
Miserere a verso a verso" ("singing *Miserere* verse by verse," 5.24): they
appropriate the psalm's cry of penitence at the same time that they learn to
ask God for mercy. Likewise, the souls who died in a state of excom-
munication from the church, who were spiritual sheep without a shepherd
to guide them, are compared in an extended simile to a "mandra fortunata"
("fortunate flock," 3.86) all huddled together, their eyes and muzzles bent
to the ground. As sheep that now have a divine shepherd, they are in the
first stages of becoming a community.

Among all the pilgrims-in-the-making within antepurgatory, the group
most interesting to Dante are those who neglected their spiritual condition
because of political cares. To represent them the poet chose a number of
thirteenth-century European rulers who were bitter enemies in life but
who now comfort one another in common grief over their failed past.
Behind this group portrait of monarchs involved in a penitential healing
process there may well stand, as Le Goff suggests, two precursor texts. In
one of them, the vision of purgation ascribed to Charles the Fat, a living
man sees his father's lords "and the lords of my uncles and brothers" poised
between two pools, one boiling and the other cool. He learns that these
princely ancestors can be rescued from the agony of the former by "masses,

offerings, psalmodies, vigils and alms." Likewise in the second possible precursor, the vision of Tundale, once-warring kings of Ireland—legendary enemies like Domachus and Conchobar—appear gently reconciling themselves one to another in friendship.[15]

Dante's "Valley of Princes" (*Purgatorio* 7–8) is especially striking both for the paradisiacal beauty of the setting and for its profoundly liturgical dimension. In this valley princes become monks, spending their days in prayer, song, and the regulated labor of repentance. Thus, as the sun sets on the poet's first day in purgatory, he sees the princes interrupt their sorrow over things done and left undone in order to sing the evening antiphon, Salve Regina. In doing so, presumably, they remind themselves *in hac lacrimum valle* that they are children of Eve in exile from their true *patria* in heaven.[16] Later, one of their company rises up, assumes the *orans* position, and sings the compline hymn, Te Lucis Ante. "[E] l'altre poi dolcemente e devote / seguitar lei per tutto l'inno intero, / avendo li occhi a le superne rote" ("Then the rest joined him sweetly and devoutly through the whole hymn, keeping their eyes fixed on the supernal wheels," 8.16–18). The poet does not include the text of the hymn in his poem; he counts instead on the reader to supply the familiar words attributed to St. Ambrose and commonly invoked to protect against the terrors of the night:

> Procul redant somnia
> Et noctium phantasmata;
> Hostemque nostrum comprime,
> polluantur corpora.
>
> (From all ill dreams defend our eyes
> From nightly fears and fantasies;
> Tread under foot our ghostly foe,
> That no pollution we may know.)[17]

Even before the princes close their eyes in sleep, moreover, the petition of the Te Lucis Ante is fulfilled. As if bidden by the words of the hymn, a drama unfolds before our eyes: two angels with flaming swords descend from the "bosom of Mary" (8.37) and take positions before the assembled princes. They await "our adversary," "una biscia, / forse qual diede ad Eva il cibo amaro" ("a snake perhaps such as gave to Eve the bitter food," vv. 98–99). In this brief pageant, with its nightly reenactment of heaven's conquest of evil, the angels cleave the air with their wings and repel the serpent. In so doing they remind the princes that the petitions of the compline hymn, "Hostemque nostrum comprime," have indeed been granted.

In antepurgatory, the poet shows the power of ritual to foster a separation from secular reality, to inaugurate life in the realm of the sacred. The hymns they sing become the dramas they watch and the redemption in which they trust. Moreover, by singing hymns that were left unsung in life, by reminding themselves of their status as *exules filii Evae*, by viewing again and again this theological pageant of their redemption—in short, by learning to see themselves not as powerful men of the world but as souls rescued from "nostro avversaro" (8.95)—the souls begin to let go of their past and long for God's future. When the time comes that they burn to know what awaits them after their exile, they will be ready to enter purgatory proper.

That entrance is strongly marked in canto 9 by a literal threshold that signals *Purgatorio's* second and most obviously liminal stage: a gate, three steps leading up to it, and an angelic guardian who wields a brilliant sword. As Dante sees his true spiritual likeness mirrored in the steps to the angel's throne, he is prepared for his initiation into purgatory by what amounts to a ritual scarring: the angel inscribes on his forehead seven P's, one for each of the deadly sins. Thus marked by the "courteous doorkeeper" (9.92) and prepared for the gradual erasure that will take place along the terraces of the mountain—"See that you wash away these wounds when you are within" (9.114)—Dante crosses over into purgatory proper with the Te Deum Laudamus ringing in his ear. Again, the choice of liturgical text is important in context. Thought by tradition to have been composed by Ambrose for Augustine's baptism, this hymn was sung in Dante's day "when a man depart[ed] from this world and enter[ed] a religious order."[18] Sung at this particular threshold, therefore, it commemorates more than one ritual initiation into a sacred life.

Once Dante is inside the gate, the poem begins its exploration of liminal transformation in earnest, as Dante becomes a "pilgrim" and joins vicariously in a purgatorial process that stretches from cantos 10–27. Throughout the seven terraces of the mountain, each redressing one of the deadly sins, the penitents learn the realities of a new life in God. Together they separate from worldly identifications and detach themselves from old definitions of self and society. As the newcomer to this reorientation, the pilgrim is inevitably the initiate who stands to be corrected. On the terrace of the avaricious and prodigal, for instance, when Dante kneels to reverence the soul of Pope Adrian V, he uses the honorific "you" ("voi") in addressing the former pontiff. Adrian at once reminds him, however, that he has crossed over the threshold of purgatory and is now in a realm of redeemed *communitas*:

> "Drizza le gambe, lèvati sù, frate!"
>   rispuose; "non errar: conservo sono
>   teco e con li altri ad una podestate."
>   (*Purg.* 19.133–35)

("Straighten up your legs, rise up, brother," the pope tells him; "do not err: I am a fellow servant with you and the others unto one Power.")

Here we find what Turner speaks of as the margin's "leveling process."[19] Pope and layman are brothers and fellow servants, united by a spiritual bond quite over and above the hierarchies that once differentiated and separated them.[20]

While, as we have seen, the terraces of *Purgatorio* demonstrate the first two major components of the liminal process—the "recombination of cultural traits and constituents" and the fostering of *communitas*—they give even more attention to the third, what the Turners call "the communication of the *sacra*."[21] In discussing the latter, they borrow classicist Jane Harrison's division of *sacra* into three kinds: exhibitions ("what is shown"), actions ("what is done"), and instructions ("what is said"). Thus, an initiate may be shown holy objects or relics, may witness or participate in the performance of sacred drama, and may formally receive the teaching of spiritual guides or adepts. Initiation, therefore, entails the handing on of lore and the movement from skills to wisdom; it is a kind of catechumenate.

Perhaps the most striking feature of the *Commedia*'s purgatory is how these *sacra* claim more of our attention than the mechanics, or even the experience, of penitential pain. This might be seen as part of the poet's overall refusal to infernalize purgatory, his choice to view suffering as only one element in expiation's rite of passage rather than as its predominant feature. It may also represent his interest in the power of art—his own very much included—both to transform people and to mediate sacred reality to them. For by emphasizing the importance of the *sacra* on the terraces of the holy mountain, Dante is not only inventing a liminal purgatory but also in effect underwriting his own enterprise in art.

Harrison's tripartite classification is helpful in seeing how the purgatorial process of Dante's terraces "works." To take the terrace of pride, for instance, "what is shown" is a series of art works created by God, the divine craftsman, that illustrate first the virtue of humility and then the vice of *superbia*. Exemplifying the former are bas-reliefs (or "intaglios") that show Mary at the Annunciation, David dancing naked before the Ark, and the emperor Trajan administering justice to a widow. All are made with such skill and perfection so that "non pur Policleto,/ma la natura lì avrebbe scorno" ("not only Polycletus but Nature herself would be put to shame," 10.32–33). Portraying the wages of pride, on the other hand, is a carved pavement recalling the "storiated" tombstones that often cover the floors of medieval churches. The pavement is covered with images of the mighty that have fallen.[22] In their purgation, therefore, the souls are called first to look up and aspire to the virtues depicted on the terrace's wall, and then to look down and trample images of vice underfoot. Viewing God's art, which is brought to us entirely by the artistry of Dante's poem, they are "renovated" and "renewed" (to recall the closing lines of the second canticle). The images they "read" on the mountain help the souls toward their rebirth.

This same terrace of pride also offers an illustration of what Harrison speaks of as "what is done." The penitents each shoulder more or less heavy stones, which must be carried for as long as they continue to be burdened by their own pride; when no longer so afflicted, they are released from their burdens and can stand tall. In that moment, presumably, they experience the same erasure of the forehead *peccati* that Dante comes to know at the conclusion of each round of purgation. At all those threshold crossings, an appropriate Beatitude is sung (here "Beati pauperes spiritu," *Purg.* 12.110), and a brush of an angel's wing effaces the mark of sin.

Finally, examples of "what is said," Harrison's category of instruction, range widely on the terraces. Some instruction comes from the penitent souls, as when the artist Oderisi speaks at length about the folly of artistic fame or "nominanza" (11.100–117). Elsewhere on the mountain, sight is impeded so that oracles are heard in passing or "rain down" without mediation from heaven's own light of imagination (17.13–18). Then, of course, teaching is offered continuously by Dante's purgatorial guides—Virgil for the most part, but also Sordello, Statius, Matelda, and finally Beatrice herself. Each of these "adepts" imparts a different degree of revelation, affording another glimpse of the "veduta etterna" ("eternal view," 25.31) into which all of purgatory is an initiation. Each of them guides Dante's pilgrimage to an appointed end.

This communication of the *sacra* along the various terraces ends in the third and final stage of the purgatorial pilgrimage, when the penitents emerge free of their sin and are able to enter the Garden of Eden (*Purg.* 27–33). At the completion of this journey of transformation, in other words, the original birthplace of humanity becomes the site of the soul's rebirth. Yet because Eden also continues the terraces' work of exhibition, action, and instruction, the earthly paradise is filled with the singing of psalms and liturgical songs, as well as with a variety of theological dramas. For it is here that Dante sees an allegorical Pageant of Revelation (canto 29), watches the griffin's symbolic reenactment of Christ's redemption (canto 32), and receives a vision of apocalypse (canto 32). Here too he learns for the first time that the purpose of his pilgrimage is not limited to himself. Rather, he is charged upon his return to earth to write down everything that he has seen "in pro del mondo che mal vive" ("for profit of the world that lives ill," 32.103). His liminal transformation, as recorded in the *Purgatorio*, is meant to transform others as well.

In addition to being shown and told many things in Eden, the pilgrim must undergo two quasi-sacramental washings that effectively complete his initiation. First, he is cleansed of all guilty memory in the waters of the river Lethe, even as the Asperges Me is sung (31.98); later, immersed in the river Eunoe and swallowing its "sweet draught" (33.138), he is "d'ogne ben fatto la rende" ("restored to the memory of every good deed," 28.129; cf. 33.115–29). At the conclusion of purgatory's liminal process, therefore, we find the symbolic enactment of birth and renewal that the Turners identify as typical of reaggregation rites. Except that here in Eden, the pilgrim has been readied to rise to the heavens, not to return to the mundane world. In the final leg of his journey, he has still to cross over the final boundary into humanity's true home—the *patria* for which all of purgatory has been but the preparation. "For a little time," Beatrice tells him in *Purgatorio* 32.100–102, he will be a "forester" in the Garden; his eternal goal, however, is paradise, "quella Roma onde Cristo è romano" ("that Rome where Christ is a Roman").

Purgatory functions, therefore, as the margin between two cities, the earthly and the heavenly. At the end of his afterlife pilgrimage, the transformed pilgrim must return to the world he left behind, to remain there until the undisclosed end of his mortal life. Nevertheless, because of his journey, he knows that ultimately he belongs elsewhere, in the "Rome" that is above and free. His pilgrimage will continue on earth until he can again rejoice to see the temple of his vow—forever.

In his epistle to Can Grande della Scala, Dante proclaims to his patron that his poem is intended "to remove those living in this life from the state of misery and to lead them to the state of happiness." For this reason, he wanted it to be considered a branch of moral philosophy or ethics, "inasmuch as the whole and the part have been conceived for the sake of practical results, not for the sake of speculation."[23] What he might equally have said, however, is that he meant the *Commedia* to lead readers through a Christian rite of passage, to offer them a pilgrimage through the life to come that is, in fact, an initiation into a more conscious and God-centered understanding of the life already at hand. For to read the poet's text on its own evangelical terms—that is, to follow Dante's lead in undertaking the spiritual journey he describes—is in essence to become an initiate and pilgrim oneself. It is to enter the *Commedia*'s "betwixt and between" in order to discover a mystery of spiritual transformation that begins in a dark wood of confusion and ends in the light of the Blessed Trinity. The "practical results" of such a journey will inevitably vary from person to person. Just as pilgrims do not remember the temple of their vow in the same way, any more than they see it with the same eyes, so too with Dante's readers. Each of us finds what he or she needs, takes away what seems of value. Nonetheless, it was the poet's hope, no doubt, that the reader who crossed over the threshold of his *Commedia* might in the end be changed by the experience of reading: dislodged from the status quo, exposed to a new ordering of reality, even brought closer to the eternal one "who is blessed in the world without end."[24]

CHAPTER 14

"Out upon Circumference": Discovery in Dante

I saw no Way—The Heavens were stitched—
I felt the Columns close—
The Earth reversed her Hemispheres—
I touched the Universe—
And back it slid—and I alone—
A speck upon a Ball—
Went Out upon Circumference—
Beyond the Dip of Bell—

—*Emily Dickinson*

In the first book of the *Convivio*, a work that sets out to explore the human desire to know, Dante gives the reader a portrait of himself not as a philosopher secure in his academy but as a displaced person. Writing in the early years of his exile from Florence, he describes himself as unjustly thrown out into the world, forced to wander as a man without a country, "peregrino, quasi mendicando" (1.3). "Truly," he says, "I have been a ship without a sail and without a rudder, cast about to different harbors and inlets and shores by the dry wind of wretched poverty."[1] Elsewhere he attempts to turn this nightmare into a sign of his universality. In *De vulgari eloquentia* he boasts that it is through his displacement as well as through his wide reading in the works of poets and other writers that he has come to know all the world's diverse regions. He is, therefore, "one for whom the world is fatherland as the sea is for fish" ("cui mundus est patria velut piscibus equor," 1.6).

Yet for all this bravado, with its transparent effort to portray an uprooted Tuscan landsman as a happy *gyrovagus* of the world's seas, the metaphor that appeals to him most deeply in his exile is that of the sailor coming home to port. This is the metaphor he deploys, in fact, at the end of the *Convivio*. Thinking about the fourth and final stage of human life, he imagines the soul as a navigator negotiating his way through the waters of our three score and ten, who then comes home to God at the end of his days—to God, the safe harbor from which the soul first set forth at birth.[2]

This miniature allegory is the one Dante will later expand into the narrative of his *Commedia*, where he takes a Neoplatonic commonplace—the progress of the soul as a sea voyage—and turns it into a figure that drives forward the hundred cantos of his poem. But instead of having the good mariner hoist up his sails in old age, "in years that bring the philosophic mind," he will present himself at the outset of the *Inferno* as someone shipwrecked in the middle of the journey of our life, to recall the *Commedia*'s first simile.

> E come quei che con lena affannata
>   uscito fuor del pelago a la riva,
>   si volge a l'acqua perigliosa e guata,
> così animo mio, ch'ancor fuggiva,
>   si volse a retro a rimirar lo passo
>   che non lasciò già mai persona viva.
>
> (*Inf.* 1.22–27)

(And as he who with laboring breath has escaped from the deep to the shore turns to look back on the dangerous waters, so my mind which was still fleeing turned back to gaze upon the pass that never left anyone alive.)[3]

He will show himself to be a desperate *homo viator*, sailing his way into a heavenly port at the end of his journey, but only after undergoing the crisis of conversion and an arduous passage across the landscapes of sin and purgation.

The journey Dante describes is neither a dream nor a vision but what the poet claims to be an actual "historical" event—an exploration of what his epistle to Can Grande calls the "state of souls after death."[4] Because in the early fourteenth century both hell and purgatory could still be treated as domains of geographical science—that is, actual terrestrial sites—Dante was able to show much of the hereafter as occupying the topography of the here and now. He could situate his exploration of the life to come in unknown and inaccessible regions of *this* life. For all but the final stage of his journey, therefore, he travels through territory that, if strictly off-limits to flesh and blood, could be charted in the material heavens or located on an earthly map. Indeed, what the *Commedia* essentially unfolds for the reader is a literary *mappamundi*, a complex map of words that builds upon (and by and large reflects) a contemporary cartographer's notion of the world and its position in the cosmos. The general picture holds few surprises. As might be expected, it is drawn from reading rather than from observation and from a stock of familiar authorities that includes Orosius, Albertus Magnus, Alfraganus, Isidore of Seville, and (more immediately) Brunetto Latini.[5] Dante views the earth as a ball, a "palla," that is largely covered by ocean—what he refers to in *Paradiso* 9.84 as "quel mar che la terra inghirlanda" ("the sea that circles the world"). The dry land thus surrounded by water is restricted to the Northern Hemisphere; it is also kept within clear bounds. As Dante writes in the *Quaestio de aqua et terra* (his unique effort as a professional geographer): "It is commonly held by all that this habitable earth extends in longitude from Gades, which lies on the western boundaries of Hercules, and as far [east] as the mouths of the Ganges, as Orosius states."[6]

Although Dante was well aware of the diversity of opinion on the possibility of life at the antipodes, he follows Augustine's lead in rejecting it outright. Even if there were dry land there, no one could ever have navigated the waters stretching between the hemispheres, across what Augustine describes with a shudder as "Oceani immensitate traiecta," the vast expanse of the ocean. Because of this impassable gulf, the existence of people in the Southern Hemisphere would require another father than Adam, and therefore be a different kind of humanity altogether. Such an idea for Dante is not only false according to Christian faith ("appo la nostra fede"); it is also contrary to ancient law *and* the teaching of the Philosopher: "And doubtless Aristotle would laugh heartily if he heard speak of two different species of human generation, as if we were talking about horses and asses: for they who hold this opinion (may Aristotle forgive me) might well themselves be called asses" (*Convivio* 4.15).[7]

In all these regards, the "prose" Dante follows a conventional, even conservative, line. When we come to the *Commedia*, on the other hand, his picture of the world changes radically, at least in one major respect. It is as if in the relatively few years between the breaking off of the *Convivio* and his writing of the poem he had made a geographic discovery that warranted a revision of the world's map. All of a sudden, in what had formerly been taken as the utterly vacant waters of the Southern Hemisphere, he describes a solitary landmass, an "isoletta," or small island, located at the antipodes from Jerusalem's Mount Zion. From its shores rises a mountain of almost incalculable height.

It takes an effort of the imagination to consider what effect the appearance of this "dilettoso monte" would have had on Dante's first readers. For what he does in the *Commedia* is report a "discovery" that no other writer before him had made, one that purported to resolve not only the vexed question of Eden's whereabouts—in the *De vulgari eloquentia* he had placed it (as had many others) in the east, "in oris orientalibus" (1.8)—but also the much-debated location of purgatory. With the confidence of the traveler who has seen it all for himself firsthand, he shows both sites to occupy the same mountain, the one atop the other, and precisely on the other side of the globe from the holy city where Christ died.

Elements of this new configuration are to be found elsewhere.[8] The earthly paradise was often represented (in texts and on maps) as an island in the ocean, or as a place made inaccessible by a wall of fire, even as a place "planted" (according to the Venerable Bede) on a mountain so high it touched the sphere of the moon. Likewise purgatory was occasionally imagined as insular (as in the *Voyage of St. Brendan* and the legend of St. Patrick), or as hidden within the depths of a mountain, be it in Scotland or the wastes of Norway. Purgatory had even been linked allegorically to Eden by virtue of an association made by Ambrose and Rupert of Deutz, an interpretative bridge that joined the cherubs' flaming swords of Genesis 3:24 and the refining fires spoken of by St. Paul in 1 Corinthians 3:12–15.[9]

But as even the most cautious of the *studiosi* have had to admit, Dante reworked these traditions with striking originality, and in the process discovered more than one new thing under the sun. Single-handedly, as it were, he removed Eden to the Southern Hemisphere and discovered within it not the requisite four rivers of paradise but two—and two that no one had ever placed there: Lethe, flowing out of Virgil's Elysian Fields, and Eunoe, flowing entirely out of Dante's imagination.[10] He also brought purgatory up from the horrors of the underworld and delivered it into the bright light of day. No one before him had ever joined these two locations so concretely (or described them in such unforgettable detail); no one had placed them together at the antipodes to Jerusalem; and no one else records the *felix culpa* of their genesis.

I am referring to the origin of the mountain as related in the last canto of the *Inferno*.[11] There Dante tells how Satan, when he was expelled from heaven, plummeted to earth, plunged through its surface at the Antarctic pole, and buried himself at the dead center of the universe. Upon his impact the dry land that once covered the Southern Hemisphere fled to the north. The land at the core of the earth not only shrank from his presence (thereby creating the pit of hell around his giant body) but also rushed upward to fill the watery vacuum at the southern pole. The result was a mountain "che si leva più da l'onda" ("which rises highest from the sea," *Par.* 26.139). With Eden planted at its peak, that mountain became the birthplace of humanity, and after Adam's sin, an unpeopled world off-limits to mortals. After the redemption of Christ, however, its steep slopes and garden summit again took on life, not as a place where flesh and blood were permitted to return but as a purgatory where the penitent souls of the dead might work their way up the mountain, through sin and into virtue—where they might reenter Eden en route to the celestial paradise.

What we find in this extraordinarily dense act of mythmaking is a blend of topography, sacred history, and belief—a treatment of geography as a kind of scriptural exegesis—that links Dante to the cartographers of the *mappaemundi*.[12] In the art of both, theology generates landscape, and faith has the power to invent mountains as well as to cast them into the midst of the sea. No space is neutral. Rather, it becomes the occasion for Christian doctrine to take on a local habitation and a name, for event to become place. Or to put it another way, because the second Adam redeemed the first Adam's sin, "Christs Crosse and Adams tree" stand at the antipodes from one another. Jerusalem and Eden share a common horizon line on the globe of Dante's imagining, so that geography shows the redeeming link between one Testament of Scripture and the other.

The purpose of Dante's mapmaking, however, is more than a description of the physical world as shaped by Christian theology; it is to chart the route of pilgrimage. From the opening canto of the *Inferno* Dante is told that the purpose of his itinerary through hell and purgatory is to reach God's heavenly city. When in the last cantos of the *Paradiso* he finally arrives there, it is quite explicitly as "peregrin che si ricrea / nel tempio del suo voto riguardando, / e spera già ridir com' ello stea" ("a pilgrim who is refreshed within the temple of his vow as he looks around, and already hopes to tell again how it was," 31.43–45). He compares himself openmouthed in the Empyrean to some barbarian from the north come for the first time to

Rome, someone "wonder-struck" upon seeing St. John Lateran rise up "above all mortal things" (31.34–35). He is like a bumpkin from Croatia who gapes in wonder at the sacred image of Veronica's Veil (31.103–5).

As I show at greater length in the previous chapter, "Crossing Over," Dante clearly wanted to relate the actual travel experience of contemporary pilgrims to his own arrival in the Empyrean, "quella Roma onde Cristo è romano" (*Purg.* 32.102). Indeed, he goes out of his way to establish this correspondence by setting the poem's journey in Holy Week of 1300, the Jubilee year when the plenary indulgence offered by Pope Boniface VIII could make a pilgrimage to Rome as spiritually efficacious as one to the Holy Land. Whether from Croatia to the Lateran, or from a "selva oscura" to the heavenly Jerusalem, the journey is an *itinerarium mentis in Deum.* Indeed, the poem offers itself to the reader as an allegorical invitation to precisely this kind of spiritual voyage. To turn its pages is to set sail for God.

It is striking, therefore, that within the *Commedia* Dante should feature an account of a voyage (and the identity of a voyager) so apparently at odds with his personal enterprise. Over against all the characteristics of his own pilgrimage—the finding of a "vera via," the need for guidance along the way, a known (not to mention sacred) destination, a return home with the fruits of the experience—over against pilgrimage itself, Dante offers the counterexample of Ulysses.[13] In a poem that defines Adam's original sin as a "trapassar del segno" (*Par.* 26.117), an overpassing of a boundary, Ulysses is used not only to reenact the primal trespass against mortal limitation but to do so specifically in the form of a navigational transgression, as if in deliberate refutation of that "good mariner" described in the fourth book of the *Convivio.* Rather than venturing out in order to return home to the soul's safe harbor in God, Ulysses exemplifies the choice to take another direction entirely, to sail off the map of the known world and into forbidden seas. He breaks boundaries without looking back, making a voyage that goes "Out upon Circumference—/Beyond the Dip of Bell."

The account of this journey is given in the 26th canto of the *Inferno,* when at Dante's passionate and repeated request, Virgil engages the tormented soul of Ulysses in conversation, asking him to "tell where he went, lost, to die" ("dove, per lui, perduto a morir gissi," v. 84).[14] What follows is a spellbinding narration that utterly takes over the canto and brings it without interruption to a close. Ulysses describes how, when he left Circe after more than a year's stay, none of the familial loves or civic obligations that should have drawn him home could in fact conquer the deeper longing within him to gain experience of the world, and of human vice and worth. And so, taking with him a single boatload of faithful (if aged) companions, he sets forth on the open sea of the Mediterranean, "per l'alto mare aperto" (v. 100). But rather than sailing eastward to his home in Ithaca, he heads instead for the western edge of the known world, to "dov' Ercule segno li suoi riguardi / acció che l'uom più oltre non si metta" ("that narrow outlet where Hercules set up his markers, so that man should not pass beyond," vv. 108–9). Poised at the threshold of Gibraltar, at the geographical boundary that represents the spiritual limits to human aspiration and knowledge, Ulysses then urges his men to break through the *ne plus ultra* ("più oltre non," v. 109). In words that are often quoted out of context simply because they defy the infernal setting in which they ring out, he says to his crew:

> "O frati," dissi, "che per cento milia
>   perigli siete giunti a l'occidente,
>   a questa tanto picciola vigilia
> d'i nostri sensi ch' è del rimanente
>   non vogliate negar l'esperïenza,
>   di retro al sol, del mondo sanza gente.
> Considerate la vostra semenza:
>   fatti non foste a viver come bruti,
>   ma per seguir virtute e canoscenza."
>   (*Inf.* 26.112–20)

("O brothers," I said, "who through a hundred thousand dangers have reached the west, to this so brief vigil of the senses that remains to us, choose not to deny experience, following the sun, of the world that has no people. Consider your origin: you were not made to live as brutes, but to pursue virtue and knowledge.")

Such was the power of this little speech, this "orazion picciola" (v. 122), that Ulysses' companions lost their will in his, refusing even to wait for favorable winds to set out upon the open seas. Instead, as he remembers, "we made of our oars wings for the mad flight" ("de' remi facemmo ali al folle volo," v. 125). Turning their boat's stern to the morning and gaining always on the sinister left—that is, sailing due southwest—they find themselves come to the other side of the equator, traveling under the stars of the Southern Hemisphere. After five months of navigating through the unfathomed waters of this "alto passo" (v. 132), they suddenly (and with the joy of all mariners) discover land. Before them is a mountain, dark in the distance, and rising up from the ocean higher than anything seen in our world. Ulysses calls it, after the fashion of discoverers, "la nova terra" (v. 137). But even as he and his companions rejoice to see this new-found land, a storm whips up from its shore, striking the boat three times and whirling it in the waters for a fourth and final spin.

> a la quarta levar la poppa in suso
> e la prora ire in giù, com' altrui piacque,
> infin che 'l mar fu sovra noi richiuso.
>
> (*Inf.* 26.140–42)

(and the fourth time it lifted the stern aloft and plunged the prow below, as pleased Another, till the sea closed over us.)

With these words the canto comes to its end, in the recollection of Ulysses and his men shipwrecked at landfall. Having discovered the antipodes of the Southern Hemisphere—the same mountain Dante will climb in *Purgatorio*—they are prevented by Another's pleasure from gaining experience of its "mondo sanza gente." Over their enterprise death has the last word: "richiuso."

It is possible that behind this canto there stands an actual event in the history of navigation: the ill-fated expedition of the Vivaldi brothers, who in search of India set sail from Genoa in 1291, and passed through the straits of Gibraltar into the waters of the Atlantic. They were never heard from again.[15] Twenty years after Dante's death, Alfonso IV of Portugal would sail the same route, discover the Canary Islands, and safely return to tell the tale in 1341. But this latter event (although nearly contemporaneous with the *Commedia*) took place in what was indeed another world from the one in which Dante lived. Nor is there the slightest indication anywhere in his writings that he would conceive of such a sailing "out upon circumference" as anything other than what he has Ulysses call it—a "folle volo," a mad flight.[16]

It is also important to add that this "madness" has a great deal less to do with actual navigational transgression than it does with other kinds of voyaging and other kinds of trespass. Had Dante wanted simply to ground humanity within geographical boundaries he could easily have followed his general practice in the *Inferno* and chosen contemporary Italians like the Vivaldi brothers to make the point. Instead he chose Ulysses. Why?

Although Dante did not have direct access to Homer's poetry—the text of the *Odyssey* would not be rediscovered in the West until 1362—he inherited from Latin literature a complex notion of Ulysses, the man skilled in all ways of contending, that in turn informs the complexity of his own account.[17] Virgil, Ovid, and Statius all treat the worker of Troy's ruin as a brilliant scoundrel in the Greek (which is to say, duplicitous) mode. He is a wordsmith of deceit ("fandi fictor") to Virgil; "fallax," "audax," "experiens" in Ovid; an inciter to evil deeds, "hortator scelerem," for Statius.[18] At the same time, however, there is also a rich allegorical tradition that treated Ulysses as a model of wisdom and fortitude, as "nobis exemplar Ulixen." Transformed by the Stoics into a figure of wisdom, into a man skilled in all ways of *knowing*, Ulysses is praised (by Seneca) for riding out the storms of the spirit, for being so fixed on the high calling of *sapientia* (according to Horace) that he could hold his own against a sea of troubles in order to return home. This *in bono* allegorical treatment was not limited to pagan authors. For many patristic writers, too, Ulysses became, as Hugo Rahner has shown, a type of the Christian *homo viator*, who sails in the ship of the church, bound to the mast of the cross, and able finally to reach the port of heaven, his true *patria*.[19] To be Ulysses, in this view, was to be a pilgrim.

But not for Dante. Aware, even without having Homer's text, of Ulysses' determination to sail home, he rewrites an ancient script of return and in so doing rejects a venerable allegorical tradition. The experienced navigator, piloted by wisdom and valiantly keeping his course, becomes in Dante's hands a shipwrecked madman. Some of the finest Dante scholarship of the last few decades has stressed the medieval orthodoxy of this boldly revisionist move: its repudiation of *curiositas*, of wandering, of philosophical presumption, of rhetorical power when it is cut off from a commitment to truth and community, of the wisdom of this world which knows nothing of the wisdom of God. John Freccero has even suggested that Dante's sabotage of Ulysses in the *Commedia* may be a palinode on his own philosophical ambitions in the *Convivio*, a rejection of philosophy as the pole star, and a chastened look back on the foundering of Dante's own "ship without a sail and without a rudder."[20] What all of these readings examine in their various ways is how Dante places the intellectual boundary-breaker within bounds, even as he pockets Ulysses in the eighth *bolgia* of lower hell. As on earth, so in the mind: there are mountains meant to be "frightful, sheer, no-man-fathomed."

There can be no doubt that the *Commedia* intends the reader to see Dante's voyage as an explicit correction of the wanderer, as the triumph of pilgrimage over sheer exploration.[21] In the first canto of the *Purgatorio*, for instance—and just before Dante is girded with the reed of humility—we are told that he came "in sul lito diserto, / che mai non vide navicar sue acque / omo, che di tornar sia poscia esperto" ("to the desert shore, that never saw any man navigate its waters who afterwards had experience of return," vv. 130–32). The comparison implicit in these lines is unmistakable. Dante lands where Ulysses could not, and returns to tell the tale.

While there are other such recollections along the way (*Par.* 13.136; 26.61–63), certainly the most explicit contrast between pilgrim and wanderer comes in *Paradiso* 27, when Dante looks down through the universe from his lofty vantage in the heaven of the Fixed Stars. Sighting the puny semblance of the earth's globe at the still center of the cosmos, he sees the whole of the habitable world. At its western extremity, beyond Cadiz, he notes "il varco/folle d'Ulisse" (vv. 82–83), the mad track of Ulysses. From this celestial perspective the ambition of the explorer "to gain experience of the world, and of human vice and worth" is meant to seem small, or at least to appear infinitely less than the "esperïenza piena" (*Inf.* 28.48) that Dante comes to know in his journey to God. Instead of a "folle volo"—a madness Dante feared in himself at the outset ("temo che la venuta non sia folle," *Inf.* 2.35)—divine grace affords him an "alto volo" (*Par.* 25.50), a lofty flight into regions of knowledge beyond the grasp even of high fantasy. Ulysses burned to see the unpeopled world and failed; but Dante, soaring above the mark of that desire, claims to have seen God face to face, and lives to tell what he can remember of that vision.

Given all this, it is possible to see the poet of the *Commedia* connecting the dots of tradition in a new but essentially reassuring way, to watch him break some boundaries (narrative and exegetical) in order to reinforce others. But at the same time that we can assert the "orthodoxy" of his handling of Ulysses, the containment of the wanderer within the poetic structure of pilgrimage, it is important not to lose sight of the provocative audacity of the treatment itself. For, in fact, Dante is at his most inventive and exploratory exactly when he is upholding the importance of limit. At the same time in *Inferno* 26 that he is overtly controlling the impulse to cut loose and go it alone, he is also performing an act of extraordinary authorial daring. Not only does he give us the revolutionary "discovery" of Ulysses' final voyage—a tale told by no one else—but he has his navigator ship-wrecked off the shores of a mountain in the Southern Hemisphere that is utterly his own invention, that is *his* "nova terra." Dante places the bound-ary breaker within infernal bounds, yes; but it is also true that he draws the circumference of legitimacy on his own. *He* is that Other who wills that Ulysses should drown on the brink of discovery.[22]

If the *Commedia* presents a clear dichotomy between the success of one voyager and the disaster of the other, the poet's settling of his own personal account is nonetheless both complicated and fraught. For the danger of a "trapassar del segno," an overpassing of a boundary, is not entirely disposed of by the narrative triumph of pilgrimage over exploration. There is still the precarious nature of Dante's whole poetic enterprise to deal with, especially as the claims for the "poema sacro" (*Par.* 25.1) escalate with the move to the final canticle. In the dedicatory epistle to Can Grande, Dante violates a fundamental barrier between God's Book and any human text by claiming that the *Paradiso* (and by extension his entire work) can be read according to a fourfold exegesis heretofore held to be uniquely applicable to Scrip-ture. In the opening of the *Paradiso* itself he swears to have been enraptured like St. Paul into the "third heaven" of God's presence. Then, quite unlike St. Paul, he breaks the interdiction of silence that guards the ineffable words. He does this, moreover, in a vernacular language that had not as yet been deemed worthy of philosophy, let alone theology—an Italian rich in neologisms, as sublime as Latin, and Dante's own linguistic "discovery."[23]

No wonder, then, that in the *Paradiso* our attention shifts away from the arduous journey of the pilgrim and turns more and more to the voyage of the poet, to his literary navigation of new and dangerous waters. In the extended address to his readers that opens the second canto of the *Paradiso*, for instance, Dante returns again to the nautical metaphor that he used for himself at the outset of the *Purgatorio* (1.1–3), but that also figured promi-nently among his personal tropes as early as the *De vulgari eloquentia* and the *Convivio*. He is a mariner, and his poetic career a ship under sail.[24] Speaking to his readers as if he were the captain of a diverse crew, not all of whom may prove to be seaworthy, he announces a literary expedition into fathomless waters. It will be a voyage into depth and danger ("in pelago," "per l'alto sale"), in which the text of the *Paradiso* becomes a forbidden ocean stretching out beyond the straits of all previous literature:[25]

> O voi che siete in piccioletta barca,
>> desiderosi d'ascoltar, seguiti
>> dietro al mio legno che cantando varca,
> tornate a riveder li vostri liti:
>> non vi mettete in pelago, ché forse,
>> perdendo me, rimarreste smarriti.
> L'acqua ch'io prendo già mai non si corse;
>> Minerva spira, e conducemi Appollo,
>> e nove Muse mi dimostran l'Orse.
> Voialtri pochi che drizzaste il collo
>> per tempo al pan de li angeli, del quale
>> vivesi qui ma non sen vien satollo,
> metter potete ben per l'alto sale
>> vostro navigio, servando mio solco
>> dinanzi a l'acqua che ritorna equale.
> Que' glorïosi che passaro al Colco
>> non s'ammiraron come voi farete,
>> quando Iasón vider fatto bifolco.
>>>> (*Par.* 2.1–18)

(You that are in your little bark, eager to hear, following behind my ship that singing makes her way, turn back to see again your shores. Do not commit yourselves to the open sea, for perchance, if you lost me, you would remain astray. The water which I take was never coursed before. Minerva breathes and Apollo guides me, and nine Muses point out to me the Bears.

You other few who lifted up your necks betimes for bread of angels, on which men here subsist but never became sated of it, you may indeed commit your vessel to the deep brine, holding to my furrow ahead of the water that turns smooth again. Those glorious ones who crossed the sea to Colchis, when they saw Jason turned plowman, were not as amazed as you shall be.)

In this prolonged confrontation with his audience, Dante first reminds his readers that they stand on a perilous threshold and then asks them to consider what it will mean, what it will cost, to step over. Echoing within this text, moreover, are the words of Ulysses' speech to his men in *Inferno* 26.112–20, that "orazion picciola" delivered at the Pillars of Hercules and meant to turn the oars of aging sailors into wings for the mad flight. Indeed, Dante's description of his "legno che cantando varca" ("ship that singing makes her way," v. 3) not only uses vocabulary closely associated with Ulysses—"legno," "varca"—but presents the singing poet (like Ulysses himself) as a kind of siren. Except that *this* Ulysses does not use his powers of language to seduce his audience unawares; instead he shows himself employing a full array of rhetoric to enjoin a choice. Asking his readers to consider the danger of the voyage rather than taking pride in their origins, Dante warns his crew—who like Ulysses' men are also "eager to hear"—that there are real consequences to going further. Those who are not capable of the *Paradiso* should look back to the shore of the second canticle and hold off committing themselves to the open seas ("pelago") of the third. If they decide to proceed, they must be wary of the danger they face in getting lost ("smarriti"). That the words of Dante's warning here ("pelago," "smarriti") recall the poem's prologue scene, and with it the spiritual shipwreck of the pilgrim, suggests that reading may in fact be dangerous, a matter of risk and potential loss.

And yet, of course, the poet's address to his readers shows more than concern for the well-being of those who follow in his wake. It is also a strategy calculated to heighten the importance of the final canticle, its author, and that fit audience though few who decide to take an unprecedented voyage of discovery. For quite as important as Dante's insistence on the danger of the *Paradiso*'s enterprise is his announcement that his writing is an exploration of virgin territory. As Ulysses himself might have said, "The water which I take was never coursed before." The claim is characteristically bold, perhaps even outrageous. Certainly there had been other portrayals of the blessed, elegantly drawn in Virgil's Elysian Fields, more crudely in some vernacular accounts of the thirteenth century.[26] But of course Dante is laying claim to direct experience, speaking where St. Paul remained resolutely silent, and inventing an illustrious Italian vernacular to explore that "great sea of being" (*Par.* 3.86) who is God.

On the brink of his narrative ascent, then, the poet takes the occasion to insist on his absolute novelty, on the charting of unexplored ocean and "nova terra." It is as if the Ulysses who could not deny experience had lived to tell the tale. Except that Dante, rather than breaking boundaries of his own volition, wants to insist that he has been piloted all the way. Minerva breathes wisdom into him; Apollo gives him guidance; and all "nove Muse"—the nine Muses of the new[27]—help him navigate the stars toward the divine love that governs all. Anticipating the claim of *Paradiso* 25.1–2 that his sacred poem has been at least partly the result of heaven's hand, he bolsters his authority from the outset of the canticle by stating where that authority comes from. He announces that his poetic voyage, like the pilgrimage it describes, is his response to a divine call.

To those readers who crave the "bread of angels," who are driven by that "inborn and perpetual thirst" for God (*Par.* 2.20–21), the poet says, "you may indeed commit your vessel to the deep brine, holding to my furrow ahead of the water that turns smooth again." They alone are capable of following a layman and poet who speaks the *arcana verba* of theology— in Italian rather than in Latin—and who in this very canto leads them into the deep water of Beatrice's discourse on the moon spots. Referring to his poem as if it were the great ocean itself, Dante asks his readers to watch the path he inscribes in his wake before the surface of the sea once again turns calm. This is not only a suggestion that they should hold on tight to his intellectual lead. It is also an invitation to marvel over the poetics of the *Paradiso*: to catch its brilliant metaphors in the brief moment of their articulation, before they dissolve once again into the silence beneath the surface ripples of language, below and beyond the mark of his boat. Dante knows that in the final canticle he is writing on water.

He also makes it clear that the proper response to this evanescent script is nothing less than wonder. And so at the end of the address he rewrites the disaster of Ulysses and his men by associating his own effort with that of another ancient sailor and another crew. He compares his readers to "those glorious ones who crossed the sea to Colchis" and compares himself to Jason. E. R. Curtius speculates that Dante received the story of the Argonauts through a complex line of literary transmission that runs from Pindar, through Latin poetry (Valerius Flaccus, Statius), and into the *Roman de la Rose*. But he judges Ovid's account in the *Metamorphoses* to be the most likely source, with its story of the Argonauts' journey "vellera cum Minyis nitido radiantia villo/per mare non notum prima petiere carina" ("over an unknown sea in that first ship to seek the bright gleaming fleece of gold," *Met.* 6.721).[28]

It is easy to recognize the appeal of this epic story of innovation to the poet of the *Paradiso*. As the hero who (unlike the Dantean Ulysses) actually succeeds in returning home, Jason is an appropriate exemplar for the pilgrim. As the first navigator of the "mare non notum," he also prefigures Dante's poetic voyage through waters never coursed before, in a poem that wants to present itself as the first boat, the "prima carina." But instead of explicitly underscoring the thematic of discovery—and without emphasizing the crucial fact that Jason came back from the unknown sea alive, with the Golden Fleece in tow—Dante chooses to let these associations remain implicit. Rather, he focuses on a single incident in Ovid's extended narrative, the moment "quando Iasón . . . fatto bifolco" ("when . . . Jason turned plowman").

The reference is to one of the ordeals put upon Jason in his quest for the Fleece. Harnessing the fierce iron-tipped bulls of King Aeëtes, "suppositosque iugo pondus grave cogit aratri/ducere et insuetum ferro proscindere campum" ("[he] made them draw the heavy plow and cut through the field that had never felt steel before," *Met.* 7.118–19). Ovid says that the local onlookers were amazed at the feat ("mirantur Colchi, Minyae clamoribus augent / adiciuntque animos," vv. 120–21). Dante transfers this wonder to the Argonauts themselves and therefore to his "heroic" readers, whose astonishment will not only equal that of the ancient worthies but even (or so we are told) surpass it: "Those glorious ones who crossed the seas to Colchis . . . were not as amazed as you shall be." Not only does the poet sail waters never navigated before; he also cultivates ground not yet touched by pen. As Dante plays with a commonplace metaphor that turns plowing into writing, he allows his own identification with Jason "fatto bifolco" to draw our attention once again to the novelty of his final canticle.[29] Reaching far beyond the georgic poet's cultivation of well-known fields, Dante is instead an epic plowman whose pen makes one "versus" after another. In so doing he breaks open *terra incognita*, canto by canto. He is the unabashed master of the new.

In the final canto of the *Paradiso*, however, Dante dramatizes the limits of that mastery as he discovers with poignancy an outer circumference beyond which nothing can be remembered or said. At the end of the journey the poet confesses his own failure, the dissolution of his literary achievement, as "al vento ne le foglie levi/si perdea la sentenza di Sibilla" ("in the wind, on the light leaves, the Sibyl's oracle was lost," 33.65–66). Nonetheless, even as the *Commedia* seems to self-destruct in the very moment of its completion, the poet sails on, describing the pilgrim's initial vision of God as a "volume" in which all the scattered pages of the universe are bound together with love. He tells us that the vision behind this metaphor lasted but an instant; it was "un punto solo" (v. 94). And in trying to remember it "now," at the present point of recollection and writing, his oblivion stretches before him. His rapturous vision, now lost except as metaphor, seems to have taken place longer ago than the 25 centuries that stand between his poetic efforts and "la 'mpresa / che fé Nettuno ammirar l'ombra d'Argo" ("the enterprise that made Neptune wonder at the shadow of the Argo," vv. 95–96).

At the end of the *Paradiso* as at its beginning, Dante remembers Jason and once more associates his own literary boat with the *Argo* on its maiden voyage. As in the address to his readers in *Paradiso* 2, he again underscores the appropriate reaction to such achievement by repeating the verb of wonder used earlier: *ammirare*. He also continues and refines the metaphorical play between sailing, plowing, and writing. Punning on the word *impresa*, "enterprise," a noun used three other places in the *Commedia*— twice in reference to the pilgrim's journey (*Inf.* 2.41, 47) and once to describe the poet's writing (*Inf.* 32.7)—Dante asks us to imagine the venture of the *Argo* as an imprint ("impressa"; cf. *Par.* 33.59), as a watery script no more substantial or enduring than a shadow or "ombra" cast on the sea. Thus the earlier metaphor of the poem as a boat whose rudder incises the blank surface of the ocean ("mio solco/dinanzi a l'acqua che ritorna equale," *Par.* 2.14–15) here dematerializes into even greater evanescence. The poem is an "ombra" floating on water. By the hundredth canto of Dante's *Argonautica*, the text is hardly on the page at all. The mighty venture barely leaves an impression.

It is when we note the identity of the admiring onlooker, moreover, that the poet's handling of this navigational scenario becomes almost as remarkable as his claims. For the one who stares in astonishment at the voyage of the *Argo* (and thus the one who beholds the final canto of the poem with equal amazement) is none other than a god! From the depths of the sea Neptune looks up to behold a new thing, sailing high above him and skimming the surface of waters never coursed before; he sees the trespass of Dante the explorer. At the beginning of the *Paradiso* a merely human audience would suffice, but here at the end Dante will settle for nothing less than a god—and for yet another tour de force of innovation.

The tradition of the *Argo* had always included the element of astonishment, be it that of the Olympian deities and nymphs of Pelion (Apollonius), of the Nereids (Catullus), or of Thetis (Statius). But never before had wonder been assigned to Neptune, for whom (as Curtius has shown) the tradition reserved instead the emotion of wrath.[30] Dante converts this divine opposition by a daring fiat of mythic revision. He makes it pleasing to the divine Other not to rage against the interloper upon his seas, nor to shipwreck the shadow that has presumed so much. Whereas the "mad flight" of Ulysses ended in disaster, "com' altrui piacque," Dante shows his pilgrim sailing on to safe harbor in the Empyrean. So too the poet of the *Paradiso*, who, in the midst of imagining the beatific vision *per verba*, gives us the image of a god looking up in wonder—at him.

Nine cantos earlier, in the autobiographical disclosure of *Paradiso* 25.1–12, Dante imagined himself returning to Florence after his extraordinary journey through the Other World, as if he were a triumphant (if travelworn) Jason, bearing the Golden Fleece of the *Commedia* in his hand: "con altra voce omai, con altro vello / ritornerò poeta" (vv. 7–8). Until this moment in the poem the title "poeta" had been reserved for the masters of antiquity. But here he claims it for himself, as if in recognition of his own vernacular voice ("voce") and the hundred-canto Fleece ("vello") that is his prize. What seems to matter most in the strategic identification with Jason, however, is the sheer fact of the traveler's return: it is not the going out upon circumference alone that Dante emphasizes in the end, but the going out and coming back. What matters is the return to the "monstrous races" of his own countrymen, for whom this journey to the unpeopled world of the afterlife might serve as a map for pilgrimage, an invitation to the voyage of conversion.

We do Dante a disservice, however, if we simplify the enterprise he himself refused to make less complicated. For while it is true that the Ulysses within him—the transgressor against the sign—is openly reined in throughout the *Commedia*, the impulse to explore nonetheless pulls the poem along, beyond established boundaries, in order to discover all that is possible for a self-proclaimed poet of the new. Even Dante's turn in the end to Jason as a counter to Ulysses does not resolve the problem of his own identity as a boundary-breaker; on the contrary, it keeps that identity intensely problematic. Jason's status as the first to sail or to plow *nova terra* marks the legendary hero as a master of novelty, an epoch-maker. Therefore, he is an apt model for both pilgrim and poet. But it is also true that in Virgil and Ovid the innovations of boat and plow are associated quite specifically with the passing away of the Golden Age, and therefore with a "fall" into experience, history, and loss. The *Argo*'s accomplishment, if indisputable, is also tainted, its *ombra* an ambiguous foreshadowing.[31] So too (according to Ovid in *Met.* 7.121–42) when Jason "turned plowman" and opened virgin territory, he sowed the serpent's teeth and reaped a harvest of destruction. His heroism came at a terrible price.

Nor does the *Commedia* present Jason exclusively in triumph. When the captain of the *Argo* actually appears in the poem, it is not in the *Paradiso*'s figural context of success and wonder—as the first sailor of the first ship, the plowman of virgin territory, and the cause of Neptune's admiration. It is, rather, as one of the damned imprisoned in the second ditch of Malebolgia. Although retaining his regal bearing even in lower hell, Jason is nonetheless placed in the vile company of the seducers, among those who made a career of deception specifically through their artful use of language, "con segni e con parole ornate" (*Inf.* 18.91). "With him," says Virgil, "go all who practice such deceit" ("Con lui sen va chi da tal parte inganna," v. 97).

It is customary in Dante studies to separate one Jason from the other, so that the seducer of Hypsipyle remains discretely in hell, with no particular relevance to pilgrim or poet. Dante's exemplar, on the other hand, is the voyager who claims the Golden Fleece, who takes his symbolic place in paradise. Certainly the placement of these references seems to enjoin such a distinction, with one Jason in the first canticle, observed in passing, and the other in the *Paradiso*, twice claimed by Dante as an avatar of himself. The poem, however, does not necessarily work so neatly. Rather than moving from a Jason *in malo* to another *in bono*, we may instead be confronting a single figure that is an ambiguous confusion of possibilities, a "polysemous" mixture of seduction and discovery that the poet condemns in Ulysses, makes ambiguous in Jason, and celebrates in himself.

Giuseppe Mazzotta has suggested, in fact, that Dante does not ignore a comparison of himself with Jason the seducer, but in *Paradiso* 25.7–8 deliberately marks the radical difference between Jason's "signs and ornate speech" and Dante's own Golden Fleece, an alterity signified by the poet's description of himself with an "*altra* voce" and an "*altro* vello."[32] The point is well taken, yet the marking of difference can also be seen as the masking of a perceived identity, the veiled exposure of ambivalence. In any case, condemnation and wonder seem to sail together in the *Commedia*, with the poem's judgment on exploration paradoxically authorizing its own discovery of the high seas. Jason offers the example of a successful homecoming, but carries with him liabilities of association that Dante may have wanted to exploit rather than avoid in the development of his own highly complex persona.

This is not to say that either "fair words" or the artful speaker are inevitably undermined. On the contrary, Dante goes out of his way to establish from the outset of the *Commedia* that even pagan poetry can be commissioned by heaven to do God's work. And so Beatrice goes to Virgil in Limbo and asks him to use his "parola ornata" (*Inf.* 2.67)—the same phrase used to describe Jason's seductions—for the work of salvation. Dante's larger point, however, seems to be that all language, all the tokens and fair words of poetry, are by nature as ambiguous (and as perilous) as discovery itself. As the poem shows in its contrast between Ulysses and the pilgrim, a voyage beyond mortal boundaries can be either an act of transgression or a journey to God. Likewise, the poet as siren can seduce us into an epic of narcissism or call us away from whatever "Florence" we call home, to follow a way of life more "just and sane" (*Par.* 31.39).

Dante neither shipwrecks the reader in a sea of indeterminacy nor allows his text to wander unmoored. Instead, he makes discovery the subject and indeed the nature of his poem. Interpretation becomes navigation, and the poem a map to be read critically, vigilantly—read even against its author. Inveighing constantly against the peril of overreaching, Dante at once conceals and confesses his own presumption. He establishes his authority as a seaworthy guide by the sheer force of his claim, yet strategically includes the necessary critique of that authority. Perhaps nowhere more powerfully than in the figure of Ulysses, he issues a warning against the demonic possibilities of his own talent. It is a warning that words, whether spoken or written, have the power to create worlds no less dangerous than one in which we live and through whose waters we navigate our course. The *Commedia* asks us to go out upon circumference in order to see the center. But it does so all the while alerting us to the risks of the enterprise, to the shadowy nature of all language—even that of a "sacred poem."

Reference Matter

Notes

1. For the most recent consideration of this scene, see Stock, pp. 102–11, which builds on the extensive work of Courcelle. See also Bolgiani, esp. pp. 110–17, which discusses possible sources; Préaux; and O'Donnell, 3: 59–61. See also Ferrari; Chadwick.

2. Bel Geddes, p. 248.

3. Ibid. Bel Geddes projected a theatrical company of 523 persons and drew up plans for a production in Madison Square Garden, as well as for various university auditoriums and open-air amphitheaters. "But as the second year of my occupation with *The Divine Comedy* drew to a close, I began to realize that it would never be produced" (p. 252). Nonetheless, his concept for such a production had its reviewers, who saw Bel Geddes as making an unprecedented, one might say Dantesque, move. Thus Sheldon Cheney in *Century Magazine*: "Not only does it pose in theatrical form things that have never been posed before, things dramatic and spiritual, but it presupposes an entirely new type of stage and theater, a structure independent of the picture-frame idea of the current traditional playhouse. The project is built on the two foundations of imagination and practical knowledge" (cited in Bel Geddes, p. 252).

4. Sayers, p. 2. A book-length study of Sayers's Dante work is offered by Reynolds in *Passionate Intellect*; see also Reynolds's account of Sayers's initial discovery of the *Commedia* in her *Dorothy L. Sayers*, pp. 353–56.

5. Reynolds, *Passionate Intellect*, pp. 196–97, cites a May 8, 1952, letter from Sayers to Norah Lambourne: "I really must go *sometime* to Ravenna, having become suddenly obsessed (as if I hadn't enough to cope with already) by a novel about Dante and his daughter, which has been simmering for some time at the back of my mind." Sayers never finished the novel, many of whose

chapters are only rough drafts. For a consideration of the effort, see Reynolds, *Passionate Intellect,* pp. 191–206.

6. For the universe that Dante both inherited and invented, see Boyde. Although the Ptolemaic vision of the universe has been out of date since the Renaissance, Peterson argues in "Dante and the 3-Sphere" that the poet's "spherical cosmology" not only is "unbelievably apt and accurate" but is "in essence the same vision" as Einstein's (p. 1031). He offers a consideration of Dante's physical theories in "Dante's Physics."

For Wallace Stevens's "Evening Without Angels," which I take to be a rejection of Dante's imagined world, see Stevens, pp. 136–37. The poem opens as follows:

> Why seraphim like lutanists arranged
> Above the trees? And why the poet as
> Eternal *chef d'orchestre*?
>   Air is air,
> Its vacancy glitters round us everywhere.
> Its sounds are not angelic syllables
> But our unfashioned spirits realized
> More sharply in more furious selves.

7. For a full analysis of this passage, see Herzman and Townsley.

8. According to Edward Rothstein ("Is Destiny Just a Divine Word Game," *New York Times,* Aug. 12, 1997, pp. C11–12), Michael Drosin's recent book, *The Bible Code* (New York: Simon and Schuster, 1997), has proven "that if the first 304,805 letters of the Hebrew translation of Dostoevsky's *Crime and Punishment* are laid end to end and arranged into rows of 4,772 letters, in the midst of this array one can find, in crossword fashion, the name of John Fitzgerald Kennedy." On the subject of codes, biblical or otherwise, Rothstein notes that they are "seemingly grounded in nature, not culture, in divinity, not humanity; and although Mr. Drosnin's code is particularly fantastical, the need for finding such governing codes is common in our time" (p. C11).

9. The Dantista who has shed most light here is Kleiner, while Bloom is consistently drawn to Dante's "strangeness."

10. The quoted text in Latin reads, "quod finis totius et partis est, removere viventes in hac vita de statu miseriae, et perducere ad statum felicitatis," para. 15. Dante's epistle to Can Grande is from *Dantis Alagherii Epistolae,* Latin on p. 178, translation p. 202.

11. I consider the inadequacy of this Kierkegaardian antithesis with regard to Dante in "What Is Truth?"

12. The earliest "life" of Dante is by Boccaccio. See also Anderson; Mazzotta, "Life of Dante."

13. The quoted text in Italian reads, "non solamente maschi ma femmine, che sono molti e molte in questa lingua, volgari e non litterati."

14. For an overview of the church's censure of Dante and in particular of his *Monarchia*, see Comollo, pp. 41–54; also Anderson's chapter on the *Monarchia* and its reception, pp. 209–25.

15. Anderson's chapter "The Grace of Inspiration," pp. 295–319, offers a number of theories concerning the "birth" of the *Commedia* and places Dante in the context of other visionaries. See also Barolini, Ferrante, and Hollander, "Why Did Dante Write the *Comedy*?"; as well as Mazzotta, "Why Did Dante Write the *Comedy*?" I personally like Merrill's account in "Divine Poem," p. 88: "The *Comedy*'s energy and splendor suggest that Dante indeed 'saw the light' in a timeless moment. Its prophetic spleen and resonant particulars hint at something not quite the same, that like Milton or Yeats he had mediumistic powers—a sustaining divinatory intelligence which spoke to him, if only (as Julian Jaynes would have it) from that center of the brain's right hemisphere which corresponds to Weinecke's area on the left. This much granted, it would still remain to be amazed in the usual fashion when faced by a masterpiece: How on earth was it brought safely into being and on to the page?"

16. Lerner, pp. 56–57, describes the proliferation of "lay claims to spiritual intelligence" in the thirteenth century, and, after mentioning Fra Dolcino, Arnold of Villanova, and the Provençal Beguin Na Prous Boneta, adds the following parenthesis: "(Perhaps one ought not to rule out a certain Dante Alighieri as still another case)."

17. Boccaccio, pp. 42–43.

18. Guido da Pisa, p. 4.

19. Leo, p. 60. See also Curtius, *European Literature*, p. 358: "The conception of the *Commedia* is based upon a spiritual meeting with Virgil. In the realm of European literature there is little which may be compared with this phenomenon. The 'awakening' of Aristotle in the thirteenth century was the work of generations and took place in the cool light of intellectual research. The awakening of Virgil by Dante is an arc of flame which leaps from one great soul to another."

20. Alighieri, *Vita nuova*, chap. 42, p. 99.

21. For the relevance of this vision literature to the poet, see Morgan. Translations of the major texts are found in Gardiner. For the relevance of *St. Patrick's Purgatory* in particular, see de Pontfarcy.

CHAPTER 1

1. Foundational studies on the place of the Bible in the Middle Ages include Smalley, *Study*; Spicq; and de Lubac. For more recent studies, see Leclercq; Danielou and Devoto; Lourdaux and Verhelst; Riché and Lobrichon; Levy; and Gameson. The *CHB* is also an indispensable resource.

2. Ferrante reminds us that biblical culture in the Middle Ages was not always pious. See her essays "Bible as Thesaurus" and "Usi e abusi della Bibbia."

3. For a general consideration of Dante's appropriation of the book of Daniel, see Pézard.

4. See Alford, "The Scriptural Self."

5. Alford gives the example of Richard Rolle, pp. 16–20. See his note 34 on p. 16. Also see Kuczynski's chapter "Imitating David," pp. 51–77.

6. Gregory the Great, *Moralia in Iob*, in *PL*, vol. 75, col. 542C, quoted and translated by Taylor in Hugh of St. Victor, p. 220n.

7. The phrase is used by John of St. Arnulf to describe the *ruminatio* of John of Gorze, in *PL*, vol. 137, col. 280, cited by Leclercq, p. 90.

8. Leclercq, pp. 93–94, notes: "The memory, fashioned wholly by the Bible and nurtured entirely by biblical words and the images they evoke, causes [the monks] to express themselves spontaneously in a biblical vocabulary. Reminiscences are not quotations, elements of phrases borrowed from one another. They are the words of the person using them; they belong to him."

9. For what we know or can infer about Dante's education, see Davis, "Education in Dante's Florence," in his *Dante's Italy*, pp. 137–65.

10. In addition to Vauchez, *Laity*, see Swanson, esp. 42–135; and Manselli.

11. Bolton, pp. 73–82, quote from p. 80. See also d'Avray, pp. 13–63, esp. pp. 26–28. A succinct account of the heresies in question is offered by Oakley, pp. 178–202.

12. Cited by Swanson, p. 22.

13. For the connection between the Mendicant orders and the rise of the vernacular Bible, see Foster, "Vernacular Scriptures," esp. p. 462, as well as Minocchi. See also Vauchez, "Pastoral Transformation of the Thirteenth Century," in his *Laity*, pp. 95–106; Rusconi, pp. 114–99, esp. 114–24; and both essays by Folena. On the other hand, Evans, pp. 82–84, argues that although the Mendicants made the Bible intelligible to the laity through their preaching mission, they were nonetheless "the loudest opponents of the translation of the Bible into languages which ordinary people could understand" (p. 82). D'Avray notes that the Mendicant preachers geared themselves to a sophisticated urban audience: "In the towns, most of all in the Italian towns, the higher end

of lay culture overlapped to a considerable extent with the lower end of clerical culture" (p. 62).

14. The quote is from Thomas of Spalato's *Historia episcoporum salonitanorum*, cited by Lesnick, p. 137. Lesnick explains what it meant for Francis to preach *secundum modum concionandi*: "The medieval *concionatores* spoke in public assemblies in which the citizens made important decisions for their commune. According to this mode of public speaking, persuasion was achieved by appropriate gestures and some act designed to provoke the audience's attention or stimulate their imagination. . . . The political or religious harangue addressed a popular audience, most likely a middlebrow audience, not the elite" (p. 137).

15. Cited by Vauchez, *Laity*, p. 100, from Vicaire's translation of Dominic's canonization proceedings, pp. 75–91.

16. Henry of Susa, in the *Summa aurea*, cited by Vauchez, *Laity*, p. 113.

17. On "the potential for a lay religious life," see Swanson, pp. 102–35. Also see Lynch, pp. 186–92; and Vauchez, "Confraternities and Lay Piety," in his *Laity*, pp. 107–17: "As different from one another as these groups may have been, they all shared the same preoccupations. . . . Their common goal was to bring together pious laymen and laywomen who desired to ensure their salvation while remaining *in domibus propriis*, that is to say, in the world and in the midst of other people. This meant adopting a certain number of exterior signs, beginning with distinctive clothing, to indicate one's membership, for, at least in the beginning, there was no profession in the juridical or canonical sense of the term, but simply a *professio in signis*: all it took to be recognized as a penitent was to wear a certain habit, for the exterior would bear witness to the interior. Poverty, asceticism, and periodic continence, all prescribed by the famous *Memoriale propositi fratrum de penitentia* of 1221, were the virtues required of the brethren" (p. 113). For the specific place of the Bible in the life of these confraternities, see Vauchez, "La Bible dans les confréries."

18. See Martini. The "corda intorno cinta," which Dante removes in *Inf.* 16.106–8, has often been associated with the poet's alleged standing as a third-order Franciscan, even though, as Bosco and Reggio point out in their commentary on *Inf.* 16.106–8, members of the third order typically wore belts (*cinghie*) and not ropes (*corde*).

19. Zink, esp. pp. 305–88, describes the ways in which vernacular preaching was "a bridge between two cultures," clerical and lay.

20. These characterizations are from *De eruditione praedicatorum*, a thirteenth-century manual for preachers written by the Dominican Humbert of Romans; cited by Delcorno, *Giordano da Pisa*, p. 31. For the method and influence of the Dominican *artes praedicandi*, see Delcorno, ibid., pp. 29–37,

and Lesnick, pp. 96–108, esp. pp. 100–101 for the particular importance of Humbert of Romans.

21. In addition to Delcorno's chapter "Società e pubblico nella predicazione giordaniana," in *Giordano da Pisa*, pp. 29–80, see Lesnick, pp. 103–8 and pp. 111–33. For a brief discussion of the common ground between the friar and the poet, see Aldo Vallone's entry, "Giordano da Pisa," in *ED*, 3: 174.

22. Davis explores possible connections between Dante's thought and that of Remigio in *Dante's Italy*, pp. 157–65 and pp. 198–223.

23. On the connection between Dante and the Franciscans at Santa Croce, see Davis, *Dante's Italy*, pp. 152–54; Comollo, pp. 39–40; and Raoul Manselli's entry "Profetismo," in *ED*, 4: 696–97. On the importance of Joachim of Fiore, see Reeves's book *Influence of Prophecy* and her essay in Lee, Reeves, and Silano, pp. 17–26. See also McGinn, *Calabrian Abbot*; and Emmerson and Herzman, "Apocalypse and Joachim of Fiore," in their *Apocalyptic Imagination*, pp. 1–35.

24. In addition to Davis's essay "Education in Dante's Florence," in his *Dante's Italy*, pp. 137–65, see his entry "Scuola," in *ED*, 5: 106–9. Busnelli and Vandelli, in Alighieri, *Il Convivio*, 4: 185–86 n. 2, distinguish between the "schools of the religious" and the "disputations of the philosophers," and write more confidently than does Davis about the educational opportunities Dante would actually have had. Smalley, *English Friars*, pp. 30–44, gives a succinct account of the "basic training for scholar preachers" (p. 30) in such schools.

25. Davis, *Dante's Italy*, pp. 158–59. See also Delcorno, *Giordano da Pisa*, p. 19: "Florence, and in particular Santa Maria Novella, was the most propitious ambiance for the vernacular preaching of Fra Giordano. Here, in fact, was a school open to the needs of laypeople (among whom was Dante), and here there was gathered a rich network of lay confraternities, which had placed preaching at the center of their devotional activity."

26. On the matter of the books that were available to monks at both Mendicant schools, see Davis, "Florentine *Studia*." Davis declines, however, to speculate about whether Dante might have had access to these resources. On the subject of Dante's own books, see Petrucci, pp. 212–13: "[Of Dante's] library we do not yet have a trace. We cannot, however, disguise the fact that at the base of his Latin and vernacular production there is a fundamental problem of reading, or rather of libraries—private, courtly, or religious as they may have been. It is not possible today to resolve this problem, behind which is hidden a turning point, a key moment in the process of modifications that were occurring in fourteenth-century Italian culture. Dante certainly read (but where? how?) Latin texts of scholastic authors and classical texts, collections of Provençal poets and of vernacular Italian poets, French romances and medieval au-

thors, Church Fathers, rhetorical treatises and encyclopedias, crossing various strands of book tradition and written culture and forcefully joining them as no one had been able to do before and few would be able to do after. But the new model of library was not complete until Petrarca arrived to set upon it the seal of his own strong personality, of his prestige as a master independent of the universities, and of his genius in creating cultural models."

27. See Delaruelle.

28. See d'Avray, p. 172. See also Lesnick, pp. 96–98.

29. Lesnick contrasts the two styles of Mendicant preaching (pp. 93–95), as well as the social and class biases of each order. His study of the Franciscan *sermo humilis* is grounded in the c. 1300 *Meditations on the Life of Christ* by Giovanni de Caulibus; the Dominican "sermo modernus" is looked at primarily in terms of Giordano da Pisa's Florence sermons (c. 1303–7).

30. According to De Hamel, *History of Illuminated Manuscripts*, p. 123: "The rivalry between the two orders can be exaggerated, and no doubt both groups used similar kinds of manuscript. As a generalization, however, the Dominicans zealously promoted traditional scholarship while the Franciscans tended to be concerned with more humble social problems and popular piety. St. Bonaventura, the great Franciscan theologian teaching in Paris between 1248 and 1257, remarked that the Dominicans put learning before holiness, but that the Franciscans put holiness before learning. Both orders [however] were important in the history of the university."

31. For discussions of interdependence and harmony in the heaven of the sun, *Par.* 10–13, see Dronke, *Dante*, pp. 82–102; Ferrante, *Political Vision*, pp. 273–80; and Mazzotta, *Dante's Vision*, pp. 197–218, esp. pp. 205–12. On the other hand, Barolini, "The Heaven of the Sun as a Meditation on Narrative," in her *Undivine Comedy*, pp. 194–217, explores "the linguistic and ultimately temporal obstacles to representational parity" (p. 195).

32. For a discussion of "Dante e la laicizzazione della cultura," see Paparelli, pp. 17–27, esp. pp. 25–27. D'Avray argues against the characterization of the laity as universally ignorant: "In the towns, most of all in Italian towns, the higher end of the lay culture overlapped to a considerable extent with the lower end of clerical culture. . . . Even in the countryside, the friars would not always have been talking to congregations composed solely of simple and uneducated men" (p. 62). See also his chapter "Mendicant Preaching and the World of Learning," pp. 132–203. Likewise Gill, who argues that a far greater number of laypersons preached and translated than scholars thus far have acknowledged: "they give too stark an impression of high/low and clerical/lay segregation" (p. 86).

33. Petrucci, p. 140. See also his chapter "Reading and Writing *Volgare* in

Medieval Italy," pp. 169–235. Gillerman is helpful in deducing the poet's earliest audience.

34. Cited by Rusconi: "Non è commesso ad ogni uomo l'ufficio del predicare; ché, innanzi innanzi, a tutte le femmine è vietato in tutto e per tutto; appresso, tutti i laici e idioti che non hanno lettera; onde niuno può essere predicatore, se non è letterato e scientifico; e di questo è grave scomunicazione ed è grave peccato; però che la Scrittura è grave, e profonda, e sottilissima ad intendere, e non è da ogni persona" (p. 110). For Giordano's reservations about "le persone secolari e grosse," see Delcorno's treatment of "Società e pubblico nella predicazione giordaniana" in his *Giordano da Pisa*, pp. 29–80.

35. The homiletic strain in Dante is treated by Delcorno in "Cadenze e figure."

36. See Herzman and Stephany.

37. For the connection between Dante and Jeremiah and the relevance of the Temple sermon of Jer. 7 to *Par.* 27, see Jacoff, "Dante, Geremia e la problematica profetica."

CHAPTER 2

1. Manetti, p. 122.

2. Jerome, *Commentarium in Esiam liber xi*, p. 446, cited by Battaglia Ricci in her informative reading of Isaiah 38 (in *DB*, p. 318) as one of the "pretexts" for the *Commedia*'s opening.

3. Dante's epistle to Can Grande, in *Dantis Alagherii Epistolae*, p. 199.

4. A *florilegium* is a collection of quotations from the church fathers (as well as some more contemporary theologians) arranged according to various topics. A *postilla* is a continuous gloss or commentary on a biblical text. *Exempla* are stock examples that illustrate some vice, virtue, or characteristic (i.e., Uzzah is an exemplum of temerity). *Distinctiones* are alphabetical listings of biblical nouns, for which a range of figurative or symbolic meanings are provided. For the development of these study tools, see Smalley, *Study of the Bible*, pp. 196–242 and pp. 366–68; Longère, pp. 183–202; and Rowse and Rowse.

5. According to Spicq, p. 112: "In fact, in the Middle Ages, *Glossa* designates as much the commentary as it does the actual biblical text, and it seems as well that the Scholastic text (*exemplar parisiense*) was itself the same as the Gloss." See Smalley, *Study of the Bible*, pp. 46–66; Lobrichon, "Une nouveauté"; and De Hamel, *Glossed Books*.

6. The church considered this encasement of Scripture within traditional interpretation to be a protection against error and a safeguard against heresy.

No doubt this is why Pope Alexander III prohibited all teaching of the Bible *sine Glossa*, without gloss, and why vernacular texts caused such anxiety. See Light, "New Thirteenth-Century Bible"; and Lobrichon, esp. p. 111.

7. For an excellent introduction to this complex subject, see Lowe. Also helpful are Gibson; Cahn; Light's "Versions et revisions"; Sparks on the Latin Bible, pp. 100–27; and McNally.

8. Light, "French Bibles c. 1200–30."

9. De Hamel, *History of Illuminated Manuscripts*, notes the enduring impact of the Paris Bible: "Choose a traditional printed Bible from a good bookshop today. Look at its physical layout. It is on tissue-thin paper, very like the 'uterine' vellum of the thirteenth century. It is probably octavo in size, like almost every thirteenth-century copy. It has the same order of biblical books, headings, and the same division into chapters (with verses not introduced until the sixteenth century) and—many centuries after this layout has been dropped from most other texts—it is in minute writing in two narrow columns. Look at the binding and the coloured edges. The chances are that the cover will look like leather and be black or red or blue: these are the three colours of thirteenth-century Parisian painting. It is hardly possible to find another object which was so new in 1200 and which is still made with so little modification today" (p. 120).

10. See Cahn, p. 15, and Petrucci, pp. 132–44.

11. Vauchez, *Laity*, p. 100.

12. Foster, "Vernacular Scriptures," entertains the possibility that an Italian Bible (and particularly the New Testament) was put together by heretical groups "originating north of the Alps," but says that in the later Middle Ages it was the Mendicant houses that were "the chief centers of diffusion—such as it was—of the Italian Bible" (p. 462). He speaks of Dante's interest in Bible translation—in *De vulgari eloquentia* 1.10.2 and in *Convivio* 1.7.14–17—but concludes that when Dante renders the Scripture in Italian, "it is probable that he translated the texts for himself, as he needed them, from the Vulgate" (p. 465). According to Manetti, p. 101: "During the Trecento in Italy a partial vernacular translation of the Bible was in circulation, which Dante certainly knew, as can be deduced from a passage in *De vulgari eloquentia* (1.10.2). . . . Such versions were scattered throughout northern Italy, perhaps not translated directly from the Latin text, but from the version that Valdo had done. Nevertheless, even if he knew it, Dante made no use of it; instead every time he wanted to cite some passage in his vernacular works, he himself translated the Latin text. In toto there are 74 places in the Bible that Dante translates: 51 in the *Convivio*, 22 in the *Commedia*, one in the *Vita nuova*. Usually the transla-

tion is rather close to the text, naturally more so in prose, and less so in poetry, for obvious reasons."

13. Groppi, pp. 19–55, argues: "The codices used by Dante cannot have been Jerome or 'Old Latin' translation, since this was no longer in circulation; so the text he used must have been one derived from St. Jerome's 4th century version, namely either the 11th century *Italian text*, or the 13th century *Paris text*. In Dante's time the *Paris text* of the Bible was used as a text-book by lecturers of theology, and moreover it is the text used in all early editions of the *Vulgate* up to about 1530" (p. 26). A bit earlier in her book, Groppi states: "Thousands of copies of this *Paris text* overran all Europe, and for three centuries or more it was, one might say, the only known text" (p. 24).

14. Barnes, "Vestiges of the Liturgy," gives an overview of the presence of the liturgy in the *Commedia*, as well as extensive notes and an appendix of "obvious or speculative liturgical allusions" in the poem (pp. 264–69).

15. See the several essays by Kleinhenz on modes of biblical citation in Dante.

16. Le Goff, p. 337.

17. For the importance of liturgical processions, see Tatlock's "Last Cantos," where he argues the relevance of two works, the *Gemma animae* of Honorius Augustodunensis, which explicates a papal procession, and Durandus's *Rationale divinorum*. Also see Joan Isabel Friedman, esp. pp. 126–27. For a connection to the Corpus Christi procession, see Fisher's *Mystic Vision*, where she treats Beatrice as a "sacramental *visio Dei*." (Fisher is challenged on this association with the Corpus Christi procession by Tatlock, pp. 122–23). For the Grail legend, see Vallone, esp. pp. 688–89. On the connection between Dante's Pageant and contemporary allegorical dramas, see Toschi's *Origini*, pp. 205–6, where he recalls Vilanni's account of a 1304 Florentine *rappresentazione* and wonders if Dante might have seen its like before his exile. Giving an example of life following art, D'Ancona, 1: 301–2, describes an event in Modena in the year 1583, when the city organized a dramatization of *Purgatorio* 29's Pageant, complete with white-robed elders, seven candelabra, dancing maidens, a chariot, and a representation of the griffin.

18. Bosco, *Dante vicino*, pp. 290–91, suggests that the poet of *Purg.* 29 was inspired by the mosaics at S. Apollinare Nuovo in Ravenna. Mazzoni, pp. 285–86, points both to the Roman church of Santa Prassede sull' Esquilino and to the duomo in Anagni. To this list Fallani, pp. 19–20, adds the triumphal arch of the Roman basilica of S. Paolo nella via Ostiense, as well as SS. Cosma e Damiano (before its sixteenth-century restoration).

19. Toschi, pp. 34–36. See also his chapter on liturgical and devotional

roots of Christian theater (pp. 639–714). For the relevance to Dante of the address to the spectator in medieval drama, see the commentary of Bosco and Reggio, *Inf.*, pp. 131–32, and *Purg.* pp. 486–87.

20. Text and translation of the epistle to the Italian Cardinals are found in *Dantis Alagherii Epistolae*, pp. 127–47. Further references to the epistle will be included in the text.

21. These various appropriations of the Bible all serve to shore up Dante's identity and authority. "These are the justification," he says, "of my boldness" (p. 144, para. 5). But the Scripture is also present in the epistle in less overtly strategic ways, and as much in paraphrase and echo as in direct quotation. For instance, when Dante speaks of himself as "one of the least of the sheep of the pasture of Jesus Christ," he uses a pastoral metaphor found in the Psalms (78 [79]:13 and 99 [100]:3), in Ezekiel 34, and in all four Gospels. His claim that the truth well pleasing to God is heard "even from the mouths of babes and sucklings" cites Ps. 8:3, as well as Jesus' quotation of that text (against the chief priests and scribes) in Matt. 21:16. In addition, his mention of the one born blind who confessed the truth and thereby provoked the malice of the Pharisees summons up John 9:1–41.

22. Consider, for instance, the following passage from *Confessions* 1.5, in which the italicized print of the Penguin edition (p. 24) signifies a scriptural quotation, while a parenthesized text points out a probable echo: "There is no one but you to whom I can say: *if I have sinned unwittingly, do you absolve me. Keep me ever your own servant, far from pride* (Ps. 18:13, 14 [19:12, 13]). *I trust, and trusting I find words to utter.* (Ps. 115:10 [116:10]). Lord, you know that this is true. For have I not *made my transgression known to you?* Did you not *remit the guilt of my sin?* (Ps. 31:5 [32:5])? I do not wrangle with you for judgement (see Jer. 2:29), for you are Truth itself, and I have no wish to delude myself, for fear that my malice should be self-betrayed (see Ps. 26:12 [27:12]). No, I do not wrangle with you, for, *if you, Lord, will keep record of our iniquities, Master, who has strength to bear it* (Ps. 129:3 [130:3])?" See Alford's treatment (pp. 6–9) of how the medieval saint is typically shown to "talk Bible," as in the anonymous fourteenth-century *Life of Christina of Markyate*, where Christina's prayer is "little more than a cento of biblical quotations" (p. 8).

CHAPTER 3

1. Croce, p. 169.

2. The critics who most immediately come to mind are Nardi, "Dante profeta"; Mineo; Sarolli; and (albeit with some irony) Barolini, *Undivine Comedy*, pp. 3–20. See also the entry "profetismo" by Raoul Manselli in *ED*, 4: 694–99.

3. Padoan, "La 'mirabile visione,' di Dante e l'Epistola a Cangrande," in his *Il pio Enea*, pp. 30–63, esp. pp. 48–49.

4. Dronke, *Dante and Medieval Latin Traditions*, p. 127 n. 8.

5. Battaglia Ricci examines both structure and style in *Dante e la tradizione*. See especially her treatment of *res* and *signum* in the chapter "Polisemanticità e Struttura della 'Commedia,'" pp. 65–110, and her appendix on the connection between the Vulgate and Dante's vernacular style, "Dall' 'Antico Testamento' alla 'Commedia,'" pp. 197–228.

6. Auerbach, "Figura," in his *Scenes from the Drama*, pp. 11–76, quote from p. 29.

7. Auerbach, *Literary Language*, pp. 25–66.

8. I am taking Dante to be the full author of the epistle to Can Grande, although his authorship remains in dispute. The latest arguments for and against are offered, respectively, by Hollander, *Dante's Epistle to Can Grande*; and Kelly, *Tragedy and Comedy*. The two do combat in Hollander and Kelly, "The Can Grande Dispute." Barolini gives a lucid discussion of the epistle and its use in Dante criticism in *Undivine Comedy*, pp. 3–20. For a concise treatment of the exegetical tradition appropriated by Dante in the epistle, see R. E. McNally's entry, "Exegesis, Medieval," in *NCE*, 5: 707–12. Brief considerations of the audacity of Dante's claims to fourfold exegesis are offered by Eco, pp. 160–62; and de Lubac, vol. 2, pt. 2, pp. 319–25.

9. Singleton, *Dante's "Commedia,"* pp. 15–16: "A poet has not God's power and may not presume to write as He can. But he may *imitate* God's way of writing. He may construct a literal historical sense, a journey beyond (and it too happens to be an Exodus!) to be, in the make-believe of his poem, as God's literal sense is in His book (and with God's help he will have the power to make it real)." I find the notion of "reality" to be slippery here.

10. Jack Miles, "Jesus Before He Could Talk," *New York Times Magazine* (Dec. 24, 1995), p. 33.

11. Singleton, "Irreducible Dove," p. 129.

12. Hollander, "Dante *Theologus-Poeta*," in his *Studies in Dante*, p. 86.

13. Barolini, *Undivine Comedy*, pp. 19–20: "Dante consistently manipulates narrative in ways that authenticate his text, making it appear inevitable, a 'fatale andare,' and conferring upon himself the authority that in fact we have rarely denied him. Our tendency has been to listen to what Dante says, accepting it as true—as though he were a 'theologian'—rather than looking at, and learning from, the gap that exists between what he says and what he has actually wrought."

14. Bloom has given Dante serious attention in *Ruin the Sacred Truths* and

Western Canon. A study of the critic's career-long involvement with the poet is offered by Colilli; see also McVeigh.

15. *Inferno* opens with the discovery of Virgil, Dante's "master and author," and soon leads to the pilgrim's embrace by other great classical poets in Limbo. These meetings are then followed by others that take place farther down in hell, with Pier delle Vigne in the circle of the suicides (*Inf.* 13) and the troubadour Bertran de Born among the sowers of discord (*Inf.* 28). *Purgatorio* not only continues this pattern of encounters but also intensifies it. The most important meeting involves Dante, Virgil, and the Silver Age poet Statius, and is played out over the course of two cantos (*Purg.* 21–22). All the others involve vernacular rather than Latin writers: Sordello in cantos 7–8, Bonagiunta in canto 24, Guido Guinizelli and Arnaut Daniel in canto 26.

16. For the way Dante positions himself among his peers, ancient and modern, see Barolini's *Dante's Poets*, and Jacoff, "Models of Literary Influence."

17. Bonaventure, *Breviloquium*, Prologue, sect. 2, p. 8. See Singleton, *Dante's "Commedia,"* pp. 45–60, esp. pp. 48–49, where he discusses the relevance of Bonaventure's *Breviloquium* prologue to Dante's "mystical procession."

18. Jerome's Preface to the Books of Samuel and Kings (*PL*, vol. 28, cols. 593–604), the first of the many prefaces he wrote, was often included in medieval Bibles. He calls it his *Prologus galeatus*, or "helmeted prologue," because in it he defends his principles and methods of dealing with the Hebrew text, including his limitation of the Old Testament text to 24 books, corresponding to the 24 elders John the Divine sees adoring the Lamb of God in Apocalypse (Revelation) 4. The books he excludes as apocryphal are ones the church nonetheless continued to revere as part of the canon: Wisdom, Ecclesiasticus, Judith, Tobit, the Shepherd of Hermas, and 1–2 Maccabees. Jerome's letter no. 53 to Paulinus of Nola, which, like the "helmeted prologue," was also frequently included in medieval Bibles, describes the subject of each biblical book and follows the same canonical order Dante observes in the Pageant. Both documents are published in *SL*, 2d ser., 6: 96–102, trans. W. H. Fremantle. Rocca, pp. 25–27, suggests Dante's possible debt to Jerome's epistle for the order of the Pageant procession. Regarding Jerome's inconsistency on the Apocrypha, however, see E. F. Sutcliffe, SJ, "Jerome," in *CHB*, pp. 92–93.

19. Padoan, "San Paolo in Dante," in *DB*, pp. 242–44, argues effectively that the figure Dante sees in the procession is not Paul himself (who in fact is never glimpsed in the *Commedia*) but rather a personification of the Pauline Epistles. Padoan also offers possible iconographic models for Dante's portrait of the apostle bearing a sword, both in Rome (S. Cecilia, S. Maria in Trastevere) and in Venice (S. Marco).

20. Dronke, however, challenges "the assumption that Dante was here simply making his verse a vehicle for traditional theological emblematics" ("Procession in Dante's *Purgatorio*," p. 24).

21. Battaglia Ricci, in *Dante e la tradizione*, emphasizes how Dante distances himself from classical rhetorical definitions of "realism" or "symbolism" and instead identifies with the "literary form of the Bible." The poet's insistence that what he saw was also what the biblical authors beheld, as in *Purg.* 29.94–105, shows that the reader must absolutely believe "alla volontà dantesca di porre come 'reale' la sua visione e come 'storia' il suo *poema*" ("in Dante's determination to present his vision as 'reality' and his poem as 'history,'" p. 94).

22. Pietrobono, p. 20, laments the pedantry of the passage: "Three tercets to make us know the source, from which these figures are drawn, in which [Dante] is in accord with one or another of his authorities, are truly too much." Dronke, "*Purgatorio XXIX*," p. 122, wonders if perhaps the passage reveals "Dante's ironic look at the kind of pedantry that his future commentators would perpetuate—an irony pointed by Dante's triple wordplay on the poet's way of spending."

23. Here I depart from Barolini, *Undivine Comedy*, pp. 11–12, where she says, "the Apocalypse, the prophetic text that is the most immediate precursor of *Purgatorio* 29, is hardly innocent of literary self-referencing; rather, its author repeatedly refers to himself as a writer and to us as his readers." Is this really the case? When John is told several times to "write a book" to be sent to the seven churches of Asia, he is in fact only taking dictation—not "writing" in Dante's sense of *poetando*. Similarly, his readers are meant to heed and obey the words of his prophecy—"Worship God!" (22:9)—not appreciate his language or ponder his stylistic decisions. John's words may well be highly rhetorical and crafted, but they do not draw attention to themselves as such; nor, I think, do they show self-consciousness of what Barolini calls their "status as verbal fabrications" (p. 12).

24. For the divine command to the prophets to write, see Jer. 30:2 and 36:2, Dan. 12:4, and Hab. 2:2.

25. To observe that the biblical authors do not present themselves as poets contemplating their rhymes is not to say that either Dante or the medieval church was blind to the literary quality of the Scripture. True, a number of the church fathers took account of St. Paul's rejection of "loftiness of speech" (1 Cor. 2.1) and resisted putting the oracles of heaven under the rule of the grammarians. Jerome is a case in point. In the same letter (no. 23) to Eustochium in which he worries that he may be more a Ciceronian than a Christian, he draws a firm line between the Bible and mere literature: " 'For

what communion hath light with darkness? And what concern hath Christ with Belial?' How can Horace go with the psalter, Virgil with the gospels, Cicero with the apostle?" Yet, as Kugel has noted in *Idea of Biblical Poetry*, this highly rhetorical rejection of rhetoric suggests that the Bible has literary qualities worth noting, that there is even an equivalence between Scripture and pagan literature: Horace and the Psalter are both lyric poetry, Virgil and the Gospels both epics, Cicero and Paul both rhetoricians. Indeed, many church fathers (like Jerome himself elsewhere) celebrate the Bible's literary eloquence and beauty, its identity as what Kugel calls "literature plus": "[Scripture] boasted all the merits of classical Greek and Latin writings *plus* true doctrine and all spiritual good." ("Bible as Literature," p. 39). Thus, Augustine in *On Christian Doctrine* counsels the would-be preacher to turn to the Bible as a textbook for rhetoric, a fit replacement for the works of Cicero. Bede not only sees in Scripture the same literary devices found in pagan authors but also classifies books of the Bible according to their literary genre as lyric, epic, or drama. And Cassiodorus goes so far as to suggest that the great poets and grammarians of antiquity must have had access to the Psalter: nowhere else could they have found tropes and figures to inspire their own work. See Kugel's "Bible as Literature."

26. Augustine is probably the likely source for the equation of six wings with six historical ages (*On the Trinity* 4.4, 7–8, and *City of God* 22.24). See also Bonaventure's *Breviloquium*, Prologue, sect. 2, p. 9. According to Richard of St. Victor, *In Apocalypsim Joannis libri septem* (in *PL*, vol. 196, col. 752), however, the six wings signify the knowledge of the Scriptures: "Prima ala est in lege naturae, secunda in lectione legis scriptae, tertia in lectione prophetiae, quarta in lectione legis evangelicae, quinta in institutionis apostolicae, sexta in scientia doctorum apostolos tempore sequentium, et obscura loca Scripturarum exponentium." ("The first wing is [knowledge] in the law of nature, the second in the reading of scriptural law, the third in the reading of the prophets, the fourth in the reading of the evangelical law, the fifth in the instruction of the apostles, the sixth in the knowledge of the apostolic doctors in the succeeding age, and the exposition of obscure passages in Scripture.") So too the *Glossa ordinaria* (in *PL*, vol. 114, col. 719).

27. See Hardie; Dronke, "Procession in Dante's *Purgatorio*," pp. 25–26; and Armour, pp. 46–73.

28. Bloom, *Western Canon*, p. 94.

29. Serravalle, commentary on *Purg.* 29.105.

30. While I am turning primarily to Hollander here, I want also to acknowledge Battaglia Ricci's work on *Purg.* 29.100–105, both in *Dante e la tradizione*, pp. 93–95, and in "Scrittura Sacra," pp. 297–98. In the latter essay

(p. 298) she argues that the references to Ezekiel and John not only establish the biblical antecedents for the vision of Dante Pilgrim but also reveal how the poet wants to add his own work "in this chain of cultural transmission, as third among the sacred books, with which he establishes a rapport made at one and the same time of continuity and integration: 'John is with me.' "

31. Hollander, "Dante *Theologus-Poeta*," in his *Studies in Dante*, pp. 76–77. Hollander makes a related observation with regard to the figure of Geryon in *Inf.* 16.124–32, where a "poetic object that has every appearance of being a lie" becomes Dante's occasion to swear he is telling the truth. Thus, says Hollander, the poet "puts his entire *Comedy* behind the claim that he actually saw this actual Geryon. . . . One senses behind Dante's passage an authorial wink, lest we take it for a nod: 'I know you won't believe this (why should you?—I don't either), but the convention of my poem compels me to claim historicity even for such as Geryon" (p. 76).

32. Following closely the narrative sequence of Ovid's account in the *Metamorphoses*, where a description of the chariot and its errant course is followed by earth's prayer and heaven's response, Dante's telescoped allusion leaves off (and leaves out) the epitaph that marks the end of Phaeton's story with an admonitory postscript: "HERE PHAETON LIES; IN PHOEBUS' CAR HE FARED, / AND THOUGH HE GREATLY FAILED, MORE GREATLY DARED" ("HIC SITVS EST PHAETON CVRRVS AVRIGA PATERNI / QVEM SI NON TENVIT MAGNIS TAMEN EXCIDIT AVSIS," 2.327–28). By recalling this daring failure in the midst of his own visionary assertions (however "arcanamente"), Dante at once acknowledges the danger he runs and, in so doing, distances himself from the reckless course of the "falsus auriga Phaeton." The title "falsus auriga Phaeton" occurs in the epistle to the Italian Cardinals, where he accuses the prelates of being false charioteers who have taken the car of the church off its proper track. Later on he clears himself of any identification of his temerity with the presumption of Uzzah. See Brownlee, "Phaeton's Fall."

33. For Aquinas on prophecy, for instance, see *ST* II-II, 171–78; in question 174, 6, ad 3, he speaks about how the prophetic vocation continues to exist in the life of the church: "At each period there were always some who had the spirit of prophecy, *not for the purpose of setting out new doctrine to be believed, but for the governance of human activities*" (emphasis mine). See the several appendices on prophecy and revelation in volume 45 of the Blackfriars *ST.*

34. Battaglia Ricci writes persuasively about the essential "contamination" of Dante's poem in "Scrittura sacra," p. 321: "Truly in this contamination of materials both literary and nonliterary, to which is entrusted the function of resemanticizing the literary typos in a Christian sense, one can, I think, recognize the sign and mark of the reinvention and resemanticization in a

sacred sense of the allegorical poem; but in this one can also recognize, on the contrary, the sign and mark of the 'literaturization' of the sacred book." She goes on to speak about the "extraordinary reciprocity between the two codes from which is born 'the sacred poem to which heaven and earth have so set hand.' "

35. Speaking boldly, "cum fiducia," is a characteristic of apostolic speech throughout the Book of Acts. But most especially it is the hallmark of St. Paul, who from the moment of his conversion (9:29) to the closing words of Acts, is said to speak "cum omni fiducia, sine prohibitione" ("with all confidence, without prohibition," 28:31). See also Paul's remarks in Eph. 6, where, after enjoining the Christian to take up the "sword of the Spirit" (6:17), he says, "[Pray] for me, that speech may be given me, that I may open my mouth with confidence, to make known the mystery of the gospel. For which I am an ambassador in chains, so that therein I may be bold to speak according as I ought" (6:19–20). On this bold speech, see Schnapp, *Transfiguration of History*, pp. 215–31.

36. The central argument of Mazzotta's *Dante's Vision* is that Dante's poetry "recognizes the importance of a rational theology such as Aquinas's, but this cannot mean, for Dante, poetry's subordination to a dominant theological structure other than the one he forges. On the contrary, Dante is engaged in a creative polemic with St. Thomas, who, in many ways, is his privileged inter-locutor. Yet, against Aquinas—who relegates poetry to the corner of the merely delightful and inconsequential, in the belief that the depths of the divinity can be fathomed only through the rigor of rational investigation; whose own thought bypasses the Augustinian and Victorine legacy of history and symbolic theology; who opposes allegory and the mythologization of knowledge— against Aquinas, Dante writes a poem that retrieves history, the passions of his own life, fables, and theology together in the conviction, first, that poetry is the path to take to come to the vision of God and, second, that the poetic imagina-tion is the faculty empowered to resurrect and glue together the fragments of a broken world" (p. 14). See also Franke, esp. his "recapitulatory prospectus" in his chapter "A New Hermeneutic Horizon for Religious Revelation in Poetic Literature?" pp. 233–38. Minnis argues to the contrary (pp. 118–45) that it was the Scholastics' recognition of the literary power of the Scripture to move "the *affectus* to goodness" that actually fostered an appreciation of rhetoric and poetry.

37. A generation after Dante, Boccaccio wrote in his *Trattatello in laude di Dante* (chap. 10): "Theology and poetry can be considered as almost the same thing when their subject is the same. Indeed I go further, and assert that theology is simply the poetry of God" (p. 54). About this change of mind,

Anderson writes, "There was, in fact, a revulsion against this [negative, Scholastic] attitude in Dante's time. Albertino Mussato speaks of poets as having been the theologians of ancient times. The movement grew after Dante's death, most notably with Boccaccio's praise of poetry as theology in his life of Dante and with other writings. Coluccio Salutati was so convinced of the divine origins of poetry that he tried to convince a skeptical Dominican on this point by saying that if the Dominican denied the authority of inspiration to poets he should deny it also to the scriptures. Landino finally settled the question by placing poetry high above the liberal arts and describing the inspiration of the poet as a divine fury. To him God is the supreme poet and the world is his poem. Dante did not enter specifically into this debate; he simply overrode it in practice" (p. 305). See also Curtius, *European Literature*, pp. 214–27; and Paparelli, pp. 53–138. See Minnis's "Scriptural Authority and Pagan Authority" (in *Medieval Theory*, pp. 112–17); also his discussion (pp. 137–45) of how the Mendicants' emphasis on preaching as the goal of biblical study had an impact on late-medieval literary theory.

38.

Ultima Cumaei venit iam carminis aetas;
magnus ab integro saeclorum nascitur ordo.
iam redit et Virgo, redeunt Saturnia regna;
iam nova progenies caelo demittitur alto.
tu modo nascenti puero, quo ferrea primum
desinet ac toto surget gens aurea mundo,
casta fava Lucina: tuus iam regnat Apollo.
(Virgil, Eclogue IV, vv. 4–10)

(Now is come the last age of the song of Cumae; the great line of the centuries begins anew. Now the Virgin returns, the reign of Saturn returns; now a new generation descends from heaven on high. Only do thou, pure Lucina, smile on the birth of the child, under whom the iron brood shall first cease, and a golden race spring up throughout the world! Thine own Apollo now is king!)

39. St. Jerome, letter no. 53, in *SL*, 2d ser., 6: 101, trans. W. H. Fremantle.

CHAPTER 4

1. Foucault, p. 160. Barthes, pp. 143–50, speaks about the "removal" of the author and, with him or her, the removal of any claim to decipher a text. As a result, "everything is to be *disentangled*, nothing *deciphered*. In precisely this way literature (it would be better from now on to say *writing*), by refusing to

assign a 'secret,' an ultimate meaning, to the text (and to the world as text), liberates what may be called an anti-theological activity, an activity that is truly revolutionary since to refuse to fix meaning is, in the end, to refuse God and his hypostases—reason, science, law" (p. 147).

2. I am thinking here in particular of Barolini's works *Dante's Poets* (1984) and especially *The Undivine Comedy* (1992), as well as of three essays by Albert Ascoli that address the topic primarily in terms of Dante's prose treatises.

3. The first quote is from Bloom, *Ruin the Sacred Truths*, p. 46, and the second from his *Western Canon*, p. 95.

4. Jacoff discusses the ways in which Dante appropriates and supersedes his poetic precursors, and in particular how he uses biblical typology to position himself as their "fulfillment," in "Models of Literary Influence."

5. Schnapp speaks, with special regard to *Par.* 17.124–32, of "Cacciaguida's prophetic empowerment," in *Transfiguration of History*, pp. 236–37. See Mineo, pp. 254–96, on "investitura profetica," and Sarolli, pp. 395–98. In *Ruin the Sacred Truths*, Bloom finds nothing in Cacciaguida's lines other than Dante's celebration of himself: "With a poet so preternaturally strong as Dante, we should look for what is not there, and what is absent in this magnificent accolade is any reference to a biblical trope, whether prophetic, as in Isaiah or Jeremiah, or relating to Christ, in the Gospels or in Paul. Dante's revelation is his own, and will be of himself" (p. 49).

6. Mazzeo's chapter "Dante and the Pauline Modes of Vision," in his *Structure and Thought*, pp. 84–110, gives a full account of Dante's reliance on Paul throughout the *Commedia*. See also the brief but compelling treatment that Jacoff and Stephany (pp. 61–64) give to the importance of the "vessel of election" (*Inf.* 2.28, Acts 9:15–16). Dante appropriates a Pauline identity for himself in the opening lines of the *Paradiso* when he refers several times to Paul's "man in Christ" who was "caught up into paradise, and heard such secret words, which it is not lawful to man to utter" (2 Cor. 12:4). This oft-noted verse, moreover, is part of a larger strategy whereby Paul works first to undo the slander of his rivals in evangelism and then to establish his own authority with the Corinthians. Acknowledging his weakness in the eyes of others (10:10), he turns his enemies' charges against him into his own self-defense, claims his mortal frailty to be an occasion to glory in God's grace. This argument is then followed by a veiled reference to his rapture into the third heaven. However oblique his description to his own experience ("I know a man in Christ," 1 Cor. 12:2), he claims this journey *in paradisum* as his own—and as a final warrant for his apostolic witness. God raised him to an incalculable height, in other words, to render insignificant the depths he has plumbed. And no matter how few may be listening to him with respect, he radiates complete confidence in the

words he speaks. I believe Dante had much to learn from Paul's strategy with the Corinthians.

7. In *Par.* 25.43–45 James tells Dante that heaven has allowed him so extraordinary an experience "sì che, veduto il ver di questa corte, / la spene, che là giù bene innamora, / in te e in altrui di ciò conforte" ("so that, having seen the truth of this Court, you may strengthen in yourself and others the Hope which rightly enamors." In 25.129 John tells him that he did not ascend bodily into heaven, "e questo apporterai nel mondo vostro" ("and this you shall carry back into your world"). And in 27.65–66 Peter concludes his denunciation of the papacy by saying, "apri la bocca, / e non asconder quel ch'io non ascondo" ("open your mouth and do not hide what I hide not").

8. Minnis, p. 374.

9. In addition to the commentaries of Sapegno and Bosco and Reggio (who are especially sensitive to the place of Scripture), I have found the following critics most useful in my work on these cantos: Tartaro; Brownlee, "Why the Angels Speak Italian"; Mazzotta's chapter "Theology and Exile," in his *Dante's Vision*, pp. 174–96; Chiavacci Leonardi, "Il tema della resurrezione nel 'Paradiso," in *DB*, pp. 249–72; and Durling and Martinez, *Time and the Crystal*, pp. 240–58.

10. The actual simile in *Par.* 23.121–26 is as follows:

E come fantolin che 'nver' la mamma
    tende le braccia, poi che 'l latte prese,
    per l'animo che 'nfin di fuor s'infiamma;
ciascun di quei candori in sù si stese
    con la sua cima, sì che l'alto affetto
    ch'elli avieno a Maria mi fu palese.

(And as an infant which, when it has taken the milk, stretches its arm toward its mother, its affection glowing forth, each of these splendors stretched upward with its peak, so that the deep love they had for Mary was made plain to me.)

11. The simile (*Par.* 24.46–51) that places Dante in this academic context is as follows:

Sì come il baccialier s'arma e non parla
    fin che 'l maestro la question propone,
    per approvarla, non per terminarla,
così m'armava io d'ogne ragione
    mentre ch' ella dicea, per esser presto
    a tal querente e a tal professione.

(Even as the bachelor arms himself—and does not speak until the master propounds the question—in order to adduce the proof, not to decide it, so, while [Beatrice] was speaking, I was arming myself with every reason, to be ready for such a questioner and for such a profession.)

For analysis of the academic setting, see Barbi; Onder, "Baccialiere," in *ED*, 1: 493; and the excellent note by Bosco and Reggio on *Par.* 25.46: "The comparison here presents a scene from university life, which, belonging also to the Italian theological schools, does not serve as a proof of Dante's supposed going to Paris. What is recalled, moreover, is that the *baccalarius* read biblical texts in the schools: hence, perhaps, Dante's choice of the comparison, since all three cantos of the 'exam' are based on the necessity of the direct reading of the sacred texts. Over time, such reading was abandoned in favor, for example, of the *Sententiae* of Peter Lombard, something Roger Bacon lamented ('Baccalarius who reads the text succumbs to the reading of the *Sentences*')." Bosco and Reggio acknowledge an essay by T. Gregory.

12. In their commentary on *Par.* 26.38–39 ("colui che mi dimostra il primo amore / di tutte le sustanze sempiterne," "[he] who demonstrates to me the first love of all the eternal substances"), Bosco and Reggio suggest that among the various philosophers who have been advanced as this unnamed "he"—Aristotle, Plato, Dionysius the Areopagite, and even Virgil—Aristotle is the most likely.

13. Earlier in this same discussion, Aquinas writes: "Argument from authority is the method most appropriate to this teaching in that its premises are held through revelation; consequently it has to accept the authority of those to whom revelation was made. Nor does this derogate from its dignity, for though weakest when based on what human beings have disclosed, the argument from authority is most forcible when based on what God has disclosed" (*ST* I-II, 1, 8, resp. ad 2). See app. 7, "Revelation," in vol. 1 of the Blackfriars edition of *ST*.

14. The verse from Heb. 11:1 is "Now faith is the substance of things hoped for, the evidence of things that appear not." In 2 Pet. 3:15, Peter speaks of "our most dear brother Paul." The use of "quiditate" ("quiddity") in *Par.* 24.66 reflects Scholastic discourse.

15. The text in Latin reads as follows: "Est autem spes virtus qua spiritualia et aeterna bona sperantur, id est, cum fiducia expectantur. Est enim spes certa expectatio futurae beatitudinis, veniens ex Dei gratia et meritis praecedentibus, vel ipsam spem, quam natura praeit charitas, vel rem speratam, id est, beatitudinem aeternam. Sine meritis enim aliquid sperare, non spes, sed praesumptio dici potest."

16. *ST* II-II, 18, 4 s.c.: "On the other hand Peter Lombard teaches that

'hope is the certain expectation of future beatitude' [II *Sent.* 26, 2, 4; *De spe* 2 ad 4], and the same truth is to be found in the Second Epistle to Timothy, 'I know in whom I have believed, and am certain that he is able to guard the trust committed to me [2 Tim. 1:12].' "

17. *ST* II-II, 17, 2 resp.: "For it belongs to [God's] limitless power to bring us to limitless good. Such a good is life eternal, consisting in the joyful possession of God himself. This is simply to say that we should hope for nothing less from God than his very self; his goodness, by which he confers good upon creaturely things, is nothing less than his own being. And so the proper and principal object of hope is indeed eternal blessedness."

18. *ST* II-II, 18, 4 resp.: "Hope does not put its trust primarily in grace already received but in the divine omnipotence and mercy, when grace can come even to one who does not yet have it, and make it possible thereby for him to reach eternal life. To anyone having faith, this omnipotence and mercy of God are certainties."

19. Jacoff, "Models of Literary Influence," p. 175.

20. See Minnis, "Authorial Roles in the 'Literal Sense,' " in his *Medieval Theory*, pp. 73–117.

21. See Barolini, *Dante's Poets*, pp. 275–78; Minnis, *Medieval Theory*, pp. 43–49, 103–11; and Kuczynski.

22. Augustine, *Expositions in the Book of the Psalms*, in *SL*, 1st ser., 8:80, trans. A. Cleveland Coxe.

23. Chiavacci Leonardi notes the exegetical bridge between Isaiah and John provided by St. Gregory's *Dialogue* 2, 26. In *DB*, note 25 on pp. 266–67, Chiavacci Leonardi also cites Innocent III, *In sabbatum IV Temp.*, in *PL*, vol. 217, col. 381; and Bonaventure, *Sermo de Assumptione B. Verginis Mariae*, 5, II.

24. Here Dante may be invoking the idea of the *duplex causa efficiens* popular among thirteenth-century commentators on Scripture. God is always to be regarded as the first author of the Bible, the unmoved mover of the sacred text. Second in command are the canonical writers. In his prologue to the Book of Wisdom, for instance, Bonaventure distinguishes between these two distinct kinds of authorship. At the highest level, God is the efficient cause "by the mode of inspiring," since he is the ultimate source of all Solomon's wisdom. But Solomon himself is the efficient cause "by mode of devising," not just because the actual words of Wisdom are his but because he is responsible for what is said by them. See Minnis's discussion "The Human *Auctor* as Efficient Cause," in his *Medieval Theory*, pp. 75–94. The quotations are from pp. 79 and 78 respectively.

25. In *Convivio* 1.2.12–14 Dante made a case for speaking about oneself

either when there is no one else to rise up in defense (as with Boethius in his *Consolation*) or when personal example "is so instructive as to be of the greatest help to others" (as with Augustine in the *Confessions*). Dante continues: "If each of these reasons justifies my conduct, the bread made from my grain may be regarded as fully purified of its first blemish. I am moved to speak by both the fear of disgrace and the desire to give instruction which no one else is in a position to give."

26. Brownlee, "Why the Angels Speak Italian," pp. 602–9, is especially acute on Dante's valorization of the word *poeta* and its significance in his works from *Vita nuova* 25, to the *Inferno* and *Purgatorio*, to *Par.* 25.8, where the word appears for the 30th and final time in the *Comedy*. "The claims made in *Vita Nuova* XXV for the elevated status of the vernacular poet (implicitly and in a secular context) can be fully realized by Dante himself only in the most explicitly Christian context of the theological examination of *Paradiso* XXIV–XXVI. This display of theological mastery coincides with and guarantees Dante's self-presentation in *Paradiso* XXV as vernacular *poeta*" (p. 609).

27. In his tractate on John 21:19–25 (*Tractates*, pp. 83–84), Augustine recognized that Christians in his own day continued to ignore these words of the Evangelist: they "assert that the Apostle John is living, and . . . contend that in that sepulchre of his which is at Ephesus he is sleeping rather than lies dead." Augustine then recounts a story "found in certain scriptures, although apocryphal": that John was buried alive and will remain in the grave, sleeping, until Christ comes again in glory. According to some accounts, the dust above his tomb regularly stirred with the rise and fall of the living man's breath. Augustine himself clearly does not believe these stories and therefore declines to "wrestle" further with them. Still, he does not dismiss them out of hand: "For, let those who know the place see whether the ground does this there or sustains what is said, for in fact we have heard this from persons [who are] not irresponsible."

Aquinas, in "Of the Time and Manner of the Resurrection" (*ST* III, supp., 77, 1), recalls yet another story about St. John still current in his own day, namely, that like the Virgin Mary, John was bodily assumed into heaven shortly after Christ's own resurrection and ascension, in token of his extraordinary grace and merit. Thomas does not mention the tale told in the *Golden Legend*, how visitors to John's deathbed found manna, as well as a fountain of dust, where his body had once reposed. Instead, he refers only to "pious belief," then decides, on good theological principle, *not* to affirm it. Nonetheless, he does not close the door on the matter. Although the dead will be raised up only at the time of the Last Judgment, there may possibly have been some exceptions to this rule: "and if it has been granted to others that their resurrection should not be delayed until the general resurrection, this has been a special privilege of grace, and not as due on account of [their greater] conformity to Christ" (*ST* III, supp., 77, 1, resp. ad 2).

Rachel Jacoff considers all these perspectives and their relevance for the *Commedia* in "Dante and the Legend(s) of St. John."

28. The poet of the *Commedia* "definitively" resolves not only the vexed status of St. John's body but also other questions of belief debated within the medieval church. About the ascension of Christ in his glorified body there could be no doubt; however, it was not until 1950 that Pius XII declared the Virgin Mary's physical assumption a dogma binding on all the faithful. Commentators suggest that in this matter Dante was following the Franciscans, demonstrating how deeply he imbibed Florentine liturgical piety, or taking as his own position the teaching of this or that theologian. There is no reason to dismiss these possible influences, but to use them as a gloss on what John says in *Paradiso* 25 would be to misrepresent how the *Commedia* presents Dante's claims. He is, after all, reporting what was told to him: his heaven (as James Merrill has it in *Changing Light*) is "pure Show and Tell." Moving beyond faith into fact, in other words, he is not "with" the Franciscans or "with" the *Summa*; he is "with John." Therefore, as the beloved disciple makes crystal clear, Dante is to understand that only Christ and Mary ascended into heaven, that until the general resurrection only they enjoy the double portion of body and soul, "le due stole nel beato chiostro" ("the two robes in the blessed cloister," v. 127). No other possibility can be taken seriously, not even Enoch and Elijah, despite a solid basis in Scripture to believe that both these Old Testament figures had "walked with God" rather than suffered death and the grave.

29. Botterill formulates this point in "Doctrine, Doubt, and Certainty," where he discusses the degrees of beatitude Dante accords the baptized infants of *Paradiso* 32: "[Bonaventure and Aquinas] both hold that, although equality of grace is the norm, there exists a possibility that it will be set aside on occasion. Dante, however, goes a step further. For him the diversity in degrees of grace is the norm—is, indeed, a structural principle in the Empyrean—and to this extent his doctrine clearly differs from that of either of his two predecessors. . . . [But] it is highly probable that one or both of these authors, by admitting the possibility of differing degrees of beatitude, laid the foundations for Dante's audacious attempt to elevate that possibility into a principle. It would not be the first time Dante had taken a hint and derived a characteristically original conclusion" (pp. 22, 24).

30. In *City of God* 22.5 Augustine unfolds this argument at length: "Here then we have those incredibilities; and yet they happened. It is incredible that Christ rose in the flesh and with his flesh ascended into heaven. It is incredible

that the world believed so incredible an event; and it is incredible that men of no birth, no standing, no learning, and so few of them, should have been able to persuade so effectively, the whole world, including the learned men. . . . [This] one overpowering miracle is enough for us—that the whole world has come to believe in it without any miracles at all!" Aquinas makes a similar argument in *Summa contra Gentiles* 1.6.

CHAPTER 5

1. For the history of the clause *descendit ad inferos,* see Kelly, pp. 378–83; also Schaff, *Creeds of Christendom,* 2: 46.

2. Christ's statement in Matt. 12:40, for instance, was taken as a prophecy of his own stay in the underworld: "For as [Jonah] was in the whale's belly three days and three nights so shall the Son of Man be in the heart of the earth three days and three nights." Other New Testament texts fill in the picture more or less directly. St. Paul writes in Rom. 14:9 that Christ died "that he might be Lord both of the dead and of the living"; there is also the passage in Eph. 4:8–10 where the apostle argues that, if the savior ascended to heaven, it is "because he also descended first into the lower parts of the earth" (v. 9). What Christ accomplished during his sojourn in those lower depths was suggested by some cryptic verses in the First Epistle of Peter: "he preached to those spirits that were in prison . . . [and] for this cause was the gospel also preached to the dead: that they might be judged indeed according to men, in the flesh; but may live according to God, in the Spirit" (3:19, 4:6). Elsewhere, in Acts 2:24–31, Peter proclaims that God raised Jesus from the grave, "having loosed the sorrows of hell, as it was impossible that he should be holden by it" (v. 24). His proof text here (quoted at v. 27) is David's "prophecy" of Christ in Ps. 15 (16):10: "Because thou wilt not leave my soul in hell; nor wilt thou give thy holy one to see corruption" (a text quoted in Acts 2:27). Even more explicit in its "foretelling" is Ps. 106 (107): 13–16: "Then they cried to the Lord in their affliction: and he delivered them out of their distresses. And he brought them out of darkness and the shadow of death; and he broke their bonds in sunder. Let the mercies of the Lord give glory to him, and his wonderful works to the children of men. Because he hath broken gates of brass, and burst iron bars."

The roughly twenty biblical "sources" for the story of the descent are given by MacCulloch, pp. 45–66. See also Miller, pp. 25–55, esp. pp. 27–29; Chaine, esp. cols. 410–20; J. D. Quinn, "Descent of Christ into Hell," in *NCE,* 4: 788–89. Miller, pp. 31–34, describes the Reformation's "demythologizing" of the descent, when it was taken variously as a harmless element of folk religion (by Luther), as a way simply of affirming that Christ had truly died (by Zwingli), and as a "fable" (by Calvin). According to Reformed Christianity's Heidelberg Catechism, the descent served as a metaphor for Christ's "unspeakable distress, agony, and horror, which He suffered in His soul, and previously."

3. The earliest of these accounts is probably the Odes of Solomon, dating from the end of the first century. Miller lists other sources: "the Gospel of Peter, the Epistles of the Apostles, the Ascent of Isaiah, the Testament of the Twelve Patriarchs, the Sibylline Graces, the Acts of Thaddeus, and the Acts of Thomas, not to mention the later Anaphora of Pilate and Questions of Saint Bartholomew . . . [and] the Gospel of Nicodemus" (p. 26). For a fuller account of these apocryphal sources, see MacCulloch, pp. 131–73, and Chaine, cols. 395–410.

4. For the various versions of the descent narrative in the Gospel of Nicodemus (Greek, Latin A, Latin B), see *Apocryphal NT*, pp. 185–204. Unless otherwise noted, I will be citing the earliest (Greek) version of the text. For background on the Gospel of Nicodemus, in addition to the introduction offered by *Apocryphal NT*, pp. 164–69, see Barnstone, pp. 359–61; and Monnier, pp. 91–107.

5. In the Gospel of Nicodemus the harrowing is recounted by two brothers, sons of the priest Simeon (Luke 2:22–35), who together with their father were among those imprisoned in Hades "with all who have died since the beginning of the world" (in *Apocryphal NT*, p. 186). The tale they tell, therefore, is the account of their own rescue from death, firsthand testimony of events that took place after the crucifixion, when, according to the Gospel of Matthew, "the earth quaked, and the rocks were rent. And the graves were opened: and many bodies of the saints that had slept arose" (Matt. 27:51–52). In the apocryphon the brothers recall that at "the hour of midnight there rose upon the darkness there something like the light of the sun, and it shone and lit us all, and we saw one another" (in *Apocryphal NT*, p. 186). One by one these Old Testament figures interpret this light by reference to the foretelling in Hebrew Scripture. Thus Abraham rejoices to see the fulfillment of the promise long ago made to him in Gen. 12:3, while David and Isaiah are filled with joy to have confirmation of what they "foresaw by the Holy Spirit." Suddenly a voice like thunder proclaims the words of Ps. 23 [24]:7, "Lift up your heads, O ye princes, and be lifted up, O eternal gates, and the King of Glory shall enter in." This prospect throws the forces of darkness into panic: Hades and Satan bicker between themselves, and a swarm of demons rushes to secure the massive doors of their city. But the gates of hell cannot prevail against the divine intruder: "the gates of brass were broken in pieces and the bars of iron were crushed and all the dead who were bound were loosed from their chains, and we with them. And the King of Glory entered as a man, and all the dark places of Hades were

illuminated" (p. 188). After his spectacular entrance, Christ banishes Satan to hell's lowest region. Then, starting with the very first human being, he delivers the saints of the Old Testament to their reward: "the King of Glory stretched out his right hand, and took hold of our forefather Adam and raised him up. Then he turned to the rest and said, 'Come with me, all you who have died through the tree which this man touched. For behold, I raise you all up again through the tree of the cross' " (p. 189). All whom Christ delivered are raised up with him on the third day. Once baptized in the river Jordan, they are given white robes and "carried up in the clouds." When the two brothers finish writing their transcript for Caiaphas, Annas, and the other astonished leaders of the temple, they too are "seen no more."

6. Monnier, p. 96, speaks of the Gospel of Nicodemus as "a veritable Mystery Play *avant la lettre*, depicting what will later become the way of representing the Resurrection in the Mystery Plays. It divides itself into perfectly resolved scenes. The characters appear with their characteristic traits, their tirades, their replies. The literature of different Christian peoples will adopt this scenario without changing anything essential." For the motif of the harrowing in medieval Latin liturgical drama, see Young, pp. 149–77; in secular drama, see Kolve, pp. 192–97. On the development of Italian theater, see D'Ancona; De Bartholomaeis. Iannucci, "Limbo," esp. pp. 84–89, draws attention to a particular *devozione*, "Hec Laus Sabbati Sancti," dating from Dante's time, which was based on the Gospel of Nicodemus, and incorporated into their Holy Saturday liturgy by lay companies of Disciplinati. His citation of this work comes from V. De Bartholomaeis, *Laude drammatiche e rappresentazioni sacre* (Florence, 1943), 1: 243–58. See also Monnier, pp. 211–45.

7. Brief considerations of the iconographic tradition are offered by Monnier, pp. 193–209; H. Quillet, "Descente de Jésus aux enfers," cols. 610–11; and P. Verdier, in *NCE*, 4: 789–93. For a book-length study of the motif, albeit one limited to the Byzantine tradition, see Kartsonis, esp. pp. 227–36.

8. Demus, p. 72.

9. Augustine, letter no. 164, "To my lord Evodius," in *SL*, 1st ser., 1: 516, trans. J. G. Cunningham.

10. In addition to Quillet, "Descente de Jésus aux enfers," cols. 597–605, see Monnier, pp. 69–192; and Kelly, pp. 378–83; also, app. 5, "Descent into Hell," in vol. 54 of the Blackfriars *ST*. R. Turner provides an excellent discussion of Dante's "position" within this tradition.

11. Augustine, letter to Evodius (no. 164), in *SL*, 1st ser., 1: 516, trans. J. G. Cunningham.

12. Ibid.

13. Augustine, *De Haeresibus*, para. 79, p. 115: "Another heresy believes that upon Christ's descent into hell the unbelievers believed and all were liberated from hell [incredulos et omnes exinde existimat liberatos]." See also Kelly, p. 381.

14. In addition to R. Turner, see S. Harrent, in *DTC*, vol. 7, pt. 2, cols. 1748–49.

15. *ST*, vol. 54, app. 5, pp. 214–15, provides a succinct summary of Thomas's various considerations of the descent. A brief version of his theology is found in a sermon he preached on the Apostles Creed during Lent 1273, close to the end of his life; it is found in Thomas Aquinas, *Sermon Conferences*, pp. 78–85.

16. Aquinas discusses the Bosom of Abraham in *ST* III, 52, 2, resp. ad 4, and distinguishes between the *limbus patrum* and the *limbus puerorum* in *ST* III, supp., 69, 5–6. See also Fausto Montanari, "Limbo," in *ED*, 3: 651–54; P. J. Hill, "Limbo," in *NCE*, 8: 762–65; and, perhaps most useful of all, Foster, *Two Dantes*, pp. 169–74.

17. For a similar discussion of these issues, see *ST* II-II, 2, 7 resp.: "Revelation about Christ was in fact given to many of the pagans, as is clear from their own prophecies. In Job we read, 'I know that my redeemer liveth'; and, as Augustine says, the Sibyl foretold certain truths about Christ. Moreover, it is recorded in the history of the Romans that, in the reign of Constantine Augustus and his mother Irene, a tomb was discovered in which there lay a man with a gold medallion on his chest, inscribed thus, Christ will be born of a virgin and I believe in him. 'O sun, you shall see me again in the reign of Irene and Constantine.' However, had any been saved who had received no revelation, they were not saved without faith in the mediator. The reason: even if they did not have an explicit faith in Christ, they did have an implicit faith in God's providence, believing that God is man's deliverer in ways of his own choosing, as the Spirit would reveal this to those who know the truth, according to the text of Job, 'Who teaches us more than the beasts of the earth.' "

18. In addition to R. Turner's review of these various positions, esp. pp. 173–91, see the overview offered by Padoan in his excellent 1969 essay, "Il limbo Dantesco," in his *Il pio Eneo*, pp. 103–24, esp. pp. 108–10. Also see Durling's note 16, "Christ in Hell," in his edition of *Divine Comedy*, pp. 580–83.

19. Peter Abelard, *Theologia Christiana* 1.5, and *PL*, vol. 178, cols. 1140–66. For a good summary of Abelard's thought and its influence on later theologians (including Vivès and Zwingli), see Harrent, cols. 1748–52.

20. Comparetti, pp. 96–118, esp. pp. 99–103.

21. Dante alludes to this passage in *Par.* 17.31–33, where he contrasts Cacciaguida's "chiare parole e . . . preciso latin" ("clear words and . . . precise

discourse," v. 34) with the Sibyl's baffling message: "per ambage, in che la gente folle / già s'inviscava pria che fosse anciso / l'Agnel di Dio che le peccata tolle" ("dark sayings, such as those in which the foolish folk of old once ensnared themselves before the Lamb of God who takes away sins was slain"). See Schnapp's discussion of these lines, *Transfiguration of History*, pp. 140–41. Also, for a larger treatment of Virgil and the Sibyl, see Hollander, *Il Virgilio Dantesco*, esp. pp. 138, 145–51; and Allevi.

22. Padoan, *Il pio Enea*, p. 105, argues that Dante opposed himself "drastically to the entire theological tradition of his time (as well as those coming afterward) by saying that in Limbo there are to be found not only children who died at a most tender age but also adults. The innovation is enormous, indeed extraordinary." A similar assessment is made by Paparelli (pp. 147–48) with regard to Dante's particular departure from Aquinas. The predicament of the unbaptized is treated indirectly in *Par.* 32.49–84, where St. Bernard details the different ways an infant could be saved, depending on the historical era in which he or she lived: "In the early ages, their parents' faith alone, with their own innocence, sufficed for their salvation. After those first ages were complete [i.e., after the covenant with Abraham], it was needful for males, through circumcision, to acquire power for their innocent wings; but after the time of grace had come, without perfect baptism in Christ such innocence was held there below [i.e., in Limbo]" (vv. 76–84). For a discussion of the theological traditions behind this doctrine of the three ages, as well as Dante's singular position on the unequal distribution of grace among unbaptized infants, see Botterill, both "Doctrine, Doubt, and Certainty" and *Dante and the Mystical Tradition*, pp. 96–101.

23. In his extensive commentary on *Inferno* 4, Manzoni contrasts the positions of Aquinas and Bonaventure, and establishes Dante's particular reliance on Bonaventure with regard to the Limbo dwellers' melancholy awareness of living "in hope without desire" (pp. 85–93)—what Paparelli refers to as Limbo's "atmosfera tutta virgiliana" (p. 148).

24. In addition to the many pre-Christian figures in Limbo, Dante includes three Moslems who were themselves "medievals": Avicenna (d. 1037), Averroes (d. 1198), and the Saladin (d. 1193). The first two are there, no doubt, because of their work on Aristotle; the last, because of his reputation for magnanimity.

25. Foster, *Two Dantes*, pp. 174–253, offers the most sustained theological sorting out of "Virgil and the Limbo-Dwellers" in light of the varied expositions given in the first two canticles, i.e., in *Inf.* 1.124–26 and 4.33–42; and in *Purg.* 3.34–45, 7.7–8, and 7. 25–36. See also Hollander, *Il Virgilio Dantesco*, pp. 125–28; and Iannucci, "Limbo," pp. 74–81. Both Foster (*Two Dantes*, pp. 250–

53) and Hollander (pp. 126–27) grapple with Virgil's confession that he was "ribellante" against God's law (*Inf.* 1.125), which stands in striking contrast to his other protestations of innocence. According to Iannucci, "In Limbo Dante is not so much interested in the idea that God endows man with a free will potentially capable of securing salvation, an idea expressed by Aquinas and upheld by Dante in the rest of the *Commedia*, as in the mystery of elective grace and predestination" (p. 81).

26. Aquinas, for example, could not be more clear on this matter in *De veritate*: "It is not possible for an adult without grace to be only in original sin, because as soon as he has attained the use of free choice, if he has prepared himself for grace, he will have grace; otherwise his very negligence will be imputed to him as a mortal sin" (*Truth* 24, 12, ad 2). Likewise, in 28, 3, ad 4: "The opinion that an adult may have original sin without any actual sin is held by some [e.g., Albertus Magnus] to be an impossible position. For when he begins to be an adult, if he does what he can, there will be given to him the grace by which he will be free of original sin; but if he does not do what he can, he will be guilty of a sin of omission. Since everyone is obliged to avoid sin and he cannot do this without setting his aim upon the due end, as soon as anyone is in the possession of his faculties he is obliged to turn to God and make Him his end. By so doing he is disposed for grace. Furthermore, Augustine says that the concupiscence deriving from original sin makes infants disposed to experience concupiscence, and adults actually to do so; for it is unlikely that one who is infected with original sin will not submit to the concupiscence of sin by a consent to a sin."

27. Padoan argues (*Il pio Enea*, pp. 113–15) that the poet's contemporaries were outraged by his "shattering" ("rottura") of theological tradition in *Inf.* 4: "tradizione qui non è infranta: è volutamente ignorata, distrutta, annullata" ("here tradition is not broken: it is willfully ignored, destroyed, annulled") (p. 113). He goes on to cite the fulminations of St. Antonino, bishop of Florence in the late fourteenth century, who dismissed the entirety of Dante's vision as "nothing but poetry" (p. 114). See also Mésoniat, pp. 81–83.

28. This might well have been the place to mention Cato, who would have been "old" in Limbo's condition at the moment of Christ's descent, and who must have been among the "many others" Christ made blessed on that occasion. In the opening canto of *Purgatorio*, in fact, Virgil recognizes that Cato "at the last day" will be resurrected in a glorified body and therefore be among the blessed: "la vesta ch'al gran dì sarà sì chiara" (v. 75). What Virgil does not understand is that neither Cato's Roman antiquity nor his former residency in Limbo make a lasting bond between him and any of the pagans who remain there, not even his former wife, Marcia. Of her Cato tells Virgil,

"Or che di là dal mal fiume dimora, / più muover non mi può, per quella legge / che fatta fu quando me n'usci' fora" ("Now that she dwells beyond the evil stream no more may she move me, by the law which was made when I came forth from there," vv. 88–90).

29. The commentary tradition has long noted that Virgil's listing of Old Testament exempla follows Augustine's division of world history into six ages, found in his explication of Ps. 92:1: "For the first period as the first day, was from Adam until Noah: the second, as the second day, from Noah unto Abraham: the third, as the third day, from Abraham unto David: the fourth, as the fourth day, from David unto the removal to Babylon: the fifth period, as the fifth day, from the removal to Babylon unto the preaching of John. The sixth day beginneth from the preaching of John, and lasteth unto the end: and after the end of the sixth day, we shall reach our rest. The sixth day, therefore, is even now passing." *Exposition on the Book of the Psalms*, in *SL*, 1st ser., 8: 457, trans. A. Cleveland Coxe.

30. This reversal is central to Iannucci's reading of *Inf.* 4: "The structure of medieval depictions of Limbo is comic. So profoundly entrenched was the association between the redemption and the harrowing in the mind of medieval man that it was well nigh impossible to conceive of Limbo in any other terms. Only a man like Dante, who possessed a sense of tragedy as well as comedy, a humanistic sympathy for pagan culture, and, most of all, a broad vision of history which set the sacred and profane side by side, could overturn this structure." "Limbo," pp. 104–5.

31. See Schnapp's discussion of this passage, *Transfiguration of History*, pp. 22–23, as well as the wider consideration offered by his chapter "History in the Grip of Mars," pp. 14–35.

32. In his note to *Inf.* 12.42, Singleton suggests that Dante is following Thomas Aquinas in his exposition of Aristotle's *Metaphysics* (*Exp. Metaphys.*, bk. 3, lect. 2, n. 478): "For Empedocles said that there exists in the world a certain alternation of hate and friendship, in such a way that at one time love unites all things and afterward hate separates them. But as to the reason why this alternation takes place, so that at one time hate predominates and at another time love, he said nothing more than that it was naturally disposed to be so [*ut quodam tempore dominaretur odium, et alio tempore amor, nullam aliam dicebat, nisi quia sic aptum natum est esse*]." See Giorgio Stabile, "Empedocle," in *ED*, 2: 666–67.

33. In *Purg.* 3.34–45, Virgil contrasts the condition of those who have faith in the Trinity and in the Incarnation of Christ (i.e., in "the infinite course taken by One Substance in Three Persons," the need for "Mary to give birth"),

with those who desire fruitlessly, and in that way experience eternal grief. He says that he is speaking of "Aristotle and of Plato and of many others," no doubt including himself in that latter group of "molt' altri."

34. Iannucci makes a careful correlation between Christ's descent into hell and that of Beatrice, first in "Limbo," pp. 95–97 (esp. p. 95 n. 45), and then in a related essay, "La discesa di Beatrice," in *Forma*, pp. 53–81.

35. Hollander wonders (*Il Virgilio Dantesco*, p. 128) whether in this somewhat frantic moment of doubt Virgil gives us some sense of his lack of faith: "In his refusal to believe in what he knew to have been promised (in the final verses of the preceding canto he announced the coming of the angelic intercessor which Beatrice promised precisely in view of this difficult moment), we are perhaps witnesses of a repetition of the sin that has relegated Virgil to Inferno. If this situation is analogous to Virgil's position on earth, we are led to think that he had probably possessed a far greater understanding than we have wanted to attribute to him and therefore an understanding sufficient to bring him to conversion, but that he did not know how or did not want to act accordingly." Hollander seems to be relying here on a notion of implicit faith at work in the *Commedia*, and sees Virgil as failing to "carry through" on his superior consciousness. But does this situation also describe Plato, Aristotle, and "many others"? Dante presents us with explicit faith in the cases of Trajan and Ripheus, is silent on the matter of Cato, and offers no other examples of pre-Christian saved pagans.

36. Quint makes the following contrast: "Beatrice summons Virgil up to earth to lead Dante down through hell. Erichtho sends Virgil to the bottom of Hell to bring a spirit up to earth" (p. 202).

37. Schnapp's formulation is as follows: "[Despite] the essential role performed by the *Aeneid* in the disclosure of Christ's historical mission, Virgil remains in death as in life a tragically flawed reader. The concrete signs of the Christ-event (the immediate carnal presence of the actual harrower of Hell), and the fact of Classical Elysium's topographical marginality to Christian paradise, have no real impact: the ultimate meanings of all events and signs, so long as Christ remains hidden in anonymity, will be a mystery to classical man" (*Transfiguration of History*, p. 4).

38. In *Inf.* 8.43–45, for instance, Virgil acclaims Dante's violent rejection of Filippo Argenti by apparently citing Luke 11:27, where a woman praises Christ by blessing the "womb that bore you." Christ's reply to her in Luke 11:27 is a correction if not a reproof: "Rather, blessed are those who hear the word of the Lord and keep it." For the significance of this rejoinder to Virgil's situation in the *Commedia*, see my essay "Virgilio cita le scritture," as well as Kleinhenz's

"Dante and the Bible: Intertextual Approaches," where he identifies six different types of biblical reference in the *Commedia*. See also his " Dante and the Bible: Biblical Citation."

39. The original of Anonimo Fiorentino's comments on *Inf.* 23.124–26 is as follows: "Virgilio si potea maravigliare dello errore di costui che, avendo innanzi Cristo signore del Cielo e della terra, com' egli nol conobbe, dolendosi ancora di sè, che non era a quel tempo che lo avrebbe conosciuto." See Pietro Mazzamuto, "Caifas," in *ED*, 1: 751–52.

40. Vellutello writes on *Inf.* 23.124–26 that Virgil is lost in wonder because he realizes that he and Caiaphas made the same prophecy. The line of his own that he recalls is "Unum pro multis dabitur caput"—a line he wrote without understanding what he was saying until this moment.

41. See Stephany, "Biblical Allusions," and my essay "Resurrecting the Word."

42. "Coperchio," translated here as "covering," may refer to a lid of any kind. But more particularly in Dante, as Rachel Jacoff has pointed out, it means a sepulchral slab, the "lid" that covers a tomb. Dante in fact uses the word in this sense three times in the *Inferno* (9.121, 10.9, 11.6), all in reference to the tombs of the heretics, "who make the soul die with the body" ("che l'anima col corpo morta fanno," 10.15). This earlier usage may well be encoded here. If so, it suggests that Virgil's Eclogue rolled away the "stone" that blocked Statius in his ability to believe.

43. See Allen and Barolini's response in "Critical Exchange."

44. See the essays by Putnam, Hawkins, and Jacoff in *PA*, pp. 94–144.

45. For instance, see the Christological use of Ps. 117 (118):22—"The stone which the builders rejected; the same is become the head of the corner"—in Matt. 21:42; Mark 12:10; Luke 20:17; Acts 4:11; and 1 Pet. 2:7.

46. Rachel Jacoff, in an unpublished manuscript on *Purg.* 30 scheduled to appear in vol. 2 of the forthcoming California Lectura Dantis, argues that the way Christ's resurrection frames the arrival of Beatrice and the departure of Virgil is "absolutely strategic, for it is the hope and, for Dante, the 'fact' of the Resurrection that authorizes the transfiguration of the Virgilian lilies of mourning into the lilies of welcome. There is a perfect gloss on the key word 'inani' (the word which describes the uselessness of Anchises' gesture) in a comparable context in 1 Corinthians 15:12–24 where St. Paul uses the same word repeatedly to describe what would be the case if Christ had not risen from the dead: 'Si autem Christus non resurrexit, inanis est ergo praedicatio nostra, inanis est fides vestra' ('If Christ has not been raised from the dead, then our preaching is in vain and your faith is in vain')."

CHAPTER 6

1. When Virgil tells the pilgrim in *Inf.* 4.15, "Io sarò primo, e tu sarai secondo" ("I will be first, and you second"), he is announcing an order that obtains throughout the journey, from the entrance into hell (*Inf.* 2.141–42) until the crossing over into Eden (*Purg.* 27). The last time Virgil's precedence is specified is *Purg.* 27.46, where we are told, "Poi dentro al folco innanzi mi si mise" ("Then he entered the fire in front of me").

2. For the significance of moves to left or right, see Freccero's "Pilgrim in a Gyre," in his *Dante: Poetics of Conversion*, pp. 70–92. The move "a la sinistra" in *Purg.* 30.43 is of interest to many of the early commentators. Buti (in Biagi, 2: 635) associates the leftward direction with Virgil and the rightward with Statius. The one represents reason, the other the intellect. Reason is relegated "a la sinistra" because it is less reliable than the intellect ("e perchè lo intelletto più dirittamente e più altamente indica che la ragione alcuna volta s'inganna"). The distinction Buti makes here is between the natural faculty of reason, exemplified in Virgil, and intellect, exemplified in Statius, as the capacity to know God, who is (to recall *Inf.* 3.18) "il ben de l'intelletto," "the good of the intellect."

3. Gmelin, *Göttliche Komödie: Kommentar*, 2: 477.

4. See Pöschl's treatment of Dido, along with W. R. Johnson's reading of *Aen.* 4.68–73, pp. 78–84. Padoan's entry "Didone," in *ED*, vol. 2, offers a useful summary of Dido's presence throughout Dante's work.

5. Bono devotes her first chapter to Virgil's Dido and Aeneas; she then follows with a study of three "transvaluations," of which the last two—Augustine and Dante (pp. 41–61)—are of relevance here. See also Mazzotta, *Dante, Poet of the Desert*, pp. 147–91, esp. pp. 160–70.

6. Fulgentius, p. 105.

7. Dante's one positive portrayal of Dido occurs in *Monarchia* 2.3, where she is treated second in a sequence of Aeneas's three wives, between Creusa and Lavina. Here Dante seems to take Dido at her own word in *Aen.* 4.171–72, using her "marriage" to Aeneas as a way of legitimating Rome's claims to Africa. Creusa represents Asia and Lavinia Europe.

8. Mazzotta, *Dante, Poet*, pp. 170–71, discusses how Dante identifies Carthage with Babylon, to Dido's detriment, while "clearing" the Rome that Augustine maligns throughout *The City of God*.

9. Beatrice, in *Purg.* 30.109–45, takes Dante to task for not having been able to grow in his love and understanding for her after her death, when, instead of following her with his heart, he turned away ("e volse i passi suoi per via non vera," v. 130) to pursue "imagini . . . false" (v. 131). This inability to

"read" Beatrice at an earlier time is paralleled here by his preoccupation with her beauty after "la decenne sete" (32.2). And so at the beginning of *Purg.* 32, as if in preparation for the apocalyptic vision soon to follow, the pilgrim is told that his fixation on the *bellezza* of Beatrice is "Troppo fiso!" (32.9). He must learn to "read" her spiritually, in terms of her revelatory significance; to look within and beyond her personal beauty.

CHAPTER 7

1. Hollander, "Tragedy in Dante's *Comedy*."

2. Sowell, "Dante's Nose," in his *Dante and Ovid*, p. 44, notes that " '*lo 'nvidio*' contains the name *Ovidio* within it and that Ovid's name is dismembered and remembered in every 'io vidi'—'Ovidii,' Latin genitive for 'of Ovid'—as in verses 48, 112, and 142 of *Inferno* 25 but also throughout the *Commedia*."

3. Paratore, "Ovidio," in *ED*, 4: 227, "un insegnamento provvidenziale in grado non molto inferiore a quello dell'*Eneïde*."

4. Barolini, *Dante's Poets*, pp. 195–96, 223–26.

5. Paratore, "Ovidio," p. 226.

6. Hoffman and Lasdun speculate on the current appeal of Ovid to contemporary poets and suggest that his stories "have direct, obvious and painful affinities with contemporary reality. They offer a mythical key to most of the more extreme forms of human behaviour and suffering, especially ones we think of as peculiarly modern: holocaust, plague, sexual harassment, rape, incest, seduction, pollution, sex-change, suicide, hetero- and homosexual love, torture, war, child-beating, depression and intoxication form the bulk of the themes" (p. xi). They describe the structure of the *Metamorphoses* as "not merely like a Russian doll, one story inside another . . . [but] like a snake pit, in which an indeterminate number of snakes are devouring and being devoured by one another" (pp. xii).

7. Galinsky, p. 19.

8. In an unpublished manuscript on Dante's relation to his Latin sources, Jacoff notes the simultaneous attribution and concealment of Ovid in *Inf.* 25.97–99: "Dante's address to Ovid points to two specific metamorphoses, that of Cadmus and Arethusa. The mention of Cadmus is apropos since Cadmus is changed into a serpent and since Dante clearly follows Ovid's description of Cadmus' transmutation in his own rendering of the man who becomes a snake. However, Arethusa is not particularly relevant to the immediate context and makes us wonder why Dante would want to adduce her story and not the more germane tale of Salamacis and Hermaphrodite which, as the commen-

tary tradition shows, is clearly the major source for the Ciafra-Agnello meta-
morphosis, where two forms come together to form an *imagine perversa*.
Dante's language is very close to Ovid's here, and he even uses the simile of ivy
intertwined with a tree, which Ovid had used to render the blending of forms.
Commentators often wonder why Dante mentions Arethusa, but it seems clear
that by doing so Dante, in the boast, manages to represent himself as both
announcing an Ovidian source and hiding one: that is, Dante shows himself
engaged in an activity which is not quite as up front as it sounds, an activity
which masks its own potential for theft."

9. See Brownlee's "Pauline Vision" and "Ovid's Semele."

10. Lanham, p. 36. Lanham's second chapter, "The Fundamental Strat-
egies: Plato and Ovid," is especially relevant. See also Solodow.

11. Quintilian's *Istitutio oratorio*, written c. 95 and therefore roughly 75
years after Ovid's death, contains a number of interesting assessments of the
poet's character and work. I single out only two: "Ovid has a lack of seriousness
even when he writes epic and is unduly enamoured of his own gifts, but
portions of his work merit our praise" ("Lascivius quidem in herois quoque
Ovidius et nimium amator ingenii sui, laudanus tamen in partibus," 10.1.88)
and "the Medea of Ovid shows, in my opinion, to what heights the poet might
have risen if he had been ready to curb his talents instead of indulging them"
("Ovidii Medea videtur mihi ostendere, quantum ille vir praestare potuerit, si
ingenio suo imperare quam indulgere maluisset," 10.1.98). Since the *Istitutio*
was discovered only in 1416, Dante's own assessment of Ovid could not have
been formed directly by Quintilian.

12. Ghisalberti, "Giovanni del Virgilio," p. 18.

13. Ghisalberti, "Medieval Biographies of Ovid," p. 35. See also Robathan;
S. Battaglia; and Monteverdi.

14. See, for instance, *Tristia* 4.10.125–32, where Ovid concludes an ex-
tended catalogue of woe with the following:

nam tulerint magnos cum saecula nostra poetas,
non fuit ingenio fama maligna meo,
cumque ego praeponam multos mihi, non minor illis
dicor et in toco plurimus orbe legor.
si quid habent igitur vatum praesagia veri,
protinus ut moriar, non ero, terra, tuus.
sive favore tuli, sive hanc ego carmine famam,
iure tibi grates, candide lector, ago.

(For although this age of ours has brought forth mighty poets, fame has
not been grudging to my genius, and though I place many before myself,

report calls me not their inferior and throughout the world I am most read of all. If then there be truth in poets' prophecies, even though I die forthwith, I shall not, O earth, be thine. But whether through favour or by very poetry I have gained this fame, 'tis right, kind reader, that I render thanks to thee.)

15. Mazzotta, "Theology and Exile," in his *Dante's Vision*, pp. 174–96.

16. Brownlee, "Why the Angels Speak Italian."

CHAPTER 8

1. For the *locus amoenus*, see Curtius, *European Literature*, pp. 183–202; Gmelin, *Göttliche Komödie: Kommentar*, 2: 434–39; and Giamatti, pp. 1–119, whose survey of the earthly paradise in ancient and medieval thought includes a chapter on Dante (pp. 94–119).

2. Sapegno, 2: 308, glosses *Purg.* 28.44 with *Vita nuova* 15.5, while Bosco, "Il canto XXVIII," pp. 142–43, speaks of *stilnovist* echoes throughout the pilgrim's approach to Matelda. See also Stambler, pp. 244–45.

3. Gmelin, *Göttliche Komödie: Kommentar*, 2: 308, identifies Matelda as "eina *figura* von Eva vor dem Sudenfall"; for Singleton, *Journey to Beatrice*, pp. 184–201, she is an image of "Virgo or Justice," and therefore akin to "Astrea, star-maiden" (p. 200).

4. Aside from the mirror images of forest landscape, there is also in each case—in "selva oscura" and "selva antica"—the pilgrim's inability to remember how he entered the wood. In *Inf.* 1.10 he says, "Io non so ben ridir com' i' v'intrai" ("I cannot rightly say how I entered it"), and in *Purg.* 28.23–24 we read, "ch'io / non potea rivedere ond' io mi 'ntrassi" ("I could not see back to where I had entered it").

5. For *disviare*, see not only *Purg.* 16.82 and 28.38 but also *Par.* 6.116, 9.131, and 12.45. For *sviare*, see *Purg.* 29.118, *Par.* 18.126 and 27.141.

6. The Cavalcanti poem is found in Goldin, pp. 330–33. See Barolini, *Dante's Poets*, pp. 148–53, for a reading of Cavalcanti's presence in *Purg.* 28. See also Contini, pp. 143–58; Bosco, "Il canto XXVIII," pp. 472–73; and Singleton's treatment of Dante's "primo amico" in *Journey to Beatrice*, pp. 204–21. Barolini argues that since Cavalcanti provided Dante with the specific "intertext" for the pilgrim's meeting with Matelda, it would seem "that a measure of textual redemption is indeed accorded Cavalcanti in the *Commedia*" (p. 152). Because allusions taken from Cavalcanti's work are concentrated in *Inf.* 10 and *Purg.* 28, Barolini sees Dante placing Cavalcanti between damnation and redemption. I have taken the presence of the "pastorella" *ballata* in a different way, namely as a text (and a view of love) meant to be rewritten.

7. See Sapegno, 2: 314–15, on *Purg.* 28.139–41, for instance, or Poggioli, pp. 2–6, where he emphasizes Dante's specific indebtedness to Ovid's description of the Golden Age, even as he establishes the distinctness of Eden as a present reality from the "irrevocable past" described by Ovid.

8. Holloway, in her introduction to Latini, *Il tesoretto,* speculates on possible connections between Dante and Latini but does not note the disparity between Latini's choice of Ovid as guide and Dante's of Virgil.

9. Curtius, *European Literature,* pp. 194–95, notes that while Virgil's "ideal" forest is poetically felt and harmonized with the composition of the epic's succession of scenes, in Ovid, "poetry is already dominated by rhetoric . . . descriptions of nature become bravura interludes, in which poets try to outdo one another."

10. All quotations in this paragraph are from Singleton, *Journey to Beatrice,* p. 213.

11. Ibid., p. 216.

12. Hollander, *Allegory in Dante's "Commedia,"* p. 156.

13. Matelda's appearance in the meadow of *Purg.* 28 is preceded by the appearance of her dream double, Leah, who gathers flowers into garlands and sings as she "works." In the dream, Leah describes herself as satisfied with her doing: "e me l'ovrare appaga" (*Purg.* 27.108). The rhyme scheme of lines 27.104, 106, 108 is *smaga-vaga-appaga,* all but identical to the scheme of the Siren's song in *Purg.* 19.20, 22, 24 (*dismago-vago-appago*). Dante seems, on the one hand, to be linking Leah and Matelda with the prelapsarian activity of Adam in the Garden ("ut operaretur, et custodiret illum," Gen. 2:15), while on the other hand contrasting their innocence with the Siren's seduction. It is worth noting that "vago"—an adjective of desire whose moral ambivalence is reinforced by its use by both Leah and the Siren—is the opening word of *Purg.* 28, where it describes the eagerness of the pilgrim to explore what awaits him within the "divina foresta." My thanks to Professor Ron Martinez for once pointing out the etymological play between *deligo* and *delecto.*

14. Abelard, quoted in Singleton, *Journey to Beatrice,* pp. 206–7, trans. Singleton.

15. Bonaventure, *The Mind's Road to God,* p. 13.

16. In the third volume of his *Compendium theologiae veritatis* (in *Opera omnia,* 8: 132) Bonaventure uses Ps. 91 to discuss the nature of creaturely delectation: "Voluntaria duplex est, quia alia est in Creatore, alia in creatura. Delectatio, quae in Creatore est, bona est, de qua Psalmus: *Memor fui Dei, et delactus sum,* etc. Quae autem in creatura est, duplex est: quaedam enim est propter Deum, et haec bona est; sed hic sumitur delectatio pro opere rationis,

non pro passione: de qua Psalmista: *Delectasti me, Domine, in factura tua?*"
("Delight that is willed is of two kinds. One kind is in the Creator, the other in
created things. The delight that is in the Creator is good—of it the Psalm says,
'I remembered God and was delighted,' and so forth [Ps. 76:4, Douay version].
That which is in created things is two kinds. One kind is because of God, and
this is good—delight is taken here as a work of the reason, not as an emotion
[*passio*]. The Psalmist says of it, 'You have given me, Lord, a delight in your
doings' [Ps. 91:5].") To employ an Augustinian distinction, one could say that
Adam (and Matelda) "use" the creation properly by enjoying God through it.

17. Poggioli, pp. 13–14, compares Rabelais's Abbey of Thélême and Dante's
earthly paradise (though without developing their contrasts), and sees both as
places that stand for "a cultivation of the self made of speculation and con-
templation, of the earnest wisdom of philosophy and of the 'merry wisdom' of
poetry and . . . of both the creation and the enjoyment of music and the arts.
Leah's and Matelda's garlands may suggest the lovely handiwork of either
painting or sculpture; as for music, let's not forget that Matelda sings and dances
before us. All this proves again that the Garden of Eden is a place of both
pleasure and leisure: of a disinterested and productive *otium*."

18. See Vickers, "Claudel's Delectation."

19. Vickers, "Seeing Is Believing," p. 36.

20. It would be a naive reading of the *Commedia*, however, that did not
take into account the authorial self-referentiality of all these passages. For in
both *Inf.* 5 and *Purg.* 10, evidence of the power of art to delight ultimately asks
us to reflect on Dante's own literary achievement. Be it in the creation of
Francesca's siren song (with its echo not only of Guido Guinizelli's "Al cor
gentil" but also of *Vita nuova* 20), or in the ecphrastic moments on the terrace
of pride, the actual "fabbro" we are confronting is none other than the poet of
the *Commedia*. On this point see Barolini's chapter "Re-presenting What God
Presented: The Arachnean Art of the Terrace of Pride," in *Undivine Comedy*,
pp. 122–42.

CHAPTER 9

1. Sapegno, in his commentary on *Purg.* 28.139–41 (2: 315), notes Dante's
extensive reliance on *Met.* 1.90–111.

2. Paratore, p. 79: "come una storia dell'umanità dalle origini al termine
provvidenziale di Cesare, e cioè come una ripresa in tono minore dell'*Eneïde*."
See also Paratore's "Ovidio," in *ED*, 4: 225–36.

3. Hawkins, "Virtue and Virtuosity."

4. The tree of *Purg.* 32 has occasioned many interpretations. Moore,

"Symbolism and Prophecy in *Purg.* XXVIII–XXXIII," in his *Studies, Third Series*, pp. 178–220, suggests that Dante may be drawing on a legendary connection between Eden's Tree of the Knowledge of Good and Evil and the wood of the cross. Foster, "*Purgatorio* XXXII," takes it as "symbolic of an ideal order of relationship holding between God and his rational creation" (p. 144). Nardi, *Nel mondo di Dante*, pp. 107–59, sees the tree as a representation of God's justice, particularly as manifested in the political realm.

5. Hollander, *Allegory in Dante's "Commedia,"* suggests that in the sequence of dreams that structure the second canticle (in *Purg.* 9, 19, and 27), there is a fourth in Dante's encounter with Beatrice in *Purg.* 30–32: "That Dante thought of the vision atop the mountain as a 'fourth dream' is attested by the fact that the Pilgrim falls asleep (*Purg.* 32.64–72) after the appearance of the griffin. As before he has fallen asleep and had dreams, now he has been vouchsafed a vision then falls asleep. The reversed order sets the 'fourth dream' above the first three, for, although it is itself a veiled vision in that what he sees is a symbolic version of the Christ, it has nevertheless greater reality than what he had previously seen in dream; he sees the real Beatrice, although she is still veiled" (p. 158 n. 26). While I find this reading plausible, the emphasis in *Purg.* 32 is on the Ovidian simile of sleep that takes the place of dream and that differs so strikingly from the biblical simile of waking.

6. Porena, commentary on *Purg.* 32.69, p. 311.

7. Cioffi, p. 97, says of these two metamorphoses, "Just as Syrinx lives on in Pan's music, so Argus endures in the plumage of a species [the peacock]." She also mentions Ovid's remarks about "Philomela's post-trauma creativity, 'grande doloris / ingenium est, miserisque venit sollertia rebus' ['from great pain, genius stems, and cleverness comes out of wretched things']." In Dante's treatment of Argus in *Purg.* 32, however, I find no such interest in the ameliorative aspects of the transformation, let alone an interest in the redemptive aspects. To me, Dante's emphasis is on the cost of Argus's sleep ("costò sì caro," v. 66), on its danger.

8. Barolini, *Undivine Comedy*, pp. 160–61, grants that the final cantos of *Purgatorio* "indicate the superiority of Christian to classical visions," but then makes the following discrimination: "Argus . . . simply slept, and [his] sleep led to his death, [while] Dante refers to a less simple condition, a wakeful sleep that gives life, like the 'letargo' that overcomes the pilgrim in the poem's last instant, as he perceives the form of the universe in a visionary instant." She connects Dante's falling asleep in *Purg.* 32 to John the Divine's "walking trance" in the mystical procession of *Purg.* 29.144. See also her "Arachne, Argus, and St. John."

9. The fullest study of the importance of Dante's engagement with the Transfiguration story is Schnapp's *Transfiguration of History*, esp. pp. 90–106 (biblical sources) and pp. 114–20 (*Purg.* 32). See also his "Trasfigurazione e metamorfosi." Chamberas offers a useful overview of the theological tradition.

10. Foster, "*Purgatorio XXXII*," pp. 143–45, discusses connections between the Song of Songs, the tree of Eden, and Christ's Transfiguration.

11. Schnapp, *Transfiguration of History*, p. 97.

12. Augustine, *Sermo* 78 ("De Diversis 69"), in *PL*, vol. 38, col. 493 (Latin); and *SL*, 1st ser., 6: 348, trans. R. G. MacMullen.

13. Apoc. 1: 19. For the importance of the Apocalypse to Dante, see Herzman, "Dante and the Apocalypse"; and Cristaldi. While Herzman can only speculate that Dante directly understood and consciously took the Apocalypse as a model for his poem, "what is not speculative is that Dante saw himself writing in imitation of the Bible" (p. 413).

14. Augustine, *Sermo* 78 ("De Diversis 69"), in *PL*, vol. 38, col. 493 (Latin); and *SL*, 1st ser., 6: 348, trans. R. G. MacMullen.

15. Brownlee, "Dante and the Classical Poets," p. 118.

CHAPTER 10

1. For an enumeration of Augustinian references and citations in Dante's work, see A. Pincherle, "Agostino," in *ED*, 1: 80–82; Moore, *Studies, First Series*, pp. 291–94; Gardner; Calcaterra; and Chioccioni.

2. Dante's epistle to Can Grande, para. 28, in *Dantis Alagherii Epistolae*. In discussing theological debate over the possibility of a mortal's seeing God *per speciem*, Mazzeo, *Structure and Thought*, pp. 84–110, emphasizes the importance of Augustine's qualifiedly positive verdict on Dante's claims. On this issue see also Foster, "Dante's Vision of God"; and Tonelli, pp. 207–14.

3. Calcaterra gives a summary of the state of the question in 1931 before advancing his own essentially aesthetic rationale that the imagination has its own reasons ("la fantasia ha i suoi diritti," p. 446). For later discussions see Chioccioni; and Fallani, pp. 185–203, where he draws attention to the frequent references to Augustine in Pietro Alighieri's 1340 *Commentarium*, although with a caveat (p. 193): "L'intero commento ha 142 citazioni dirette da S. Agostino, e non è poca cosa in confronto agli altri autori: S. Tommaso ne ha cinquanta. Arbitrarietà di Pietro Alighieri, predelizione personale a un autore, o non, piuttosto, una controllata misura, rispetto ai libri che vida più spesso in mano al padre, e da lui consultati?" ("The entire commentary has 142 direct citations from St. Augustine, and that is not a little thing in relation to other authors. St. Thomas has fifty. Is this an arbitrary choice of Pietro Alighieri's, a

personal predilection of an author, or is it not rather a quite deliberate measure given the books he often saw in his father's hand, and often consulted by him?")

4. No one has written more convincingly about Dante's departure from Augustine's vision of Rome (or about the poet's indebtedness to Augustine's notion of providential history) than has Charles Till Davis, in both *Dante and the Idea of Rome* and *Dante's Italy*, pp. 198–289. Davis not only clarifies Dante's revision of Augustine but also considers that reworking in the light of several trecento political theorists. See also Ferrante, *Political Vision*.

5. In addition to this hasty positioning of Augustine in eternity at 32.35, the *Paradiso* mentions the saint only one other time, invoking his name to identify someone else in the heaven of the theologians: "quello avvocato de' tempi cristiani / del cui latino Augustin si provide" ("that defender of Christian times, of whose discourse Augustine made use," 10.120).

6. Moore, *Studies, First Series*, p. 294.

7. See, for instance, Freccero's chapters "The Prologue Scene" and "The Firm Foot on a Journey Without a Guide," in his *Dante: Poetics of Conversion*. See also Chiarenza; Newman.

8. Mazzotta, *Dante, Poet of the Desert*; Schnapp, *Transfiguration of History*; Martinez, "Dante, Statius, and the Earthly City."

9. In sermons on Stephen as the first martyr for the name of Christ (*PL*, vol. 38, cols. 1425–26), Augustine emphasizes the correspondence between the protomartyr and Christ in their common return of forgiveness for wrath. The spiritual antecedent of both is Abel, "quem primum iustum impius frater occidet" ("the first righteous man slain by an ungodly brother"), whose lineage continues until the end of human history, "usque in huius saeculi finem inter persecutiones mundi et consolationes Dei" ("right up to the end of history, with the persecutions of the world on the one side and on the other the consolations of God") (*City of God* 18.51).

10. Pietro Alighieri cites Augustine's text in his *Commentarium*, as did Jacopo della Lana more than a decade before him (c. 1324–28). The citation remains a constant in twentieth-century commentary. Nardi, *Il canto XV*, attributes the concept of Virgil's speech to *City of God* 15.5 and remarks the appearance of the term *consorte* (p. 13). Some suggest Gregory the Great's *Moralia* 4.31 as an intermediate source.

11. Calcaterra, p. 440, building on the work of others, observes that Augustine applies the adjective phrase "falsi et fallaces" to the gods of pagan Rome in *City of God* 2.29 and 4.1, as well as in *De consensu evangelistarum* 1.25.

12. The accusation that Virgil was a liar comes from Augustine's sermon on the fall of Rome (in *PL*, vol. 38, col. 623), a text that Davis rightly describes

as "revealing the abyss between Augustine and Dante in their estimates of Virgil and Rome" (*Dante and the Idea of Rome*, p. 55). See also Augustine's rewrite of *Aeneid* 1.279 ("imperium sine fine dedi") in *City of God* 2.29, where God's pledge of eternity to the church replaces Jupiter's corresponding promise to Rome.

In the prologue to the *City of God* Augustine compares a verse of Scripture (James 4:6) with a line from the *Aeneid* (6.853) in order to contrast Christian humility with Roman arrogance. In the opening chapter of Augustine's work, and indeed *passim*, it is Virgil, as Rome's theologian-poet, whom Augustine takes to task for the delusions of an entire civilization. Or, as Cochrane puts it, in Virgil's poem "we may perceive the spiritual foundations of the City of Man, over which Augustine was to oppose its antitype in the shape of a city not built with human hands" (p. 71). Mazzotta's treatment of Virgil and Augustine (*Dante, Poet of the Desert*, pp. 147–49) offers a probing exploration not only of Augustine's objections to the *poeta nobilissimus* of Rome but of Dante's transformation of those objections into his own vision of history. For an altogether different assessment, see Rand.

13. In *City of God* 15.22, Augustine considers the mingling of the sons of God with the daughters of men (Gen. 6.2) as a seduction of the soul away from the primary good and its fall into enthrallment with what is secondary. Using terms that seem to inform Virgil's speech in *Purgatorio* 17, he goes on to say: "If, however, the Creator is truly loved, that is, if he himself is loved, and not something else in his stead, then he cannot be wrongly loved. We must, in fact, observe the right order even in our love for the very love that is deserving of love, so that there may be in us the virtue, which is the condition of the good life. Hence, as it seems to me, a brief and true definition of virtue is 'rightly ordered love.' That is why in the holy Song of Songs Christ's bride, the City of God, sings, 'Set love in order in me.'" Dante may also have had in mind Augustine's *On Christian Doctrine* 1.27: "He lives in justice and sanctity who is an unprejudiced assessor of the intrinsic value of things. He is a man who has an ordinate love: he neither loves what should not be loved nor fails to love what should be loved; he neither loves more what should be loved less, loves equally what should be loved less or more, nor loves less or more what should be loved equally."

14. Augustine, *City of God* 5.16: "[Rome] had this further purpose, that the citizens of that Eternal City, in the days of their pilgrimage should fix their eyes steadily and soberly on those examples, and should observe what love they should have toward the City on high, in view of life eternal, if the earthly city had received such devotion from her citizens, in their hope of glory in the sight of men." In 5.17 Augustine notes a similar "shadowy resemblance" ("per umbram quandam simile") between the remission of sins in the city of God and

"that refuge of Romulus, where the offer of impunity for crimes of every kind collected a multitude which was to result in the founding of Rome." Roman virtue provides Augustine's pilgrims with a flawed simulacrum of proper citizenship, whereas Dante makes no such qualification. For him, Roman virtue and vice get equal billing with scriptural exempla along the terraces of purgatory. See my essay "Polemical Counterpoint."

15. Chioccioni draws attention to the Augustinian presence in *Purgatorio* 16 and notes the specifically Augustinian resonance of the phrase "la vera città" (pp. 124–30; see also pp. 40–42). What he fails to register is Dante's revisionary Roman departure from the polemic of the *City of God*.

16. See Schnapp, " 'Sì pïa l'ombra d'Anchise si porse': *Paradiso* 15.25," in *PA*, pp. 145–56.

CHAPTER 11

1. Augustine's major treatment of the rapture is found in *De Genesi ad litteram libri xii*, bk. 12, esp. chaps. 27–37. (Cf. Thomas Aquinas, *ST* II-II, 175, 3–6). For a survey of varying patristic and medieval interpretations of Paul's experience, see Mazzeo, *Structure and Thought*, pp. 84–110. McGinn, in *Foundation of Mysticism*, gives an overview of Augustine's thought on the *visio Dei* on pp. 232–43, and considers the ineffable and the apophatic throughout his study. See also Butler, pp. 78–87.

2. In *Confessions* 11.6, for instance, Augustine contrasts God's inner, silent Word with the "outer" words of his utterance through the mediation of angels or in Scripture: "These words, which you had caused to sound in time, were reported by the bodily ear of the hearer to the mind, which has intelligence and inner hearing responsive to your eternal Word. The mind compared these words, which it heard sounding in time, with your Word, which is silent and eternal, and said, 'God's eternal Word is far, far different from these words which sound in time. They are far beneath me; in fact, they are not at all, because they die away and are lost. But the Word of my God is above me and endures for ever' " (trans. Pine-Coffin). Two relevant studies are Mazzeo's "St. Augustine and the Rhetoric of Silence" and Lossky.

3. Dante's epistle to Can Grande, para. 29, in *Dantis Alagherii Epistolae*. Further references to the epistle will be given in the text.

4. See Kirkpatrick, pp. 36–43.

5. Augustine, epistle to Paulinus (no. 147, "Liber de videndo Deo"): "To the extent that you understand these words of the saintly man, which are not carnal but spiritual, and recognize that they are true, not because he said them, but because truth clamors in them without noise of words, to that extent you

prepare yourself inwardly as in the incorporeal place of His dwelling, to hear the silence of his discourse, and to see his invisible form [*ad audiendum silentium narrationis eius, et videntum invisibilem formam eius*])." *Letters of Saint Augustine*, 3: 222.

6. Freccero, "Paradiso X: The Dance of the Stars," in his *Dante: Poetics of Conversion*, p. 221.

7. For an excellent study of Dante's coined words, see Schildgen.

8. Donoghue, pp. 372–73.

9. Fish, p. 4.

10. Tonelli, pp. 207–14, includes the Ostia episode among the *Paradiso's* "precedenti filosofici e letterari," though without any specific literary analysis of possible connections. See also Chioccioni; and Foster, "Dante's Vision of God," p. 34: "Clearly the pith of [the Ostia vision] is a longing to pass from relative being to absolute, from derived to Original, and the connection of these terms is not only analysed but contemplated in a meditation moving around it from one pair of opposites to another—passing away and stability, time and eternity, effects and their cause, signs and the unsigned. In Dante too we find these contrasts, but in the *Commedia* most especially the latter one, the passage through signs and symbols to substance. And this was natural to a poet whose self-assumed task, *figurando il paradiso*, it was to make spiritual order imaginable. Images had to be Dante's starting point; a system of signs that both hid and half-revealed a reality 'chiuso e parvente del suo proprio riso.'"

11. For critical considerations of the Ostia episode, see Courcelle, *Recherches sur les "Confessions"*; O'Donnell, 3: 127–33; and Stock, pp. 116–21. For discussion of the nature of the ecstasy, especially with regard to its mixture of Plotinus and Paul, see Mandouze; O'Maera, pp. 202–3; Bonner, pp. 98–99; and Louth, pp. 133–41.

12. See Freccero, "An Introduction to the *Paradiso*," in his *Dante: Poetics of Conversion*, pp. 195–208; Chiarenza; Murtaugh; and Ferrante, "Words and Images."

13. Chiarenza, pp. 85–86, describes this imagistic dissolve and writes about the *Paradiso's* predilection for "anti-images": "There are, then, stages in the development of Dante's imagery in the *Paradiso*. Three of them are those already mentioned, in which we find, first, concrete shapes which can barely be perceived, then shapes in which symbolic meaning overshadows concrete form, and at last purely conceptual shape not found in the material universe. These stages lead the poet to the point where he can go no further but must end his poem in order that it become fully imageless."

14. Singleton, *Divine Comedy*, Commentary 3, p. 571.

CHAPTER 12

1. "Sub infusione Saturni due species hominum cadunt: una quarum grossa est et inculta: puta illorum grosse, nigre et inculte capillature sunt dicentes, vestes spernentes; alia est qui in heremis et in solitudine religiose ad contemplativam vitam se dant, monastice et hermitice abominantes omnia singularia, ac silentio et castitate viventes." *Il codice cassinese della "Divina Commedia,"* p. 493.

2. The first and most extensive of these transitions is found in *Par.* 1.64–99.

3. See Brownlee, "Ovid's Semele."

4. Boethius, bk. 1, prose 1, pp. 133–34. "Her dress was made of very fine, imperishable thread, of delicate workmanship: she herself wove it, as I learned later, for she told me. . . . On its lower border was woven the Greek letter P (P), and on the upper, Θ (Th), and between the two letters steps were marked like a ladder, by which one might climb from the lower letter to the higher."

5. Benedict, pp. 38–39.

6. See, for instance, Bosco and Reggio, 3: 346.

7.

Gemma coelestis pretiosa Regis,
norma justorum, via monachorum,
nos ab immundi, Benedicte, mundi
    subtrahe coeno.
        (*PL*, vol. 145, col. 957)

(Precious ornament of the King of heaven, pattern of righteousness, pathway of monks, draw us, Benedict, away from the filth of the unclean world.) (trans. John Leinenweber)

Peter Damian's "Carmina sacra et preces" are found in *PL*, vol. 145, cols. 917–86; the above quote from "De Benedicto abbate, hymnus, ad vesperas" is found in col. 957. See also O. J. Blum, in *NCE*, 11: 214–15; and Lokrantz.

8. See Sapegno's commentary on *Par.* 21.134 (3: 270).

9. "Nam loqui et docere magistrum condecet: tacere et audire disciplinum convenit." Benedict, pp. 36–37.

10. "[Li] contemplativi pensano tutte l'alte cose d'Iddio, contemplando la creatura s'inalzano a contemplare lo creatore: e perché l'anima umana è fatta a similitudine sua, però anno desiderio li contemplativi di vedere l'essenzia dell'anima umana più che di niuna altra cosa creata; e però finse l'autore che tale pensieri li venisse in questo luogo." Buti, p. 611.

11. "Perhaps God will be known to us and visible to us in the sense that he will be spiritually perceived by each of us in each of us, perceived in one another, perceived by each in himself." Augustine, *City of God* 22.30.

12. Benedict, pp. 12–13.

13. St. Gregory, *Life and Miracles*, chap. 36, p. 75.

14. "Mira autem res valde in hac speculatione secuta est: quia, sicut post ipse narravit, omnis etiam mundus velut sub uno solis radio collectus, ante oculos ejus adductus est" (*PL*, vol. 66, col. 198). ("Another remarkable sight followed. According to his own description, the whole world was gathered up before his eyes in what appeared to be a single ray of light," Gregory, *Life and Miracles*, chap. 35, p. 71). Gregory then goes on to explain this phenomenon as an interior flooding of light that caused the exterior universe to be seen in miniature: "All creation is bound to appear small to a soul that sees the Creator. Once it beholds a little of His light, it finds all creatures small indeed. The light of holy contemplation enlarges and expands the mind in God until it stands above the world. In fact, the soul that sees Him rises even above itself, and as it is drawn upward in His light all its inner powers unfold." *Life and Miracles*, chap. 35, pp. 72–73. Cf. *Par.* 22.151 and 27.85–87.

15. "Sed omissa subtili investigatione, dicendum est breviter quod finis totius et partis est, removere viventes in hac vita de statu miseriae et perducere ad statum felicitatis." Dante's epistle to Can Grande, para. 15, in *Dantis Alagherii Epistolae*.

CHAPTER 13

1. Van Gennep, p. 3.

2. V. Turner and E. Turner, *Image and Pilgrimage*, p. 2. Other relevant works by V. Turner are "The Center Out There," *Dramas, Fields, and Metaphors*, "Liminality and *Communitas*," "Variations on a Theme," and, again with E. Turner, "Religious Celebrations." Critical assessment of V. Turner's methods and conclusions can be found in the essays collected in Earle and Sallnow.

3. V. Turner, "Variations on a Theme," p. 37: "A *limen* is a threshold but at least in case of protracted initiation rites or major seasonal festivals it is a very long threshold, a corridor, almost, or a tunnel which may indeed become a pilgrim's road or, passing from dynamics to statics, may cease to be a mere transition and become a set way of life, a state, that of an anchorite or monk."

4. V. Turner and E. Turner, *Image and Pilgrimage*, pp. 6–7.

5. Despite the free-ranging aspect of their analysis in *Image and Pilgrimage*

of pilgrimage as a rite of passage, the Turners are careful to qualify their use of van Gennep. Because pilgrimage is voluntary, "not an obligatory social mechanism to mark the transition of an individual or group from one state or status to another within the mundane sphere, pilgrimage is probably better thought of as 'liminoid' or 'quasi-liminal,' rather than as 'liminal' in van Gennep's full sense" (pp. 34–35). Likewise, though pilgrimage has initiatory features, strictly speaking it is not initiatory, that is, not "an irreversible, singular ritual instrument for effecting a permanent, visible cultural transformation of the subject" (p. 31).

6. For a general consideration of "pilgrim" and "pilgrimage" in all of Dante's works, see the entry "pellegrino" in *ED*, 4: 369–70. The most extensive treatment of the subject is by Demaray, who argues that the "Great Circle" pilgrimage route from Rome to Egypt/Sinai to Jerusalem and back to Rome again underwrites the structure of the three canticles and provides a "key" to interpreting the poem. While Demaray's thesis strikes me as far-fetched, he offers many useful insights about the importance to the *Commedia* of actual pilgrimage practice. For other treatments, see Sumption; Zacher; Labarge; Mominis; Davidson and Dunn-Wood; and Webb, pp. 33–55.

7. In addition to Demaray, pp. 37–43, see Thurston; and Le Goff, pp. 330–31.

8. The fourteenth-century chronicler Villani reports that Rome was filled with "200,000 pilgrims" who came from "distant and divers countries, both far and near" (p. 320). Rops gives the estimate of two million pilgrims for the first Jubilee year (p. 64).

9. In his commentary on these verses, Singleton agrees that Dante was himself in Rome during the holy year and saw the "remarkable organization" (*Divine Comedy*, Commentary 1, p. 315) that he describes in the poem. The bridge mentioned in these lines was the only one in Dante's day to serve the section of the city where St. Peter's is located. The "Castle" is the Castel Sant'Angelo, the "Mount" Monte Giordano.

10. For the history of purgatory's theological formulation and popular reception, see Le Goff. Of all the theologians he surveys, Bonaventure (pp. 250–56) is most interesting in connection with Dante's own purgatorial "innovations," e.g., the greater proximity of purgatory to heaven than to hell, the direction of penance by angels rather than demons, and the liberation of the soul from purgatory prior to the Last Judgment.

11. Le Goff, p. 334.

12. For Dante's theological geography, see Morgan, pp. 144–65.

13. La Favia argues that by means of the Psalms and hymns cited throughout the second canticle, the poet intended a program of parallels between the

canonical hours of an earthly day and Dante's experience of purgatory. He provides a useful summary of the liturgical texts cited: "From the Mass Dante mentions the *Asperges* (*Purg.*, XXXI, 98), *Gloria in excelsis Deo* (*Purg.*, XX, 136), *Benedictus* (*Purg.*, XXX, 19), *Osanna* (*Purg.*, XXIX, 51), and *Agnus Dei* (*Purg.*, XVI, 19). From the Divine Office he mentions the following psalms: *In exitu Israel de Aegypto* (*Purg.*, II, 46), *Miserere* (*Purg.*, V, 24), *Adhaesit pavimento anima mea* (*Purg.*, XIX, 73), *Labia mea, Domine* (*Purg.*, XXIII, 11), *Delectasti* (*Purg.*, XXVIII, 80), *Beati quorum tecta sunt peccata* (*Purg.*, XXIX, 3), *In te Domine speravi* (*Purg.*, XXX, 83), and *Deus venerunt gentes* (*Purg.*, XXXIII, 1). From the hymns of the Divine Office, he names the *Salve regina* (*Purg.*, VIII, 82), *Te lucis ante* (*Purg.*, VII, 13), *Te Deum laudamus* (*Purg.*, IX, 140), and *Summae Deus clementiae* (*Purg.*, XXV, 121). It should be noted how the poet distributes the single songs along his journey, actually according to the liturgical time of the Church: the parts of the Mass are proclaimed in the morning hours; the first two mentioned hymns, which belong to Compline, are sung in the evening hours, and the other two, which belong to Matins, in the early morning hours; and the psalms are recited variously during the entire day. Consequently, all the liturgical parts respect the same liturgical time as on earth" (p. 55). See also Ardissino.

14. On the relevance of this psalm, see Singleton, "*In exitu Israel de Aegypto*"; Tucker; and Danielou, "Figures du baptème."

15. Le Goff, pp. 118–22, 190–93; quotations from p. 120.

16. Ardissino (p. 52) notes the penitential character of the Salve Regina and its assignment to the office of Holy Saturday eve, after vespers. The antiphon was relatively recent in Dante's day, and became extremely popular through its introduction into the Office by the Franciscans toward the middle of the thirteenth century.

17. Quoted in Britt, pp. 39–40; trans. Britt.

18. Francesco da Buti (1385–95), cited by Singleton in *Divine Comedy*, Commentary 2, p. 195.

19. In "Religious Celebrations," V. and E. Turner note that in *communitas* "there is a direct, total confrontation of human identities which is rather more than the casual camaraderie of ordinary social life. It may be found in the mutual relationships of neophytes in initiation, where *communitas* is sacred and serious, and in the great seasonal celebrations" (p. 205). In this instance, Dante and Adrian are both purgatorial neophytes, but whereas Dante's transformation is only provisional and "initiatory," Adrian is undergoing a true initiation, that is, "an irreversible, singular ritual instrument for effecting a permanent, visible cultural transformation of the subject" (*Image and Pilgrimage*, p. 31).

20. Adrian cites Scripture in support of this new *communitas*: "If ever you have understood that holy gospel which says, '*Neque nubent*,' you may well see why I speak thus" (*Purg.* 19.136–38). Part of the power of this interaction with a former pope derives from the parallel conversation with the soul of Nicholas IV in *Inferno* 19. There, in the inverted world of the simonists, the layman poet plays the role of prophet and priest to a pontiff likened in simile to an assassin.

21. V. and E. Turner, "Religious Celebrations," pp. 202–6.

22. Dante was counting on the reader's familiarity not only with this feature of medieval churches but with the pious uses that these tombstones were put to: "As, in order that there be memory of them, the stones in the church floor over the buried dead bear figured what they were before [*portan segnato quel ch'elli eran pria*]; wherefore many a time men weep for them there, at the prick of memory that spurs only the faithful: so I saw sculptured there, but of better semblance in respect of skill, all that for pathway juts out from the mountain." *Purg.* 12.16–24.

23. Dante's epistle to Can Grande, paras. 15 and 16, in *Dantis Alagherii Epistolae*.

24. Dante's epistle to Can Grande ends with a description of the "aim" of the *Paradiso* that gives as well the trajectory of the entire *Commedia*: "And since, having reached the beginning or first cause, which is God, there is nothing further to seek, he being Alpha and Omega, or the first and the last (as he is designated in John's vision), the treatise comes to an end in God himself, who is blessed in the world without end." *Dantis Alagherii Epistolae*, p. 211, para. 33.

CHAPTER 14

1. *Convivio* 1.3: "Veramente io sono stato legno sanza vela e sanza governo, portato a diversi porti e foci e liti dal vento secco che vapora la dolorosa povertade."

2. In *Convivio* 4.28, where Dante speaks about the fourth (and final) stage of life, he refers to the soul's return to God, "si come a quello porto onde ella si partio quando venne ad intrare nel mare di questa vita" ("as to the port from which it departed when it came to set sail on the sea of this life"). He goes on to develop this metaphor of navigational return at some length, as he will (at large) in the *Commedia*, perhaps most provocatively in *Inferno* 26–27. For Dante's use of nautical metaphors in general, see Curtius, *European Literature*, pp. 28–30.

3. Introduced into the lexicon of the poem in this, its first simile, are two

words, "pelago" and "passo," that will both gather weight as the *Commedia* progresses and continually point the reader back to this opening moment of Dante's spiritual "naufragio."

4. Dante's epistle to Can Grande, para. 8, in *Dantis Alagherii Epistolae*, p. 200. Campbell, *Witness*, suggests that the literary situation of the traveler who writes is "a limit case for such intertwined literary issues as truth, fact, figure, fiction, even genre. How, for instance, does one distinguish fact from fiction, either as writer or as reader, in the case of unverifiable records of private experience taking place in profoundly unfamiliar surroundings?" (p. 2). Her question can be used to examine the literal truth claims of the *Commedia* quite apart from any discussion of the "allegory of the theologians"—as an absolute "limit case" in the history of travel literature. See also Campbell's "Nel mezzo del cammin di nostra vita."

5. For a study of Dante's geography, see Moore, *Studies, Third Series*. A concise appendix on the subject is found in Kimble, pp. 240–44. See also Boyde's chapter "Land and Sea."

6. Alighieri, *Quaestio de aqua et terra*, para. 19, in his *Tutte le opere* (p. 381): "Nam, ut communiter ab omnibus habetur, hec habitabilis extenditur per lineam longitudinis a Gadibus, que supra terminos occidentales ab Hercule positos ponitur, usque ad hostia fluminis Ganges, ut scribit Orosius." In *Par.* 27.80–81, from the heaven of the Fixed Stars, Dante surveys "tutto l'arco / che fa dal mezzo al fine il primo clima" ("[the] whole arc which the first climate makes from its middle to its end"). The *Quaestio* purports to be a disquisition delivered by Dante to a gathering of scholars in Verona in January of 1320, a "scientific" inquiry into the relative levels of land and water on the surface of the globe. Dante concludes that the elevation of heavy earth above lighter water is a result of the attraction of the stars. Although the authenticity of the *Quaestio* has been challenged, it is now largely accepted as Dante's work. See Manlio Pastore Stocchi's entry in *ED*, 4: 761–65, which includes a bibliography. Also see Toynbee, pp. 534–35; and Alexander.

7. *Convivio* 4.15: "E sanza dubbio forte riderebbe Aristotile udendo fare spezie due de l'umana generazione, si come de li cavalli e de li asini; che, perdonimi Aristotile, asini ben si possono dire coloro che cosi pensano."

8. A standard overview of Dante's terrestrial paradise in relation to the larger tradition is found in Patch; for a fuller account, see Coli's study, esp. pp. 189–90, where he discusses at length Dante's peculiar positioning of Eden and purgatory on the same invented mountain. Nardi has explored this territory in even greater depth in his impressively erudite essay "Intorno al site del Purgatorio." See also Boyde, pp. 96–111, who underscores the originality of Dante's

conception. The poet's "remaking" of purgatory is discussed by Le Goff, pp. 334–55, and perhaps most acutely by Morgan, pp. 144–65.

9. Nardi, "Intorno al site del Purgatorio," pp. 352–54, quotes from Ambrose, *Ennaratio in Psalm. 118* (17.1), and Rupert of Deutz, *De Trinitate* 1.32–33.

10. Nardi, "Intorno al site del Purgatorio," pp. 372–73, masks the sheer surprise of Eunoe by saying that Dante was led ("fu condotto") to imagine a companion stream to Virgil's Lethe, whose name (as well as whose existence) he "coined." The point is that Eunoe is Dante's own discovery, what Le Goff refers to as the poet's "invention" (p. 479), and what Patch calls "an astonishing change for Dante to make from the traditional picture of Eden, a point in his originality and in the classical influence to which he was subject" (p. 185). See Vittorio Russo's entry "Eunoe," in *ED*, 2: 765–66; and Singleton, *Journey to Beatrice*, pp. 159–83, where he discusses Eunoe as "a striking departure from scriptural authority." Dronke, *Medieval Poet*, pp. 402–4, wonders if an observation by Pliny regarding two fountains in Boethia (*Historiae naturalis* 31.11) may be the source of Dante's "originality."

11. Both Moore, *Studies in Dante, Third Series*, pp. 119–20, and Kimble, pp. 241–42, regard Dante's origination of the mountain as the poet's own myth; so too does the commentary tradition in general. Nardi argues in *La caduta di Lucifero*, however, that Dante is working from three biblical texts—Isa. 14:11–16, Rev. 12:7–16, and Luke 10:18.

12. An excellent discussion of the *mappaemundi* as "largely exegetic" is given by Woodward, "Medieval Mappaemundi." See also John Block Friedman's first chapter, which notes that the medieval map was "likely to be a hodgepodge of biblical, classical, and fabulous history mixed with the names of true places, cities, and peoples" (p. 38). His description recalls something of the "hodgepodge" of the *Commedia* itself.

13. For a discussion of the difference between pilgrimage and wandering, see Zacher, esp. chaps. 1–2. Zacher calls Dante's Ulysses "probably the most striking medieval depiction of the *curiosus* as wanderer" (p. 35). See also Ladner, esp. p. 251.

14. The bibliography on Dante's treatment of Ulysses is extraordinarily extensive. For an overview of the figure himself, see Stanford. A masterful summary of critical work up through the 1960s can be found in Scott; Fido brings the bibliography more up to date. See also Mario Fubini's entry "Ulisse," in *ED*, 5: 803–9, which surveys critical positions and provides a bibliography.

15. That the ill-fated expedition of the Vivaldi brothers may have been in Dante's mind when he told his version of the Ulysses story has become something of a commonplace among commentators. Rogers offers an extended study of the subject and maintains a reverse order of influence: Dante's Ulysses

framed the way the Vivaldi expedition came to be treated. "In other words, just as Dante's passage has inspired many later poets, so there is a reminiscence of the *Divina Commedia* in historical scholarship concerning European exploration and discovery" (p. 45).

16. Ever since Francesco De Sanctis, in the late nineteenth century, it has been *de rigeur* among Italian critics of a certain stripe to see Ulysses as anticipating (and perhaps even inspiring) what we call the "Age of Discovery." Thus De Sanctis says of Ulysses' speech to his men: "We feel that burning curiosity to know which assailed the men of that era. We seem to be taking part in a voyage of Columbus: sin becomes virtue. Dante the logical Ghibelline puts the besieger and traitor of Troy into Hell, for Troy was the root of the Holy Roman Empire, but Dante the poet raises a statue to this forerunner of Columbus, who stretches wide his arms to new seas and new worlds" (1: 208).

17. Against this romantic identification of Ulysses (and Dante, his maker) as Renaissance explorers *avant la lettre*, Scott demonstrates impressively, by a broad look at Dante's works, that there is nothing in the poet himself "of the intrepid explorer, another Marco Polo, let alone a precursor of Columbus" (p. 157); that Dante clearly acknowledged limitations to the habitable world (p. 164); and that he respected restraints on human intellect: "The idea of exceeding certain natural or divinely-appointed limitations is basic to Dante's view of human nature and one which is implied in the use of the term *follia*" (pp. 167–68). See Bosco, "La 'follia' di Dante," in his *Dante vicino*, pp. 55–76; and Nardi, "La tragedia d'Ulisse."

18. Padoan offers a comprehensive look at the Ulysses traditions at Dante's disposal in his "Ulisse 'Fandi Fictor.'" Barker covers some of the same source material in "Dante and the Last Voyage of Ulysses" (in his *Traditions of Civility*, pp. 53–73) as does Freccero in "The Prologue Scene" and "Dante's Ulysses" (both in his *Dante: Poetics of Conversion*). Thompson argues (pp. 43–50) that Dante would have known of Ulysses' return even without the text of Homer, through allusions to that homecoming in Latin literature, medieval mythography, and commentary.

19. See Rahner.

20. Freccero writes in *Dante: Poetics of Conversion*: "[It] seems safe to presume that the figure of Ulysses, for all of its apparent historicity, is at the same time a palinodic moment in the *Divine Comedy*. As Bruno Nardi once suggested, it implies a retrospective view of Dante himself both as poet and as man, when with confidence ('ingegno') he embarked upon the writing of the *Convivio*, a work never completed, which began by stating that all men desire to know and that ultimate happiness resides in the pursuit of knowledge. Ulysses would then stand for a moment in the pilgrim's life . . . for the

disastrous prelude to the preparation for grace, a misleading guide before the encounter with Virgil" (p. 146).

21. Shankland, pp. 28–31, shows how linguistic similarities in certain details of the journeys of Ulysses and Dante constantly contrast the "folle volo" of one with the "alto volo" of the other.

22. I like Barolini's formulation in *Undivine Comedy*, p. 52: "Ulysses is the lightning rod Dante places in his poem to attract and defuse his own consciousness of the presumption involved in anointing oneself God's scribe. In other words, Ulysses documents Dante's self-awareness: Dante *knows* that, in constructing a system whose fiction is that it is not fictional, he has given himself a license to write the world, to play God unchecked."

23. Auerbach, *Literary Language*, maintains that Dante merged all the forms of his Latin heritage into his own vernacular and made Italian "(not as such but as one of the vernacular languages) into the language of the European spirit" (p. 314). See Curtius, *European Literature*, pp. 350–57, on Dante's fusion of Latin and the vernacular.

24. Major studies of Dante's addresses to the reader are found in Gmelin, "Die Anrede an den Leser"; Spitzer, "Address to the Reader"; and Auerbach, "Dante's Address" and *Literary Language*, pp. 296–301. All touch on the opening of *Paradiso* 2.

25. In their commentary on *Par.* 2.5, "non vi mettete in pelago," Bosco and Reggio restrict the reference of "pelago" to the high seas of the Mediterranean and deny that it can apply to the ocean itself, "because a voyage in the ocean was for Dante inconceivable: only Ulysses ventured forth there, contravening divine prohibition" (3: 29). I am suggesting that the final canticle is not speaking of navigation but of writing, and that it announces itself as a trespass from the outset, before then going on to claim that its literary venture is a discovery made licit by virtue of divine call. See also Boitani, pp. 250–78.

26. Bosco and Reggio (3: 25) mention the thirteenth-century vernacular descriptions of the blessed by Giacommino da Verona and Bonvesin de la Riva as precedents for the waters that Dante was coursing in the final canticle. They go on to assert that the poet's originality lies in his taking on theological and philosophical issues so boldly (and with such sophistication). Perhaps the most ardent defense of Dante's novelty, however, is offered by Benvenuto da Imola in his commentary on the *Commedia*, written between 1373 and 1380. Beginning his lengthy gloss on Dante's claim in *Par.* 2.7 to travel uncharted seas, he asks, "Quis enim unquam excogitavit facere unum coelum artificiale, quale hic poeta mirabilis" ("Who indeed ever devised so accomplished a heaven as this marvellous poet?"). His answer is, no one else.

27. Sapegno (3: 19) notes that since Daniello's 1568 commentary, the

"nove Muse" have often been taken to refer not to all nine Muses but to new and Christian (rather than antique pagan) revelation. But following on the assertion that "L'acqua ch'io prendo già mai non si corse," the poet may well be playing with the full range of the adjective "nove." The Muses invoked, therefore, not only may be nine in number or Christian in inspiration, but indeed may be altogether new, never before called upon—the muses of novelty invoked to help the poet express what is presented as "quella vista nova" (*Par.* 33.136).

28. See Curtius, "Ship of the Argonauts."

29. For the metaphor of writing as plowing, see Curtius, *European Literature*, pp. 313–14.

30. Curtius, "Ship of the Argonauts," p. 491; see also Dronke, *Medieval Poet*, p. 436. Hollander, *Allegory in Dante's "Commedia,"* pp. 220–32, gives an extensive reading of the Jason material in *Paradiso.* He does not, however, consider the conversion of the sea god's traditional wrath into awe. Instead, he emphasizes Jason and Neptune as two figural identities of Dante, Pilgrim and Poet (pp. 230–31). Boitani discusses the sublimity of Dante's poetic navigation but not its trespass (pp. 275–78).

31. Virgil's Eclogue IV, vv. 31–40 refers to the *vestigia fraudis* in terms of sailing the seas and cleaving the earth. With the return of the Golden Age, however, "even the trader will quit the sea, nor shall the ship of pine exchange wares"; "the earth shall not feel the harrow." Likewise in *Met.* 1.89–100, Ovid defines the Golden Age as free of navigation and of plowing. See also Curtius, "Ship of the Argonauts," pp. 490–91.

32. Mazzotta, *Dante, Poet of the Desert*, p. 142. Hollander glosses *Par.* 25.7–9 as meaning "not only that Dante, the lamb, will have another pelt, but that Dante, the poet, shall return from heaven with a new Fleece, not the Golden Fleece of Jason, but the true *vello*, granted by the Grace of God" (*Allegory in Dante's "Commedia,"* p. 224).

Bibliography

Alexander, David. "Dante and the Form of the Land." *Annals of the Association of American Geographers* 76 (1986): 38–49.

Alford, John A. "The Scriptural Self." In Bernard S. Levy, ed., *The Bible in the Middle Ages*, pp. 1–21. Binghamton, N.Y.: Medieval and Renaissance Texts and Studies, 1992.

Alighieri, Dante. *The Banquet.* Trans. Christopher Ryan. Stanford French and Italian Studies 61. Saratoga, Calif.: ANMA Libri, 1989.

——. *Dante, Monarchia.* Ed. and trans. Prue Shaw. Cambridge Medieval Classics 4. Cambridge, Eng.: Cambridge University Press, 1995.

——. *Dante, La vita nuova (Poems of Youth).* Trans. Barbara Reynolds. Harmondsworth, Eng.: Penguin Books, 1969.

——. *Dante Alighieri, Il Convivio.* Ed. G. Busnelli and G. Vandelli. 2d ed. Rev. A. E. Quaglio. Vols. 4–5 of *Opere di Dante.* Florence: Le Monnier, 1964.

——. *Dantis Alagherii Epistolae.* Ed. and trans. Paget Toynbee. 2d ed. Oxford: Clarendon, 1966.

——. *De vulgari eloquentia: Dante's Book of Exile.* Trans. Marianne Shapiro. Lincoln: University of Nebraska Press, 1990.

——. *The Divine Comedy.* Trans. Allen Mandelbaum. New York: Bantam Books, 1984.

——. *The Divine Comedy.* Ed., trans., and comm. C. S. Singleton. 6 vols. Bollingen Series 80. Princeton, N.J.: Princeton University Press, 1972–75.

——. *Tutte le opere.* Ed. Luigi Blasucci. Florence: Sansoni, 1981.

Allen, Mowbray. "Does Dante Hope for Virgil's Salvation?" *MLN* 104 (1989): 193–205.

Allen, Mowbray, and Teodolinda Barolini. "Critical Exchange." *MLN* 105 (1990): 138–43.

Allevi, F. *Con Dante e la Sibilla ed altri d'agli antichi al volgare.* Milan: Edizioni Scientifico-Letterario, 1965.

Anderson, William. *Dante the Maker.* New York: Crossroad, 1982.

Anonimo Fliorentino. *Commento alla "Divina Commedia" d'Anonimo Fioren- tino del secolo XIV, ora per la prima volta stampato a cura di Pietro Fanfani.* 3 vols. Bologna: G. Romagnoli, 1866–74.

The Apocryphal New Testament. Ed. J. K. Elliott. Oxford: Clarendon, 1993.

Ardissino, Erminia. "I Canti liturgici nel *Purgatorio* dantesco." *DSARDS* 108 (1990): 39–65.

Armour, Peter. *Dante's Griffin and the History of the World: A Study of the Earthly Paradise ("Purgatorio," Cantos xxix–xxxiii).* Oxford: Clarendon, 1989.

Ascoli, Albert. "'Neminem ante nos': Historicity and Authority in the '*De vulgari eloquentia.*'" *Annali d'Italianistica: Dante and Modern American Criticism* 8 (1990): 186–231.

——. "The Unfinished Author: Dante's Rhetoric of Authority in *Convivio* and *De vulgari eloquentia.*" In Jacoff, *Cambridge Companion to Dante,* pp. 45–66.

——. "The Vowels of Authority (Dante's *Convivio* IV.vi.3–4)." In K. Brownlee and W. Stephens, eds., *Discourses of Authority in Medieval and Renaissance Literature,* pp. 23–46. Hanover, N.H.: University Press of New England, 1989.

Auerbach, Erich. "Dante's Address to the Reader." *Romance Philology* 7 (1953– 54): 268–78.

——. *Literary Language and Its Public in Late Latin Antiquity and in the Middle Ages.* Trans. Ralph Manheim. New York: Pantheon Books, 1965.

——. *Scenes from the Drama of European Literature.* Trans. Ralph Manheim. New York: Meridian Books, 1959.

Augustine of Hippo, Saint. *City of God.* Trans. Henry Bettenson. Ed. David Knowles. Harmondsworth, Eng.: Penguin, 1972.

——. *Confessions.* Trans. R. S. Pine-Coffin. Harmondsworth, Eng.: Penguin, 1961.

——. *The Confessions.* Trans. William Watts. 2 vols. Loeb Classical Library. London: Heinemann, 1912.

——. *The "De Haeresibus" of Saint Augustine.* Trans. and comm. L. G. Müller, OFM. Washington, D.C.: Catholic University Press, 1956.

——. *Letters of Saint Augustine.* Ed. and trans. Sr. Wilfred Parson. 6 vols. New York: Fathers of the Church, 1951–89.

——. *On Christian Doctrine.* Trans. D. W. Robertson, Jr. The Library of Liberal Arts. New York: Macmillan, 1958.

——. *Tractates on the Gospel of John.* Trans. John W. Rettig. Vol. 3. Washington, D.C.: Catholic University Press, 1995.

Barbi, Michele. "La similtudine del baccelliere (*Par.* XXIV, 46–48)." *Studi danteschi* 12 (1927): 79–82.

Barker, Ernest. *Traditions of Civility.* Cambridge, Eng.: Cambridge University Press, 1948.

Barnes, John C. "Vestiges of the Liturgy in Dante's Verse." In Barnes and Cuilleanain, *Dante and the Middle Ages,* pp. 231–69.

Barnes, John C., and Cormac O. Cuilleanain, eds. *Dante and the Middle Ages.* Dublin: Irish Academic Press, 1995.

Barnstone, Willis, ed. *The Other Bible: Ancient Alternative Scriptures.* San Francisco: Harper San Francisco, 1984.

Barolini, Teodolinda. "Arachne, Argus, and St. John: Transgressive Art in Ovid and Dante." *Mediaevalia* 13 (1989): 201–26.

——. *Dante's Poets: Textuality and Truth in the "Comedy."* Princeton, N.J.: Princeton University Press, 1984.

——. *The Undivine Comedy: Detheologizing Dante.* Princeton, N.J.: Princeton University Press, 1992.

Barolini, Teodolinda; Joan Ferrante; and Robert Hollander. "Why Did Dante Write the *Comedy?*" *DSARDS* III (1993): 1–25.

Barthes, Roland. "Authors and Writers." In *Critical Essays,* trans. Richard Howard, pp. 143–50. Evanston, Ill.: Northwestern University Press, 1972.

Battaglia, Salvatore. "La tradizione di Ovidio nel Medio Evo." In *La coscienza letteraria medioevo,* pp. 23–50. Naples: Liguori, 1965.

Battaglia Ricci, Lucia. *Dante e la tradizione letteraria medievale: Una proposta per la "Commedia."* Pisa: Giardini, 1983.

——. "Scrittura sacra e 'Sacrato Poema." In *DB,* pp. 295–422.

Bel Geddes, Norman. *Miracle in the Evening.* Garden City, N.Y.: Doubleday, 1960.

Benedict, Saint. *The Rule of St. Benedict.* Ed. and trans. J. McCann. Westminster, Md.: Newman, 1952.

Benvenuto. *Benvenuti de Rambaldis de Imola Comentum super Dantis Aligherij "Comoedium," nunc primum integre in lucem editum sumptibus Guilielmi Warren Vernon, curante Jacopo Phlippo Lacaita.* Florence: Barbèra, 1887.

Biagi, Guido, ed. *La "Divina Commedia" nella figurazione artistica e nel secolare commento.* 3 vols. Turin: Unione tipografico-editrice Torinese, 1924–39.

Bibliorum Sacrorum iuxta vulgatam clementiam. Nova editio. Ed. Aloisius Gramatica. Vatican City: Typis Polyglottis Vaticanis, 1929.

Bloom, Harold. *Ruin the Sacred Truths: Poetry and Belief from the Bible to the Present.* Cambridge, Mass.: Harvard University Press, 1989.

——. *The Western Canon: The Books and the School of the Ages.* New York: Harcourt Brace and World, 1994.

Boccaccio, Giovanni. *Trattatello in laude di Dante. The Earliest Lives of Dante.* Trans. J. R. Smith. New York: Frederick Ungar, 1963 [1901].

Boethius. *Boethius, "The Theological Tractates," "The Consolation of Philosophy."* Trans. H. F. Stewart, E. K. Rand, and S. J. Tester. Cambridge, Mass.: Harvard University Press, 1978.

Boitani, Piero. *The Tragic and the Sublime in Medieval Literature.* Cambridge, Eng.: Cambridge University Press, 1989.

Bolgiani, Franco. *La conversione di S. Agostino e l'VIII libro delle "Confesioni."* Pubblicazioni della Facoltà di Lettere e Filosofia 8.4. Turin: Università di Torino, 1956.

Bolton, Brenda. "Innocent III's Treatment of the *Humiliati.*" In G. J. Cuming and D. Baker, eds., *Popular Belief and Practice,* pp. 73–82. Studies in Church History 8. Cambridge, Eng.: Cambridge University Press, 1972.

Bonaventure, Saint. *"Breviloquium" by St. Bonaventure.* Trans. E. Nemmers. St. Louis, Mo., and London: B. Herder, 1946.

——. *The Mind's Road to God.* Trans. George Boas. Indianapolis, Ind.: Bobbs-Merrill, 1953.

——. *Opera omnia.* Ed. PP. Collegii a S. Bonaventura. 11 vols. Quaracchi: Ex typ. Colegii S. Bonaventurae, 1882–1902.

Bonner, Gerald. *St. Augustine of Hippo: Life and Controversies.* Philadelphia: The Library of History and Doctrine, 1963.

Bono, Barbara. *Literary Transvaluation: From Vergilian Epic to Shakespearean Tragedy.* Berkeley: University of California Press, 1984.

Bosco, Umberto. "Il canto XXVIII del *Purgatorio.*" *Nuove lettere dantesche* 5 (1972): 131–48.

——. *Dante vicino.* Caltanisetta-Rome: Sciascia, 1966.

Bosco, Umberto, and Giovanni Reggio. *Dante Alighieri, "La Divina Commedia" con pagine critiche.* 3 vols. Florence: Le Monnier, 1979.

Botterill, Steven. *Dante and the Mystical Tradition: St. Bernard of Clairvaux in the "Commedia."* Cambridge, Eng.: Cambridge University Press, 1994.

——. "Doctrine, Doubt, and Certainty: *Paradiso* XXXII.40–84. *Italian Studies* 43 (1987): 20–36.

Boyde, Patrick. *Dante Philomythes and Philosopher: Man in the Cosmos.* Cambridge, Eng.: Cambridge University Press, 1981.

Britt, Matthew, OSB, ed. *The Hymns of the Breviary.* Rev. ed. New York: Benziger Brothers, 1955.

Brownlee, Kevin. "Dante and the Classical Poets." In Jacoff, *Cambridge Companion to Dante,* pp. 100–119.

——. "Ovid's Semele and Dante's Metamorphosis: *Paradiso* 21–22." In *PA,* pp. 224–32.

——. "Pauline Vision and Ovidian Speech in *Paradiso* 1." In *PA*, pp. 202–13.

——. "Phaeton's Fall and Dante's Ascent." *DSARDS* 102 (1984): 135–44.

——. "Why the Angels Speak Italian: Dante as Vernacular *Poeta* in *Paradiso* XXV." *Poetics Today* 5 (1984): 597–610.

Buti, Francesco da. *Commento di Francesco da Buti sopra la "Divina Commedia" di Dante Allighieri . . . per cura di Crescentino Giannini.* 3 vols. Pisa: Nistri, 1858–62.

Butler, Dom Cuthbert. *Western Mysticism: The Teaching of Saints Augustine, Gregory, and Bernard on Contemplation and the Contemplative Life.* 2d ed. London: Constable, 1922.

Cachey, Theodore J., Jr. *Dante Now: Current Trends in Dante Studies.* Notre Dame, Ind.: University of Notre Dame Press, 1995.

Cahn, Walter. *Romanesque Bible Illustration.* Ithaca, N.Y.: Cornell University Press, 1982.

Calcaterra, Carlo. "Sant' Agostino nelle opere di Dante e del Petrarca." *Rivista di filosofia neo-scholastica*, Spec. supp. to 23 (1931): 422–99. (Reprinted in *Nella selva di Petrarca.* Bologna: Capelli, 1942.)

Campbell, Mary Baine. " 'Nel mezzo del cammin di nostra vita': The Palpability of *Purgatorio*." In S. Tomasch and S. Gilles, eds., *Text and Territory: Geographical Imagination in the European Middle Ages*, pp. 15–28. Philadelphia: University of Pennsylvania Press, 1998.

——. *The Witness and the Other World: Exotic European Travel Writing, 400–1600.* Ithaca, N.Y.: Cornell University Press, 1988.

Chadwick, Henry. "History and Symbolism in the Garden at Milan." In F. X. Martina and J. A. Richmond, eds., *From Augustine to Eriugena: Essays on Neoplatonism and Christianity in Honor of John O'Maera*, pp. 42–55. Washington, D.C.: American University Press, 1991.

Chaine, J. "Descente du Christ aux enfers." In F. Vigouroux, ed., *Dictionnaire de la Bible, Supplément*, vol. 2, cols. 395–431. Paris: Letouzey, 1934.

Chamberas, Peter A. "The Transfiguration of Christ: Study in Patristic Exegesis of Scripture." *Saint Vladimir Theological Quarterly* 14 (1970): 48–65.

Chiarenza, Marguerite Mills. "The Imageless Vision and Dante's *Paradiso*." *DSARDS* 90 (1972): 109–24.

Chioccioni, Pietro. *L'Agostinismo nella "Divina Commedia."* Florence: Olschki, 1952.

Cioffi, Caron Ann. "The Anxieties of Ovidian Influence: Theft in *Inferno* XXIV and XXV." *DSARDS* 112 (1994): 77–100.

Cochrane, Charles. *Christianity and Classical Culture: A Study of Thought and Action from Augustus to Augustine.* Rev. ed. Oxford: Oxford University Press, 1972 [1940].

Il codice cassinese della "Divina Commedia" per la prima volta letteralmente messo a stampa per cura dei monaci benedettini della Badia di Monte Cassino. Monte Cassino: Tipographia di Monte Cassino, 1865.

Coli, Edorado. *Il paradiso terrestra dantesco.* Florence: Carnesecchi, 1897.

Colilli, Paul. "Harold Bloom and the Post-Theological Dante." *Annali d'italianistica: Dante and Modern American Criticism* 8 (1990): 132–43.

Colish, Marcia L. *The Mirror of Language: A Study in the Medieval Theory of Knowledge.* Rev. ed. Lincoln: University of Nebraska Press, 1983 [1968].

Comollo, Adrianna. *Il disenso religioso in Dante.* Florence: Olschki, 1990.

Comparetti, Domenico. *Vergil in the Middle Ages.* Trans. E. F. M. Benecke. Princeton, N.J.: Princeton University Press, 1997 [1896].

Contini, Gianfranco. *Un' idea di Dante.* Turin: Einaudi, 1970.

Courcelle, Pierre. *Les "Confessions" de saint Augustin dans la tradition littéraire: Antécédents et posterité.* Paris: Etudes augustiniennes, 1963.

——. "L'enfant et les 'sorts biblique.'" *Vigiliae Christianae* 7 (1953): 194–220.

——. *Recherches sur les "Confessions" de saint Augustin.* Rev. ed. Paris: de Boccard, 1968 [1950].

——. "Source chrétienne et allusions païennes de l'épisode de 'Tolle-lege.'" *Revue d'histoire et de philosophie religieuses* 32 (1952): 171–200.

Cristaldi, Sergio. "Dalle Beatitudini all' *Apocalisse.* Il Nuovo Testamento nella *Commedia.*" *Letture classensi* 17 (1988): 24–67.

Croce, Benedetto. *La poesia di Dante.* Bari: Laterza, 1921.

Cuming, G. J., and D. Baker, eds. *Popular Belief and Practice.* Studies in Church History 8. Cambridge, Eng.: Cambridge University Press, 1972.

Curtius, E. R. *European Literature and the Latin Middle Ages.* Trans. Willard R. Trask. New York: Harper and Row, 1963 [1953].

——. "The Ship of the Argonauts." In *Essays on European Literature,* trans. Michael Kowal, pp. 486–92. Princeton, N.J.: Princeton University Press, 1973.

D'Ancona, Alessandro. *Origini del teatro italiano.* 2 vols. Turin: Loescher, 1891.

Danielou, Jean. "Les figures du baptème: La traversée de la Mer Rouge." In *Bible et Liturgie,* pp. 119–35. Paris: Editions du Cerf, 1958.

Danielou, Jean, and Giacomo Devoto, eds. *La Bibbia nell' alto medio evo.* Spoleto: Centro italiano di studi, 1963.

Davidson, L. K., and M. Dunn-Wood. *Pilgrimage in the Middle Ages: A Research Guide.* New York: Garland, 1993.

Davis, Charles T. *Dante and the Idea of Rome.* Oxford: Clarendon, 1957.

——. *"Dante's Italy" and Other Essays.* Philadelphia: University of Pennsylvania Press, 1984.

——. "The Florentine *Studia* and Dante's Library." In Di Scipio and Scaglione, *"Divine Comedy" and the Encyclopedia*, pp. 339–66.

d'Avray, D. L. *The Preaching of the Friars: Sermons Diffused from Paris Before 1300*. Oxford: Clarendon, 1985.

De Bartholomaeis, Vincenzo. *Origini della poesia drammatica italiana*. Bologna: Zanichelli, 1924.

De Hamel, Christopher. *Glossed Books of the Bible and the Origins of the Paris Booktrade*. Woodbridge, Eng., and Dover, N.H.: D. S. Brewer, 1984.

——. *A History of Illuminated Manuscripts*. London: Phaidon, 1986.

Delaruelle, Etienne. "San Francesco d'Assisi e la pietà popolare." In Raoul Manselli, ed., *La religiosità popolare nel Medio Evo*, pp. 231–50. Bologna: Mulino, 1983.

Delcorno, Carlo. "Cadenze e figure della predicazione nel viaggio Dantesco." *Letture Classensi* 15 (1986): 41–60.

——. *Giordano da Pisa e l'antica predicazione volgare*. Florence: Olschki, 1975.

de Lubac, Henri. *Exégèse Médiévale: Les quattre sens de l'écriture*. 2 vols. in 4. Paris: Aubier, 1959–64.

Demaray, John. *The Invention of Dante's "Commedia."* New Haven, Conn.: Yale University Press, 1974.

Demus, Otto. *The Mosaic Decoration of San Marco in Venice*. Ed. Herbert L. Kessler. Chicago: University of Chicago Press, 1988.

de Pontfarcy, Yolande. "The Topography of the Other World and the Influence of Twelfth-Century Irish Visions on Dante." In Barnes and Cuilleanain, *Dante and the Middle Ages*, pp. 93–115.

De Sanctis, Francesco. *History of Italian Literature*. Trans. Joan Redfern. 2 vols. New York: Harcourt, Brace, 1931.

Dickinson, Emily. *The Complete Poems of Emily Dickinson*. Ed. T. H. Johnson. Boston: Little, Brown, 1960.

Di Scipio, G., and A. Scaglione, eds. *The "Divine Comedy" and the Encyclopedia of the Arts and Sciences*. Amsterdam and Philadelphia: John Benjamins, 1988.

Donoghue, Denis. "On the Limits of Language." *Sewanee Review* 85 (1977): 371–91.

Dronke, Peter. "Apocalisse negli ultimi canti del Purgatorio." In *DB*, pp. 81–94.

——. *Dante and Medieval Latin Traditions*. Cambridge, Eng.: Cambridge University Press, 1986

——. *The Medieval Poet and His World*. Rome: Edizioni di Storia e Letteratura, 1984.

———. "The Procession in Dante's *Purgatorio*." *Deutsches Dante-Jahrbuch* 53–54 (1978–79): 18–45.

———. "*Purgatorio* XXIX." In Foster and Boyde, *Cambridge Readings in Dante's "Comedy,"* pp. 114–37.

Durling, Robert M., ed. *The "Divine Comedy" of Dante Alighieri. "Inferno."* Ed. and trans. Robert M. Durling. Introduction and notes by Ronald L. Martinez and Robert M. Durling. Oxford: Oxford University Press, 1996.

Durling, Robert M., and Ronald L. Martinez. *Time and the Crystal: Studies in Dante's "Rime Petrose."* Berkeley: University of California Press, 1990.

Earle, John, and Michael J. Sallnow, eds. *Contesting the Sacred: The Anthropology of Christian Pilgrimage.* New York: Routledge, 1991.

Eco, Umberto. *The Aesthetics of Thomas Aquinas.* Trans. Hugh Bredin. Cambridge, Mass.: Harvard University Press, 1988.

Emmerson, Richard K., and R. Herzman, eds. *The Apocalyptic Imagination in Medieval Literature.* Philadelphia: University of Pennsylvania Press, 1992.

Evans, G. R. *The Language and Logic of the Bible: The Road to Reformation.* Cambridge, Eng.: Cambridge University Press, 1983.

Fallani, Giovanni. *L'esperienza teologica di Dante.* Lecce: Milella, 1976.

Ferrante, Joan. "The Bible as Thesaurus for Secular Literature." In Levy, *Bible in the Middle Ages*, pp. 23–50.

———. *The Political Vision of the "Divine Comedy."* Princeton, N.J.: Princeton University Press, 1984.

———. "Usi e abusi della Bibbia nella letteratura medievale." In *DB*, pp. 213–25.

———. "Words and Images in Dante's *Paradiso*: Reflections of the Divine." In Aldo S. Bernardo and Anthony L. Pellegrini, eds., *Dante, Petrarch, Boccaccio: Studies in the Italian Trecento in Honor of Charles S. Singleton*, pp. 115–32. Binghamton, N.Y.: Medieval and Renaissance Texts and Studies, 1983.

Ferrari, Leo. "Truth and Augustine's Conversion Scene." In J. C. Shnaubelt, ed., *Augustine: Second Founder of the Faith*, pp. 9–19. New York: Peter Lang, 1990.

Fido, Franco. "Writing Like God—Or Better? Symmetries in Dante's 26th and 27th Cantos." *Italica* 63 (1986): 2250–64.

Fish, Stanley E. *Self-Consuming Artifacts: The Experience of Seventeenth-Century Literature.* Berkeley: University of California Press, 1972.

Fisher, Lizette Andrews. *The Mystic Vision in the Grail Legend and in the "Divine Comedy."* New York: Columbia University Press, 1917.

Folena, Gianfranco. "Textus testis: Caso e necessità nelle origini romanze." In Vittorio Branca, ed., *Concetto, storia, miti e immagini del Medio Evo*, pp. 483–507. Florence: Sansoni, 1973.

——. " 'Volgarizzare' e 'tradurre': Idea e terminologia della traduzione dal medio evo italiano e romanzo all' Umanismo europeo." In Giuseppe G. Petronio, ed., *La traduzione: Saggi e studi*, pp. 57–120. Trieste: LINT, 1973.

Foster, Kenelm. "Dante's Vision of God." *Italian Studies* 14 (1959): 21–39.

——. "*Purgatorio* XXXII." In Foster and Boyde, *Cambridge Readings in Dante's "Comedy,"* pp. 138–54.

——. *The Two Dantes.* Berkeley: University of California Press, 1977.

——. "Vernacular Scriptures in Italy." In *CHB*, pp. 452–65.

Foster, Kenelm, and Patrick Boyde, eds. *Cambridge Readings in Dante's "Comedy."* Cambridge, Eng.: Cambridge University Press, 1981.

Foucault, Michel. "What Is an Author?" In *Textual Strategies: Perspectives on Post-Structuralist Criticism*, ed. and trans. Josué V. Harari. Ithaca, N.Y.: Cornell University Press, 1979.

Franke, William. *Dante's Interpretive Journey.* Chicago: University of Chicago Press, 1996.

Freccero, John. *Dante: The Poetics of Conversion.* Ed. Rachel Jacoff. Cambridge, Mass.: Harvard University Press, 1986.

——, ed. *Dante: A Collection of Critical Essays.* Englewood Cliffs, N.J.: Prentice-Hall, 1965.

Friedman, Joan Isabel. "La processione mistica di Dante: Allegoria e iconografia nel canto xxix del *Purgatorio*." In M. Picone, ed., *Dante e le forme dell' allegoresi*, pp. 125–48. Ravenna: Longo, 1987.

Friedman, John Block. *The Monstrous Races in Medieval Art and Thought.* Cambridge, Mass.: Harvard University Press, 1981.

Fulgentius. "Expositio virgilianae continentiae secundum philosophos moralis." In R. Helm, ed., *Fabii Planciadis Fulgentii V.C. opera*, pp. 81–107. Leipzig: Teubner, 1898.

Galinsky, Karl. *Ovid's "Metamorphoses": An Introduction to the Basic Aspects.* Oxford: Basil Blackwell, 1975.

Gameson, Richard, ed. *The Early Medieval Bible: Its Production, Decoration and Use.* Cambridge, Eng.: Cambridge University Press, 1994.

Gardiner, Eileen, ed. *Visions of Heaven and Hell Before Dante.* New York: Italica, 1989.

Gardner, Edmund G. *Dante and the Mystics.* London: Dent, 1913.

Ghisalberti, Fausto. "Giovanni del Virgilio: Espositore delle '*Metamorfosi*,' " *Giornale dantesco* 34 (1933): 1–110.

——. "Medieval Biographies of Ovid." *Journal of the Warburg and Courtauld Institutes* 9 (1946): 10–59.

Giamatti, A. B. *Earthly Paradise and the Renaissance Epic.* Princeton, N.J.: Princeton University Press, 1966.

Gibson, Margaret T. *The Bible in the Latin West.* Notre Dame, Ind.: University of Notre Dame Press, 1993.

Gill, Katherine. "Women and Religious Literature in the Vernacular." In E. Ann Matter and John Coakley, eds., *Creative Women in Medieval and Early Modern Italy,* pp. 64–104. Philadelphia: University of Pennsylvania Press, 1994.

Gillerman, Dorothy. "Dante's Early Readers: The Evidence of Illuminated Manuscripts." In Di Scipio and Scaglione, *"Divine Comedy" and the Encyclopedia,* pp. 65–80.

Gmelin, Hermann. "Die Anrede an den Leser in Dantes Göttlicher Komödie." *Deutsches Dante-Jahrbuch* 29/30 (1951): 130–40.

———, comm. *Die Göttliche Komödie: Kommentar.* 3 vols. Stuttgart: Klett, 1955.

Goldin, Frederic, ed. and trans. *German and Italian Lyrics.* Garden City, N.Y.: Anchor/Doubleday, 1973.

Gregory, Saint. *Life and Miracles of St. Benedict (Book Two of Dialogues).* Trans. Odo John Zimmerman and Benedict R. Avery. Collegeville, Minn.: St. John's Abbey Press, 1949. Reprint, Westport, Conn.: Greenwood Press, 1980.

Gregory, T. "Filosofia e teologia nelle crisi del XIII secolo." *Belfagor* 19 (1966): 1–16.

Groppi, Felicina. *Dante as Translator.* Trans. Camilla Roatla. Rome: Herder, 1966.

Guido da Pisa. *Guido da Pisa's Expositiones et Glose super Dantis, or Commentary on Dante's "Inferno."* Ed. Vincent Cioffari. Albany: State University of New York Press, 1974.

Hardie, Colin. "The Symbol of the Gryphon in *Purgatorio* XXIX 108 and following Cantos." In Oxford Dante Society, ed., *Centenary Essays on Dante,* pp. 1013–31. Oxford: Oxford University Press, 1965.

Harley, J. B., and David Woodward, eds. *Cartography in Prehistoric, Ancient, and Medieval Europe and the Mediterranean.* Chicago: University of Chicago Press, 1987.

Harrent, S. "Infidèles (salut des)." In *DTC,* vol. 7, pt. 2, cols. 1726–1930.

Hawkins, Peter S. "Polemical Counterpoint in *De civitate Dei.*" *Augustinian Studies* 6 (1975): 97–106.

———. "Resurrecting the Word: Dante and the Bible." *Religion and Literature* 16 (1984): 59–71.

———. "Virgilio cita le scritture." In *DB,* pp. 351–59.

———. "Virtue and Virtuosity: Poetic Self-Reflection in the *Commedia.*" *DSARDS* 98 (1980): 1–18.

———. " 'What Is Truth?' The Question of Art in Theological Education." *Anglican Theological Review* 76 (1994): 364–74.

Herzman, Ronald B. "Dante and the Apocalypse." In Richard K. Emmerson and Bernard McGinn, eds., *The Apocalypse in the Middle Ages*, pp. 398–413. Ithaca, N.Y.: Cornell University Press, 1992.

Herzman, Ronald B., and William A. Stephany. " 'O miseri sequaci': Sacramental Inversion in *Inferno* XIX." *DSARDS* 96 (1978): 39–65.

Herzman, Ronald B., and Gary W. Townsley. "Squaring the Circle: *Paradiso* 33 and the Poetics of Geometry." *Traditio* 49 (1994): 95–125.

Hoffman, Michael, and James Lasdun, eds. *After Ovid: New Metamorphoses.* New York: Farrar, Straus and Giroux, 1994.

Hollander, Robert. *Allegory in Dante's "Commedia."* Princeton, N.J.: Princeton University Press, 1969.

——. "A Checklist of Commentators on the *Commedia* (1322–1982)." *DSARDS* 101 (1983): 181–92.

——. *Dante's Epistle to Can Grande.* Ann Arbor: University of Michigan Press, 1993.

——. *Studies in Dante.* Ravenna: Longo, 1980.

——. "Tragedy in Dante's *Comedy*." *Sewanee Review* 91 (1983): 240–60.

——. *Il Virgilio Dantesco: Tragedia della "Commedia."* Biblioteca di 'Lettere italiane' Studi e Testi 28. Florence: Olschki, 1983.

Hollander, Robert, and Henry Ansgar Kelly. "The Can Grande Dispute." *Lectura Dantis* 14–15 (1994): 61–115.

The Holy Bible. Douay/Rheims Version. Baltimore: John Murphy, 1899.

Hugh of St. Victor. *The "Didascalion" of Hugh of St. Victor.* Trans. Jerome Taylor. Records of Western Civilization. New York: Columbia University Press, 1961.

Iannucci, Amilcare A. *Forma ed evento nella "Divina Commedia."* Rome: Bulzoni, 1984.

——. "Limbo: The Emptiness of Time." *Studi Danteschi* 52 (1979–80): 69–128.

——, ed. *Dante: Contemporary Perspectives.* Toronto: University of Toronto Press, 1997.

Jacoff, Rachel. "Dante and the Legend(s) of St. John." *DSARDS*, forthcoming.

——. "Dante, Geremia e la problematica profetica." In *DB*, pp. 113–24. Florence: Olschki, 1988.

——. "Models of Literary Influence in the *Commedia*." In L. A. Fincke and M. B. Shichtman, eds., *Medieval Texts and Contemporary Readers*, pp. 158–76. Ithaca, N.Y.: Cornell University Press, 1987.

——, ed. *The Cambridge Companion to Dante.* Cambridge, Eng.: Cambridge University Press, 1988.

Jacoff, Rachel, and William Stephany. *Inferno II.* Lectura Dantis Americana. Philadelphia: University of Pennsylvania Press, 1989.

Jerome, Saint. *Commentarium in Esiam liber xi.* Corpus Christianorum series latina 73. Turnholt: Brepols, 1963.

Johnson, W. R. *Darkness Visible: A Study of Vergil's "Aeneid."* Berkeley: University of California Press, 1976.

Kartsonis, Anna D. *Anastasis: The Making of an Image.* Princeton, N.J.: Princeton University Press, 1986.

Kelly, Henry Ansgar. *Tragedy and Comedy from Dante to Pseudo-Dante.* Berkeley: University of California Press, 1993.

Kierkegaard, Søren. *"The Present Age" and "Of the Difference Between a Genius and an Apostle."* Trans. A. Dru. New York: Harper and Row, 1962.

Kimble, George H. T. *Geography in the Middle Ages.* London: Methuen, 1938.

Kirkpatrick, Robin. *Dante's "Paradiso" and the Limitations of Modern Criticism.* Cambridge, Eng.: Cambridge University Press, 1978.

Kleiner, John. *Mismapping the Underworld: Daring and Error in Dante's "Comedy."* Stanford, Calif.: Stanford University Press, 1994.

Kleinhenz, Christopher. "Dante and the Bible: Biblical Citation in the *Divine Comedy*." In Iannucci, *Dante,* pp. 74–93.

——. "Dante and the Bible: Intertextual Approaches to the *Divine Comedy*." *Italica* 63 (1986): 225–36.

——. "Dante and Citation." In Cachey, *Dante Now,* pp. 43–62.

Kolve, D. A. *The Play Called "Corpus Christi."* Stanford, Calif.: Stanford University Press, 1966.

Kuczynski, Michael P. *Prophetic Song: The Psalms as Moral Discourse in Late Medieval England.* Philadelphia: University of Pennsylvania Press, 1995.

Kugel, James. "The 'Bible as Literature' in Latin Antiquity and the Middle Ages." *Hebrew University Studies in Literature and the Arts* 11 (1983): 20–70.

——. "David the Prophet." In James Kugel, ed., *Poetry and Prophesy: The Beginnings of a Literary Tradition,* pp. 45–55. Ithaca, N.Y.: Cornell University Press, 1990.

——. *The Idea of Biblical Poetry.* New Haven, Conn.: Yale University Press, 1981.

Labarge, Margaret Wade. *Medieval Travellers.* London: Hamish Hamilton, 1982.

Ladner, Gerhart B. "Homo Viator: Medieval Ideas on Alienation and Order." *Speculum* 42 (1967): 233–59.

La Favia, Louis M. " '. . . Chè quivi per canti . . .' (*Purg.*, XII, 113), Dante's Programmatic Use of Psalms and Hymns in the *Purgatorio*." *Studies in Iconology* 10 (1984–86): 53–65.

Lanham, Richard A. *Motives of Eloquence: Literary Rhetoric in the Renaissance.* New Haven, Conn.: Yale University Press, 1976.

Latini, Brunetto. *Il tesoretto*. Ed. and trans. Julia Bolton Holloway. New York: Garland, 1981.

Leclercq, Jean, OSB. *The Love of Learning and the Desire of God: A Study of Monastic Culture*. Trans. C. Misrahi. New York: Fordham University Press, 1961.

Lee, Harold; Marjorie Reeves; and Giulio Silano, eds. *Western Mediterranean Prophecy:* The School of Joachim of Fiore and the Fourteenth-Century *Breviloquium*. Toronto: Pontifical Institute of Medieval Studies, 1989.

Le Goff, Jacques. *The Birth of Purgatory*. Trans. Arthur Goldhammer. Chicago: University of Chicago Press, 1984 [1980].

Leo, Ulrich. "The Unfinished *Convivio* and Dante's Rereading of the *Aeneid*." *Medieval Studies* 13 (1951): 41–64.

Lerner, Robert E. "Ecstatic Dissent." *Speculum* 67 (1992): 33–57.

Lesnick, Daniel R. *Preaching in Medieval Florence: The Social World of Franciscan and Dominican Spirituality*. Athens, Ga.: University of Georgia Press, 1989.

Levy, Bernard S., ed. *The Bible in the Middle Ages: Its Influence on Literature and Art*. Binghamton, N.Y.: Medieval and Renaissance Texts and Studies, 1992.

Light, Laura. "French Bibles c. 1200–30: A New Look at the Origin of the Paris Bible." In Gameson, *Early Medieval Bible*, pp. 155–76.

——. "The New Thirteenth-Century Bible and the Challenge of Heresy." *Viator* 18 (1983): 275–88.

——. "Versions et revisions du texte biblique." In Riché and Lobrichon, *Le Moyen Age et la Bible*, pp. 55–57.

Lobrichon, Guy. "Une nouveauté: Les gloses de la Bible." In Riché and Lobrichon, *Le Moyen Age et la Bible*, pp. 95–114.

Lokrantz, Margareta. *L'opera poetica di s. Pier Damiani*. Stockholm: Almquist and Wiksell, 1964.

Longère, Jean. *La prédication medievale*. Paris: Etudes augustiniennes, 1983.

Lossky, Vladimir. "Les eléments de 'Théologie négative' dans la pensée de saint Augustin." In *Augustinus Magister, Congrès international augustinien Paris, 21–24 septembre 1954*, vol. 1, *Communications*, 575–81. Paris: L'année théologique augustinienne, 1954.

Lourdaux, W., and D. Verhelst, eds. *The Bible and Medieval Culture*. Louvain: University of Louvain, 1979.

Louth, Andrew. *The Origins of the Christian Mystical Tradition: From Plato to Denys*. Oxford: Clarendon, 1981.

Lowe, Raphael. "The Medieval History of the Latin Vulgate." In *CHB*, pp. 102–54.

Lynch, Joseph H. *The Medieval Church: A Brief Survey.* London: Longman, 1992.

MacCulloch, J. A. *The Harrowing of Hell.* Edingburgh: T. and T. Clark, 1930.

Mandouze, André. "L'extase d'Ostie." In *Augustinus Magister, Congrès international augustinien Paris, 21–24 septembre 1954,* vol. 1, *Communications,* pp. 67–84. Paris: L'année théologique augustinienne, 1954.

Manetti, Aldo. "Dante e la Bibbia." *Bolletino della Civica Biblioteca.* Bergamo: Studi di storia, arte e letteratura, 1984.

Manselli, Raoul, ed. *La religion populaire au Moyen Age: Problèmes de méthode et d'histoire.* Paris: Vrin, 1975.

——, ed. *Le religiosità popolare nel medio evo.* Bologna: Multino, 1983.

Manzoni, Francesco. "Saggio di un nuovo commento alla *Commedia*: Il canto IV dell' *Inferno.*" *Studi Danteschi* 42 (1965): 29–206.

Martinez, Ron L. "Dante, Statius, and the Earthly City." Ph.D. diss., University of California, 1977.

Martini, Adolfo. "Dante francescano." *Studi francescani* 18 (1921): 40–71.

Mazzeo, Joseph Anthony. "St. Augustine and the Rhetoric of Silence." In *Renaissance and Seventeenth-Century Studies,* pp. 1–24. New York: Columbia University Press, 1964.

——. *Structure and Thought in the "Paradiso."* Ithaca, N.Y.: Cornell University Press, 1958. Reprint, New York: Greenwood, 1968.

Mazzoni, Guido. *Alma luces malae cruces: Studi Danteschi.* Bologna: Zanichelli, 1941.

Mazzotta, Giuseppe. *Dante, Poet of the Desert.* Princeton, N.J.: Princeton University Press, 1979.

——. *Dante's Vision and the Circle of Knowledge.* Princeton, N.J.: Princeton University Press, 1993.

——. "Life of Dante." In Jacoff, *Cambridge Companion to Dante,* pp. 1–13.

——. "Why Did Dante Write the *Comedy*? Why and How Do We Read It? The Poet and the Critics." In Cachey, *Dante Now,* pp. 63–82.

McGinn, Bernard. *The Calabrian Abbot: Joachim of Fiore in the History of Western Thought.* New York: Macmillan, 1985.

——. *The Foundation of Mysticism.* Vol. 1 of *The Presence of God: A History of Western Christian Mysticism.* New York: Crossroad, 1992.

McNally, Robert. *The Bible in the Early Middle Ages.* Atlanta: Scholars, 1986.

McVeigh, Daniel. "*The Western Canon*: Bloom, Dante, and the Limits of Agon." *Christianity and Literature* 44 (1995): 181–94.

Merrill, James. *The Changing Light at Sandover, A Poem.* New York: Alfred A. Knopf, 1993.

——. "Divine Poem." In J. D. McClatchy, ed., *Recitative*, pp. 87–95. San Francisco: North Point, 1986.

Mésoniat, C. *Poetica Theologia: La "Lucula noctis" di G. Dominici e le dispute letterarie tra '300 e '400*. Rome: Edizione di Storia e Letteratura, 1984.

Miller, David L. *Hells and Holy Ghosts: A Theopoetics of Christian Belief.* Nashville: Abingdon, 1989.

Milton, John. *The Poems of John Milton*. Ed. J. Carey and A. Fowler. New York: W. W. Norton, 1968.

Mineo, Niccolò. *Profetismo e apocalittica in Dante*. Catania: Università di Catania, 1968.

Minnis, A. J. *Medieval Theory of Authorship: Scholastic Literary Attitudes in the later Middle Ages*. 2d ed. Middle Ages Series. Philadelphia: University of Pennsylvania Press, 1988.

Minnis, A. J., and A. B. Scott, with David Wallace. *Medieval Literary Theory and Criticism c. 1100–c. 1375*. Rev. ed. Oxford: Clarendon, 1991.

Minocchi, S. "Italiennes (versions) de la Bible." In *Dict. B.*, vol. 3, pt. 1, cols. 1012–38.

Mominis, Alan, ed. *Sacred Journey: The Anthropology of Pilgrimage*. Westport, Conn.: Greenwood, 1992.

Monnier, Jean. *La descente aux enfers: Étude de pensée religieuse d'art et de la littérature*. Paris: Librairie Fischbacher, 1904.

Monteverdi, Angelo. "Ovidio nel medio evo." In F. Arnaldi et al., eds., *Studi Ovidiani*, pp. 67–78. Rome: Istituto di Studi Romani, 1959.

Moore, Edward. *Studies in Dante, First Series. Scripture and Classical Authors in Dante*. 1896. Reprint, New York: Greenwood, 1968.

——. *Studies in Dante, Third Series. Miscellaneous Essays*. 1903. Reprint, New York: Greenwood, 1968.

Morgan, Alison. *Dante and the Medieval Other World*. Cambridge, Eng.: Cambridge University Press, 1990.

Murtaugh, Daniel. "*Figurando il paradiso*: The Signs That Render Dante's Heaven." *PMLA* 90 (1975): 227–84.

Nardi, Bruno. *La caduta di Lucifero e l'autenticità della "Quaestio de Aqua e Terra."* Turin: Società editrice internazionale, 1959.

——. *Il canto XV del "Purgatorio."* Rome: Casa di Dante, 1953.

——. "Dante profeta." In P. Mazzantini, ed., *Dante e la cultura medievale*, 2d ed., rev., pp. 265–326. Bari: Laterza, 1983 [1941].

——. "Intorno al sito del Purgatorio e al mito dantesco dell' Eden." In *Saggi di Filosofia dantesca*, pp. 349–74. Milan: Società Anonima Editrice Dante Alighieri, 1930 [1922].

——. *Nel mondo di Dante*. Rome: Edizione di "Storia e Letteratura," 1944.

——. "La tragedia d'Ulisse." In P. Mazzantini, ed., *Dante e la cultura medioevale*, 2d ed., rev., pp. 125–34. Bari: Laterza, 1983 [1941].

Newman, Francis X. "St. Augustine's Three Visions and the Structure of the *Commedia*." *MLN* 82 (1967): 56–78.

Oakley, Francis. *The Western Church in the Later Middle Ages*. Ithaca, N.Y.: Cornell University Press, 1979.

O'Donnell, James J., ed. *Augustine, "Confessions."* 3 vols. Oxford: Oxford University Press, 1992.

O'Maera, John J. *The Young Augustine: The Growth of St. Augustine's Mind up to His Conversion*. London: Longman, 1954.

Ovid, Publius Naso. *Heroides and Amores*. Trans. Grant Showerman. 2d ed. Rev. G. P. Goold. Cambridge, Mass.: Harvard University Press, 1977.

——. *Metamorphoses*. Trans. Frank Justus Miller. Rev. G. P. Goold. 2 vols. Cambridge, Mass.: Harvard University Press, 1984.

——. *Tristia, Ex Ponto*. Trans. Arthur Leslie Wheeler. 2d ed. Rev. G. P. Goold. Cambridge, Mass.: Harvard University Press, 1988.

Padoan, Giorgio. *Il pio Enea, e l'empio Ulisse*. Ravenna: Longo, 1977.

——. "Ulisse 'Fandi Fictor' e le vie della sapienza." *Studi Danteschi* 37 (1960): 21–61.

Paparelli, Gioacchino. *Ideologia e poesia di Dante*. Florence: Olschki, 1975.

Paratore, Ettore. *Tradizione e struttura in Dante*. Florence: Sansoni, 1968.

Patch, Howard R. *The Other World According to Descriptions in Medieval Literature*. New York: Octagon, 1970 [1950].

Peterson, Mark. "Dante and the 3-Sphere." *American Journal of Physics* 47 (1979): 1031–35.

——. "Dante's Physics." In Di Scipio and Scaglione, *"Divine Comedy" and the Encyclopedia*, pp. 163–80.

Petrocchi, Giorgio. "San Paolo in Dante." In *DB*, pp. 235–48.

Petrucci, Armando. *Writers and Readers in Medieval Italy: Studies in the History of Written Culture*. Ed. and trans. Charles M. Radding. New Haven, Conn.: Yale University Press, 1995.

Pézard, André. "Daniel e Dante, ou les vengeances de Dieu." *Studi Danteschi* 50 (1973): 1–96.

Pietrobono, Luigi. "Il canto xxix del *Purgatorio*." Lectura Dantis, *Purgatorio*. Florence: Sansoni, 1910.

Plotinus. *The Enneads*. Trans. Stephen MacKenna. 3d ed. Rev. B. S. Page. London: Faber, 1969.

Poggioli, Renato. "Dante *poco tempo silvano*: Or a 'Pastoral Oasis' in the *Commedia*." *DSARDS* 80 (1962): 2–20.

Porena, Manfredi. *La "Divina Commedia" di Dante Alighieri commentata da Manfredo Porena*. 3 vols. Bologna: Zanichelli, 1946–48.

Pöschl, Viktor. *The Art of Virgil*. Trans. Gerda Seligson. Ann Arbor: University of Michigan Press, 1962.

Préaux, J. "Nouvelles approximations sur l'épisode du 'Tolle, lege." In *Revue belge de philosophie e d'histoire* 33 (1955): 555–76.

Putnam, Michael J. "Virgil's Inferno." In *PA*, pp. 94–112.

Quillet, H. "Descent de Jésus aux enfers." In *DTC*, vol. 4, pt. 1, cols. 565–619.

Quint, David. "Epic Tradition and *Inferno* IX." *DSARDS* 93 (1975): 201–7.

Quintilian. *Institutio oratoria*. Trans. H. E. Butler. 4 vols. Loeb Classical Library. Cambridge, Mass.: Harvard University Press, 1980.

Rahner, Hugo. *Greek Myths and Christian Mystery*. Trans. Brian Battershaw. London: Burns and Oates, 1963.

Rand, Edward K. *Founders of the Middle Ages*. Cambridge, Mass.: Harvard University Press, 1929.

Reeves, Marjorie. *The Influence of Prophecy in the Later Middle Ages: A Study in Joachism*. Notre Dame, Ind.: University of Notre Dame Press, 1993.

Reynolds, Barbara. *Dorothy L. Sayers: Her Life and Soul*. New York: St. Martin's, 1993.

———. *The Passionate Intellect: Dorothy L. Sayers' Encounter with Dante*. Kent, Ohio: Kent State University Press, 1989.

Riché, Pierre, and Guy Lobrichon, eds. *Le Moyen Age et la Bible*. Paris: Beauchesne, 1984.

Robathan, Dorothy M. "Ovid in the Middle Ages." In J. W. Binns, ed., *Ovid*, pp. 191–207. London: Routledge, 1973.

Robinson, H. Wheeler, ed. *The Bible in Its Ancient and English Versions*. Oxford: Clarendon, 1940.

Rocca, Luigi. "Il canto xxix del' *Purgatorio.*" Lectura Dantis, *Purgatorio*. Florence: Sansoni, 1904.

Rogers, Francis M. "The Vivaldi Expedition." *DSARDS* 73 (1955): 31–45.

Rops, Henri Daniel. *Cathedral and Crusade*. Trans. John Warrington. London: Dent, 1957.

Rowse, Richard H., and Mary A. Rowse. "*Statim invenire*: Schools, Preachers, and New Attitudes to the Page." In R. L. Beson and G. Constable, eds., *Renaissance and Renewal in the Twelfth Century*. Cambridge, Mass.: Harvard University Press, 1982.

Rusconi, Roberto. *Predicazione e vita religiosa nella società italiana da Carlo Magno alla Controriforma*. Turin: Loescher, 1981.

Sapegno, Natalino. *"La Divina Commedia" a cura di Natalino Sapegno*. 2d ed. 3 vols. Florence: La Nuova Italia, 1955.

Sarolli, Gian Roberto. *Prolegomenon alla "Divina Commedia."* Biblioteca dell'Archivium Romanicum 1/112. Florence: Olschki, 1971.

Sayers, Dorothy L. " . . . And Telling You a Story." In C. S. Lewis, ed., *Essays Presented to Charles Williams*, pp. 1–37. Grand Rapids, Mich.: Wm. B. Eerdmans, 1966.

Schaff, Philip. *The Creeds of Christendom, With a History and Critical Notes.* 6th ed. 3 vols. Grand Rapids, Mich.: Baker Book House, 1983 [1886].

Schildgen, Brenda D. "Dante's Neologisms in the *Paradiso* and the Latin Rhetorical Tradition." *DSARDS* 107 (1989): 101–20.

Schnapp, Jeffrey. *The Transfiguration of History at the Center of Dante's "Paradise."* Princeton, N.J.: Princeton University Press, 1986.

——. "Trasfigurazione e metamorfosi nel *Paradiso* dantesco." In *DB*, pp. 273–92.

Scott, John A. "*Inferno* XXVI: Dante's Ulysses." *Lettere Italiane* 23 (1971): 145–86.

Serravalle, Giovanni. *Fratris Johannis de Serravalle Ord. Min. Episcopi et Principius Firmani Translatio et Comentum totius libri Dantis Alighierii.* Ed. Fr. Marcellino da Civezza and Fr. Teofilo Domenichelli. Prati: Gianchetti, 1891.

Shakespeare, William. *The Tragedy of Hamlet, Prince of Denmark.* Ed. B. Mowat and P. Werstine. The New Folger Library. New York: Washington Square Press, 1992.

Shankland, Hugh. "Dante *Aliger* and Ulysses." *Italian Studies* 32 (1977): 21–38.

Singleton, Charles S. *Dante's "Commedia": Elements of Structure.* Baltimore: The Johns Hopkins University Press, 1977 [1954].

——. "*In exitu Israel de Aegypto.*" In Freccero, *Dante: Critical Essays*, pp. 102–21.

——. "The Irreducible Dove." *Comparative Literature* 9 (1957): 129–35.

——. *Journey to Beatrice.* Baltimore: The Johns Hopkins University Press, 1977 [1958].

Smalley, Beryl. *English Friars and Antiquity in the Early Fourteenth Century.* New York: Barnes and Noble, 1960.

——. *The Study of the Bible in the Middle Ages.* Notre Dame, Ind.: University of Notre Dame Press, 1978 [1952].

Solodow, Joseph B. *The World of Ovid's "Metamorphosis."* Chapel Hill: University of North Carolina Press, 1988.

Sowell, Madison D., ed. *Dante and Ovid: Essays in Intertextuality.* Medieval and Renaissance Texts and Studies 82. Binghamton, N.Y.: Medieval and Renaissance Texts and Studies, 1991.

Sparks, H. F. D. "The Latin Bible." In Robinson, ed., *The Bible*, pp. 100–127.

Spicq, C. *Esquisse d'un histoire de l'exégèse latine au moyen âge.* Bibliothèque Thomiste 26. Paris: Vrin, 1944.

Spitzer, Leo. "Address to the Reader in the *Commedia.*" *Italica* 32 (1955): 143–65.

Stambler, Bernard. *Dante's Other World.* New York: New York University Press, 1957.

Stanford, W. B. *The Ulysses Theme: A Study in the Adaptability of a Traditional Hero.* Oxford: Blackwell, 1954.

Statius. *Thebiad.* Trans. J. H. Mozley. 2 vols. Cambridge, Mass.: Harvard University Press, 1967.

Stephany, William A. "Biblical Allusions to Conversion in *Purgatorio* XXI." *Stanford Italian Review* 3 (1983): 141–62.

Stevens, Wallace. *The Collected Poems of Wallace Stevens.* New York: Alfred A. Knopf, 1965.

Stock, Brian. *Augustine the Reader: Meditation, Self-Knowledge, and the Ethics of Interpretation.* Cambridge, Mass.: Harvard University Press, 1996.

Sumption, Jonathan. *Pilgrimage: An Image of Medieval Religion.* Totowa, N.J.: Rowman and Littlefield, 1975.

Swanson, R. N. *Religion and Devotion in Europe, c. 1215–c. 1515.* Cambridge, Eng.: Cambridge University Press, 1995.

Tanner, Norman, ed. *Decrees of the Ecumenical Councils.* 2 vols. London: Sheed and Ward, 1990.

Tartaro, Achille. "Certezze e speranza nel XXV del 'Paradiso.'" *L'Alighieri* 1 (1983): 3–5.

Tatlock, J. S. P. "The Last Cantos of the *Purgatorio.*" *Modern Philology* 32 (1934–1935): 113–23.

Thomas Aquinas, Saint. *The Sermon Conferences of St. Thomas Aquinas.* Ed. and trans. Nicholas Ayo, CSC. Notre Dame, Ind.: University of Notre Dame Press, 1988.

——. *The "Summa Contra Gentiles" of St. Thomas Aquinas.* Trans. English Dominican Fathers. 4 vols. London: Burns, Oates and Washburn, 1923–24.

——. *The "Summa Theologica" of St. Thomas Aquinas.* Trans. Fathers of the English Dominican Province. 3 vols. New York: Benziger, 1948.

——. *Truth.* Translated from the definitive Leonine text of *Quaestiones disputatae de veritate.* Chicago: H. Regnery, 1952–54.

Thompson, David. *Dante's Epic Journeys.* Baltimore: The Johns Hopkins University Press, 1974.

Thurston, Herbert. *The Holy Year of Jubilee.* London: Sands, 1900.

Tonelli, Luigi. *Dante e la poesia del ineffabile.* Florence: Barbèra, 1934.

Toschi, Paolo. *Le origini del teatro italiano.* Turin: Einaudi, 1955.

Toynbee, Paget. *A Dictionary of Proper Names and Notable Matters in the Works of Dante.* Rev. Charles S. Singleton. Oxford: Clarendon, 1968 [1898].

Tucker, Dunstan J. " '*In exitu Israel*' . . . The *Divine Comedy* in the Light of the Easter Liturgy." *American Benedictine Review* 11 (1960): 43–61.

Turner, Ralph V. "*Descendit ad inferos*: Medieval Views on Christ's Descent into Hell and the Salvation of the Ancient Just." *Journal of the History of Ideas* 27 (1966): 173–94.

Turner, Victor. "The Center Out There: Pilgrim's Goal." *History of Religions* 12 (1973): 191–230.

——. *Dramas, Fields, and Metaphors: Symbolic Action in Human Society.* Ithaca, N.Y.: Cornell University Press, 1974.

——. "Liminality and *Communitas.*" In *The Ritual Process: Structure and Anti-Structure,* pp. 94–130. Chicago: Aldine, 1974.

——. "Variations on a Theme of Liminality." In Sally F. Moore and Barbara G. Meyerhoff, eds., *Secular Ritual,* pp. 36–52. Amsterdam: Van Gorcum, 1977.

Turner, Victor, and Edith Turner. *Image and Pilgrimage in Christian Culture: Anthropological Perspectives.* New York: Columbia University Press, 1978.

——. "Religious Celebrations." In Victor Turner, ed., *Celebration: Studies in Festivity and Ritual,* pp. 201–19. Washington, D.C.: Smithsonian Institution Press, 1982.

Vallone, Aldo. "Il canto xxix del *Purgatorio.*" Lectura Dantis, *Purgatorio.* Rome: Casa di Dante, 1981.

van Gennep, Arnold. *Rites of Passage.* Trans. Monika B. Vizedom and Gabrielle L. Caffee. Chicago: University of Chicago Press, 1960 [1908].

Vauchez, André. "La Bible dans les confréries et les mouvements de dévotion." In Riché and Lobrichon, *Le Moyen Age et la Bible,* pp. 581–95.

——. *The Laity in the Middle Ages: Religious Beliefs and Devotional Practices.* Ed. D. E. Bornstein. Trans. M. J. Schneider. Notre Dame, Ind.: University of Notre Dame Press, 1993.

Vellutello, Alessandro. *La "Commedia" di Dante Alighieri con la nova espositione di Alessandro Vellutello.* Vinegia: Francesco Marcolini, 1544.

Vicaire, M.-H. *Saint Dominique: La vie apostolique.* Chrétiens de tous les temps 10. Paris: Editions du Cerf, 1965.

Vickers, Nancy J. "Claudel's Delectation in Dante." *Claudel Studies* 8 (1981): 28–41.

——. "Seeing Is Believing: Gregory, Trajan, and Dante's Art." *DSARDS* 101 (1983): 67–85.

Villani, Giovanni. *Villani's Chronicle.* Trans. Rose E. Selfe. Ed. Philip H. Wick-
steed. 2d ed. New York: E. P. Dutton, 1907.

Virgil. *Virgil: Eclogues, Georgics, Aeneid, The Minor Poems.* Trans. H. Rushton
Fairclough. Rev. ed. 2 vols. Cambridge, Mass.: Harvard University Press,
1967.

Webb, Diana M. "Saints and Pilgrims in Dante's Italy." In Barnes and Cuillea-
nain, *Dante and the Middle Ages,* pp. 33–55.

Westrem, Scott D., ed. *Discovering New Worlds: Essays on Medieval Exploration
and Imagination.* Garland Medieval Casebooks 2. New York: Garland,
1991.

Woodward, David. "Medieval Mappaemundi." In Harley and Woodward,
Cartography, pp. 286–370.

Young, Karl. *The Drama of the Medieval Church.* Vol. 1. Oxford: Clarendon,
1933.

Zacher, Christian K. *Curiosity and Pilgrimage: The Literature of Pilgrimage in
Fourteenth-Century England.* Baltimore: The Johns Hopkins University
Press, 1976.

Zink, Michel. *La prédication en langue romane: Avant 1300.* Paris: Champion,
1976.

Index

Aaron, 49

Abel, 199–206, 208

Abelard, Peter, 104, 175

Abraham, 85, 102, 108, 312n5

Acts of the Apostles, 48, 59, 67, 188, 303n35, 311n2

Adam: activity before the Fall, 177, 324n13; Christ and Satan struggling over, 101; Christ as the second Adam, 183, 269; on ephemerality of language, 86; in the harrowing, 108, 313n5; task in the Garden of Eden, 174; and the Tree of Knowledge, 183

Adrian V (pope), 261, 335n19, 336n20

Aeneid (Virgil): Caiaphas echoing language of, 117; the *Commedia* as influenced by, 14, 289n19; Dante's Christian re-vision of, 121–24; the dispersal of the Sibyl's text, 228; Elysian Fields as model for first circle of hell, 145; finding personal relevance in, 1–2; the *Inferno* as pervaded by, 99; lack of understanding in face of destiny in, 114; "Manibus, oh, date lilia plenis," 122–23, 125; Ovid's *Metamorphoses* contrasted with, 149; on Rome as empire without boundary, 209, 211; as salvific text, 192. *See also* Dido

Agnus Dei, 256

Albertus Magnus, 28, 104, 267, 302n33, 316n26

Alexander III (pope), 295n6

Alfonso IV of Portugal, 272

Alford, John, 22

Alfraganus, 267

Alighieri, Dante, *see* Dante

Alighieri, Pietro, 13, 327n3, 328n10

Ambrose, St., 48, 215, 259f, 268

Anderson, William, 289n15, 304n37

Annas, 227, 313n5

Annunciation, the, 46, 262

Anonimo Fiorentino, 319n39

Anselm, St., 28

Ante-purgatory, 257–60

Anthony of Egypt, St., 1

Antonino, St., 316n27

Apocalypse, the: Dante's citing of, 42; in Dante's Pageant of Revelation, 48, 58f, 64–66, 68, 300n23; and Dante's preview of the heavenly city, 75; Dante writing in imitation of, 327n13; and Jerome's limitation of the Old Testament, 299n18; as marking the closing of the canon, 214; on the Promised Land, 85–86; and the Transfiguration, 42, 188

Apostles' Creed, 100

Aquinas, St. Thomas: on the acceptance

Library of Congress Cataloging-in-Publication Data
Hawkins, Peter S.
    Dante's testaments : Essays on scriptural imagination / Peter S.
Hawkins.
      p. cm. — (Figurae)
    Includes bibliographical references and index.
    ISBN 0-8047-3492-5 (alk. paper). — ISBN 0-8047-3701-0 (pbk. :
alk. paper)
     1. Dante Alighieri, 1265–1321—Religion. 2. Bible—In literature.
I. Title. II. Series: Figurae (Stanford, Calif.)
PQ4419.B5H39   1999
851'.1—dc21   99-29125

◎ This book is printed on acid-free, archival quality paper.

Original printing 1999
Last figure below indicates year of this printing.
08   07   06   05   04   03   02   01   00   99

Designed by Janet Wood
Typeset in 11/14 Adobe Garamond by Keystone Typesetting, Inc.